未尝举箸忘吾蜀

I never raise my chopsticks

without remembering my dear Sichuan


陆游

Lu You

Song-dynasty poet, 1125–1209

# The Food of Sichuan

Photography by Yuki Sugiura

with additional location photography by Ian Cumming

# Fuchsia Dunlop

**W. W. NORTON & COMPANY**

*Independent Publishers Since 1923*

# Introduction

When the first edition of this book was published in 2001, Sichuanese cuisine was renowned across China but little known abroad. In Britain, there were no genuine Sichuanese restaurants, and authentic seasonings were impossible to find. Even among chefs and food experts, few outside China had experienced the lip-tingling sensation of real Sichuan pepper. Two pioneering cookbooks, Robert Delfs' *The Good Food of Szechwan* and Ellen Schrecker's *Mrs. Chiang's Szechwan Cookbook*, had introduced the flavors of Sichuan to American readers but "Chinese food," as understood in the Western world, was still dominated by the Cantonese style.

Much has changed in the intervening years. A craze for Sichuanese food began to sweep China in the late 1990s, and has since spread beyond the country's borders. Sichuanese restaurants have sprung up in Western cities, mapo tofu is now a favorite dish of discerning international eaters, and Sichuan pepper is tingling its way across the world. Sichuanese ingredients are increasingly available, and the region itself is becoming popular as a food destination. In 2010 UNESCO named the Sichuanese capital, Chengdu, as its first Asian City of Gastronomy. Finally, Sichuanese cuisine is receiving some of the global attention it so richly deserves.

I was privileged to be living in Sichuan during a period of dramatic social change in the 1990s, when for the first time it became possible for a foreigner to conduct detailed gastronomic research on the ground. In 1994, after two years of studying the Chinese language part-time, I moved to Chengdu to take up a British Council Scholarship at Sichuan University. I must admit that my choice of university was heavily influenced by the reputation of the local cuisine: on two previous trips to the region I had been bowled over by the complex flavors and warm colors of the food, and I knew I wanted to find out more about it.

When I'd been in Chengdu for a couple of months, sampling the street snacks and folk cuisine, and wandering through the vibrant local markets, I—along with a German friend, Volker—decided to make inquiries about cooking classes. One sunny October afternoon we cycled across the city in search of the famous provincial cooking school. We could hear from the street that we had arrived. Fast, regular chopping, the sound of cleavers on wood. Upstairs, in a plain white room, dozens of apprentice cooks in white overalls were engrossed in learning the art of sauces. Chiles and ginger were being pulverized with pairs of cleavers on tree-trunk chopping boards, Sichuan pepper was being ground to a fine brown powder, and the students were scurrying around mixing oils and spices, fine-tuning the flavors of the rich, dark liquids in their crucibles. The air hummed with a gentle rhythmic pounding, and the clinking of china spoons in china bowls. On long parallel tables sat bowls of soy sauce and oil, and piles of sugar and salt. Notebooks scribbled with Chinese characters lay open amid the blood-red chiles and scattered peppercorns. The light streamed in through open windows. We agreed immediately that this was where we had to study.

Over the next two months, Volker and I took private classes at the Sichuan Institute of Higher Cuisine. Our teacher was the brilliant Gan Guojian, and the school's English tutor, Professor Feng Quanxin, was on hand to help us decipher the Sichuanese dialect and explain unfamiliar culinary terms. With this foundation, a growing fluency in the Chinese language and a small repertoire of classic Sichuanese dishes, I was able to talk to chefs and restaurateurs, and to spend study days in several local restaurants.

Some months later, when I had finished my course at Sichuan University and was thinking about returning home to England, I dropped in at the cooking school. To my surprise, the principal invited me to enroll as a regular student on a professional training course: a particular privilege, since no foreigner had ever done this before. I leapt at the opportunity, promptly enrolled and paid my modest fees, and was issued with chef's whites and a Chinese cleaver.

Every day for the next three months, I studied cooking with forty-five Sichuanese young men and two young women. Mornings were spent in the classroom, covering culinary theory—the selection of raw ingredients, mixing of flavors, control of heat and different cooking methods—and then we would all move over to the demonstration room. There, we would watch our teachers, Long Qingrong and Lü Maoguo, prepare folk dishes and banquet delicacies with ease and artistry. In the afternoons, it was our turn to cook. In teams of ten we would prepare our ingredients, killing and cleaning fish, washing and chopping vegetables, collecting dried spices and pickled chiles from the nearby storeroom. Then each of us would have a turn at the wok, our classmates gathering round to tease and criticize. The finished dishes were all presented to the teacher, who would assess them for color, taste and texture. On my days off I would cycle through Chengdu, learning about street food and researching ingredients. I was also lucky enough to study in some of the city's restaurant kitchens, including traditional snack specialist the Dragon Wonton and the magical Shufeng Garden.

Ever since that period of delicious initiation, I have continued to explore the byways of Sichuan province, researching regional dishes and local culinary traditions. Nearly twenty years after the publication of the first edition, I felt it was time to revise this book, to try to satisfy the growing appetite for information about Sichuanese cuisine in the English-speaking world in the light of my own now-expanded knowledge, and to reflect the evolution of Sichuanese cuisine itself over this period.

Writing a cookbook that attempts to encapsulate the cuisine of a place is like pitching a tent on quicksand. Any living culinary culture is a moving target, constantly evolving and responding to new influences and encounters. Dishes that I knew and loved in Chengdu in the mid-1990s have all but disappeared, while new ingredients and cooking methods have seeded themselves on local menus; fresh culinary crazes sweep the city often. Even the province itself is radically altered since I first lived there, having in 1997 shed the vast metropolis of Chongqing, Chengdu's old rival, which has become a separate municipality, taking with it approximately 30 million of Sichuan's population (in culinary terms, however, Chongqing can still be considered to be part of Sichuan).

These days, amid the giddy pace of social change, many senior chefs lament the loss of kitchen skills among the young and complain that sensationalized dishes overloaded with oil, chiles and monosodium glutamate (MSG) are eclipsing the subtlety and nuance of traditional Sichuanese cooking. On the other hand, in recent years I have also met local heroes who are doing their utmost to honor and preserve their gastronomic heritage for future generations. They have inspired and encouraged me as I try to document something of Sichuanese food and food culture for English-speaking readers.

This edition contains new recipes and new information, as well as photographs that I hope will inspire readers in their kitchens and their travels. All the original recipes have been retested, revised and refined in the light of advice from local chefs and my own deepened experience of Sichuanese cooking. Some of the recipe introductions in the first edition included descriptions of an old Chengdu street life that has almost completely vanished; out of nostalgia and affection, I have left most of them intact, but please be aware that many of the places and customs I describe no longer exist.

Doing justice in a single book to a cuisine as magnificent, complex and regionally diverse as the Sichuanese remains an impossible task, but I hope this book, for readers of English, will take us a little further along the road.

*Fuchsia Dunlop, 2019*

# The Story of Sichuanese Cuisine

Sichuanese cooking is one of the great cuisines of the world. While in the West it is known mainly for being hot and spicy, in China it is legendary for its sophistication and amazing diversity: local gourmets claim that the region boasts 5,000 different dishes.

Chinese poets have glorified the region's food for the last thousand years, and the Sichuanese themselves are particularly obsessed with food, even given the tough competition in this respect from other parts of China. Surly taxi drivers wax lyrical as they describe their favorite dumplings; outbound travellers sigh, dewy-eyed, when they consider the pickled vegetables they are leaving behind; office clerks slurping a quick bowl of noodles on their lunch break recount legends of the great chefs of the 1930s.

Chinese cuisine is often treated as one tradition, with a few regional variations. Viewed from the outside, perhaps it is the unifying themes that leap to mind: the use of chopsticks, the consumption of rice, noodles or breads with shared dishes of meat and vegetables, the technique of stir-frying in a wok, the use of soy sauce as a flavoring. Viewed from the inside, however, it is the differences that seem to matter more, ranging from the bright, fresh flavors of the south to the delicate seasonal cooking of the eastern coastal areas and the spicy diet of the western provinces; between the wheaten staples of the north and the southern use of rice.

It is easy to forget that China is more of a continent than a country: its vast territory encompasses deserts and rainforests, high mountains and fertile plains, salt lakes and rolling grasslands. Sichuan (with Chongqing) is almost twice the size of Italy, and has a population nearly double that of Britain's. It has its own dialect, its own operatic style, a unique teahouse culture and, of course, an outstanding culinary tradition.

The most famous characteristic of Sichuanese cuisine, which it shares with the cooking of nearby Hunan and Guizhou provinces, is its fieriness, derived from the liberal use of red chiles, but also, in Sichuan, from numbing Sichuan pepper. In the countryside, chiles are strung up in enormous bunches from the eaves of the timber-framed farmhouses, resembling the strings of scarlet firecrackers detonated for the Chinese New Year. Dried in the sun, blood-red and lustrous, or pickled bright scarlet in salt and wine, chiles are at the heart of Sichuanese cooking. Sichuanese people have an extraordinary appetite for chiles, and they tend to find their way into at least some of the dishes served at every breakfast, lunch and dinner. Because of this, the Sichuanese have a reputation for being a bit spicy themselves, and local women are even known as "spice girls" (*la meizi*). The spicy local diet is so notorious that Chinese people will invariably ask outsiders on their way to Sichuan whether or not they are "afraid of chile-heat" (*pa la*).

Chiles are used in many local dishes, but so inventively that their taste never palls. Dried chiles, sizzled in oil, give the "scorched chile flavor" that is the base of Gong Bao chicken and innumerable vegetable stir-fries; combined with Sichuan pepper, they are used in intensely fiery "numbing-and-hot" dishes. Milder chiles pickled in brine and spices yield a more subtle heat, the base of the sensational "fish-fragrant flavor," with its mix of salty, sweet, sour and spicy tastes. Ground chiles and chile oil are used in myriad cold dishes, most famously the "strange-flavor" concoctions that combine salty, sweet, numbing, hot, sour and nutty tastes, while chile bean paste is the dominant taste in "home-style" dishes. The heat of chiles is never meant to overwhelm the flavors of the other ingredients, however, but is intended to heighten sensation and to open up the palate to a richer variety of tastes.

Sichuan chile bean paste (*doubanjiang*), a famous product of Pixian just outside Chengdu, is made, unusually in China, from fava beans rather than soy beans, which are mixed with wheat flour, allowed to become moldy, fermented in brine and then mixed with salt-fermented chiles. Traditionally, the paste is matured in open clay jars: on sunny days, it bakes in the sun, and on clear nights, it receives a libation of dew; the pots are only covered when it rains. Through this special process, they say, the paste absorbs the essences of the universe, and breathes in the spirit of the Sichuanese earth.

Despite the emphasis on chiles, hot and spicy food certainly isn't all the region has to offer. In fact, the most salient characteristic of Sichuanese cooking is its audacious combinations of different flavors in a single dish and a multitude of flavors within a meal. Some of these compound flavors are hot and spicy; many others, such as sweet-and-sour "lychee flavor," delicate "fragrant-boozy flavor" and fresh, light "ginger juice flavor," are not. So those who do *pa la*—"fear chiles"—will still find plenty to entice them within the pages of this book.

The other famous spice associated with the cuisine, Sichuan pepper (*huajiao*), is known variously as flower pepper, brown peppercorns, prickly ash or, erroneously, fagara. One of the most ancient Chinese spices, it has an extraordinary, heady aroma that carries hints of wood, citrus peel and the languid scents of summer, and produces a weird numbing effect on the lips and tongue (known in Chinese as *ma*, which also means anaesthetic and pins-and-needles). Despite this initial strangeness, the spice's taste and fragrance are incomparable, and most people seem to succumb quickly to its aromatic charms. Curiously, one folk explanation for its widespread use in Sichuanese cooking is that its numbing effects allow the consumption of more chiles than would otherwise be humanly possible!

The finest Sichuan pepper in China is grown in Hanyuan county, in the mountains of western Sichuan. Local people say its fragrance is so strong that you can rub the raw spice on your palm and still smell it on the back of your hand, through skin and bone. Hanyuan Sichuan pepper was used as a scent before it became a cooking spice, and was so highly prized that it was offered in tribute to the emperors of China. During the Han-dynasty period, the spice was actually mixed into the mud walls of the residences of imperial concubines, which became known as "pepper houses" (*jiaofang*), a term that survived into the late imperial era, unlike the practice that inspired it. According to Sichuanese scholars, the custom arose not only because of the pepper's fragrance, but because the plant bears many seeds and is thus a traditional symbol of fertility. Even today, Sichuan pepper and peanuts are thrown over brides and grooms at weddings in rural areas.

The spiciness of Sichuanese cooking is often ascribed to the muggy climate. In traditional Chinese medicine, dampness is seen as dangerously unhealthy, for it impairs the *yang* energy of the body and causes sluggishness. The best way to restore a healthy equilibrium is to eat foods that drive out moisture and dispel the cold, which makes heating foods like chiles, ginger and Sichuan pepper a vital part of the diet. Local people feel obliged to eat plenty of chiles not only during the winter, when they conquer the creeping dampness that penetrates every layer of clothing, but also at the height of summer, when they aid perspiration and dispel humidity. (Incidentally, several Sichuanese friends, reared on stereotypes of rainy, foggy London, have remarked on the suitability of Sichuanese food for the British climate!)

Sichuan is also famous for its mistiness, for the gray moistness that for much of the year shrouds trees and rivers, blotting out the sunlight. Clear skies are famously rare, so much so that they say Sichuanese dogs "bark at the sight of the sun" (*shu quan fei ri*). Against all this dismal weather, picture the colors of a typical Sichuanese meal: the chile oil dressing on a bowlful of fresh fava beans, the scarlet pickled chiles resplendent on a braised fish, the cool pinks of cold stewed meats, the dusky red of Sichuan pepper. Not only does such food restore the body, but its warm, autumnal colors also soothe the heart and offer a fitting rebuke to the perennial grayness of the sky.

## History

The Sichuan region has long been famous for its plentiful and delicious food. Carved brick panels unearthed around Chengdu that date back to the Han dynasty, some 2,000 years ago, depict scenes of hunting, cooking and lavish banqueting. A writer from the same period, named Yang Xiong, described the way cooks "blended the five flavors, creating a harmony of sweetness, preparing tonic soups of Chinese peony."

As far back as the fourth century AD, a historian called Chang Qu famously remarked on local people's liking for interesting flavors and hot-and-fragrant tastes (*shang ziwei, hao xinxiang*). By the twelfth century, during the Song dynasty, there were Sichuanese restaurants in the northern capital, Bianliang (today's Kaifeng), suggesting that the region had developed a distinctive style of food that was already becoming known beyond its borders. In the early days, however, any spiciness in the local cooking must have come not from chiles, but from a trio of pungent seasonings: ginger, Sichuan pepper and a related plant known as ailanthus-like prickly ash (*dang* or *shi zhuyu*, Latin name *Zanthoxylum ailanthoides*) that would later be totally eclipsed by chiles. Ginger from the Sichuan region has long been revered and is mentioned in the earliest Chinese gastronomic treatise, *The Root of Tastes* (*benwei pian*), written in the third century BC.

Chiles only reached China in the late sixteenth century, toward the end of the Ming dynasty, when the earliest written references to them begin to appear in botanical sources from the eastern coastal provinces of Zhejiang and Jiangsu. Probably brought to China by Portuguese traders (although some believe they came via one of the overland routes from India), this "barbarian pepper" (*fanjiao*) was described as an ornamental plant prized for its pretty white flowers and scarlet fruit; it would be at least another century before the use of chiles to flavor food was documented. During the seventeenth century, chiles took root in the inland provinces of Jiangxi and Hunan, first popping up in Hunanese records in 1684. Most sources suggest that chiles made their slow journey into Sichuan from here: according to the exhaustive research of Professor Jiang Yuxiang, of Sichuan University, despite one possible reference to chile-growing in Sichuan in the mid-1700s, it wasn't until the reign of the Jiaqing Emperor (1796–1820) that the plant became firmly established as a local crop.

By the early nineteenth century, Zhang Mu, an author from Jiangxi, noted a fashion "of recent decades" for chiles, which had "a fiery flavor and, when eaten, cause the lips and tongue to swell, but are enjoyed by a multitude of people." One can only imagine how readily chiles were adopted by the Sichuanese, who had long been accustomed to seasoning their food boldly to counter the unhealthy humors of the climate. Their use spread during the later Qing dynasty, as Sichuanese food became ever more famous for its strong tastes and intriguing use of hot-and-numbing spices. These days, chiles are indispensable in Sichuan, but their dialect name, "sea peppers" (*haijiao*), remains as a reference to their foreign origins. Strangely, the use of chiles has all but disappeared from the coastal parts of China that first encountered them.

People sometimes ascribe the distinctiveness of Sichuan's culture to geographical isolation. Look at a topographical map of China and you'll see why: the green, fertile Sichuan basin is ringed by forbidding mountains, with the vast Tibetan plateau rising to its west. The only way out is along the route of the Yangtze River, which snakes through treacherous gorges to central China and, finally, the sea. Before the advent of railways and modern transport, reaching Sichuan was quite an ordeal—not for nothing did the poet Li Bai describe the way there as more difficult than the road to heaven.

Actually, however, Sichuan has not had a history of isolation. More than 2,000 years ago, the forces of China's great unifying emperor, Qin Shihuang (he who was buried with the terracotta army), defeated the ancient western kingdoms of Ba and Shu and brought the Sichuan basin under central control. His followers, migrating to the region from the central Chinese plains, are thought to have brought with them some of their own eating customs, beginning a long process of cultural exchange between Sichuan and the rest of China.

In times of peace, Sichuan often closed in on itself, retreating behind its geographical fortifications, the flow of people slowing to a trickle. Each period of war or dynastic upheaval, however, saw great waves of immigrants entering the province, with the result that most of the population of modern Chengdu are thought to be descendants of outsiders. The most dramatic influx occurred in the early Qing dynasty, from the late seventeenth century onward. The dying days of the previous dynasty, the Ming, had seen conflict and chaos all over China; war, pestilence and natural disasters had decimated the Sichuanese population, and vast areas of valuable farmland had fallen into disuse. As the new Qing rulers worked to restore food production and bring about stability, they encouraged systematic, large-scale migration into the fertile basin, a historic movement of people from more than a dozen provinces that became known as "filling Sichuan from Hu and Guang" (*huguang tian sichuan*).

Government officials and rich merchants often brought their own chefs with them when they moved to Sichuan; with every wave of migration came new tastes and culinary techniques. By the time Western missionaries settled in Chengdu, around the turn of the twentieth century, it was a truly cosmopolitan city with a vibrant culinary scene. There were restaurants specializing in other regional cuisines, such as the delicate style of the Jiangnan, or lower Yangtze, region. Fu Chongju's *Survey of Chengdu*, published in 1909, listed banquet halls that could lay on sea cucumber or bird's nest feasts, as well as places offering Western

dishes like buttered chops, milk pudding and pheasant curry. Among Fu's lists of hundreds of local dishes and snacks can be found many that are still eaten today, including chicken with chiles, chicken in Sichuan pepper sauce and mapo tofu.

Much of what we recognize today as Sichuanese cuisine took shape in the late nineteenth and early twentieth centuries. During the Japanese occupation of China, millions of displaced people from northern and coastal areas sought refuge inland, and Chongqing became the wartime capital of the Nationalist government. Officials from all over China took up residence, US servicemen arrived to support the war effort, and new restaurants soon sprang up to cater for every taste: by 1943, there were over 250 in the city, including 30 Western-style restaurants and coffee shops.

The distinctive character of Sichuanese cuisine has grown out of this long history of immigration and cultural fusion. Today's "traditional" culinary repertoire incorporates many outside influences: most notably chiles from South America, but also roasting and smoking techniques that originated in the imperial kitchens of Beijing, and an interest in deep-frying that is said to have come from Americans in 1930s Chongqing. Even among Sichuan's most celebrated gastronomic creations, Gong Bao chicken bears the name of an official who was born in Guizhou province, Baoning vinegar was first brewed by an immigrant from northern Shanxi (a province with a strong vinegar-making tradition), and chile bean paste was the invention of a Fujianese man who settled in Pixian, near Chengdu, in the late seventeenth century. These days the pace of change is inevitably faster, and local cooks are beginning to experiment with the likes of steak, okra and salmon.

While it's possible to see this onslaught of foreign influences as a threat to regional identity, it's worth remembering that Sichuan has been a cultural and culinary melting pot for much of its history. As local people proudly attest, their province is extremely *baorong*: open, adaptable and inclusive.

## Land of Plenty

Sichuan has long been known in China as a "land of plenty" (*tianfu zhi guo*) because of its agricultural wealth. The fertile soil of the Sichuan basin, its warm climate and abundance of rain and river-water create ideal conditions for farming. Some 2,300 years ago, an imperial official named Li Bing supervised the harnessing of the rivers near Chengdu in the Dujiangyan irrigation project, an extraordinary work of engineering which brought an end to the flooding that had plagued the region, opening up the land for stable and productive agriculture, and ensuring that its people would always be well-fed.

From the fecund Sichuan earth spring forth not only rice but all kinds of fruit and vegetables, all year round. Local specialties include mandarin oranges, pomelos, lychees, longans, peaches, loquats, Chinese chives, bamboo shoots, celery, eggplants, lotus root, water spinach and gourds of all shapes and sizes. Exceptionally fine tea leaves grow in the mountains, and wild vegetables such as fiddlehead ferns (*juecai*) and the spring shoots of the Chinese toon tree (*chunya*) are also enjoyed.

Sichuan is criss-crossed by rivers and streams, once the habitat of a multitude of fish, including the esteemed rock carp (*yanli*), Ya'an snowtrout (*yayu*) and long-snout catfish (*jiangtuan*). The surrounding mountains, forests and grasslands once teemed with wildlife and exotic plants: fungi, wild frogs and all kinds of medicinal roots and herbs. Writers through the ages have raved about its exquisite produce, including, most notably, Tang-dynasty poet Du Fu and Song-dynasty poet Lu You. In the eyes of Chinese gourmets, the entire region is like a vast larder filled with the stuff of gastronomic dreams.

When it comes to chiles, the Sichuanese traditionally favor a couple of specific varieties. Most distinctive is the *erjingtiao*, a long, thin-skinned, mild chile with a curved tail and an enticing flavor, which is typically pickled or dried. In the 1990s, these chiles were mainly grown in

Mumashan, just outside Chengdu: I visited the area once at harvest time and the markets were ablaze with scarlet peppers that seemed to glow like lanterns against the overcast sky. Tragically, the chile fields of Mumashan have since been paved over, and so *erjingtiao* have become more scarce and are usually grown further afield. Other local varieties include the smaller, plumper "facing heaven" chile (*chaotianjiao*) and the squat, pointy "bullet" chile (*zidantou*). Plump, round chiles known as "lantern chiles" (*denglongjiao*) are used mainly in pickling. In recent years, local chefs increasingly rely on small, pointy dried chiles known as "little rice" chiles (*xiaomila*), which are largely grown in other regions, including Yunnan.

Sichuan pepper has been grown in Sichuan since ancient times. The spiky plant, with green pimpled berries that grow rosy in the late-summer sun, prefers mountainous terrain with bright sunlight and freezing winters. Like wine grapes, the pepper is an expression of its terroir, which is why true aficionados seek out not only pepper from western Sichuan's Hanyuan county, but pepper grown on the Ox Market Slopes (*niushipo*), a particular tract of land within that county. The new season's *niushipo* pepper has a simply incredible scent, reminiscent of kumquats—high and bright and pure. Wild green varieties of Sichuan pepper have long been used by rural people, but in the late 1990s, one such variety was domesticated, approved for sale and named "nine-leaf green" (*jiuyeqing*). Since 1998, this pepper, commonly known as "green flower pepper" (*qing huajiao*) or "rattan pepper" (*tengjiao*) has grown in popularity among Sichuanese cooks: it has a dazzling aroma that recalls the sharp freshness of lime peel, and goes particularly well with eels, frogs and fish.

Pickled vegetables also play a crucial role in regional cooking. Many people still make their own quick-pickled vegetables for daily use; other pickles, which require more complicated processing, are usually bought. The most famous is *zhacai*, a spiced, salted mustard tuber produced in Fuling, near Chongqing, but this is just one of the region's

Sichuan pepper growing in Hanyuan county in western Sichuan. The pepper shown is "tribute pepper" *(gongjiao)*, considered the finest in China and once sent in tribute to the imperial court in Beijing

"four great pickles." The others are "big-headed vegetable" (*datoucai*), a kind of salted turnip; Nanchong "winter vegetable" (*dongcai*), made from a leafy variety of mustard; and Yibin *yacai*, a dark, sweet, spiced preserve made from the tender stems of another mustard variety. (See p. 417 for more information about all of these.)

Another celebrated local product is Sichuan well salt, which is made by heating bittern extracted from salt mines deep within the earth and is prized for its purity of flavor. The salt mines founded by irrigation expert Li Bing in the third century BC were among the earliest in the world, and by the time of the Tang dynasty there were nearly 500 in the area, and the center of production, today's Zigong, became known as the "salt capital" (*yandu*).

Of course it's not only the raw materials that contribute to the diversity of Sichuanese cuisine. Local people have developed an extraordinarily sophisticated culinary tradition, with a whole armory of skills. Sichuanese chefs are well known for their cutting skills, for their subtle control of heat, and most of all for their inspired flavoring techniques, which are quite unmatched in other Chinese traditions, and possibly in global cooking. The combination of these crafts can transform even a limited range of ingredients into a banquet; with the resources available to official cooks of the great mansions of the past and high-class chefs of the present day, the possibilities are almost infinite.

Sichuanese chefs use a highly complex culinary vocabulary, some of which is next to impossible to translate into English. Recipe books identify 56 distinct cooking methods, their differences minutely analyzed (see p. 475); there are different terms for every type of slice and chunk (see p. 37) and labels for every flavor combination (see p. 471). Subtle gradations of texture or "mouthfeel" (kougan) are recognized. Professional cooking manuals preface each recipe with a note on the flavor category, cooking method and special characteristics (tedian) of the dish in question—the latter might include its appearance, fragrance and texture, and is usually expressed in a catchy "four-character" phrase.

## Different Culinary Styles

Chengdu, the ancient capital of the Shu kingdom, is in many ways also the capital of Sichuanese cuisine. It has been a political hub and a center of silk production and brocade weaving for more than two millennia, and its wealthy merchants and officials long ago developed a taste for the luxuries of life. Chengdu's mellow climate and plentiful produce made the living there easier than in many parts of China, and the local population earned a reputation for being idle pleasure-lovers, never happier than when they were playing cards or mahjong in a teahouse, or guzzling the delicious local food.

The city has changed out of all recognition in the two last decades, but still expresses the sensibility that created a cup of tea which can last for a whole afternoon, and a hotpot you can mull over from dusk to midnight.

To the east of Chengdu lies Chongqing, formerly Sichuan's second city and now a separate municipality. Clinging to the steep banks of the Yangtze River, Chongqing is a mountain city. Before the railways, the river was the region's most important transport link with the rest of China, and Chongqing is still a crucial river port, sending boats downstream through the Three Gorges to Shanghai and the sea. The Chongqing climate is even more steamy than Chengdu's—in fact, so overwhelming is the summer heat that the city is known as one of China's "furnaces" (*huolu*). Perhaps predictably, the response of local people to this heat and humidity is to eat even more chiles and Sichuan pepper than their Chengdu neighbors, so Chongqing folk cooking can be quite fiendishly hot and numbing.

In recent years, the city has become famed for its "river-and-lake cooking" (*jianghu cai*), the kind of rough, generous, spicy food enjoyed by laborers eating by the riverside. You can tell you're in a *jianghu* Chongqing restaurant when you have to pluck small morsels of chicken or eel from a colossal pile of chiles, and you're surrounded by noisy, laughing, red-faced people!

The steep hills and busy port give Chongqing a much brisker atmosphere than Chengdu, and this paciness is reflected in its culinary culture, which has been a rich source of new food trends and dynamic innovation. Many of Sichuan's more famous dishes rose to prominence here—most notably hotpot, chicken in a pile of chiles, and fish stew with pickled mustard greens. Chongqingers traditionally look down on the people of Chengdu for being lazy and out-of-date in their eating habits. The inhabitants of Chengdu habitually retort that while Chongqing people may know how to invent a good dish, their food is coarse and crude, and needs the refining touch of Chengdu chefs before it can become really great cuisine.

Beyond the longstanding rivalry between Chengdu and Chongqing, there are countless culinary differences across the Sichuan region. In the south, people adore the fast, simple "small stir-fry" cooking method and often serve their food with spicy dips. They particularly like to pair pickled chiles with pickled ginger (a clue, perhaps, to the origin of the "fish-fragrant" flavor combination), and use more fresh herbs, including spearmint (*yuxiang* or *liulanxiang*) and Korean mint (*huoxiang*). In the southeast, people sometimes season their dips with litsea oil, which has a powerful lemongrass-like aroma and is more commonly associated with the cooking of nearby Guizhou province. In the mountainous regions to the west of Chengdu, Han Chinese culinary customs mingle with those of several important minorities, including Tibetans, Qiang and Yi. (Although you will find a handful of Sichuanese Hui Muslim dishes within these pages, the cuisines of these other minority cultures are beyond the scope of the book.)

In recent years, with the revival of interest in traditional food cultures, many smaller regions are promoting their own styles of cooking. Some talk in terms of a Great River School (*dahe bang*) encompassing the Yangtze towns of Luzhou, Yibin, Li Zhuang and Leshan; a Small River School (*xiaohe bang*) centered on the Jialing River, including Nanchong and Guangyuan; and a

Zigong-Neijiang School (*zinei bang*), covering the dishes and snacks of those two places. In the salt-industry city of Zigong, locals are keen to advance their own "salt gang" style of cooking (*yanbang cai*). In truth, the whole of Sichuan is a patchwork of delicious specialties, some of them stubbornly local, others spanning regional boundaries.

Aside from regional variations, there are many different grades and types of Sichuanese cuisine. The province is best known for the glorious flavors of its folk cooking, which includes many of the dishes that make Sichuanese people dreamy with nostalgia when they're away from home: old favorites like twice-cooked pork, mapo tofu and Gong Bao chicken; home-made pickles served with a slug of chile oil; and the traditional feast dishes of rural Sichuan, such as bowl-steamed pork belly with preserved vegetable. Twenty years ago, most Sichuanese people cooked up these classic folk dishes at home, and made their own pickles and winter-cured meats. The older generation, including—strikingly—many men, can still rustle up a good mapo tofu or dry-fried green beans, but younger people, sadly, seem to be losing touch with their culinary heritage. In Chengdu, hearty traditional cooking can still be found in the cheap, backstreet eateries known as "fly restaurants" (*cangying guanzi*)—a joking reference to their supposed lack of hygiene (rather like English "greasy spoon" cafes).

Sichuan in general, and Chengdu in particular, are renowned for their street snacks: the dumplings, noodles and other delicious nibbles collectively known as "small eats" (*xiaochi*). Almost every county town has its own specialty—a kind of leaf-wrapped dumpling, perhaps, a cold-dressed meat dish or a style of noodles. These delicacies were originally sold on the streets by itinerant vendors who mostly specialized in one particular snack. Some can still be bought this way, around temples and parks in the cities and on the streets of smaller towns, although it's becoming more common to eat them in noodle shops or specialty restaurants. (For a more detailed account of Sichuan's "small eats" tradition, see pp. 370–371.)

The old town of Fubao in Hejiang
county, Luzhou, southeastern Sichuan

While Sichuanese food is often stereotyped as cheap and casual, the elegant cuisine at the top end of the social scale can also be stunning. Banquet menus often showcase virtuoso cooking skills and the exotic ingredients collectively known as "treasures from the mountains and flavors of the seas" (*shanzhen haiwei*). One classic banquet dish, for example, is duck stewed with caterpillar fungus (*chongcao yazi*), the whole duck spiked with *Cordyceps sinensis*, a fungus from the Tibetan grasslands that invades the bodies of caterpillars and grows inside them until nothing is left but their shape; the fungus, a traditional tonic food, has been eaten in Sichuan for around 300 years. Sichuanese banquet cooks also use distinctive local cooking methods to prepare some universal Chinese delicacies, creating dishes such as home-style sea cucumber and dry-braised shark's fin.

Banquet cooking often features dishes of great wit and subtlety, designed to surprise and enchant the guests. So you might be offered chicken "tofu" (*ji douhua*), which resembles the cheap-and-cheerful tofu of eastern Sichuan but is actually made with finely ground chicken breast (see p. 203); or "white cabbage in boiling water" (*kaishui baicai*), where a whole Chinese cabbage is served in broth, the joke being that the humble cabbage is served in a lavish, perfectly clear stock made from chicken, duck, ham and pork bones. In more recent years, the Chengdu chef Yu Bo has become known for his "calligraphy brushes" (*maobi su*), a dish that appears to be calligraphy brushes with a dish of red ink, but in fact consists of flaky pastries tucked into bamboo stems, alongside a dip of tomato sauce.

Historically, banquet tables often showcased intricate sculptures crafted out of vegetables, or platters of sliced, multicolored ingredients collaged in the form of elaborate tableaux: "peacock spreading its tail" (*kongque kai ping*) or "panda fighting bamboo" (*xiongmao zhan zhu*). Such laborious knifework, the Chinese equivalent of French sugar sculpture, is a dying art. Sichuanese banquets almost always supplement the exotica with expert renditions of much-loved classics and street snacks, such as bowl-steamed dishes and dandan noodles. However, the higher you rise on the social scale of banqueting, the lighter and more delicate the flavors are likely to be.

In the past, high-ranking officials and wealthy merchants often retained their own chefs, and some of China's finest dishes emerged from this tradition. In the late nineteenth and early twentieth centuries, elite Chengdu restaurants sought to re-create the elegant and intimate atmosphere of the private kitchen. Fu Chongju's *Survey of Chengdu* singled out for special mention the Zhengxingyuan, a banquet restaurant run by a Manchu chef who had previously served in the household of an imperial official and was a master of the fabled three-day Man-Han imperial banquet. After his restaurant closed in 1910, two of his former chefs opened another one called the Rongleyuan, which went on to become a byword for gastronomic excellence. These days, such elevated banquet cooking is hard to find. In Chengdu, its true heirs are two brilliant chefs who run "private kitchens" (*sifang cai*) in the traditional mold: Lan Guijun at Yuzhilan, and Yu Bo at Yu's Family Kitchen.

Another fascinating aspect of Sichuanese cuisine is Buddhist vegetarian cooking. Chinese Buddhist monasteries have a longstanding tradition of vegetarianism, and while most monks and nuns themselves exist on a simple diet, larger establishments often run special restaurants serving more elaborate vegetarian fare. Perhaps the most intriguing aspect of this grander style of temple food is that many dishes are cunningly engineered to imitate meat, poultry and fish in appearance, taste and texture. This cuisine of artful mimicry is found all over China, but Sichuanese monasteries have their own regional style, offering vegetarian versions of dishes such as twice-cooked pork, dry-fried eels and steamed rice pudding with pork belly (see pp. 260–261 for more on monastic cooking).

It's worth noting that because dairy foods are largely absent from the Chinese diet, Chinese vegetarian food is almost always vegan.

For centuries, Sichuan has had a sizeable population of Muslims. Most are of the Hui minority, descendants of traders on the old Silk Road who trace their origins to northwestern China; a few are Uyghurs, Turkic people from the western region of Xinjiang. Following the drive to repopulate Sichuan in the early Qing dynasty, Hui Muslims established a community around the old imperial heart of the city (near today's Mao statue), where they built a mosque and opened noodle shops, restaurants and other businesses. Although the old mosque was demolished in 1998, a few halal eateries have sprung up around the new one. Sichuanese halal restaurants usually serve some lamb, goat and beef dishes that are eaten by Hui Muslims across China, but they also offer glorious halal versions of classic local recipes that are more usually made with pork, such as twice-cooked beef and chicken slices in "lychee" sauce with crispy rice.

## The Art of Flavor

China is the place for food,
but Sichuan is the place for flavor
(*shi zai zhongguo, wei zai sichuan*)

Anyone who has eaten in Sichuan will know that this popular Chinese saying is no exaggeration. The Sichuanese are renowned for their ability to combine many different tastes into exquisite compound flavors (*fuhewei*). Local chefs boast of using 23 distinct flavor combinations, which, applied to a wide variety of raw ingredients, create an immense diversity of tastes: they say each and every one of a hundred Sichuanese dishes will have its own unique flavor (*yicai yige, baicai baiwei*). A Sichuanese banquet can be an intriguing culinary journey, teasing the palate with a whole sequence of contrasting flavors: strong, spicy tastes, rich sweet-and-sour sauces, gently aromatic cold meats, delicate soups . . .

From a traditional Western standpoint, there are four fundamental tastes: salty, sweet, sour and bitter. The Chinese, however, identify five, in keeping with

their theories of the five elements (metal, wood, water, fire and earth) and five directions (north, south, east, west and center), and their liking for fives in general. The five fundamental Chinese tastes, recognized since the time of Confucius, are salty (咸 *xian*, or *han* in Sichuanese dialect), sweet (甘 *gan* or 甜 *tian*), sour (酸 *suan*), hot or pungent (辛 *xin* or 辣 *la*) and bitter (苦 *ku*). The Sichuanese, who like to go their own way in so many respects, have their own version of these five fundamental tastes, often replacing bitter with numbing (麻 *ma*)—the extraordinary taste of Sichuan pepper—and sometimes also adding umami (鲜 *xian*) and fragrant (香 *xiang*).

The Chinese word *xian* (or umami, to borrow the Japanese word more familiar to English-speakers) is one of the most beautiful in the Chinese culinary language. It expresses the delicious savory tastes of fresh meat, poultry and seafood, the scrumptious flavors of a pure chicken broth, or the subtle magic of freshly rendered lard. *Xian* describes the most exalted flavors of nature; it is the Chinese cook's muse, the essence of flavor itself.

Much of Chinese gastronomy is concerned with bringing out the *xian* taste of fine ingredients, enhancing it here and there with chicken fat or fragrant mushrooms; teasing it out with small amounts of salt or sugar; using wine, ginger and scallions to dispel the sullying tastes of blood and rawness. At the giddier heights of the culinary arts, Chinese chefs lend *xian* to wonderfully textured but tasteless ingredients like shark's fin by simmering them in complex stocks made from *xian*-rich foods such as pork, duck and chicken. In more humble kitchens, people might use lard or chicken fat to stir-fry vegetables, imbuing them with sumptuous *xian* tastes that don't actually recall the flavor of the meat itself.

Of course, there is now a growing awareness of this same "fifth taste" in the West, identified in foods that are naturally rich in glutamic acid and other natural flavor enhancers, such as certain types of mushrooms and seafood. When glutamic

acid was first commercially produced in 1909, as monosodium glutamate or MSG, Chinese cooks began to use it to enhance the *xian* of dishes. When added judiciously, MSG can give a pleasurable lift to a dish, but many cooks use it and its derivative "chicken essence" (*jijing*) to excess, obscuring the natural flavors of ingredients and (in my opinion) creating such a commotion of the palate that more subtle tastes are overshadowed. It is a bitter irony that in China, of all places, where chefs have spent centuries developing the most sophisticated culinary techniques, this mass-produced white powder should have been given the name *weijing*, "the essence of flavor."

The term *xiang* also has a much richer and deeper meaning than "fragrant" does in English. The same word refers to the incense used in offerings to gods and ancestors; fragrant meats were roasted as sacrificial offerings; scent was seen as a means of communication with the spirit world. This is not to suggest that chefs and eaters are spiritually moved every time they smell some roasting pork (although they might be), but that the word for "fragrant" does have a transporting loveliness in Chinese. It is used to describe the enticing aromas of wines and liquors, spices, scented flowers, roasted nuts and citrus peel. It is often used to express the particular delightfulness of the smells and flavors created by frying and roasting (what scientists would call Maillard reactions or caramelization): for example, the sensory appeal of the lacquered skin of a roast duck or the bewitching aromas stirred up in a wok from sizzling ginger and scallions in oil.

Another concept crucial to understanding Chinese cooking is that of dispelling rankness and unpleasant odors, known collectively as *yiwei* ("peculiar smells"), and more specifically as *xingwei* ("fishy odors"), *saowei* ("foul odors") and *shanwei* ("muttony odors"). To the Chinese, the smells and tastes of raw meat and fish have an unappetizing edge to them that must be suppressed or eradicated by various means. Raw meat is usually blanched before cooking to cleanse it of blood and impurities. Salt, Shaoxing wine, Sichuan pepper, ginger and

scallions are widely used in marinades, especially those involving fish or strong-tasting meats like beef or mutton. A few pieces of crushed ginger and scallion and a scattering of Sichuan pepper are typically added to stews or stocks made with meat or poultry. (This may sound esoteric to Western cooks, but it really does improve the flavor—just try comparing the taste and smell of pork-bone stocks made with and without a little scallion and ginger.) The concern with these unpleasant raw smells in animal foods is an ancient one: they are even mentioned in the *Lu Annals*, a text dating back to the Warring States period (around the third century BC). Some vegetables also have unpleasant tastes that must be tamed—like the tongue-curling *sewei* ("astringent taste") of spinach and some types of bamboo shoots, or the pepperiness of daikon.

Cantonese cooks are famously preoccupied with preserving and bringing out the natural tastes of their fresh ingredients. They tend to add seasonings with a light and delicate touch, in order to enhance but not overwhelm their raw materials. Sichuanese cooks, by contrast, are renowned for their creation of intense (*nong*) and complex flavors through the audacious mixing of the basic tastes. The lavish use of chiles, Sichuan pepper, garlic, ginger and scallions, however, is not meant to obliterate the natural flavors of ingredients, and you should be able to taste their *xian* at the heart of all this spiciness (*la zhong you xianwei*).

Sichuanese cooks often refer to saltiness as the foundation, the essential background against which the colors of a complex flavor are sketched. Saltiness brings out the natural qualities of raw ingredients—there is even a saying that you cannot make a dish without it (*wu han bu cheng cai*). The most important salty flavoring is Sichuan well salt, with soy sauce, fermented black beans and chile bean paste being key secondary sources of salt. Sweetness, from white, brown or crystal sugars, maltose syrup and sometimes honey, is a significant note in some compound flavors, but can also be used in tiny amounts to round out savory tastes.

Sourness comes from vinegar or pickled vegetables, and historically from salted unripe plums (*meizi*). Bitterness appears occasionally, in the use of tangerine peel and certain vegetables like bitter melon and bamboo shoot. Chiles in various forms are the most famous source of Sichuanese hotness, but local cooks also place white pepper, ginger, garlic, scallions and mustard in the same *la* ("spicy-hot") flavor family. The numbing *ma* taste, of course, comes exclusively from Sichuan pepper.

These basic tastes are combined into a vast array of complex flavors, and Sichuanese cooks and gourmets have precisely labeled at least 23 of them. Each has its own distinct characteristics, its balance of sweet and sour, its degree of spiciness, its effect on the tongue and palate. This highly organized approach to the theory of flavor does not imply any rigidity: in fact, Sichuanese cooks are amazingly inventive, and every chef I know stresses the importance of a spirited, flexible (*linghuo*) approach to cooking. The "official" flavors are just a template, to be played with and augmented. Food writers talk of expanding the canon to include newly popular flavors like "fruit juice flavor" (*guozhi wei*) and "tomato sauce flavor" (*qiezhi wei*).

Some of these complex flavors are unique to Sichuan and deserve separate mention here. The most fascinating is "fish-fragrant flavor" (*yuxiang wei*), a stunning combination of pickled chile paste, ginger, garlic, scallions, sugar and vinegar that can be used for both hot and cold dishes. There is no fish involved, and the term is rarely used for actual fish dishes. Most local experts insist that the name arose because this combination of flavors is used in local fish cooking (which it is, particularly in southern Sichuan) and so a fish-fragrant sauce reminds everyone who eats it of fish. An alternative but disputed explanation is that the name comes from the practice of popping a few whole, raw crucian carp into jars of pickling chiles to enhance their flavor. Old cookbooks do include recipes for "pickled fish chiles" made in this way (*pao yu lajiao*), but they are rarely seen these days. Whatever the truth of its origins, and however old

its roots in folk cooking, the fish-fragrant flavor seems to have a fairly recent history for a "classic" Sichuanese style. Fu Chongju made no mention of the flavor in his 1909 *Survey of Chengdu*, but a few fish-fragrant dishes do appear in one of the earliest Sichuanese cookbooks, the Sichuan volume of *Famous Chinese Dishes*, which was first published in 1960—with the explanation that they are made with seasonings commonly used when cooking fish.

Another key Sichuanese combination is the "home-style flavor" (jiachang wei), a gorgeous, belly-warming mix of chile bean paste, sweet flour sauce, fermented black beans and some related seasonings, all of them intensely savory. One of the most common home-cooking methods involves sizzling chile bean paste in oil with ginger and garlic, perhaps with a little ground meat, adding plenty of vegetables and a little liquid, covering the pot and then letting the ingredients cook until the flavors have been absorbed: this appears to be the root of home-style dishes.

Finally, and most sensationally, the *mala* or "numbing-and-hot" flavor combination of chiles and Sichuan pepper is essential to Sichuanese cuisine, and is its best-known calling-card all over China and abroad. (For a description of all the "official" flavor combinations, see pp. 471–474.)

Given Sichuan's fiery reputation, it's worth stressing that plain, understated tastes are no less important in Sichuanese cuisine than the clamorous, wild sensations of chile heat and pepper tingle. A dramatic dish like Chongqing chicken in a pile of chiles begs to be complemented by plain white rice and a gentle, refreshing broth; a rich, spicy beef stew by some simple stir-fried greens. The high notes of Sichuanese cooking may be more electrifying than those of other cuisines, but, as in any other part of China, good eating is all about balance, and plainness and piquancy go hand in hand. This is part of the comfort of food, which, even in Sichuan, is not just about scintillating sensation, but about restoring and sustaining the equanimity of mind and body.

## Texture

For the Chinese in general and the Sichuanese in particular, texture is an integral part of the appeal of any dish, and the very limited grasp of texture in Western gastronomy may be the greatest obstacle to profound Western appreciation of Chinese cuisine. To Chinese palates, the texture of a dish is every bit as important as its color, taste and aroma. There is even a special word for the sensation that a piece of food creates in the mouth: *kougan*, literally "mouthfeel." The concept of *kougan* covers not only texture in the English sense of crispness, softness, chewiness and so on, but also the pleasurable feeling that one gets from eating a stir-fried dish in which all the ingredients are cut harmoniously into slivers, or the satisfaction derived from eating meatballs from which every last wisp of stringy tendon has been carefully removed.

Certain types of texture are particularly enjoyed in Sichuan: the crisp, rubbery bite of tripe and other offal; the slithery crunch of jellyfish and silver ear fungus; the silky tenderness of the flesh pocketed in a fish's cheek. This is partly why Chinese people derive such immense pleasure from eating foods that some Westerners find weird or even revolting. My Chinese friends positively relish using their tongues and teeth to separate the bones and skin in a chicken's foot or wing, and appreciate the subtle balance of slipperiness and tautness in a strand of pea-starch jelly. Texture is one of the main attractions of Chinese exotica like shark's fin and sea cucumber, and partially explains why Chinese cooks are prepared to spend hours, or even days, making these rare and gristly ingredients palatable.

Some of the terms used to describe texture in Chinese are untranslatable because the concepts they express are simply overlooked by Western gourmets. *Cui* is the first among these—it refers to a certain quality of crispness, a texture that offers resistance to the teeth, but finally yields, cleanly, with a pleasant, snappy feeling. This is a quality of kidneys, cut finely and then cooked swiftly over a fierce flame; of goose intestines, scalded briefly in

a Sichuan hotpot; of chicken gristle, fresh celery and raw snow peas. The Sichuanese love of this particular texture is why you might find a dish named "three *cui* ingredients with pickled chile" (*paojiao sancui*, a stir-fry of goose intestines, duck gizzards and wood ear mushrooms) on a menu.

*Su* refers to a different kind of crispness: the dry, friable quality of deep-fried dumplings or baked puff pastry. *Nen* expresses the delicate tenderness of young leaves and flesh, and is commonly used to describe succulent foods like deftly stir-fried meat and fish. *Lao* literally means "old" and conveys the opposite of *nen*: the toughness of mature flesh and fibrous leaves, or the dryness of tender foods that have been overcooked. *Pa*, in local dialect, describes what happens to food cooked for a long time, to the point when meat falls away from bones and root vegetables become soft and pulpy. *Nuo* is the soft, springy stickiness of ingredients like glutinous rice.

Learning to appreciate texture in the Chinese way takes a little time and dedication, but adds an extra dimension to gastronomic pleasure. If you're a novice, it's best not to start with the more obscure types of offal or the most expensive delicacies. Cold jellyfish, served in most Chinese restaurants, makes a good beginning: it is slithery and crunchy, but most Westerners find it fairly easy to enjoy. Wood ear mushrooms, which appear in many stir-fries, have an equally interesting, but not disturbing, texture. Try as you eat these things to allow your tongue, teeth and mouth to share in the pleasure, to treat the texture as something to be enjoyed in itself. Slowly, you will find the door opening wider to a more profound enjoyment of Chinese food.

## Drinks

Sichuan is famous not only for its food, but also for the excellence of its wines and teas. The wines are strong, vodka-like concoctions made from various grains and drunk in tiny china cups. When I first lived in Sichuan, women scarcely touched them, so when a woman did indulge there was a whiff of scandal and danger in the air. Men would quaff cup after cup, ritualistically, in formal toasts or casual drinking games.

Sichuan's most famous wine is *wuliangye* ("five-grain liquid"), an intensely fragrant clear liquor that is made from sorghum, rice, glutinous rice, wheat and corn, and traditionally brewed using water from the Min River. The wine, produced in Yibin in southern Sichuan, is 60 percent proof (though apparently toned down for export). Some of the wine cellars in Yibin are thought to date back about 500 years, to the Ming dynasty. A more recent arrival on the Sichuan wine scene is Quanxing wine, a strong sorghum liquor that has been made in Chengdu since the early nineteenth century.

These days, grape wines, particularly dry reds (*gan hong*), are becoming increasingly fashionable for formal occasions. If you wish to drink grape wines with Sichuanese food, oaky whites and tannic reds are best avoided. Classic choices include floral and aromatic white wines such as Riesling or Gewurztztraminer, sometimes with an edge of sweetness. Whisky can work surprisingly well with Sichuanese dishes.

At informal meals, Sichuanese people often sip beer or soft drinks. More traditionally, drinks might not be offered at all with simple meals, since the light broth served at the end has a similar function, to quench the thirst and rinse the palate.

In the Sichuan countryside, poorer people sate their thirst with the water left over from cooking rice (*mitang*), which is both delicious and nourishing.

Tea may be served before or after meals, but not usually while they are in progress. One exception is the herbal tea known as "red-and-white tea" (*hongbai cha*) or "eagle tea" (*laoying cha*): a specialty of the holy Daoist Qingcheng Mountain, its cooling properties are particularly enjoyed in hot weather. In recent years, an infusion of roasted tartary buckwheat, served hot like tea, has become extremely popular as a drink.

Teahouses are part of the fabric of Sichuanese life. In villages and old quarters of the cities they are intimate places, clusters of bamboo chairs in a leafy courtyard or the ground floor of a timber-framed house, where older people gather to gossip, or to play and sing traditional Sichuan opera. In the grounds of Buddhist and Daoist temples, teahouses buzz with the chatter of tourists and pilgrims, their courtyards and colonnades secluded from the bustle of the streets. In city parks, too, teahouses extend over huge areas, encompassing pagodas, bamboo groves and lakeside promontories.

From the late Qing dynasty until the 1940s, teahouses were at the center of social life. Some were frequented by members of Sichuan's secret societies (*paoge*), who used the arrangement of their tea cups as an elaborate secret code. Teahouses often had an air of political subversion—many establishments of this period displayed signs urging their clients to avoid discussing national affairs (*wu tan guoshi*). Some teahouses specialized in theatrical performances or story-telling; others in Chinese chess or Go (*weiqi*). Certain establishments gained notoriety as places of rendezvous for prostitutes and their clients. Many traditional teahouses have disappeared in the course of modernization, but it is still possible to stumble across an old-school place, with roving masseurs and ear-cleaners, and even, on rare occasions, a Sichuanese opera group.

According to Chinese legend, the Divine Farmer Shen Nong discovered tea as a drink some five millennia ago, when tea leaves drifted into a pot of water he was boiling in the open air. Shen Nong is said to have enjoyed the fragrance of this infusion and appreciated its medicinal benefits. The historical origins of tea-drinking are unclear, although many scholars believe that the wild tea plant was first domesticated in what is now Sichuan. One fourth-century text, Chang Ju's *Treatise on the Kingdom of Huayang*, mentions that tea was given in tribute to King Wen, the twelfth-century-BC founder of the Zhou dynasty, by tribal heads of the district; the same text also describes the cultivation of tea in several parts of the region.

These days, Sichuan is one of the centers of Chinese tea production. The most famous local varieties are all green teas, including Mengding sweet-dew tea (*mengding ganlu*) from Mingshan county, Maofeng tea from Ya'an county (*maofeng cha*), green bamboo-leaf tea (*zhuye qing*) from Emei Mountain, and snow-shoot tea from Qingcheng Mountain (*qingcheng xueya*). The Sichuanese themselves have a particular penchant for jasmine teas, which are thought to be the most refreshing and best suited to the sultry local climate. They are made by heating green tea with fresh jasmine flowers from the eastern Sichuan hills until the floral fragrance infuses the leaves. Sichuanese jasmine tea (known colloquially as "flower tea"—*huacha*) is far lovelier than the jasmine tea one usually finds outside China. It is wonderfully fragrant, with unfurling long, green leaves and drifting, tender blossoms.

The manner of serving tea in Sichuan is also distinctively local. The Sichuanese rarely use teapots, but brew loose tea leaves in china bowls with lids and saucers (known as "lid-bowl tea," *gaiwancha*). The saucer catches spills and protects the drinker from the heat, the bowl is the drinking vessel, and the lid is used to keep the tea hot— and also, with a gentle sweeping motion, to help the water circulate as the leaves infuse. Sichuanese tea-drinkers also use the lid as a filter, fanning away any floating leaves as they raise the bowl to their lips. In traditional teahouses, the water is topped up by tea attendants bearing copper kettles, some with the famous yard-long spouts, that are handled with flamboyance and amazing dexterity. The same cup of tea can last for as long as you wish, although the flavor of the leaves dims with each refilling.

Chinese green tea has an intensely pleasing fragrance and clarity. It is also thought to focus the mind, and Chinese monks have drunk it for centuries as an aid to meditation. There are many different ways of drinking tea, from the casual consumption of long-brewed infusions on trains and buses, to the eastern Chinese *gongfu cha*, with its special implements and soothing rituals.

To my mind, however, sitting on a bamboo chair in a tranquil Sichuan teahouse, inhaling the scent of tea leaves and jasmine flowers, while gazing at the reflection of trees on the surface of the amber liquid, is one of life's great pleasures.

Traditional production at the Shaofenghe chile bean paste factory in Pixian, which is run by descendants of the original inventor of the paste, a Fujianese immigrant named Chen Yijian

# The Sichuanese Kitchen

The simplicity of the equipment used in traditional Sichuanese kitchens is striking. A cleaver, a wooden chopping board and a few bowls and plates to hold ingredients are all you really need for food preparation, and most cooking can be done with little more than a wok, a steamer, a rice cooker or cooking pot, a pair of chopsticks and a ladle.

A few other tools do come in useful—a wok scoop, a strainer, a rolling pin or two—but the whole paraphernalia is much simpler and more compact than its Western equivalent. Some recipes call for the use of ordinary saucepans, frying pans and kitchen utensils, a few for less common utensils like meat hooks (these are introduced in the recipes that require them). In general, you can cook Sichuanese food with Western kitchen utensils, but the traditional tools—in particular the wok and cleaver—are wonderful to use.

When it comes to the actual cooking, a gas stove is ideal because it gives you immediate control over temperature and because gas flames lick nicely up around the base of a traditional rounded wok; if you have an electric stove, you will need to use a flat-bottomed wok. You can also use an induction cooktop, ideally one with what they call a "wok dimple"—a hollow into which you can fit a wok. In China, you can buy induction cooktops that are compatible with a traditional Chinese wok, but these are hard to find abroad. An induction stove offers superb control of heat and extremely high temperatures, but requires slight adjustments in cooking technique: the heating only works when the pan is in contact with the stovetop, so tossing a wok is impractical, and with a "wok dimple" you need to take into account that the heat source extends up the sides of the wok, rather than being concentrated around the base, as it is with a gas stove. Whatever your stove, a hood with powerful extraction to draw away the smells of frying is extremely useful.

## The Essentials

The following are the kitchen utensils I would find it hard to live without. They can be found in most large Chinese supermarkets and kitchenware shops and can also be bought online.

### Cleaver (caidao 菜刀)
The one essential knife in a Chinese kitchen is the cleaver. Nothing matches its versatility, and once you become accustomed to it you will find you rarely want to use anything else. It can be used for slicing, mincing, chopping, peeling, crushing, mashing, gutting fish, boning poultry, and even carrying food around. Almost all these jobs can be done with an ordinary slicing cleaver, known in Chinese as a "vegetable knife" (*caidao*), which has a thin, light blade, but it's useful also to have a heavier chopping cleaver (*kandao* or *zhandao*) if you wish to chop poultry or ribs on the bone. Cleavers are made of carbon steel or stainless steel; the former must be kept oiled to prevent rusting, but are easier to sharpen.

You can buy cleavers in Chinese supermarkets and, increasingly, in department stores and kitchenware shops: select one of a size and weight that feels comfortable to you, and make sure it's not a heavier bone-chopping sort of cleaver if you want to use it for everyday slicing. In Sichuan, the finest cleavers were traditionally said to be made in Dazu, a town that is famous for its ancient Buddhist carvings.

### Taking care of your cleaver
It's important to keep the blade sharp. The best way is to use a whetstone regularly. Whetstones can usually be bought along with your cleaver. To sharpen the blade, wet the stone under the faucet and then secure it, coarser side up, on a work surface—I usually place it on a damp dish towel to keep it from moving around. Holding the cleaver handle in your

dominant hand and the end of the blade in your other hand, place the blade facing away from you on the whetstone at a very narrow angle and rub it backward and forward, moving the blade from side to side to ensure even sharpening. Turn the cleaver and sweep it flat across the stone to remove any shavings on the other side. When the blade feels sharp, you can turn the whetstone over and use the finer-grained side to bring it to a keener edge. Keep moistening the stone as you go along, and add a drop of dish soap if necessary to banish any oil. If you sharpen your cleaver regularly, the process won't take long. If you're unsure whether it is sharp enough, gently press the blade into a tomato: if it's sharp, it should cut easily through the skin.

Try to keep the cleaver in a place where it won't get bashed or cause accidents. Sichuanese people tend to keep theirs in a wooden rack hanging on the kitchen wall, as do I. If you have a carbon-steel blade, rinse and dry it immediately after use, and rub it with a little cooking oil to prevent rust.

## Chopping board (caidun 菜墩)
The traditional Sichuanese chopping board is a thick, round slab of tree trunk, treated with salt and vegetable oil, which lasts for many years. In restaurant kitchens these can be enormous, but for home kitchens a section of trunk 12 inches (30cm) in diameter and about 4 inches (10cm) thick is ample. After a good session of chopping, the cook will use a cleaver blade to scrape clean the surface of the wood before rinsing and drying it: thus the board is gradually eroded, so it's important to rotate it from time to time to keep the surface even. The best boards are made of tight-grained wood like Chinese honey locust (*zaojiao shu*), ginkgo (*baiguo shu*) or Chinese olive (*ganlan shu*), but birch, willow and several other types are also used. Ordinary chopping boards can, of course, be used instead.

## Bowls and dishes
It's always useful to have a selection of little bowls, plates and dipping dishes on hand, for the mixing of sauces, marinating of meats and arranging of prepared seasonings like chopped garlic and ginger.

## Wok (chaoguo 炒锅)
A traditional wok is ideal for stir-frying because its curved base allows for even heating and for the easy movement of food around the hot metal surface. It can also be used for deep-frying, boiling, steaming and dry-roasting. Most Chinese woks are made from carbon steel, or crude or cast iron, all of which cook superbly but must be seasoned to prevent rusting. They vary in size from about 12 inches (30 cm) in diameter for an all-purpose home kitchen wok to more than 40 inches (1 meter) for use in commercial kitchens. Some have one long handle, which makes for easy tossing, but the most common in Sichuan are those with two small metal "ear" handles. Although these must be held with an oven mitt or kitchen towel, they are more stable—a boon when boiling or deep-frying.

You can also buy flat-bottomed woks, which work well on electric stoves but are less versatile than the traditional kind, and non-stick woks, which may be convenient but lack the wonderful patina of a seasoned-metal wok. These days you can buy woks in many kitchen stores, but they are generally much cheaper (and just as good) in Chinese supermarkets.

## Seasoning a new wok
Carbon-steel or iron woks must be seasoned before use. To season a new wok, scour it thoroughly with wire wool to remove any rust or coating, give it a good scrub under the faucet, dry it and then heat it over high heat. When it is extremely hot, carefully smear it all over with a good wad of paper towels soaked in cooking oil. Repeat this procedure twice more with fresh paper towels and oil. When the wok has cooled down, wipe or rinse it and dry it thoroughly.

## *Regular re-seasoning of a wok*
This very simple process is an essential part of stir-frying with a classic Chinese wok because it creates a non-stick surface, ensuring that food can be moved around easily. If you find that food, especially meat, poultry and fish, is sticking to your wok, it's most likely because it has not been seasoned properly.

1 Perforated ladle
2 Fine-mesh strainer or "spider"
3 Chinese cooking ladle
4 Long cooking chopsticks
5 Wok stand
6 Carbon-steel wok with
  one long handle
7 Bamboo wok brush
8 Wok lid
9 Trivet for steaming in a wok
10 Wok scoop
11 Bamboo steamer and lid
12 Carbon-steel wok with
  two "ear" handles

To re-season the wok, heat it over high heat until it is extremely hot. Add a few tablespoons of cooking oil and carefully swirl it around all parts of the wok that will be in contact with food. When the oil is hot and smoke is rising around the edges, pour it off into a heatproof container. You can then add some fresh oil, heat it up to the desired temperature and begin to cook. If you are making a series of dishes, give the wok a quick rinse or scrub with a bamboo brush after each dish, and re-season the surface before you start the next one. The same seasoning oil can be re-used many times, so if you cook Chinese food regularly, as I do, just keep it in a heatproof container next to your stove and pour it in and out of the wok as you need it.

*Cleaning your wok*

After cooking, a quick rinse with water and a gentle scrub with a wok brush will usually suffice. If you do have to scrub the wok hard, exposing the surface of the metal, or if it becomes rusty, you must season it again, as you would with a new wok (see p. 31) before storing it. If you use the wok for boiling or steaming, re-seasoning is also needed to restore the surface. It is not usually necessary to clean the underside of a wok.

## Wok lid (guogai 锅盖)

Wok lids are usually sold separately from the wok itself. They are not used in frying but are needed for steaming and sometimes for simmering.

## Wok stand (guojia 锅架)

Many modern stovetops have built-in wok stands or cradles; if yours doesn't, you will need a wok stand to use a round-bottomed wok—especially for steaming, boiling and deep-frying. A wok stand is also useful if you wish to stabilize a round-bottomed wok full of oil or water on a work surface.

## Wok brush (zhushua 竹刷)

Bamboo wok brushes, which are made from bundles of bamboo splints, are used for cleaning the wok between dishes. When you have finished cooking one dish and are ready to begin another, just rinse the wok with cold water, using the brush to scrub away any bits of food. The advantage of using a bamboo rather than a plastic brush is that you can scrub the wok while it is still very hot.

## Wok scoop (guochan 锅铲) or ladle (piaozi 瓢子)

Most Sichuanese chefs use a ladle for cooking because it is so versatile. It can be used to stir food around the wok, ladle stock into sauces, ladle food into serving bowls, and also to measure out ingredients and mix up last-minute sauces. Home cooks tend to use wok scoops instead, as these are better for turning ingredients and scraping the base of the wok.

## Perforated ladle (loupiao, loushao 漏瓢, 漏勺)

A perforated ladle or slotted spoon is used for fishing dumplings and noodles out of their cooking water, and for lifting deep-fried foods out of hot oil. Many Sichuanese cooks use a large, shallow strainer (8–12 inches [20–30cm] in diameter) with a short handle, which is perforated by many quite large holes.

## Fine-mesh strainer with bamboo handle (zhaoli 笊篱)

These strainers, also known as spiders, are used for lifting deep-fried foods out of cooking oil.

## Cooking chopsticks (kuaizi 筷子)

Long-handled chopsticks are used to move food around the wok and separate pieces of food while deep-frying; long-handled tongs can be used instead. Ordinary chopsticks are used for tasting and mixing.

## Steamer (zhenglong 蒸笼), trivet (蒸架)

Steaming has been an important cooking method in China since antiquity. In Sichuan, it is widely used, especially in rustic cooking and for making dumplings and snacks. For best results, use a traditional bamboo steamer with a lid: choose one that will fit into your wok, leaving a little space around the sides. You can use a metal steamer, but condensation may form on the lid and fall onto the food. You can also steam in a wok without a steamer: just place the food in a dish on a trivet, an inverted bowl or even an empty tuna can with both ends removed, and cover the wok with a lid.

### Rice cooker (dianfanguo 电饭锅)

These wonderful machines not only make perfect rice every time, but keep it warm until you wish to eat it. More sophisticated models have settings for different kinds of rice and congee. The great advantage of an automatic rice cooker is that it allows you to concentrate on the other dishes as you cook without having to worry about the rice drying out or sticking to the bottom of the pan. The rice and water can be measured out long before the meal, and you need only push the button when you want the machine to start steaming.

### Pressure cooker (gaoya guo 高压锅)

Many Chinese cooks use a pressure cooker for stews and steamed dishes; I'm a recent but wildly enthusiastic convert. These days, with my 1½-gallon (six-liter) Kuhn Rikon (a sturdy, simple, safe and beautiful piece of equipment), I can make a magnificent stock in just over half an hour and sumptuous stews from tough cuts of meat in a similar time. Most excitingly from a Sichuanese point of view, a pressure cooker is perfect for making steamed dishes such as pork in ricemeal, because you don't have to keep a constant eye on the wok to make sure the water doesn't boil dry. If at first it all seems intimidating (as it did to me), I recommend Catherine Phipps' *The Pressure Cooker Cookbook*.

### Rolling pin (ganmianzhang 擀面杖)

This is needed for some pastry dishes. The Sichuanese use fairly thin rolling pins that taper at both ends. They come in a number of sizes: thin ones for dumpling skins, medium-thick for flatbreads, and thicker pins for rolling out noodle pastry. Pieces of dowelling can be used instead, or ordinary Western rolling pins.

### Bamboo baskets (shaoji 筲箕)

Most Sichuanese kitchens are equipped with an assortment of shallow bamboo baskets, round or horseshoe-shaped. They are wonderfully versatile: they can be used as colanders, storage baskets for vegetables and trays for sun-drying small amounts of herbs or spices. When they are not in use, they are simply stacked up or hung on the walls.

These baskets are woven on a small scale by specialist craftsmen, and then touted around the markets, usually strung up on a wooden frame attached to a bicycle; some of them are woven with beautiful patterns. Metal or plastic colanders and ordinary trays can do the same job.

## The Art of Cutting (daogong 刀功)

Cutting has been fundamental to Chinese cooking since ancient times. A traditional term for the preparation of food was *gepeng* ("to cut and to cook"), and knife skills are still the essential starting point for any would-be Sichuanese chef. On my first day at the Sichuan cooking school, like every other student, I was given a cleaver, along with my chef's white overalls. It was mine, to bring to class with me every day, to become familiar with, to sharpen often on the enormous whetstone in the yard, to keep clean and free from rust. Every lesson would include instructions for the chopping or slicing of the raw ingredients—not an optional extra, but a fundamental part of the character of each individual dish.

There is beauty in the process of cutting, if you choose to look for it. Watching an artful cutter at work, wielding a cleaver as delicately as though it were a scalpel, is a real joy. And although some of the techniques can be accomplished using a mandoline or food processor, there is a certain rhythm and meditative quality to doing everything by hand that I find most soothing. My first teacher at the Sichuan cooking school, Gan Guojian, would come up and correct my posture as I hunched over the chopping board, slicing ginger with a cleaver. "Stand straight," he'd say. "Relax your shoulders and let the chopping movement involve your whole arm, not just your wrist and fingers." Cutting is not just a means to an end, it is part of the pleasure of Chinese cooking.

There are some meat and poultry dishes, mostly steamed or stewed, where the main ingredient is left whole, but the vast majority of dishes require food that is cut into smaller pieces. This is partly because many of them are cooked quickly over high heat, so the pieces of food must be small and regular if the heat is to penetrate evenly. Uneven cutting of the ingredients for a chicken stir-fry, for example, will make the smaller pieces tough and "old" (*lao*) by the time the larger pieces are cooked through. Smaller pieces, with a higher ratio of surface area to volume, also absorb the flavors of sauces and marinades more readily than larger ones.

Again, speed is important here: most Sichuanese cooks will add the marinade ingredients to meat just before they cook it; and sauces are frequently added to the wok just before the food is tipped out onto the serving dish.

Eating with chopsticks also makes its own demands: knives are never seen on the Chinese dining table, so all the cutting must be done in the kitchen. When the food is served, it should either be in manageable pieces, or, in the case of whole fowl or steamed meats, soft enough to tear apart with chopsticks. It is acceptable in Chinese etiquette to hold a larger piece of food in your chopsticks, take a bite and then return it to your rice bowl, but many foods are actually served in bite-sized pieces.

The most interesting aspect of the Chinese art of cutting, however, is the aesthetic. When Chinese cooks talk about the qualities of the dish, they often refer to "color, fragrance, flavor and form" (*se xiang wei xing*). A fine dish will first assail the eyes with its beauty, then the nose with its scent; the tongue is the next to be delighted, along with the inside of the mouth. The awareness of mouthfeel (*kougan*) contributes to the diversity of Sichuanese cooking because it opens up so many permutations.

A skillful cook can transform pork, the most common of meats, into countless different dishes by varying not only the flavorings and the cooking method but also the form. The meat can be sliced, ground, slivered, cut into chunks or chopped into little cubes. Every type of slice, every thickness of sliver, every kind of chunk will produce a different

sensation in the mouth and a different-looking dish, so much so that it's possible to incorporate pork in a number of dishes served at the same meal without its becoming tedious.

The cutting technique used for a particular dish is determined by the nature of the ingredient and the cooking method. Crisp vegetables like radish and kohlrabi can be sliced with a swift, clean up-and-down motion; sinewy meat or steamed buns requires a gentle sawing movement. Poultry on the bone can be chopped into chunks, chicken breast made into cubes or slivers. Beef and lamb are almost always sliced across the grain to break up the fibers of the meat; delicate chicken is cut along the grain, so it doesn't disintegrate in the wok.

Whatever the method, there are two essential rules. One is that the cutting is as regular as possible, to ensure even cooking and a pleasant appearance and mouthfeel. The other is that all the ingredients of a single dish are cut in harmony with one another as much as possible, again for aesthetic reasons. In Gong Bao chicken, for example, the cubed chicken meat is complemented beautifully by the small chunks of scallion; for fish-fragrant pork slivers, the celery or celtuce and wood ears are both cut into narrow strips to match the meat. As local cooks say, "cubes with cubes, slivers with slivers" (*ding pei ding, si pei si*). This aesthetic is one that I find so pleasing that it has permeated much of my non-Chinese cooking, and now influences the way in which I make up a salad or a Western stew.

Sichuanese cooks use an astonishingly sophisticated vocabulary to describe the art of cutting. There are at least three basic ways of using the cleaver, known as vertical slicing (*qie*), horizontal slicing (*pian*) and chopping (*zhan* or *kan*), and when the direction of the cut and the angle of the knife are taken into account, these multiply into at least fifteen permutations, each with a different name. Another dozen or so terms refer to other knife techniques, including pounding (*chui*), scraping (*gua*) and gouging (*wan*). The latest encyclopedia of Sichuanese cooking lists 33 distinct terms, and that's without even considering the techniques used in more esoteric food arts like vegetable carving.

A similarly diverse collection of terms, some quite poetic, describe the shapes into which ingredients can be cut: the same cooking encyclopedia describes no fewer than 63. Some are specific to particular ingredients, like pickled chiles or scallions; others are general. A basic term like "slice" (*pian*) has at least ten permutations, including "domino slices" (*gupai pian*), "thumbnail slices" (*zhijia pian*), "axe-blade slices" (*fuleng pian*) and "ox-tongue slices" (*niushe pian*). Strips (*tiao*) are named after chopsticks (*kuaizi tiao*), elephant's tusks (*xiangya tiao*) or phoenix tails (*fengwei tiao*), depending on their precise dimensions. Scallion rings are "flowers" (*cong hua*) or "fish eyes" (*yuyan cong*) according to their length, and scallions sliced at a steep angle are called "horse ears" (*ma erduo*)—just make a few and you'll see why. There are nine different ways of cutting scallions alone. Knowledge of the finer points of cutting is not required for home cooking, of course, but an understanding of its basic principles can make anyone a better cook.

The following section introduces the basic Chinese knife skills you will need to make most recipes in this book. Although I'm a fervent cleaver advocate and rarely use any other knife in my own kitchen, you can, of course, use a Western-style knife instead.

## Using a Chinese cleaver

Westerners often see the typical Chinese kitchen knife as a clumsy, violent instrument, suitable only for butchery. In fact, the common kitchen cleaver, or slicing cleaver, is the most versatile and sensitive of knives. The blade can be used to slice and chop all kinds of meat and vegetables; to peel ginger and even to bone a duck; the sharp back corner of the blade can be used to crack open a fish-head to release its flavors; the flat of it can crush garlic, ginger and scallions with a whack. Turn the knife upside down, and the blunt back edge of the blade can be used to pummel raw meat or fish to a paste; hold it flat and use it to scoop up chopped vegetables and transfer them to the wok. Any heavier chopping is best done with a chopping cleaver.

There are three essential rules for using a cleaver safely and effectively:

1. Keep it sharp (see pp. 30–31); a blunt cleaver is unwieldy, inaccurate and frustrating to use.
2. Hold the cleaver correctly to protect your fingers (see below).
3. Concentrate on what you are doing.

## Basic cutting (qie 切)

This fundamental technique is the simplest and most commonly used in the Sichuanese kitchen. Grasp the handle of the cleaver in your dominant hand, with your forefinger extending along the side of the blade. Use your other hand to hold the food steady on the chopping board: curve your fingers so that the middle joint of the middle finger presses against the side of the knife and the fingertips are tucked safely away, and always, always keep your thumb behind the curved fingers. The knife can now be moved in an up-and-down or sawing motion, or eased gently into the food, but it will always be kept in check by the middle finger joint. Move your hand backward as you cut, gradually exposing the food to the blade. Never raise the blade higher than your knuckles.

## Horizontal cutting (pian 片)

This technique is a little trickier to learn but is particularly useful for slicing boneless meat, fish and poultry. It requires a very sharp knife. Place the food flat on the chopping board. Turn the cleaver onto its side, parallel to the board. Ease the blade into the side of the block of food, guiding the knife-edge with the middle and index fingers of your non-dominant hand. Work slowly at first, taking care to slice off an even layer from the top of the pile. (You can also take the slices from the bottom of the pile instead, inserting the blade just above the chopping board and pressing the food down firmly with your left hand, but it's more difficult to achieve slices of an even thickness if you work this way.)

1 Chinese slicing cleaver
2 Scallion "flowers" (*hua*)
3 "Grains" (*li*)
4 Small cubes (*ke*)
5 Slivers or "silken threads" (*si*)
6 "Thumbnail" slices
7 Cubes (*ding*)
8 Scallion "cubes"
9 Strips (*tiao*)
10 "Horse ears"
11 Garlic cloves, slivers of ginger
12 Roll-cut chunks

## Chopping (zhan, kan 斩, 砍)

To chop meat, fish or poultry on the bone, hold the food firmly in your non-dominant hand as for basic cutting, but for safety's sake a little further away from the place where you intend to make the cut. Raise the cleaver and bring it straight down with considerable force. If you are not absolutely confident of the accuracy of your chopping, it's best to hold the food with a fork or other implement rather than your hand; not very professional maybe, but much safer. Do use a heavier chopping cleaver for this kind of work or—even easier—ask your butcher to do the chopping for you.

## Fine-chopping (duo 剁)

To fine-chop ingredients like garlic or cilantro, begin by slicing them into reasonably small pieces and then simply hammer the cleaver down on them repeatedly, keeping your wrist and arm supple and relaxed. You don't need to hold the food with your other hand if you use this technique. Some cooks will use two cleavers for this, holding them about ½ inch (1cm) apart and whacking them down alternately. You can also do this kind of chopping by rocking a cleaver backward and forward rather like a mezzaluna.

## Pummeling (chui 捶)

Instructions for using the back of the cleaver to pummel meat to a paste are given in the recipe for chicken balls in clear soup (see p. 318).

## Some useful shapes

The following list serves as an introduction to some of the common forms into which food is cut before cooking. Instructions for cutting ingredients into more complicated shapes are given in the few recipes that require them.

## Slices (pian 片)

The most basic shape, and the first stage for making other shapes such as slivers, strips and cubes. Slices can be cut vertically or horizontally, and vary greatly in dimensions—various different types of slice are introduced in the relevant recipes throughout the book.

## Slivers (si 丝)

The Chinese name for food cut into fine shreds or slivers literally means "silk" or "silken thread." The finest slivers, which can be cut only from crisp vegetable ingredients like radish and potato, are known as "silver-needle silken threads" (*yinzhen si*). To cut food into slivers, first cut it into slices the thickness of the desired final sliver; then make an overlapping pile of slices on your board like a shallow flight of steps (or, in Chinese, like "pages of a book," *yi feng shu*) and cut them into slivers.

## Strips (tiao 条)

The basic strip is cut in the same way as a sliver, but is shorter and thicker (usually 2–2½ inches [5–6cm] long and about ½ inch [1cm] thick).

## Chunks (kuai 块)

This term covers all kinds of chunks of vegetables, poultry and meats, either on or off the bone, rectangular, lozenge-shaped or roll-cut (see below).

## Cubes (ding 丁)

Made by cutting food into slices, then strips, and finally into ½ inch (1–1.5cm) cubes.

## Tiny cubes (ke 颗)

The same as cubes, but less than ½ inch (1cm) in size.

## Grains (li 粒)

Small, irregular pieces of chopped food—about the same size as rice grains, mung beans or soy beans, depending on the recipe.

## Fine choppings (mo 末)

Similar to grains, but more finely chopped.

## Roll-cut chunks or slices
## (gundao kuai, gundao pian 滚刀块, 滚刀片)

This technique is used for cutting long, thin root vegetables like radishes and carrots, and sometimes small potatoes and pieces of taro. It maximizes the surface area of the chunks so they can absorb flavors more readily. Steady the peeled, trimmed vegetable firmly on the chopping board, and hold the cleaver blade vertically but at a steep angle to the vegetable. Cut a diagonal chunk or slice from one end of the vegetable, and then roll it toward you by 90 degrees and cut another chunk or slice, as if you were sharpening a pencil. Repeat.

### "Horse ears" (ma erduo 马耳朵)

Used for long, thin vegetable ingredients like scallions, Chinese leeks and pickled chiles. Trim the vegetables and then cut them at a very steep angle into slices. Each slice will look remarkably like a horse's ear.

## Preparations for Cooking

Many ingredients require some preparation or pre-cooking before you begin to assemble a dish. The following are a few of the more common preparatory techniques.

### Soaking (paofa 泡发)

Dried ingredients must be soaked before use, and then rinsed if at all gritty. For speed, most dried ingredients can be soaked in hot water from the kettle; however, if you use hot water, they cannot be kept for any length of time. If you want them to last for a day or two, soak them for several hours in cold water and then store in the fridge until you need them.

### Marinating (mawei 码味)

Marinades are often added to raw fish, meat and poultry to dispel any lingering rank, raw tastes and give the food a base flavor. Salt, Shaoxing wine, ginger, scallions and Sichuan pepper are particularly efficacious in dispelling rank tastes. Soy sauce is sometimes added where color is required as well as flavor. For most stir-fried dishes (where the food is finely cut), marinade seasonings are added to the ingredients just before cooking. A related technique is salting, where a little salt is added to crisp vegetables to draw out some of their excess water and make them pliable.

### Coating in starch or batter (maqian 码芡)

Light batters made from starch mixed with water or egg are used to keep food tender and to seal in juices and flavors. Thicker batters may be used to cloak food before deep-frying (this is called "putting on some clothes," chuanyi). Both can be made from potato starch, pea starch, cornstarch or wheat flour bound with water, egg white or whole beaten egg.

### Passing through the oil (guoyou 过油)

This refers to deep-frying as a preliminary stage in cooking. Sometimes small pieces of meat, fish or poultry are coated in an egg-white batter and deep-fried at a fairly low temperature to separate the pieces and cook them through while preserving their tenderness. Very hot oil is used to fix the shape of ingredients and to make them crisp on the outside while keeping them tender within.

### Blanching (chaoshui 焯水)

Meat and poultry are often blanched before cooking to remove any bloody juices and give a cleaner dish. Vegetables may be blanched to "break their rawness" (duansheng) before a turn in a hot wok.

## Cooking Methods

When Westerners think of Chinese cooking, the first thing that comes to mind is often a fast stir-fry in a smoking wok. Stir-frying and other kinds of wok cooking are certainly essential methods, but they are only part of a more complex picture. Sichuanese chefs claim to use 56 cooking methods. Some of these are variations on the broader themes of stir-frying (chao), braising (shao), deep-frying (zha) and steaming (zheng), distinguished from one another by subtle differences in temperature or the amount of liquid used. Others, like pickling (pao) and oven-roasting (kaoxiang kao), are more obviously distinct. Steaming is particularly important in the cooking for old-fashioned village feasts.

Behind all these cooking methods lies the crux of Chinese cuisine, the command of heat and timing, known in Chinese as huohou (literally, "fire and waiting"). An accomplished cook will develop a sixth sense for the strength of heat and time required to cook ingredients to the desired texture and appearance. Thousands of years ago, the legendary chef Yi Yin said "the control of fire is fundamental to nurturing the inherent qualities of all ingredients"; in the late eighteenth century, the gourmet and scholar Yuan Mei wrote that once a chef had conquered *huohou*, he had more or less mastered the art of cooking.

The detailed categorization of cooking methods is a fascinating illustration of the complexities of Sichuanese cuisine, but luckily you don't need to know them all to make delicious home-cooked food. For reference, descriptions of the 56 "official" cooking methods can be found on pp. 475–478. But for those who want to leap straight into the kitchen, the following is a brief introduction to the basic Sichuanese cooking techniques, as well as a few key cooking methods that are distinctive to the region.

### Frying-fragrant (chaoxiang 炒香)

This is a key technique in Sichuanese and Chinese cooking. Aromatic ingredients—typically chile bean paste, dried and pickled chiles, Sichuan pepper, garlic and ginger—are sizzled in a wok until the cooking oil has acquired their flavors and, in the case of chile bean paste and pickled chiles, their rich red color. Other ingredients are then tossed in the fragrant oil. The key is to avoid burning the aromatics, so it's safest to add them before the oil is smoking-hot (dried chiles and Sichuan pepper can be briefly moistened before frying to inhibit burning). If the oil seems to be overheating, hold the wok away from the heat for a few seconds, stirring constantly, until it has cooled down slightly. If you do burn the aromatics, it's best to start again with fresh oil and seasonings.

Some seasonings benefit from a slow, coaxing frying, like chile bean paste, while others, like chopped garlic, require only seconds in the wok. Dried chiles and Sichuan pepper are often "fried-fragrant" together: for an even better result, give the chiles a bit of a sizzle before you add the Sichuan pepper. Trust your nose to tell you when the aromatics are ready: they should smell wonderful.

### Stir-frying (chao 炒)

Stir-frying usually begins by "frying-fragrant" a few aromatics in the cooking oil (see above). Other foods are then added in stages, depending on the time they need to cook. Sauces and seasonings are added during the cooking process. With stir-frying, the heat must be swift and even, and you need to keep the food moving constantly. A wok scoop can be used to scrape the food from the base of the wok and turn it over repeatedly. Sichuanese chefs tend to use a ladle to push the food around, and will also toss the wok to dramatic effect.

### Thickening sauces (gouqian 勾芡)

Chinese cooks thicken sauces with various starches. The starch becomes transparent and glossy when cooked, and this is what gives many Chinese dishes their characteristic luster. The starch paste is added at the end of cooking and will thicken the sauce in just a few seconds. Sichuanese restaurant kitchens have a bowlful of ready-mixed starch-and-water paste sitting by the side of the stove, to be used as needed. My advice is always to err on the side of caution when adding this paste: you can add a little more if you need to, but you cannot take it away, and nothing ruins a Chinese dish like the gluey sauce that is the consequence of excessive starch. As a rule, starch thickening is used more in restaurants than in home cooking.

### Small stir-frying (xiaochao 小炒)

This method, particularly beloved in southern Sichuan, involves frying marinated and starch-coated meat in hot oil until the pieces separate, flinging in secondary vegetable ingredients, then adding a sauce and tossing just once or twice more before serving. There are no initial stages of cooking: it's all done quickly, in a single wok, over very high heat. Gong Bao chicken (see p. 182) is probably the best known example of the small stir-fry method.

### Dry-frying (ganbian 干煸)

Food cut into slivers or strips is turned constantly in a wok, typically with very little oil, over medium heat, until slightly dried out and beautifully fragrant. Seasonings are added toward the end of cooking, often with a little extra oil. There is no marinade, starch coating or sauce, and the cooking is leisurely. Restaurant chefs often cheat by deep-frying the main ingredient instead of dry-frying it, because it's quicker, as in the well-known dish of dry-fried green beans (see p. 274).

### Dry-braising (ganshao 干烧)

In this method, used primarily for fish and seafood, the main ingredient is simmered with flavorings over medium heat until the liquid has been totally absorbed or reduced to a dense sauce. Starch is never added as a thickener. The classic example of this method is dry-braised fish with pork in spicy sauce (see p. 226).

### Home-style braising (jiachang shao 家常烧)

This method begins by stir-frying chile bean paste until the cooking oil is red and fragrant, then adding stock and other ingredients. Everything is simmered gently over low heat until the food has absorbed the rich "home-style" flavors. The liquid may be thickened with starch before serving, as with fish braised in chile bean sauce (see p. 218).

### "du" cooking (untranslatable! 㸆)

This traditional Sichuanese cooking method is used mainly for fish and tofu dishes. It is really a dialect word for a kind of braising: the food is simmered gently in liquid until it has absorbed the flavors. The name is said to be an onomatopoeia capturing the *gudu-gudu-gudu* bubbling sound of the sauce. Mapo tofu (see p. 245) is made by this method.

### Frying with spices (qiang 炝)

This is a type of stir-frying that begins by sizzling dried chiles and Sichuan pepper in a little oil until the oil is fragrant and spicy, then tossing other ingredients—usually crisp, juicy vegetables—in the flavored oil. It can be used, for example, for cucumber, lotus root and many leafy greens.

### Deep-frying (zha 炸)

Many Sichuanese recipes make use of deep-frying, either as a preliminary stage of cooking or as the main cooking method. Deep-frying can be done in a deep-fat fryer, a regular pan or a Chinese wok: the advantage of using a wok with a curved base is that you won't need as much oil. However, it is imperative, when using a wok with a curved base, to make sure that it is stable (a wok stand will do the trick). Different recipes require different oil temperatures. As a general rule, cooler oil is used for preliminary deep-frying when a tender, slippery mouthfeel is required, and hotter oil when a crisp texture is the aim. It's easiest to use a deep-frying or sugar thermometer to gauge the temperature of the oil. If you don't have one, here is a rough guide for assessing temperature, which is based on the advice of Chengdu chef Lan Guijun. Simply heat the oil with a 2½ inch (6cm) length of scallion white. Note that as the oil approaches 210°F (100°C), bubbles of increasing size will appear at both ends of the scallion as the water evaporates, producing a crackling sound.

300°F (150°C): by the time the oil reaches this temperature, both ends of the scallion will have started to become golden with caramelization, but its length should be mainly uncolored. You will start to smell its aroma around now.

355°F (180°C): at this temperature, the whole scallion should be golden and slightly wrinkled, with dark brown or even blackened ends, and you should be able to smell its aroma.

390°F (200°C): the whole scallion will be dark brown and wrinkled, with blackened ends.

### Oil-sizzling (youlin 油淋)

A number of Sichuanese recipes end with the pouring of sizzling-hot oil over spices and aromatics to unleash their flavors. The oil for this must be hot enough to produce a dramatic sizzle. An easy way to assess the temperature is to pile some offcuts of scallion into a bowl, then ladle over a little drizzle of oil and see if you get a vigorous sizzle, a minor hiss or no sound at all. When you get a vigorous sizzle, the oil is ready to be poured over the aromatics.

# The Sichuanese Larder

This section includes information on almost all of the specialty ingredients you will need to make the recipes in this book. (A few of the more unusual ingredients are described in the introductions to particular recipes.) Please don't be daunted by the size of the chapter, because the following will set you up for making most dishes:

• soy sauces (light and dark)
• Sichuan chile bean paste
• dried chiles
• whole Sichuan pepper
• fermented black beans
• Chinkiang vinegar
• Shaoxing wine
• sesame oil
• a few spices (cassia bark or cinnamon sticks and star anise will do as a start)
• potato starch
• fresh ginger, garlic and scallions
• ground white pepper.

## A note on storage

If you want to keep ingredients completely dry and crisp (for example, fried or roasted nuts), store them in an airtight jar with one of the little desiccation sachets you find in packets of many Japanese and other East Asian foods (I keep a supply of these in a jam jar).

## Basic Ingredients

### Salt (chuanyan 川盐)

Sichuanese gourmets attach great importance to the use of local well salt, which has been mined in the Zigong area since the Han dynasty. Lauded for its intense, pure taste, it is seen as an essential ingredient, especially for pickled vegetables. The difference between Sichuan salt and a good rock or sea salt is subtle, so don't worry if you can't find the real thing. If you want to enter into the Sichuan spirit, just use mineral-rich rock or sea salt rather than refined table salt. I always use fine-grained salt for Chinese cooking because it dissolves more quickly into a sauce or dressing.

### Sugar (tang 糖)

Sugar is used to give a sweet taste and also, in smaller quantities, to "harmonize" (hewei) or round out complex flavors. The most common sugar is a fine white sugar, similar to superfine sugar, which dissolves easily: this is the sugar used in the recipes in this book, unless otherwise specified. These days, some chefs make a dense sugar syrup from white sugar to use in sauces for cold dishes, so the sugar is already dissolved. Brown sugar (known in Chinese as "red sugar," hongtang), which has a more complex flavor with caramel notes, is used in some sweet dishes.

### Rock sugar (bingtang 冰糖)

This pale yellow sugar comes in large crystals, has a pleasant flavor and is used in sweet soups, dumpling stuffings and some meat dishes, as well as medicinal stews and infusions. It can be found in East Asian food shops: most places now sell rock sugar in manageable crystals about the size of peanuts; if you can only find much larger crystals, you will need to break them down before use.

### Soy sauce (jiangyou 酱油)

The Chinese have been fermenting soy beans for more than 2,000 years, but liquid soy sauce is a (relatively) recent innovation: the first written mention of it was in the thirteenth century. Since the late eighteenth century, however, it has been one of the key seasonings of the Chinese kitchen. In the 1990s, most Sichuanese cooks used one type of soy sauce that was both salty and dark. More recently, they have taken to Cantonese light and dark soy sauces. Because these are the soy sauces most readily available in the West, I have used them in testing my recipes. Please be aware of their different uses: light soy sauce (*shengchou*) is the main seasoning, with its salty-umami flavor and relatively pale color. Dark soy sauce (*laochou*) is dark and syrupy, and is used mainly to give a rich, dark "red" color to Chinese dishes. Do make sure you buy soy sauces that are naturally rather than chemically fermented.

### Vinegar (cu 醋)

This is an essential flavoring in Sichuanese cooking. The finest Sichuanese variety is Baoning vinegar, made in northern Langzhong from wheat bran, rice, various other grains and a starter concocted from medicinal herbs. It has a dark red-brown color and a deep, mellow fragrance with a slightly sweet aftertaste. Baoning vinegar is hard to find outside China, but Chinkiang vinegar (from Jiangsu province) is widely available and makes an excellent substitute. Other dark Chinese vinegars can also be used. Clear vinegar made from glutinous rice is good for cold dishes where a pale color is required.

### Chinese cooking wines (liaojiu 料酒)

Mild, amber-colored cooking wines, usually known simply as "cooking wine" (*liaojiu*), are used to dispel "fishy tastes" and refine the flavors of meat, poultry and fish. Shaoxing wine (*shaoxingjiu*) from eastern Zhejiang province, which is 14.5 percent alcohol and made from glutinous rice, is the most highly regarded, though Sichuanese cooks often use local versions. Shaoxing cooking wine is widely available in Chinese supermarkets and has been used when testing the recipes in this book. (Some food writers recommend medium-dry sherry as a substitute.) Stronger vodka-like wines (*qujiu, baijiu*) made from various grains, and around 50 percent alcohol or even higher, are occasionally used in cooking; a slug of hard liquor is an indispensable ingredient in home-made pickled vegetables.

### Ground white pepper (hujiao mian 胡椒面)

Ground white pepper is particularly used in "white-flavored" (*baiwei*) dishes, which are pale in color and often simply seasoned with salt and pepper. It is also the source of hotness in some hot-and-sour soups. Black pepper is rarely, if ever, used in traditional Sichuanese cooking—its dark grains are considered unsightly.

### Potato starch (qianfen 芡粉)

Flavorless white starch is a key ingredient in Sichuanese cooking. A slurry of starch and water is used to coat raw meat, poultry and fish before cooking and to thicken sauces; dry starch is used to coat food before deep-frying. In Sichuan, cooks use pea starch, but potato starch and cornstarch are perfectly acceptable substitutes. I use potato starch, which is sold in most Chinese shops.

Different starches have slightly different thickening properties: if you wish to use cornstarch, increase my quantities by about half as much.

### Sesame oil (xiangyou 香油)

The Chinese name for this oil, made from toasted sesame seeds, is "fragrant oil," and its deep, nutty aroma is highly prized. Sesame oil is used in dressings for cold dishes and also to enhance the fragrance of hot dishes. For the latter, because of the volatility of its fragrance, it is almost always added right at the end of cooking, off the heat.

Toasted sesame oil is readily available in Chinese shops and mainstream supermarkets. Do make sure you choose a pure sesame oil and not one blended with other, plainer oils. This oil is used in tiny quantities, so a small bottle lasts a long time.

### Sesame paste (zhima jiang 芝麻酱)

The toasted sesame paste used in Sichuanese cold dishes has a wonderful nuttiness. If you can, choose sesame paste that is dark rather than light brown, and avoid tahini, which has a very different flavor. Sesame paste separates in the jar into a layer of thick paste and a layer of oil. Before use, you need to mix it well and then thin it down with some vegetable oil or water until it has a runny, creamy consistency. Alternatively, you can make your own (see p. 457).

1 Chinese green garlic (*suanmiao*)
2 Scallions
3 Garlic
4 Ginger
5 Tianjin preserved vegetable
6 Sesame oil
7 Clear rice vinegar
8 Strong Chinese *baijiu* grain liquor
9 Shaoxing wine
10 Chinkiang vinegar
11 Fermented black beans, Cantonese
   (above right) and Sichuanese (below)
12 Soy sauces, dark and light
13 Sesame paste
14 Sichuan preserved mustard tuber
   (*zhacai*)
15 Fermented glutinous rice wine
   (*laozao*)
16 Spicy fermented tofu
17 Yibin *yacai* (preserved vegetable)
18 Sweet flour sauce
19 Packet of sweet flour sauce
20 Pickled mustard greens (*suancai*)
21 Spices: Chinese black cardamom
   and sand ginger (in dish), star anise,
   fennel seeds, sliced licorice root,
   cassia bark

### Sesame seeds (zhima 芝麻)

The Sichuanese use both white and black sesame seeds. Toasted white sesame seeds are mainly used as a garnish, while toasted black sesame seeds are typically used in sweet dishes. To toast raw sesame seeds, stir them in a dry wok over very low heat for a few minutes, until they are fragrant, brittle and (in the case of the white ones) tinged with gold (see p. 457). In this book, sesame seeds refers to white sesame seeds unless otherwise specified.

### Fermented black beans (douchi 豆豉)

These intensely savory fermented beans, the main ingredient of Chinese black bean sauce, are made by steaming soaked dried soy beans, allowing them to become moldy, then mixing them with salt, liquor and spices and leaving them to ripen and ferment for several months—a method that dates back nearly two-and-a-half millennia, to the time of Confucius. The final flavor of the beans is reminiscent of a good soy sauce, and they will keep indefinitely (the 2,000-year-old beans in the Hunan Provincial Museum, excavated from a nobleman's tomb, look much the same as those in my kitchen!). The finest Sichuanese black beans, made in the county of Tongchuan, are plump, glossy and powerfully fragrant. The Cantonese black beans available in most Chinese supermarkets are smaller and drier, but they can be used interchangeably. For best results, rinse Cantonese beans in cold water before use.

### Sweet flour sauce (tianmianjiang 甜面酱)

This thick, dark, glossy paste is made from a fermented wheat-flour dough and is a descendant of the thick fermented sauces that were the key savory seasoning in China until the advent of liquid soy sauce. It is used in some stir-fried dishes and in the curing of winter meats, and can also be used as a dip for delicacies such as fragrant and crispy duck. It is similar to the "sweet bean sauce" that is also sold in Chinese shops. As the English translations of the names of these sauces are inconsistent, it's best to take an image of the Chinese characters above on your phone when looking for sweet flour sauce.

### Cooking oils and fats

Rapeseed oil (*caizi you* 菜籽油), which is made from toasted yellow rapeseeds and has a deep amber color, is the traditional Sichuanese vegetable oil. It has a glorious, toasty aroma that adds an extra dimension to chile oil and all kinds of dishes. In recent decades, however, artisanal rapeseed oil has been gradually eclipsed by refined oils made from rapeseeds, soy beans, sunflower seeds and peanuts, which are often cheaper and lighter but have less character.

Pork lard is used for its luxurious flavor in stir-fried dishes and many sweet confections, and beef tallow is an essential ingredient in Sichuanese hotpot. Chicken fat, a delicious luxury, is used occasionally, especially in banquet cooking. Many chefs use a mixture of rapeseed oil and lard ("blended oil," *hunheyou*) for cooking.

For stir-frying, you need to use an oil that is stable at high temperatures: I recommend rapeseed oil, peanut oil, sunflower oil or lard. Coconut oil is a good vegetarian substitute for lard, especially in sweet dishes—although it is not generally used in Sichuan.

## Chiles and Sichuan Pepper

### Dried chiles (gan lajiao 干辣椒)

Sun-dried chiles are indispensable in Sichuanese cooking. Several varieties can be found in the region's markets. The classic local variety, the long, broad *erjingtiao*, has a mild heat and a wonderful flavor but is increasingly hard to find because of the loss of local farmland; traditionally, it is favored for pickling and for chile oil. More common are smaller dried chiles, either the plump "facing-heaven chile" (*chaotianjiao*), which is moderately hot, very fragrant and named because its fruits grow upward, facing the sky, and the smaller "little rice chile" (*xiaomila*), a thin, pointy variety typically grown in Yunnan, Guizhou and Henan provinces. Short, squat, pointy chiles are known as "bullets" (*zidantou*), while rounder, plumper chiles are called "lantern chiles" (*denglongjiao*). Other local types include "seven-star" chiles (*qixingjiao*), named for the way the chiles cluster in bunches of about seven. In general, there's a degree of confusion and inconsistency over the labeling of chile varieties, both in Sichuan and abroad. What you do need is chiles that are red and lustrous, fragrant and not overpoweringly hot (hot Indian or Thai chiles can be unpalatable when used in Sichuanese quantities). With the growing international popularity of Sichuanese food, many Chinese supermarkets stock large bags of chiles suitable for Sichuanese cooking: mostly small, pointy chiles, but also the plump "facing heaven" or "bullet" types. Any of these can be used in the recipes in this book.

In southern Sichuan, two interesting dried-chile preparations are widely used. One is *ciba* chiles: dried chiles soaked, pounded to a paste and then mixed with other flavorings (see p. 468). The other is *cuo* or "rubbed" chiles: dried chiles gently toasted over the embers of the stove, dusted off and rubbed into coarse flakes for use as a seasoning.

### Ground chiles (lajiao mian 辣椒面)

A coarse powder made by toasting and then pounding sun-dried chiles with their seeds. In Sichuan, this is typically made from mild, fragrant *erjingtiao* or "little rice" chiles. Ground chiles are used both in cooking and as a dip for cooked meats and poultry. They are also the key ingredient in chile oil, an essential seasoning in many Sichuanese cold dishes. Grinding your own chiles is easy (see p. 454), but if you wish to save time, a good option is coarsely ground Korean chiles. While they are not as hot or fragrant as the Sichuanese version, they can easily be found in East Asian supermarkets and give a wonderful ruby-red color to chile oil.

### Chile oil (hongyou 红油)

Chile oil, literally "red oil," is mostly used in cold dishes and dips, but can also be added to hot dishes for extra color and luster. The Cantonese chile oil commonly sold in Chinese supermarkets often includes dried shrimp and other ingredients, and can be excessively hot; you may wish to reduce the quantities suggested in the recipes if you use store-bought chile oil. It's much better to make your own (see p. 455), which is quick and easy, and it will keep for ages. Some Sichuanese chefs flavor their chile oil with a number of other aromatics and spices, but purists insist that it should contain nothing but pounded chiles, a few sesame seeds and oil.

### Sichuan chile bean paste
### (pixian douban, doubanjiang 郫县豆瓣, 豆瓣酱)

This rich paste, made from fermented fava beans and *erjingtiao* chiles, is indispensable in Sichuanese cooking, lending its savory flavor, gentle heat and deep red color to many hearty local dishes. It is made in Pixian, just outside Chengdu, where it is available in several stages of maturity. The freshest paste, just a year old, is bright red, the most mature a dark purple, although it's most often used when it's a deep red-brown color, after 2–3 years. (For more information, see pp. 429–430.)

Outside China, the most widely available chile bean paste is the Lee Kum Kee version, which is fairly smooth, with a deep orange color, but includes non-traditional ingredients such as soy beans and garlic. For more authentic flavors, seek out real Pixian paste, which should be a reddish brown and contain only chiles, fava beans, salt and wheat flour. Many Chinese chefs now also use a modern version called hot fava bean paste or "red-oil" bean sauce (*hongyou douban*), which has an oily appearance and gives a gorgeous red color to dishes, but is seen as less authentic; this is increasingly available in Chinese supermarkets. The saltiness and heat vary from brand to brand, and you may want to adjust the amount of salt you use accordingly. Real Pixian paste often contains chunky pieces of bean and chile, so is best finely chopped before use: you can do this with a knife on a board, or, for convenience, blitz a whole bagful in a food processor and then use as needed.

I recommend following Sichuanese practice and using young chile bean paste (or hot fava bean paste) for stir-fried dishes and dips, and darker Pixian paste for mapo tofu and red-braised stews.

## Pickled chiles (pao lajiao 泡辣椒)

Red chiles pickled in brine with a dash of liquor and a few spices are used in many Sichuanese dishes. The most important type is the long, mild, horn-shaped *erjingtiao*, which has a glorious scarlet color and a lovely fruity taste with a teasing hotness. The chiles may be cut into sections and used to add color to a dish or finely chopped to make a scarlet paste. If you can lay your hands on pickled *erjingtiao*, cut off and discard their tops, place them on a chopping board and then use the blunt side of a knife blade to gently squeeze out as many seeds as possible before cutting.

Unfortunately, Sichuanese pickled chiles are almost impossible to find outside the region. As a substitute, I recommend using strips of red pepper as a colorful garnish, and Indonesian sambal oelek (which can be found in many East Asian food shops) instead of the pickled chile paste: it has a similar heat level and lends a good red color to dishes, although it lacks the fruitiness of the Sichuanese chiles. Hunan-style chopped salted chiles (see below) can also be used. Alternatively, use Lee Kum Kee chile bean sauce (*toban djan*) or, if you can find it, hot fava bean paste or "red-oil" bean sauce (*hongyou douban*), which has a brighter color and a wonderful pickled chile flavor—both will give the cooking oil a spicy aroma and ruby tint much like Sichuan pickled chile paste.

Aside from *erjingtiao*, tiny, pale green, pickled "wild mountain chiles" (*yeshanjiao*) are also popular in Sichuan, particularly in fish dishes, and they can be extremely hot. They are sold in jars in Chinese supermarkets, preserved in brine.

## Chopped salted chiles (duolajiao 剁辣椒)

This gorgeous scarlet pickle, which consists of roughly chopped chiles pickled (with their seeds) in salt, is actually a specialty of Hunan province, but has become popular in Sichuan in recent years. It is widely available in Chinese supermarkets abroad. With its vibrant color and salty, sour and spicy taste, the pickle makes a good substitute for Sichuan pickled chiles in some dishes. Do taste before use, though, as heat levels vary and you may wish to adjust my suggested quantities.

## Sichuan pepper (huajiao 花椒)

This ancient spice is still the region's most distinctive flavoring (see p. 14 for a detailed description). The berries of a woody shrub that grows in mountainous areas (*Zanthoxylum simulans* and some other varieties), Sichuan pepper is actually a member of the citrus family, and it is unrelated to regular pepper. The dried berries are pink and pimply on the outside, pale within. Sometimes you will see the glossy black seeds too, but they have no taste and can be discarded.

The pepper is sizzled in oil, often with dried chiles, to flavor wok-cooked dishes. It can also be roasted and ground, then used as a dip or a sprinkle for hot or cold foods. Sichuan pepper is also used in spice mixes, and added to stocks and marinades to dispel the rankness of meat, poultry and fish.

Good Sichuan pepper should have a powerful and seductive aroma, and if you chew on it, your lips and mouth should begin to buzz after a few seconds, and then a great crescendo of tingliness should build up and last for several minutes. With low-quality Sichuan pepper, nothing will happen! In the past, the quality of Sichuan pepper sold abroad was generally poor, but the growing popularity of Sichuanese food means that the zingy stuff can increasingly be found in Chinese shops. If it's not zingy, it's not worth using in the Sichuanese way.

Sichuanese gourmets are becoming interested in the provenance and variety of different Sichuan peppers, because the flavor of the spice is so strongly influenced by what the French would call its terroir: some companies now sell precisely labeled peppers from specific locales.

## Green Sichuan pepper (qinghuajiao, tengjiao 青花椒, 藤椒)

Green Sichuan pepper, also known as "rattan pepper" (*tengjiao*) is a relative newcomer on the Sichuan culinary scene: a formerly wild variety that was approved for sale and consumption in 1998. Its dried berries are greenish and have a vibrant scent reminiscent of lime peel. Like red Sichuan pepper, it should make your mouth tingle.

Green Sichuan pepper is used particularly with river fish, eels and rabbit. It is often added at the end of cooking, for example by sizzling some pepper in hot oil and then pouring the whole lot over a dish. It can also be paired with chiles in stir-fries, just like regular red Sichuan pepper. It is rarely roasted and ground. Some Chinese shops in the West now sell chilled, vacuum-packed sprigs of fresh whole green Sichuan pepper, which, after a quick sizzle in hot oil, make a fantastic final flourish for dishes such as fish stew with pickled greens (see p. 221).

When I received my original culinary training in Chengdu, green Sichuan pepper was not available, and I still tend to use red Sichuan pepper in most dishes. I've specified green Sichuan pepper where I particularly recommend it, but please do feel free to substitute red pepper with green pepper if you wish, and to experiment.

### Ground roasted Sichuan pepper (huajiaomian 花椒面)

This common seasoning is made by gently toasting and then grinding regular red Sichuan pepper (see p. 456). You may be able to buy it pre-ground, but I don't recommend this, since the fragrance of the powder quickly dulls; it's better to make it at home in small quantities as needed.

### Sichuan pepper oil (huajiao you, tengjiao you 花椒油, 藤椒油)

Sichuan pepper oil is made by infusing moderately hot oil with Sichuan pepper. Both green and red Sichuan pepper oils are now available: the green one has a fresher, fruitier aroma. Sichuanese chefs often use Sichuan pepper oil instead of ground roasted Sichuan pepper in dressings for cold dishes because it has a superior mouthfeel and appearance. When used in hot dishes, it should be added at the last minute, just before serving.

## Fresh Aromatics and Herbs

### Garlic (dasuan 大蒜)

Garlic is ubiquitous as an aromatic in Sichuanese cooking, and some varieties and parts are also eaten as vegetables. The type of garlic familiar to Westerners and North Americans is most widely used. Legend says it was brought to China by a Han-dynasty official returning from a mission to Central Asia, and was given its Chinese name *dasuan* ("big garlic") because its heads were so much larger than those of the wild native varieties. The Sichuan region is famous for its *dusuan*, or "single-headed garlic": fat, individual, purplish bulbs that are not divided into cloves. Garlic cloves may be used whole, sliced or chopped, or, in restaurants, pounded to a paste (*suanni*) with a little salt, cooking oil and water (if you are making this at home and will be using it immediately, these other ingredients are not necessary).

### Green garlic (suanmiao, qingsuan 蒜苗, 青蒜)

The Sichuanese also use a great deal of green garlic sprouts, often translated as "scallions" or "Chinese leeks"—but as an accompanying vegetable rather than a flavoring. At first glance, bunches of green garlic look like bunches of scallions, but their leaves are flat and leek-like rather than tubular. They are still hard to find abroad, so snatch them up if you find them in Chinese supermarkets; use them especially in twice-cooked pork and mapo tofu. Alternatively, grow your own substitute by allowing garlic cloves to sprout.

### Garlic shoots or scapes (suantai 蒜薹)

These long, cylindrical, green garlic stems, each topped with a miniature garlic bulb, are a delectable vegetable, and are particularly fabulous with bacon. They can be found in good Chinese supermarkets (usually with the bulbs trimmed off).

### Ginger (shengjiang 生姜)

Fresh ginger root or rhizome is an essential flavoring, and is also used in marinades for meat, poultry and fish. It is thought to have originated in Southeast Asia, but has been cultivated in China (and in Sichuan) since ancient times.

1 "Red-oil" bean sauce
2 Pixian chile bean paste
3 Lee Kum Kee chile bean sauce
  (*toban djan*)
4 Juancheng chile bean paste, from
  Pixian
5 Home-made chile oil
6 Coarsely ground Korean chiles
7 Red Sichuan pepper
8 Green Sichuan pepper
9 Ground roasted (red) Sichuan pepper
10 Sichuan pepper oil
11 Chopped salted chiles
12 Sambal oelek pickled chile paste
13 Sichuanese pickled *erjingtiao* chiles
14 Sichuanese dried *erjingtiao* chiles
15 Dried pointy chiles ("little rice chile"
  type)
16 Dried plump chiles ("facing-heaven"
  type)

The mature rhizome of the plant is the most common and indispensable variety, while the pale, tender young stems are used as a vegetable in stir-fries and can also be pickled.

The fresh ginger that is widely available in the West is suitable for most uses. When whole pieces of ginger are crushed and added to a dish, the skin is left on for maximum taste and fragrance (the ginger is not eaten, so the coarse peel doesn't matter). When ginger is sliced, slivered or finely chopped and used in dishes where it will actually be eaten, it should be peeled: the easiest and least wasteful way to do this is to scrape off the peel with a spoon—surprising, but true!

Pickled ginger (which is sold in some East Asian supermarkets) is often paired with pickled red chiles as an aromatic, particularly in southern Sichuanese cooking.

### Scallions or Chinese green onions (cong 葱)

Chinese green onions are similar to Western scallions, but with much longer leaves and without swollen bulbs. Most Chinese sources say they are native to Siberia, but they have been cultivated in China for more than 3,000 years. In China, slender green onions ("small onions," *xiaocong*) are used raw as a garnish, while thicker, older onions ("large onions," *dacong*) are typically used in marinades and cooked dishes. The quantities given in this book assume the use of normal Western scallions with straight rather than swollen bulbs.

If you are using uncooked scallion whites in cold dishes, it's worth tasting them first: if they have a very harsh oniony flavor, you can subdue this by steaming or microwaving them for a few seconds, or briefly soaking them in cold salted water.

In southern Sichuan, people also use a sort of onion known as "bitter shallot" (*kujiao*). A variety of *Allium Chinese*, these tiny white onions are the size of scallion bulbs, with thin, papery skins. Raw, they have a strong and bitter oniony taste.

### White Beijing leek (jingcong 京葱)

This is like a leek-sized version of a scallion, but with a milder flavor. In cooked dishes, baby leeks or scallion whites can be used as a substitute. For raw dishes, use scallion whites, but make sure their flavor is not too aggressive.

### Chinese chives (jiucai 韭菜)

Chinese chives have flat leaves and are much larger than common Western chives. They are native to China, where they are thought to have been cultivated for some 3,000 years. There are several varieties, including regular Chinese chives (also known as garlic chives) and flowering chive stems topped with tiny buds, as well as yellow chives.

### Cilantro leaves (xiangcai 香菜)

Cilantro (also known as *yansui*) is the main fresh herb used in Sichuanese cooking. Its strong fragrance and fresh taste are particularly used to soften and refine the flavors of red meat and other strong-tasting ingredients. The herb is also used as a colorful garnish, and its tender stems and leaves can be stir-fried or eaten as a salad. Cilantro is native to the Mediterranean, but found its way to China during the Han dynasty.

### Korean mint (huoxiang 藿香)

In southern Sichuan, Korean mint (*Agastache rugosa*) is often used, mainly in fish and eel dishes, to dispel "fishy tastes" and refine flavors. It is also known as wrinkled giant hyssop.

### Spearmint (yuxiang, liulanxiang 鱼香, 留兰香)

Another herb used in southern Sichuan is spearmint (*Mentha spicata*), which is used in dips and also in cooking fish and eels, to dispel "fishy tastes" and refine flavors.

### Fish mint or heartleaf (zhe'ergen, ze'ergen, yuxingcao 折耳根, 则耳根, 鱼腥草)

This unusual herb (*Houttuynia cordata*) has a curious, sour taste and strongly divides opinion, even in Sichuan. Its leafy stems and pale roots are both used in Sichuanese dishes. It can sometimes be found in Vietnamese shops (called *diep ca*).

## Dried Spices

"Fragrant things" (*xiangliao*) is the term commonly used to describe a range of spices used in the preparation of aromatic stewed meats, Sichuan hotpot and other dishes. The most essential are listed below. Other spices that are less widely used include cloves (*dingxiang*), galangal (*gaoliangjiang*), nutmeg (*roudoukou*), other types of cardamom, bay leaves and various more unusual spices.

### Cassia bark (guipi 桂皮)
This is the dried bark of the Chinese cassia tree (*Cinnamomum cassia*), which has a cinnamon-like flavor but is considered inferior to true cinnamon. It comes in long, thick strips, with a dark brown outer layer covering caramel-colored wood. Cassia bark should be used in small amounts to avoid giving dishes a bitter flavor. Cinnamon sticks can be used instead.

### Star anise (bajiao, da huixiang 八角, 大茴香)
The sun-dried fruit of an evergreen tree that, when ripe, pops open into a lovely eight-pointed star (the name means "eight horns" in Chinese). The stars are reddish-brown in color and have a deep anise fragrance. Use them judiciously: too much can overwhelm a dish.

### Chinese black cardamom (caoguo 草果)
The ridged, olive-shaped dried fruit of a variety of "false cardamom" (*Amomum tsao-kuo*), this spice has a cool, cardamom-like flavor. Dark brown and roughly nutmeg-sized, they are sold in Chinese supermarkets as "tsao kuo," and mainly used in aromatic stews. Smack them gently with a cleaver or a rolling pin before use to crack them open.

### Sand ginger
(shajiang, shannai, sannai 沙姜, 山奈, 三奈)
The dried, sliced rhizome of *Kaempferia galanga*, a plant in the ginger family, this spice looks like dried ginger and has a peppery taste. It is often sold in Chinese supermarkets simply as "sliced ginger." The spice, which is used in aromatic stews, is native to India but is also grown in southern China.

### Fennel seeds (xiao huixiang 小茴香)
These pale green seeds have an anise flavor, and are grown in several parts of northern China, although they are not a native spice. They are used in aromatic stews and in five-spice powder.

### Licorice root (gancao 甘草)
These thin, diagonal slices of dried licorice root are often used in spice mixes.

### Five-spice powder (wuxiang fen 五香粉)
Five-spice powder is made by grinding several spices together—not necessarily five. It typically includes the following: star anise, cassia bark, Sichuan pepper and fennel seeds. Sand ginger, cloves and licorice root are sometimes added. Many Chinese cooks also use more complex blends of spices, including "13-spice" and "18-spice."

### Tangerine peel (chenpi 陈皮)
The dried peel of mandarin oranges or tangerines is used occasionally in Sichuanese cooking. You can make it yourself by scraping the pith from strips of fragrant orange or tangerine peel and drying them in an airy place. When they are bone-dry, place them in an airtight jar and they will keep for ages, improving in flavor as they mature. Dark brown dried tangerine peel can be bought in Chinese supermarkets.

## Preserved Foods

The pickles and preserves traditionally made by Sichuanese farmers to deal with gluts have become a distinctive local flavor. Crisp vegetables pickled in brine, wine, sugar and spices are eaten as a side dish to cleanse and refresh the palate; salted vegetables with chile are used in some recipes and as a relish; pickled chiles (see p. 50) have many culinary uses. The following preserved foods are important ingredients in some Sichuanese dishes. If you want to try making your own Sichuanese preserves, recipes for some of the simpler preparations are given in the Preserved Foods chapter (see pp. 420–428).

## Preserved mustard tuber (zhacai 榨菜)

This plump vegetable, often sold in tins as "Sichuan preserved vegetable," has a crisp texture and salty, sour, spicy taste. Once opened, the pickle keeps well in the fridge and is particularly delicious stir-fried with pork. It should be rinsed thoroughly before use. "Big-headed vegetable" (*datoucai*), made from a kind of turnip, is another famous Sichuanese pickle with similar uses, but is hard to find outside China (see p. 417 for more on these pickles).

## Yibin yacai (yibin yacai 宜宾芽菜)

This dark, aromatic, salty-sweet pickle is made from the tender stems of a variety of mustard green (*erpingzhuang*). The stems are sun-dried, salt-fermented for a couple of months, then mixed with spices and a brown sugar syrup and packed into jars to undergo a second and longer fermentation (see p. 417). The pickle, a specialty of the city of Yibin, can be ordered online and is sold in some Chinese shops. (If you can't find it, Tianjin preserved vegetable, packed in earthenware jars, is more widely available—with a similar texture and taste, it makes a decent substitute.) *Yacai* can be extremely salty and is best rinsed before use; it is often stir-fried in a little oil before being added to a dish. Note that for non-Sichuanese Chinese people, *yacai* is the word for bean sprouts, which can lead to confusion when shopping!

## Pickled mustard greens (suancai 酸菜)

This leafy variety of mustard, pickled in spiced brine, has a sour and salty taste. It is often used in soups and goes particularly well with fish. Chinese and Thai versions, packaged in brine in plastic pouches, can be found in most Chinese shops.

## Preserved duck eggs (pidan 皮蛋)

Preserved duck eggs are made by curing raw duck (or sometimes quail or chicken) eggs in an alkaline mixture that "cooks" them chemically, transforming their appearance and unleashing delicious umami flavors. While Westerners call them "century eggs" or "thousand-year-old eggs," their Chinese name is simply *pidan* ("skin eggs"), and they can be found in most Chinese supermarkets. To use them, simply crack the shells and peel them off, then rinse the eggs and allow to dry. You may notice pretty, fern-like patterns below the surface of the eggs: these are created during their chemical transformation and are a sign of quality and richness of flavor. Preserved eggs can be eaten raw or used in cooked dishes. If you buy the eggs in China, they may still be coated in the thick curing paste, a mixture of mud, ash or lime, salt and rice husks: the husks are added to keep them from sticking together. The paste should be chipped and rinsed off before you crack open the eggs.

# Dried Mushrooms

## Dried wood ear mushrooms (mu'er 木耳)

Wood ear mushrooms (*Auricularia auricula-judae*), which grow on damp wood in shady places, have a pleasing texture, simultaneously slithery and crunchy, but little flavor. Try to find thinner, lighter wood ears (sometimes sold as "cloud ears"), rather than thicker, coarser varieties. These mushrooms come in small, frilly pieces which must be soaked in hot water for 15–20 minutes (or cold water for a few hours) before use. They keep indefinitely in a cool, dry place. It's hard to give accurate quantities for dried wood ears in a recipe, because they weigh almost nothing and then expand to incredible proportions after soaking, so please regard my quantities as estimates.

## Dried shiitake mushrooms (xianggu 香菇)

These dried mushrooms, known in Chinese as "fragrant mushrooms" (*xianggu*) or, less commonly, "winter mushrooms" (*donggu*), have been cultivated in China for about a thousand years. They have an intense, delicious umami flavor. There are several different varieties and they come in different sizes: the best are those with pale criss-cross fissures over their brown caps (known as "flower mushrooms," *huagu*). The mushrooms must be soaked in hot water for about 30 minutes before use, or in cold water for several hours—their tasty soaking water can be strained and added to soups and sauces. They keep indefinitely in a cool, dry place.

## Bamboo pith fungus (zhusun 竹荪)

This unusual fungus, a Sichuan specialty, has a beautiful, lacy appearance. It can be used in stir-fries, but is more often seen in rich chicken soups. Available in some Chinese supermarkets, usually under the name "bamboo fungus," it should be soaked very briefly in hot or cold water before use. Its Chinese name sounds similar to the word for "bamboo shoot" (zhusun, but with a different second character), which can cause confusion.

## Silver ear fungus (yin'er 银耳)

Also known as white wood ear fungus (baimu'er) or white ear (bai'erzi), this delicate mushroom is sold dried, each head a mass of pale yellow, papery frills that somewhat resembles a chrysanthemum. After soaking, it expands into nearly transparent waves with a texture that is both crunchy and gelatinous. Wild silver ear fungus has long been considered a delicacy, prized for its intriguing texture and nutritional benefits (it is said to soothe the lungs, among other things). In Sichuanese cooking, it is mainly used in sweet soups.

## Other Ingredients

## Fermented tofu (doufuru 豆腐乳)

Tofu is sometimes seen as the Chinese equivalent of cheese. If this is so, then this strong-tasting tofu product, with its heady fragrance, might be compared to ripe blue cheese. The two main types are "red" fermented tofu (colored by red yeasted rice) and "white" fermented tofu, though there are countless variations. In Sichuan, predictably, people love spicy fermented tofu. One wildly delicious local variety consists of chunks of fermented tofu packed in a jar with chile oil and spices: similar versions can be found in Chinese shops abroad. Fermented tofu is added to marinades and used as a relish (eat a cube or two with steamed rice, remembering that it's extremely salty).

## Fermented glutinous rice wine (laozao 醪糟)

Often made at home (see p. 460 for a recipe) or bought from artisanal producers in a market, this mildly alcoholic condiment consists of pulpy glutinous rice grains in their clear, fermented juices. It has a rich, sweet, mellow flavor. *Laozao* is mainly used in marinades for meat and poultry. It is also the main flavoring in so-called "drunken" (zaozui) and "fragrant-wine flavor" (xiangzao wei) dishes. Please note that *laozao* goes by different names in other parts of China, including "wine-brew" (jiuniang) in the Jiangnan region and "sweet wine" (tianjiu) in Hunan. Where small amounts of this wine are used in a marinade rather than as a stand-out seasoning, I have suggested using Shaoxing wine instead, for convenience.

## Red bean paste (dousha, xisha 豆沙, 洗沙)

Red bean paste is one of the classic stuffings for all kinds of Chinese and Sichuanese confections. It can be made at home, fairly laboriously, but is easy to find in Chinese supermarkets, either in tins or chilled. Store-bought red bean paste usually contains only azuki beans and sugar; the Sichuanese often fry this paste in lard to enrich it, but it can be used straight from the package.

## Litsea oil (mujiangzi you 木姜子油)

This intensely flavored oil smells very like lemongrass. It is widely used in Guizhou province, but the people of southeastern Sichuan also like to add a few drops to some dips and cold dishes.

## Glutinous rice (nuomi 糯米)

The Sichuanese don't regard glutinous rice as a staple food, but they often use it in snacks, sweet dishes and stuffings. Short-grain glutinous rice (often sold as Japanese "sweet rice") is better for sweet dishes, while long-grain glutinous rice is favored for savory dishes. The long-grained kind can be fermented with wine yeast to make glutinous rice wine (see p. 460). Glutinous rice is also ground and made into soft, squidgy doughs for all kinds of dumplings. In southern Sichuan, it is known as "wine rice" (jiumi).

## Bean-thread noodles (fensi 粉丝)

These thin, transparent noodles, made from mung bean starch, are normally sold dried, in small bundles of about 3½ oz. Before use, soak in warm water for 30 seconds or in cold water for a couple of hours to soften. They can then be added directly to the cooking pot. If you wish to use them in cold dishes, dunk the soaked noodles into boiling water for another 30 seconds or so and then cool under cold water and drain. As the noodles are long and slippery, after soaking them you might want to snip them into manageable lengths. The dried noodle bundles are hard to separate so you normally have to use a whole bunch at a time: any leftovers can be added to a salad (see p. 92) or a soup (see p. 320).

### Sweet potato noodles (fentiao 粉条)

Sweet potato noodles are typically round, about as thick as spaghetti, pale brown in color and translucent. They are sold dried, in long skeins or loops about the size of individual portions. They must be soaked before use: for a few minutes in hot water from the kettle, or several hours in cold water.

### Peanuts (huasheng mi 花生米)

Peanuts are a popular snack in Sichuan, and are also used in some stir-fried dishes (most notably Gong Bao chicken), and as a crunchy garnish for cold dishes and snacks. Raw, red-skinned peanuts can be bought in natural food stores and Chinese supermarkets: smaller peanuts are usually more delicious. Deep-fry them as a snack or garnish (see p. 458) or roast them and then rub off their skins (see p. 123); store them in an airtight jar, preferably with one of those little desiccation sachets that you find in packets of East Asian snacks.

### Bombay mix

This may seem like a surprising interloper in a Sichuanese cookbook, and it is, but it's fantastic when used as a crunchy topping for snacks like "flower" tofu and silken tofu noodles. In Sichuan, cooks traditionally use strands of *sanzi* (deep-fried noodles) and crisp, deep-fried soy beans, but I've never found these for sale in the West and it seems too much of a bother to make them at home in such small quantities, which is why I recommend Bombay mix instead. (If you'd rather stick with tradition, soak dried soy beans overnight in plenty

of water, then deep-fry until perfectly crisp; for the fried noodles, make a dough of all-purpose flour and cold water with a little salt and baking powder; rest for 20 minutes, then roll into a sheet, cut into strands and deep-fry until golden and crisp.)

### A note on MSG (weijing 味精)

Since the early twentieth century, when Japanese scientist Kikunae Ikeda discovered how to isolate glutamic acid in the laboratory, in the form of monosodium glutamate or MSG, Chinese cooks have used this fine white powder to enhance the flavor of the dishes they prepare. In moderation, this is all very well, but the temptation can be to use it as a shortcut, a substitute for properly made stocks and fine ingredients, and to the detriment of more subtle flavors.

While Western prejudice against MSG may be unfounded—there is no scientific evidence that it is harmful—it is not a traditional Chinese ingredient, and seems to have been in widespread use only since the 1960s. In general, if you use good ingredients and traditional techniques, MSG is wholly unnecessary, particularly in Sichuanese cooking, which is already quite highly flavored. Personally, I don't mind eating MSG, but I don't add it to my own cooking.

You can buy MSG in any East Asian supermarket. If you would like to use it to heighten savory flavors, here are a few tips:

• Only use it in savory dishes, never in sweet ones.
• A smidgeon of MSG can be excellent in cold dishes, particularly those with delicate flavors. Add it to taste: ¼–½ tsp is the sort of amount you might use for a recipe in this book.
• In my opinion, MSG makes oily dishes seem less oily. This is why I always add some to my seasoning dip for Sichuan hotpot (see p. 411): believe me, this is delicious!
• Add MSG to hot dishes right at the end of cooking, just before the dish is served. Again, ¼–½ tsp is the sort of amount you might add to a wokful of food.

# The Sichuanese Table

There are no hard-and-fast rules for Sichuanese menu planning. What is most important is to include a variety of colors, tastes and textures; and, from the point of view of the cook, to make the last-minute cooking as effortless as possible. Try to use a few different cooking methods, serving perhaps a slow-braised dish with a wok-cooked dish that involves a marinade and a sauce, and then just a simple stir-fried vegetable. If you're making a strongly flavored dish such as mapo tofu, serve it alongside some delicate greens. If one dish is dry and fragrant, like dry-fried chicken, complement it with something soupy. If you want to save time, you can always buy some pre-made cooked meats from a Chinese restaurant to supplement the home-cooked food. And if you want to be really Chinese about it, you should also serve a simple broth at the end of the meal.

When it comes to serving quantities, the key is to have enough rice for everyone to eat their fill, while the number of accompanying dishes is flexible. As a rule, I would aim to have around one dish per person, with one or two extra if you have time. Quantities of ingredients for cold and slow-cooked dishes can be scaled up easily; they can also be prepared in advance to make the final stages of cooking less complicated. Don't, however, try to double the quantities for a stir-fry, because the heat of a home wok will not be fierce enough to cook so much food properly.

Sichuanese dumplings or noodle dishes can be eaten as snacks or as part of an informal lunch. If you are making dumplings, make sure you stock up on plenty of wrappers and fresh stuffing ingredients: any leftovers can be frozen and used another time (you can also freeze the uncooked dumplings, and then simply cook and season them when your guests arrive). Sichuanese cold dishes make a refreshing accompaniment to a snacky dumpling or noodle meal. Sichuan hotpot is also a great party piece, and can be adapted to suit any taste and budget. All you need is a cooking ring that can be placed in the middle of your dining table, within reach of all the guests.

When I'm cooking Chinese food for friends, I rarely have the energy to make a dessert as well (and my guests are usually too full to face one). However, after the meal I do like to serve good Chinese tea and fresh fruit with something sweet like chocolates or halva.

## On saltiness and oiliness

In China, dishes are often intended to "send the rice down" (*xiafan*), which means they are eaten alongside plain, unsalted white rice. For this reason, they can seem excessively salty if eaten alone or with minimal amounts of rice. In testing the recipes in this book, I have seasoned dishes in the traditional Chinese manner: if you wish to eat them without rice, you may want to reduce the quantities of salty seasonings accordingly.

Westerners often view Chinese food as "oily," but this is not necessarily a reflection of how dishes are actually eaten in a Chinese context. In Chinese cooking, oil is an essential vehicle for heat and fragrance, but not all the oil in a dish is intended for consumption. For example, if you use chopsticks to help yourself to pieces of stir-fried food in the Chinese manner, you leave most of the oil on the serving dish; if you use a spoon, as Westerners often do, you are likely to scoop more of it onto your rice. Similarly, with dramatic, oily dishes such as spicy blood stew (see p. 170), the food is fished out with chopsticks or a slotted spoon; the oil is a flavoring but is mostly not eaten. It's also worth pointing out that these excessively oily dishes are usually only served in restaurants, and that Chinese people generally use far less oil in home cooking.

# Cold Dishes

"A Sichuanese feast always begins
with a teasing spread of cold dishes
to arouse the senses and set
the mood for the meal to come"

# Cold Dishes 凉菜类

A Sichuanese feast always begins with a teasing spread of cold dishes to arouse the senses, "open the stomach" (*kaiwei*) and set the mood for the meal to come. Often a ravishing selection of delicacies arranged with an eye to variety in color, taste and texture, these might include slivered chicken in a spicy sauce, chewy beef with numbing Sichuan pepper and cool, colorful vegetables. At traditional banquets, it is customary to start the meal with a selection of cold appetizers served in a round lacquerware hors d'oeuvre box (*cuanhe*) richly embellished with dragon and phoenix or other traditional motifs. The box is presented whole, with its decorated lid in place, and then the small dishes contained within are lifted out and arranged around the table.

The simplest *cuanhe*, which has four small dishes arranged around a larger central one, is called a "five-color" box; larger "seven-color" and "nine-color" boxes have a greater number of compartments and dishes. The finest nine-color box will amaze with its unexpected and delicious variations. The presentation of the *cuanhe* signifies the opening of the banquet, and as the guests pluck at the cold dishes with their chopsticks, the hot dishes will start to arrive, slowly but surely, from the kitchen.

The choice of dishes is a matter of the cook's discretion, local ingredients and the shifting seasons. One "seven-colored" cuanhe served to my family at the famous Shufeng Garden restaurant in Chengdu included rabbit with Sichuan pepper; chicken gizzards with pickled mountain chiles; rabbit kidneys in chile oil sauce; a type of beef offal with shredded celtuce and carrot in a mustard oil sauce; celery and tofu skin with a garlicky dressing; bitter melon with sesame oil; and sweet-and-sour red bell peppers. In Sichuan, the custom of serving food in partitioned boxes dates back at least 1,700 years; they are mentioned in a description of banquets in the Shu capital (Chengdu) written by the Western-Jin-dynasty author Zuo Si.

Cold dishes are also served at home, in less flamboyant style. A dish of cool, cooked meats or a cold-dressed vegetable is not only a pleasant contrast to stir-fried, braised or soupy hot dishes, but a great convenience to the cook, because it can be prepared in advance. Many Sichuanese hosts will also buy a few cold dishes from specialty vendors—perhaps some tea-smoked duck, stewed meats or spicy pickled vegetables—and serve them as part of an otherwise home-cooked meal. At home, the cold dishes will be on the table at the start of the meal, to be augmented by hot dishes as they emerge from the kitchen.

There's also a modern fashion for eating cold dishes with drinks as part of a casual, snacky restaurant meal. This Sichuanese version of tapas is known as *lengdanbei*, a term that resists easy translation but means something like "a few cold dishes and a glass of beer." The food is displayed on platters in restaurants open to the street and served on small round plates. Whole evenings will slide away in chatter over the beers and scattered nibbles. The dishes are simple and hearty: cold cured meats, spicy offal and stir-fried vegetables, salted eggs and aromatic peanuts. Cycling through the lively backstreets of Chengdu, it's sometimes difficult to concentrate on the road as one passes such tables of plenty, laid out under the eaves of the timber-framed houses.

One whole genre of distinctive Sichuanese snacks and appetizers is those made by a method known as *zhashou*, which leaves pieces of meat and fish chewy, glossy and aromatic with oils and spices. *Zhashou* literally means "deep-fry and receive," because it involves deep-frying small pieces of marinated meat or fish until they are crisp and golden and then simmering them in a mixture of stock and flavorings. As the water in the stock evaporates, the flavors are "received" by the meat. Such delicacies are often finished off with libations of spicy oils and sprinklings of ground spices or sesame seeds.

Street markets traditionally have stalls specializing in *zhashou* dishes: once, when I went to the county town of Pixian in search of the famous Pixian chile bean paste, I was distracted for an hour or more by one of them. Ten or twelve great platters were piled high with the most mouthwatering snacks: little wisps of intensely sweet "dragon's whiskers" beef, sesame seed-scattered pork slivers, translucent slices of "lamp-shadow" beef, and sweet-and-sour spare ribs. I nibbled, sniffed, made comparisons and chatted to the stall-holder as the bean paste factory seemed ever less interesting (I did make it there in the end).

Because their cooking methods involve several stages, *zhashou* dishes are rarely cooked at home, but rather bought in markets or enjoyed in restaurants. The basic method is not difficult, however, and the results are worth the labor, particularly if you want to make them in large quantities for a party. Examples of *zhashou* dishes in this chapter include "rabbit eaten cold" and numbing-and-hot dried beef.

A related dish, and one of Sichuan's famous old snacks, is "lamp-shadow" beef: paper-thin slices of beef laced with chile oil and numbing-and-hot spices. According to local legend, it was discovered by the celebrated Tang-dynasty poet, Yuan Zhen, who was posted as an official to the town now known as Daxian. During his tenure, drought caused a local famine and Yuan, out of concern for the suffering of the people, went out in disguise and mingled with commoners in the villages and markets. One evening, hungry and tired, he stumbled into a wine shop, where the kind owner plied him with wine and dried beef. The broad slices of beef were so thin that golden light shone through them when he held them to the lamp, and the spicy flavors were so exquisite they left him speechless. That evening, he took the recipe for "lamp-shadow" beef back to the cook at his official residence, and served it to his friends until its fame spread throughout the region.

One intriguing seasonal appetizer is "mustardy greens" (*chongcai*), which is made in early spring from the young flowering shoots of mustard greens. The shoots are sun-dried briefly to wilt them, chopped and then tossed in a hot, dry wok to reduce their water content, before being enclosed in a pot overnight to concentrate their mustardy flavor. Finally, they are dressed and eaten like a salad. They have a delightfully tingly, up-your-nose aroma: fresh, sprightly and invigorating. They are often eaten around the Chinese New Year, perhaps alongside home-made sausage and winter-cured pork.

The following chapter includes recipes for many of Sichuan's most popular cold dishes, as well as some more specifically local specialties. They are recipes I've returned to again and again, not least because they blend so well with other types of cooking. A plateful of Sichuanese cold-dressed chicken livens up any lunch; numbing-and-hot beef goes deliciously with a cool aperitif; and many of these dishes work well as Western-style appetizers. Some dishes I haven't included because they use obscure types of offal, local aquatic creatures like loach and crucian carp, and specialty Sichuanese ingredients such as seasonal bamboo shoots, which must be eaten fresh (canned ones are such a pale imitation that they're normally not worth the trouble), but many can be made with produce widely available in Western supermarkets. It's also worth remembering that many of the Sichuanese flavors and methods in this chapter can be applied to other ingredients you may have on hand.

(center): "strange flavor" bang bang chicken
(clockwise from lower left): fine green beans in ginger sauce,
"white" pork in garlicky sauce, sour-and-hot wood ear salad, rabbit
with peanuts in hot bean sauce, tea-smoked duck breast, spiced
cucumber salad, coral-like snow lotus, numbing-and-hot dried beef

COLD DISHES                                                              65

# Poached Chicken for Cold Dishes

1 x 3½–4 lb (1.6–1.8kg) chicken
  (to give you around 1¾ lb/800g boneless meat)
1-inch piece (20g) ginger, unpeeled
2 scallions, white parts only

The Sichuanese have an extraordinary flair for dressing cold chicken salads, conjuring a dozen or so basic ingredients into myriad flavors. Such dishes are easy to make, convenient to scale up for a party and remarkably quick if you cook, cool and cut the chicken in advance. Countless incredible sauces are used to dress the tender meat, and these can also be used with leftover roast chicken (or turkey: Sichuan-style turkey salads have become an essential fixture of my Boxing Day lunch table). You will find dressing recipes on the following pages: this is a master recipe for poaching the chicken.

The crux is to poach the bird at a bare simmer, so the surface of the water only quietly murmurs; if it boils, the flesh will toughen. Cantonese chefs plunge their chicken into a measured amount of boiling stock, bring it back to a boil and then switch off the heat, cover the pan tightly and let it poach gently as the boiling stock cools down. When the liquid reaches room temperature, the flesh should be just cooked, but still firm, juicy and subtly flavored, with a little raw pinkness in the bones. You do need to take care when cooking chicken this way: to make sure it is cooked to approved standards, use a meat probe thermometer to check that the innermost parts are heated to at least 165°F (74°C).

At home, I usually poach my chicken by the following easy and foolproof method—the one used by most of my Sichuanese friends, chefs and home cooks alike. But if you'd like to use the steeping method, this is given below the main recipe.

**Let the chicken come to room temperature** before you start. Lightly smack the ginger and scallion whites with the flat of a cleaver blade or a rolling pin to loosen them.

Pour enough water to submerge your chicken into a pan with a lid that will hold the bird snugly, and bring to a boil over high heat. Lower the chicken into the water, return it quickly to a boil and then skim. Add the ginger and scallion whites, half-cover the pan and turn the heat down so the liquid barely murmurs and poach for about 30 minutes, depending on the size of the chicken; if any of the bird sits above the water level, turn it halfway through.

Pierce the thigh joint deeply with a skewer to see if it is done: the juices should run clear, not pink and bloody (you will find it easiest to remove the bird from the pan to do this). When the chicken is just cooked, remove it from the pan and set aside to cool before chilling until needed (to arrest the cooking quickly and keep the skin taut, immediately submerge the bird in a large pan or bowl of ice water). The meat should be moist and silky.

*Steeping method*
*For a chicken of about 4 lb (1.8g), bring 1 gallon (4.5 liters) of water to a boil in a large stockpot and add the ginger and scallion whites. Carefully lower the chicken into the water, breast-side down, then lift it out again, letting the water drain out of its cavity (this helps to even out the temperature of the water inside and outside the bird—some recipes recommend doing it several times). Lower the bird back in, then bring the water back to a boil, immediately turn the heat down low and simmer extremely gently for 8 minutes. After this, switch off the heat, cover with a tight-fitting lid and let rest undisturbed for 20 minutes.*

*Heat again over high heat until the liquid is just beginning to boil. Remove from the heat, cover again and let steep for 15 minutes. Fill a large pan or bowl with ice water. When the chicken is ready, carefully remove it from the pot and let the hot water drain out of its cavity. Submerge it in the ice water and let rest for 15 minutes. Remove the chicken from the ice water, then drain and pat dry with paper towels. Chill until needed.*

# Cold-dressed
# Chicken

liangban ji
凉拌鸡

There is no master recipe for cold-dressed chicken: every cook makes it differently. What all the variations have in common is a backbone of savoriness from either soy sauce or a specially seasoned chicken stock, a hint of sweetness and a deep, satisfying halo of red chile oil. Often, there will also be a spritz of vinegar, a tingle of Sichuan pepper and a touch of fragrant sesame oil. Sesame paste can be added for body and fragrance (I sometimes also use smooth peanut butter, although the Sichuanese don't). Some cooks like to add chopped raw garlic or pickled chiles, while others toss the chicken with chopped scallion or Chinese celery. As you will have gathered, this is a recipe to be relaxed about, so please use the following version as a guide and feel free to improvise.

In Sichuan, rustic restaurants will chop a whole chicken into pieces on the bone, while smarter establishments will cut boned meat into slices, strips or slivers. I've suggested using boneless meat, but if you'd like to tackle the whole bird with a sharp chopping cleaver, please go ahead. It's up to you whether you include the skin: Chinese people enjoy its cool, taut slipperiness and the succulence it gives to the dish, while Westerners often dislike it. If you are making the dish with the leftovers of a roasted bird, you may wish to add extra stock to the sauce because the flesh will be drier.

14 oz (400g) cold poached chicken meat (see p. 66),
  off the bone (about half a chicken)
4 scallions
1 tsp sesame seeds
⅓ cup (50g) roasted or deep-fried peanuts (see p. 458)

*For the sauce*
½ tsp salt
2 tsp superfine sugar
2 tsp Chinkiang vinegar
2 tbsp light soy sauce
3 tbsp cold chicken stock
¼–½ tsp ground roasted Sichuan pepper
  or 1–2 tsp Sichuan pepper oil
3–4 tbsp chile oil, with or without
  sediment, to taste
1 tsp sesame oil

**Cut the chicken into bite-sized chunks.** Cut the scallions into ½–¾ inch (1–2cm) lengths (if they have a harsh oniony flavor, you can briefly steam or microwave them to subdue this). Toast the sesame seeds in a dry wok or frying pan over very gentle heat, until fragrant and tinged with gold.

For the sauce, put the salt, sugar, vinegar, soy sauce and stock into a small bowl and stir to dissolve the salt and sugar, then stir in the remaining sauce ingredients.

Place the chicken in a bowl with the scallions, peanuts and sauce and toss like a salad, then pile onto a serving dish. Just before serving, garnish with the sesame seeds.

# "Strange Flavor"
# Bang Bang Chicken

bang bang ji

棒 棒 鸡

Bang bang chicken appears on countless Chinese restaurant menus in the West, but usually only as a shadow of its authentic self. In southern Sichuan, where the dish originates, the base seasoning of sesame paste is jazzed up with sugar, vinegar, soy sauce, chile and sesame oils and Sichuan pepper to make a lip-tingling sauce. The dish is said to have originated in Hanyang Ba, a town near Leshan that was once known for its chickens: free-range birds that fed on insects, stray grains and leftovers from the local peanut crop. In the early twentieth century, Hanyang street vendors sold chunks of cooked chicken meat draped in spicy sauce as a snack. The dish became known as bang bang chicken, because of the sound their wooden cudgels made when hammered down (*bang*) on the backs of cleaver blades to help them through the meat. The dish began to feature on Chengdu menus from about the 1920s, though here the cudgels were used to whack the meat directly, loosening the fibers so it could be torn into slivers by hand.

The curious name for the sauce—"strange flavor"—derives from the unusual but deeply satisfying combination of salty, sweet, sour, nutty, hot and numbing flavors. I have found this recipe (shown in the photograph on p. 65) one of the most difficult to commit to paper, because I have enjoyed so many different versions of it. If you like, you can serve the chicken on a bed of slivered lettuce or sliced cucumber.

14 oz (400g) cold poached chicken meat (see p. 66),
  off the bone (about half a chicken)
4 scallions, white parts only,
  cut into fine slivers (optional)
3 tbsp (30g) roasted or deep-fried peanuts
  (see p. 458)
2 tsp sesame seeds

*For the sauce*
2 tbsp sesame paste
½ tsp salt
1½ tsp superfine sugar
2 tbsp light soy sauce
1½ tsp Chinkiang vinegar
¼–½ tsp ground roasted Sichuan pepper
  or 1–2 tsp Sichuan pepper oil
4 tbsp chile oil, plus 1–2 tbsp sediment
2 tsp sesame oil

**If you want to be traditional,** pummel the chicken with a rolling pin to loosen the fibers, and then tear into bite-sized slivers; otherwise, simply tear or cut into bite-sized slivers or strips. Toss with the scallion slivers, if using. Roughly chop the peanuts: the easiest way to do this is to gather them on a chopping board, place the flat of a cleaver blade over them and press firmly to break them up a bit, then chop them into smaller pieces. Toast the sesame seeds in a dry wok or frying pan over very gentle heat, until fragrant and tinged with gold.

Next make the sauce. Dilute the sesame paste with a little oil from the jar and about 2 tbsp cold water: you should end up with a paste the consistency of half-and-half—it needs to be runny enough to coat the chicken. Place the salt, sugar, soy sauce and vinegar in a small bowl and stir to dissolve the salt and sugar. Add the remaining sauce ingredients and mix well.

Shortly before serving, pile the chicken onto a serving dish and pour the sauce over it. Garnish with the peanuts and toasted sesame seeds.

# Chicken in Sichuan Pepper and Scallion Sauce

jiaoma jipian
椒麻鸡片

This is one of the lesser-known sauces in the Sichuanese canon: a *jiaoma* ("pepper-numbing") salsa that is not hot and fiery, but cool and green, with a hint of the fruity tingle of Sichuan pepper. The pepper appears here not with chile, its usual partner-in-crime, but with the pungency of scallions and the fragrance of sesame oil. It's a gorgeous and, for many people, unexpected Sichuanese flavor. Many recipes use soy sauce, but you can omit it for a more vivid green color.

You do need to chop the scallions extremely finely with a knife or mezzaluna (a food processor does not give the traditional speckly mouthfeel and appearance). Please select fresh, tender scallion greens for this dish. Traditionally, the scallions are used raw, but chefs these days sometimes prefer to soften the raw edge of their flavor, either by briefly steaming them before chopping, or chopping them with the pepper and then pouring over a little sizzling-hot oil (if using the latter method, excess oil may be discarded: the sauce should not be greasy).

Typically served with cold chicken, pork offal, fresh walnuts or beef tripe, this sauce would also go beautifully with warm new potatoes.

14 oz (400g) cold poached chicken meat (see p. 66), off the bone (about half a chicken)

*For the sauce*
½ tsp whole Sichuan pepper
1¾ oz (50g) scallion greens
 (from about 1 bunch)
1 tbsp light soy sauce (optional)
2 tsp sesame oil
7–8 tbsp cold chicken stock
Salt

**Cut the chicken into bite-sized slices.** Place in a serving dish.

For the sauce, cover the Sichuan pepper with a little warm water and let soak for about 20 minutes.

Wash the scallion greens thoroughly, shake dry and then slice thinly. Place on a chopping board with the drained Sichuan pepper and a pinch of salt, then use a sharp knife or mezzaluna to chop them together extremely finely.

Transfer to a small bowl, then add the soy sauce, if using, along with the sesame oil and 7 tbsp stock and mix well. If you are not using the soy sauce, add an extra tablespoon of stock and season with salt to taste.

Pour the sauce over the chicken. Mix well before eating.

# Fish-fragrant
# Cold Chicken

yuxiang jisi
鱼香鸡丝

So-called "fish-fragrant" sauces (see p. 24) are most commonly used in hot dishes, but the combination of flavors works just as well with cold food, as this recipe shows. It's insanely delicious, dense with fresh ginger, garlic, scallion and pickled chiles. The chiles give it a gentle kick that never overwhelms the sweet-and-sour notes of the underlying "lychee" flavor, and the red, green and pale yellow colors look beautiful together. The sauce is typically used for chicken, rabbit, pig's stomach and crisp, deep-fried green peas, but it is equally lovely as a dip for deep-fried shrimp and other tidbits. In Sichuan, the chile element comes from uncooked pickled red chiles and chile oil, but because it's impossible to find Sichuan pickled chiles abroad, I make it with sambal oelek lightly fried in oil—which, it turns out, is spectacular.

*14 oz (400g) cold poached chicken meat (see p. 66),*
*off the bone (about half a chicken)*

*For the sauce*
*2 tsp superfine sugar*
*2 tsp Chinkiang vinegar*
*1 tbsp light soy sauce*
*2 tbsp stock or water*
*4 tbsp sambal oelek and 4 tbsp cooking oil*
*(or 4 tbsp seeded, finely chopped*
*Sichuan pickled chiles and 3–4 tbsp chile oil)*
*1 tbsp very finely chopped ginger*
*1½ tbsp very finely chopped garlic*
*3 tbsp thinly sliced scallion greens*
*1 tsp sesame oil*

Cut the chicken into bite-sized slivers. Pile onto a serving dish.

For the sauce, place the sugar, vinegar, soy sauce and stock or water in a bowl and mix to dissolve the sugar.

Heat the cooking oil in a seasoned wok over low heat. Add the sambal oelek and stir-fry gently until the oil is red and wonderfully fragrant. Add this mix to the bowl of seasonings and stir, then mix in all the other ingredients and pour over the chicken. (If you are using Sichuan pickled chiles and chile oil, there is no need to cook them first.)

Variations

*The following will all dress around 14 oz (400g) cold cooked chicken.*

*"Red-oil" sauce* (hongyou wei 红油味)
*The Sichuanese name for chile oil is "red oil" (hongyou), and this "red-oil" sauce is one of the classic flavor combinations, blending chile heat with savory soy sauce and undercurrents of sugar sweetness. It is typically used for cold chicken and rabbit meat, as well as various types of offal. Combine 4 tsp superfine sugar, 3 tbsp light soy sauce and 4 tbsp cold chicken stock in a bowl and stir to dissolve the sugar. Add 1 tsp sesame oil and 4 tbsp chile oil, with or without sediment. →*

← *Numbing-and-hot sauce* (mala wei 麻辣味)
*Another classic sauce, this adds lip-tingling Sichuan pepper to the mix. Place 3 tbsp light soy sauce, 1 tbsp superfine sugar and 4 tbsp cold chicken stock in a bowl and stir to dissolve the sugar. Add 1 tsp sesame oil, ¼–½ tsp ground roasted Sichuan pepper (or 1–1½ tsp Sichuan pepper oil) and 3 tbsp chile oil, with or without sediment.*

*Chongqing sauce with bird's eye chiles and*
*green Sichuan pepper oil* (tengjiao ji 藤椒鸡)
*This sauce, based on one I first tasted in a fabulously noisy restaurant in Chongqing, draws on the current fashion for fiery, brightly colored fresh red and green chiles and green Sichuan pepper oil. In a bowl, combine 7 tbsp (100ml) chicken stock (hot or cold) with 2 tbsp light soy sauce, ½ tsp salt, 2–4 thinly sliced bird's eye chiles (red and green) to taste, 1–1½ tsp green Sichuan pepper oil, 1½ tbsp cold-pressed rapeseed oil and 1 tsp sesame oil.*

*Spicy dips* (zhanshui 蘸水)
*In southern Sichuan, they have a particular penchant for eating food with spicy dips that razzle and dazzle with fresh chile and make your lips sing with Sichuan pepper. These two dips are a homage to those served at a wildly popular little restaurant in Zigong called Kunji Dishes with Dips (kunji zhanshui cai). The owner stands at a little table near the entrance, snatching chunks of lean beef, pieces of rabbit, duck intestines, pig's tongues and rabbit stomachs from a glass cabinet and slicing them on a wooden board. His wife works like a whirlwind, stirring up dips of soy sauce, Sichuan pepper, ginger, garlic and outrageous amounts of chiles, both fresh and sizzled into chile oil. Their son wields the wok in a kitchen in the back garden, while their daughter-in-law scurries around waiting tables. The following dips can be served with cold rabbit or offal as well as chicken.*

*For a fresh chile dip, mix together 1–2 tbsp thinly sliced fresh red bird's eye chile, 3 tbsp light soy sauce, ½ tsp finely chopped ginger, 1 tbsp finely chopped garlic, ⅛–¼ tsp ground roasted Sichuan pepper and 2 tbsp cold-pressed rapeseed oil.*

*For a chile oil dip, mix together 1 tbsp chile oil plus 2 tbsp sediment, 3 tbsp light soy sauce, ½ tsp finely chopped ginger, 1 tbsp finely chopped garlic, ⅛–¼ tsp ground roasted Sichuan pepper and 1 tbsp thinly sliced scallion greens.*

# Cold Chicken with Fragrant Rice Wine

xiangzao jitiao

香糟鸡条

This unusual dish is a reminder that Sichuanese food is not just about stimulating spice and intensity of flavor. Here, steaming is used to infuse cooked chicken with the sweet, mellow fragrance of fermented glutinous rice wine, to create "fragrant wine lees flavor" (*xiangzao wei*), one of the 23 "official" flavors of Sichuanese cuisine. It is typically served cold, although you can eat it straight from the steamer.

The same method can be used to flavor duck or fish; the Sichuanese chef Yu Bo also makes a vegetarian version by heating ginkgo nuts with fermented glutinous rice wine.

*14 oz (400g) cold poached chicken meat (see p. 66), off the bone (about half a chicken)*

*⅔ cup (160ml) fermented glutinous rice wine, including both grains and liquid (see p. 460)*

*A good pinch of ground white pepper*

*About ½ tsp salt, to taste*

Cut the chicken into strips ½–¾ inch (1–2cm) wide and about 2½ inches (6cm) long. Lay the strips neatly in a bowl that will fit into your steamer. Mix together the wine, pepper and salt, then pour them over the chicken.

Place the bowl in a steamer and steam for 10 minutes over high heat. Allow the chicken to cool before serving. If you wish, you can invert the bowl on a serving dish to present the chicken as a neat dome.

# Broccoli with Sesame Oil

## xiangyou xilanhua
## 香油西兰花

*2½ cups (250g) broccoli florets*
  *(from about ¾ lbs/325g broccoli with the stalk)*
*1–2 tbsp sesame oil*
*5 tbsp cold chicken stock*
*Salt*

This dish, in its simplicity, is another reminder that any well-thought-out Sichuanese menu should include plain, understated flavors to balance the riotous excitement of oil and spice. They might appear as vegetables stir-fried with nothing more than salt and perhaps garlic, a delicate broth, or refreshing appetizers like this one. The same basic method can be used with, for example, sliced bitter melon, peas, red bell peppers or cauliflower florets. (Sesame oil is a wonderful addition to many vegetables: at home, if I'm feeling lazy, I often briefly boil a vegetable like purple sprouting broccoli and serve it, hot or cold, with little libations of sesame oil and light soy sauce.) The chicken stock adds a little umami richness; these days, many chefs would simply use a few pinches of MSG. This dish looks best if you use only the broccoli florets (I usually peel and slice the stalk and add it to a soup or stir-fry).

Bring a pot of water to a boil. Add the broccoli and blanch briefly to "break its rawness" (*duansheng*). Take care not to overcook, or the florets will start to disintegrate; the stalk should still be a little crunchy. Tip into a colander and immediately rinse with cold water to arrest the cooking, then shake dry.

Place the broccoli in a bowl, add about ¼ tsp salt, to taste, and mix well; do the same with 1 tbsp sesame oil.

Just before serving, add the stock, along with more salt and sesame oil, to taste.

# Green Soy Beans in a Simple Stock Sauce

yanshui qingdou
盐水青豆

*2 cups (300g) shelled green soy beans (edamame)*
*2 tsp sesame oil*
*3 Sichuan pickled red chiles or ¼ red bell pepper*
*4½ tbsp cold chicken stock*
*Salt*

This colorful dish (shown in the photograph on the next page) is an example of the delicate, understated flavor profile known as "salt-savory flavor" (*xianxian wei* in Mandarin, *hanxuan wei* in local dialect), which can be a pleasing contrast to bolder dishes. The same method can be used for peas, fava beans and many other vegetables.

Blanch the beans in boiling water for a minute or two until they are just cooked. Tip into a colander and refresh under cold water. Shake dry and transfer to a bowl, then add ½ tsp sesame oil and ½ tsp salt and mix well.

Cut the stem ends off the pickled chiles, if using, and squeeze out and discard the seeds as much as possible, then cut into small lozenge shapes. If using red bell pepper, briefly blanch in boiling water and refresh, then drain well and cut into small squares or lozenge shapes.

In a small bowl, combine the stock with the remaining sesame oil and salt to taste.

Mix everything together to serve.

# Spinach in Sour-and-hot Dressing

suanla bocai

酸辣菠菜

Spinach is thought to have been brought into China from Central Asia during the Tang dynasty; its Chinese name, *bocai*, includes the character *bo* from "Persia" (*bosi*), a reference to its foreign origins. The Chinese stir-fry it and use it in soups, but it's also particularly lovely in cold dishes like this one.

2 bunches (600g) spinach
4 tsp light soy sauce
2 tbsp Chinkiang vinegar
½ tsp superfine sugar
2 tbsp cold chicken stock or water
3–4 tbsp chile oil, with or
   without sediment, to taste

Bring a large pot of water to a boil.

Rinse and trim the spinach. When the water is boiling, add the spinach and blanch for just long enough to wilt the leaves. Tip into a colander and refresh under cold water. Gently squeeze to remove as much water as possible.

Place the spinach on a chopping board and cut into chopstickable lengths. Arrange these neatly on a serving dish.

Combine the remaining ingredients in a small bowl and stir well. Pour the sauce over the spinach and serve.

## Variations

*The same flavorings can be used to season other vegetables, including kohlrabi (slivered and salted to draw out excess water before it is dressed) and—more exotically—the young sprouts of the goji berry plant.*

# Preserved Eggs
# with Green Bell Peppers

## qingjiao pidan
## 青椒皮蛋

First encounters with the delicacy known in the West as "thousand-year-old eggs" can be disconcerting. I have to admit I was revolted by their gray-black color the first time I came across them in Hong Kong. But now I adore them, and most people who actually try them find them delicious: something like an exaggerated egg, with their rich, creamy yolks. The secret, I have discovered, is to close your eyes for the first bite so that you taste them without prejudice. In Sichuan, anyway, the eggs look more innocuous than the dark Hong Kong version, with their transparent, pale amber "whites" and yellow yolks surrounded by rings of different shades of gray and green.

The eggs are made by coating raw duck eggs in a paste made from salt, mud and ash or lime. Over a period of a few months, the lime in the paste chemically "cooks" the raw eggs, denaturing their proteins and causing spectacular changes in color and texture. The Chinese have been curing eggs like this for at least five centuries, originally as a method of preservation, and later to create delicious umami flavors. The historical origins of the method are obscure, but colorful legends suggest it was discovered through the accidental preservation of duck eggs in a lime pit or a pile of ash.

½ green bell pepper, raw or roasted
  (see note)
3 preserved duck eggs

*For the sauce*
2 tbsp light soy sauce
1 tsp superfine sugar
2 tbsp chile oil, with or without sediment
1 tsp sesame oil

Cut the green bell pepper into ½ inch (1cm) cubes, discarding the seeds.

Shell the preserved eggs, rinse and dry them, and then cut each one into eight wedges. Pile up the chopped peppers in the middle of a small plate and surround with slices of egg arranged like the petals of a flower.

Combine the sauce ingredients in a small bowl. Just before serving, pour the sauce over the eggs and peppers.

Note

*The green bell peppers in this dish can be either raw or cooked; some chefs insist that the best way to cook them is to roast them over a fire. (To do this at home, roast a whole pepper over a gas flame until blackened, as you might for Italian antipasti. Place in a container you can close tightly and let cool, then slip off the blackened skins.)*

Variations

*For a sour-and-hot dressing, combine 2 tsp light soy sauce, ¼ tsp superfine sugar, 1½ tbsp Chinkiang vinegar and 2 tbsp chile oil. Pour over the eggs and peppers instead of the sauce in the main recipe.*

*The dish can also be made with preserved quail eggs.*

# Coral-like
# Snow Lotus

shanhu xuelian
珊瑚雪莲

*2 sections lotus root or rhizome, about 1 lb 2 oz (500g)*
*¾-inch piece (15g) ginger, unpeeled*
*½ cup (100g) superfine sugar*
*7 tbsp (100ml) clear rice vinegar*
*A few goji berries, to garnish (optional)*
*Salt*

The lotus, or water-lily, is a traditional symbol of spiritual enlightenment for Buddhists because its roots lie in mud and filth but its stems reach skyward to blossom in pure, exquisite beauty. The plant is grown widely in Sichuan. As you drive through the lush farmland to the south of Chengdu, its broad, round leaves extend over many ponds and reservoirs. Virtually every part of the lotus is used in Sichuanese cooking.

The seeds, a symbol of fertility because their name (*lianzi*) sounds like "successive sons," are made into sweet dumpling stuffings or simmered with rice for a health-giving porridge. The underwater stem or rhizome is treated as a vegetable or candied as a confection, and the leaves can be used to wrap steamed foods, to which they impart their subtle, herby fragrance. Even the white flowers can be gently deep-fried in an egg-white batter and served with a dusting of rose-pink sugar.

The following recipe (shown in the photograph on p. 83) uses the segmented stem of the lotus, commonly known as its "root," with its bulbs of crystalline white flesh threaded with hollow tubes that, cut into slices, reveal an intricate pattern. This method of preparing the rhizome brings out its beauty, translucent whiteness and crisp texture—qualities that explain the name of the dish.

**Trim off and discard the ends** of each section of lotus root, then peel and cut into thin slices. Lightly smack the ginger with the flat of a cleaver blade or a rolling pin to loosen it. Rinse the lotus slices and then place in a bowl with the ginger; cover with lightly salted water until needed.

Bring a large pot of water to a boil. Add the drained lotus slices (discarding the ginger), return to a boil and blanch for 10 seconds or so. Tip the lotus slices into a colander, rinse under cold water and then place in a bowl.

Combine the sugar in a pan with 7 tbsp (100ml) water and a pinch of salt and warm over gentle heat, stirring until the sugar has dissolved. Set aside to cool completely.

Stir the vinegar into the sugar solution, then pour over the lotus slices. Set aside in the fridge for at least an hour, or until needed, turning the slices once or twice so they absorb the sauce evenly.

If you wish to garnish the dish, simply soak the goji berries in hot water for a minute or so before use.

# Green Beans
# in Ginger Sauce

jiangzhi jiangdou
姜汁豇豆

1½ cups (200g) green beans or yard-long beans
1½ tbsp very finely chopped ginger
1 tbsp Chinkiang vinegar
¾ tsp salt
1½ tbsp cold stock or water
1½ tsp sesame oil

Ginger sauce is one of the most delightful Sichuanese dressings for cold dishes. In Sichuan, it is often used for yard-long beans, those long, strandy beans that are sold by the bunch in Asian supermarkets, but regular green beans are equally good, if not better. The same dressing can also be used as a sauce for blanched spinach or other green, leafy vegetables, blanched snow peas, cold chicken or rabbit and various types of pork offal.

The delicacy of the sauce means you must use fine ingredients—if the ginger isn't fresh, tender and fragrant, it's not worth making. Do make sure the ginger is very finely and evenly chopped, for the sake of both appearance and texture. The sauce should have a nice "tea color" (*chase*). Some versions of the ginger sauce include soy sauce for an extra umami note. I haven't used it in the main recipe, to let the vinegar and ginger shine. If you wish to add soy sauce, use only 1 tbsp stock or water and just ¼ tsp salt, and add 2 tsp light soy sauce.

At Hao's Noodle and Tea in New York, I once had an exquisite modern dish made with this classic Sichuanese sauce: blanched Chinese chives with juicy clam meat (I think they must have used clear rice vinegar because the juices of the sauce were colorless).

**Top and tail the beans.** If using yard-long beans, cut them into shorter lengths.

Bring a large pot of water to a boil. Add the beans. Return quickly to a boil and cook for 2–3 minutes, until just tender. Tip into a colander and refresh under cold water, then shake dry. Arrange the beans neatly on a serving dish.

Combine the ginger with the vinegar, salt, and stock or water in a small bowl. Mix well, then add the sesame oil. (The vinegar should lend the sauce a light "tea color" and gentle sourness.) Pour the sauce over the beans or, for a more refined presentation, as shown in the photograph, strain the sauce over the beans and then arrange the ginger across the top.

*Spinach in ginger sauce (jiangzhi bocai 姜汁菠菜)*
*This is one of my favorite variations, and I often make it at home. Simply blanch 1 bunch (300g) spinach in boiling water until the leaves have wilted, refresh immediately under cold water and then squeeze dry. Trim off the spinach roots and cut the stems and leaves into chopstickable lengths. Dress with the ginger sauce and serve.*

# "White" Pork in Garlicky Sauce

suanni bairou
蒜泥白肉

This classic spring and summer appetizer, popular all over Sichuan, is a particular specialty of Li Zhuang, the ancient Yangtze riverside town. Here, chefs pride themselves on their knife skills. A Li Zhuang chef can place a slab of warm pork on a wooden board and use an enormous cleaver to shave off slices so broad and supple that they ripple when suspended from a pair of chopsticks. An expert local will pick up a slice, half fat, half lean, and, with a flick of the wrist, roll it up neatly around chopsticks, ready to dip. In Li Zhuang, the slices are usually placed flat on a plate so you can see them in their full translucent glory, and served with a dip made from pounded chiles. The custom of eating cool, boiled "white" pork is said to have Manchu origins.

In Chengdu, the pork is normally dressed in a classic "garlic paste" (suanni) sauce made from mashed garlic, spiced, sweetened soy sauce and chile oil. Often, the meat is paired with sliced cucumber, or, when they are in season, fresh toon tree shoots. Traditionally, the dish is made with "second-cut pork" (erdao rou), a cut of rump with a thick layer of fat and the skin still attached; pork leg may be used, but do make sure it has enough fat to give the right silky mouthfeel.

The main recipe is for a classic Chengdu garlicky sauce, but I've included a quick version that does not require the spiced, sweetened soy sauce. You might also like to try a typical Li Zhuang variation, where the "white" pork is served with a bowl of pounded ciba chile dip (see p. 468) on the side.

A thumb-sized piece of ginger, unpeeled
1 scallion, white part only
14 oz (400g) fatty pork rump, shoulder or neck,
   with skin, in one piece
½ cucumber
½ tsp salt

For the sauce
3 tbsp sweet aromatic soy sauce
   (see p. 459)
2–3 tbsp crushed garlic
2 tbsp chile oil, with or without sediment
1 tsp sesame oil

Lightly smack the ginger and scallion white with the flat of a cleaver blade or a rolling pin to loosen them.

Place the pork in a pan and cover with cold water. Bring to a boil over high heat, skimming away any froth. Then add the ginger and scallion white, turn the heat down and simmer for 10 minutes. Flip the pork and simmer for another 10 minutes. By this time the pork should be cooked through (remove from the cooking liquid and poke the thickest part with a skewer to make sure the juices run clear: this means it's done). Remove from the heat and set the pork aside to cool somewhat, uncovered, in the cooking liquid.

Trim the cucumber and slice into very thin ribbons. Sprinkle with the salt, mix well and set aside to drain.

For the sauce, combine the sweet aromatic soy sauce with 1 tbsp cold water in a bowl. Mix in the remaining ingredients.

While the pork is still warm, remove it from the liquid and place on a chopping board. Slice it as thinly as you can, trying to ensure that each piece has both fat and lean meat. Drain the cucumber ribbons, squeezing out as much liquid as possible, then pile in the center of a platter. Arrange the pork slices around the cucumber. Give the sauce a stir and pour it over the pork, then serve immediately.

## Quick "garlic paste" sauce
Combine in a bowl: 3 tbsp light soy sauce, 1 tbsp sugar, 2 tbsp crushed garlic, 2 tbsp chile oil, with or without sediment, and 1 tsp sesame oil.

# Steamed Eggplant with Scorched Green Turkish Peppers

## shaojiao ban qiezi
## 烧椒拌茄子

*2 small or 1 large (400g) eggplant*
*7 oz (200g) long green Turkish peppers*
*2–3 garlic cloves*
*4 tbsp cold-pressed rapeseed oil*
*About ½ tsp salt*
*1 preserved duck egg (optional)*

This unusual dish is a rustic specialty from southern Sichuan. In the not-too-distant past, when most country people used wood-fired stoves of a design that hasn't changed much in 2,000 years, they would tuck a few long green peppers into the smoldering embers of the fuel chamber and let them soften and pucker in the heat. Dusted off, perhaps peeled and then pounded to a thick paste with garlic, salt and raw rapeseed oil, they became one of the characteristic sauces of the region—served particularly with steamed eggplants, as in this recipe, but also as a dip for fresh "flower" tofu. In modern kitchens, some chefs fry the peppers rather than roasting them, and then mash them with their cooking oil. Many people, including Dai Shuang, half of the brilliant team behind Yu's Family Kitchen in Chengdu, add finely chopped preserved duck eggs to the sauce for extra umami richness—which sounds unlikely, but it works. Others like to season the mashed peppers with soy sauce, ginger, ground roasted Sichuan pepper, a little sugar and vinegar and/or chile oil.

At home I use Turkish green peppers to make this dish: the long, mild kind you might have grilled alongside your shish kebab. If your eggplants are plump and tender, there may be no need to peel or seed them; if you do wish to do so, you will need to add to the quantity in the recipe.

Cut the eggplant in half lengthwise and put the halves in a bowl that will fit into your steamer. Place the bowl in the steamer and steam over high heat for 20 minutes. Tip the eggplant into a colander and let any excess water drain away as it cools.

When the eggplant is cool enough to handle, if you wish peel off and discard the skin, and remove as much as possible any clumps of seeds (it's easiest to do this with your hands). Tear the eggplant lengthwise into strips ½–¾ inch (1–2cm) thick, then use a knife to cut these crosswise into chopstickable lengths. Place in a serving dish.

There are two ways to cook the peppers. You can either grill them slowly over embers until they are soft and puckered, and browned but not burned; alternatively, roast them in a 400°F (200°C) oven for 20 minutes until browned and tender.

Trim off the stem ends of the peppers. Peel away any blackened skin as much as possible. Then finely chop the peppers to a mush, or pound them with a mortar and pestle. Place the pepper mush in a bowl. Crush the garlic cloves and add them to the peppers with the oil and the salt, to taste. If you wish, you can peel, rinse and finely chop a preserved duck egg and add it to the other ingredients. Mix well. Before serving, spoon the sauce over the waiting eggplant.

## Spicy Steamed Eggplant Salad

liangban qiezi
凉拌茄子

Eggplants are so often deep-fried that it is easy to forget the way steaming brings out a completely different side to the vegetable: a pale, soft juiciness and delicate flavor. In this lovely dish (shown in the photograph on the previous page), the steamed eggplants are cut or torn into strips and then tossed with a quintessentially Sichuanese dressing, in which spicy, tingly, sweet, sour, salty and aromatic notes are blended to delicious effect. It can be made with either Chinese or Mediterranean eggplants.

Just outside Zigong, the home of Sichuan's famous well salt (and its dinosaur museum), I tasted a delicious version of steamed eggplants at the Three Tender Bites restaurant. As a side dish we were given whole steamed, cooled eggplants, wrinkled and drowsy in their dish, with a simple yet delicious dip of soy sauce with plenty of sliced scallion greens and a little chopped red bird's eye chile. (In case you are wondering, the "three tender bites" comprised fast-fried pig's liver, kidneys and stomach.)

*2 large (800g) eggplants*
*2 tbsp thinly sliced scallion greens*

*For the sauce*
*3 tbsp light soy sauce*
*2 tsp Chinkiang vinegar*
*1 tsp superfine sugar*
*2 tbsp chile oil*
*½ tsp sesame oil*
*A few good pinches of ground roasted Sichuan pepper (optional)*

Cut the eggplants in half lengthwise and pile them into a bowl that will fit into your steamer. Place the bowl in the steamer and steam over high heat for 20 minutes. Tip the eggplants into a colander and let any excess water drain away as they cool.

When the eggplants are cool enough to handle, peel off and discard the skins, and remove as much as possible any clumps of seeds (it's easiest to do this with your hands). Tear the eggplants lengthwise into strips ½–¾ inch (1–2cm) thick, then use a knife to cut these crosswise into chopstickable lengths. Place in a serving dish.

Combine the sauce ingredients in a small bowl. Mix well, then pour over the eggplants and stir gently. Before serving, scatter with the scallion greens. Any leftovers will also be delicious the following day.

# Sour-and-hot
# Wood Ear Salad

liangban mu'er

凉拌木耳

This brisk, refreshing salad (shown in the photograph on p. 65) makes a lovely contrast to heavier dishes, especially meat. The slippery-crisp mushrooms are enlivened by plenty of garlic, chile and vinegar. Many Sichuanese cooks use the tiny, pale green pickled chiles known as "wild mountain chiles" (*yeshanjiao*), either on their own or in combination with fresh red chile; if you're including pickled chiles in your salad, their brine makes a delicious addition to the dressing.

¾ oz (20g) dried wood ear mushrooms
    (5 oz/150g after soaking)
2 tbsp thinly sliced fresh red chile
    or Chinese pickled green chile
3 tbsp clear rice vinegar
    (or brine from the pickled chiles)
2 tsp finely chopped garlic
A small handful of cilantro leaves, chopped
1½ tsp sesame oil
Salt

Soak the wood ears in hot water from the kettle for at least 30 minutes (or for several hours or overnight in cold water).

Drain the wood ears and tear into bite-sized pieces, discarding any knobbly bits. Rinse well. Bring a pot of water to a boil, add the wood ears and blanch for 10–20 seconds before refreshing under cold water. Drain well.

Place the mushrooms in a large bowl. In a small bowl, combine the sliced chile, ¼ tsp salt and the vinegar or pickling brine (or a mixture of the two). Give this a stir and add to the mushrooms, along with the remaining ingredients and more salt, to taste. Mix well and serve.

# Cold Fish in Spicy Sauce

liangban xianyu
凉拌鲜鱼

It was late one evening in Chengdu, and I was tired and wanted comfort food: rice, perhaps with tofu and vegetables. But my friends had other ideas—ideas that included Zigong rabbit stomachs, fragrant-and-hot mantis shrimp, and tilefish smothered with hot chiles. It was all delicious, but a little overwhelming at that particular moment. Luckily they also ordered a version of this lovely and surprising dish, a cool, cooked fish covered in a vibrant and aromatic sauce.

There are many variations of this recipe. Some people prefer to steam the fish rather than boil it. Others add slices of fresh red and green bird's eye chiles for an extra bolt of heat and color, or garnish the dish with chopped celery or cilantro. If you are adding the fresh chiles, I suggest you taste them first to gauge the level of heat, which can vary greatly, and adjust quantities accordingly. This version is loosely based on one I tasted in the Huahua Chunyang restaurant in Chongqing.

The dish is normally made with crucian carp, which has delicate, silky flesh; in London I've used sea bream, and I think sea bass would work well too. Do make sure you choose a very fresh fish.

1 sea bream (about 1½ lb/675g)
1¼-inch (25g) piece of ginger, unpeeled, plus 1½ tbsp finely chopped ginger
1 scallion, white part only, plus 4 tbsp thinly sliced scallion greens
2 tbsp Shaoxing wine
3 tbsp cooking oil
1 tbsp finely chopped garlic
5 tbsp chopped salted chiles, to taste
A few fresh red and/or green chiles, thinly sliced (optional)
1½ tbsp light soy sauce
4 tbsp stock or water
2 tsp Sichuan pepper oil
Salt

Place the fish on a chopping board, and make diagonal slashes into the thickest part at ½ inch (1cm) intervals. Lightly smack the piece of ginger and the scallion white with the flat of a cleaver blade or a rolling pin to loosen them.

Bring some water to a boil in a wide pan or a wok. If you don't have a pan wide enough to fit the whole fish, I suggest you cut the fish in half crosswise, holding the knife at a steep angle to the board, and then slot the two pieces back together on the serving dish (if you cut at an angle, the join will be largely invisible beneath the sauce). When the water is boiling, add the same amount of salt as you would for potatoes, along with the smacked ginger and scallion white and the Shaoxing wine.

Lower the fish into the water, return to a boil, then turn the heat down and simmer gently until just cooked (7–9 minutes). Poke a chopstick into the thickest part of the fish to test for doneness: the flesh should flake easily away from the backbone. Lift the cooked fish gently out of the water and place on a serving dish.

Heat the cooking oil in a seasoned wok over high heat. Before the oil is too hot, add the chopped ginger and garlic and stir-fry very briefly until they smell wonderful. Then add the chopped salted chiles, along with the fresh chiles, if using, and continue to stir. When the chiles are piping hot, add the soy sauce and stock or water. Bring to a boil and then, off the heat, stir in the Sichuan pepper oil. Pour the sauce over the fish, scattering the solid ingredients evenly along its body. Garnish with the scallion greens. Serve warm or cold.

# Three-sliver Salad with Various Dressings

liangban sansi

凉拌三丝

The Chinese often incorporate numbers into the names of dishes: "three delicacies," "four delights," "five-spice," "two crispnesses" and, here, "three slivers." The slivers can be anything you fancy: what's important is to include a pleasing assortment of colors and textures. You might choose slivered carrot, celtuce, cucumber, daikon or bean-thread noodles. Some cooks like to add dried kelp seaweed, while I often go for kohlrabi and chayote. Other possible additions include blanched, slivered snow peas, firm tofu and blanched enoki mushrooms. You can dress the salad with whatever seasonings appeal: mustardy, sour-and-hot or a gentle sweet-and-sour dressing. I've given a few suggestions, but please feel free to improvise. The main recipe (shown in the photograph on p. 95) is an example of a sweet-and-sour dressing for cold dishes. Often, such dressings are made with sugar and clear rice vinegar, with just a hint of salt to set off the flavor. In Sichuan, some people use Chinkiang vinegar instead and add a good dash of chile oil to the sauce.

If you're using bean-thread noodles, you'll need to soak them in warm water for at least half an hour before you start (if you have leftover soaked noodles, add them to a soup). Daikon, carrot, celery, chayote or kohlrabi should be scrunched with salt, left for half an hour to become supple, then squeezed dry. Potato slivers should be briefly blanched and then refreshed under cold water.

1¾ oz (50g) dried bean-thread noodles (about half a pack)
2 large (150g) carrots
2 medium (300g) kohlrabi
2 tbsp thinly sliced scallion greens
Salt

*For the sweet-and-sour dressing*
3 tbsp superfine sugar
4 tbsp clear rice vinegar
   or Chinkiang vinegar
3 tbsp chile oil (optional)

Cover the bean-thread noodles with hot water from the kettle and set aside while you prepare the other ingredients.

Peel the carrots. Cut them lengthwise into very thin slices and then into very thin slivers. Peel the kohlrabi, slice it very thinly and then cut into very thin slivers. Add 1½ tsp salt and scrunch it into the vegetables. Set aside for 30 minutes, then drain off the water that emerges and squeeze as dry as possible.

Bring a pot of water to a boil. Add the drained noodles and blanch for 30–60 seconds. Rinse under cold water, then drain well. Combine the noodles with the slivered vegetables in a bowl and toss together.

Make the dressing. Place the sugar in a small pan with 2 tbsp water and heat gently to dissolve. Add the vinegar and a touch of salt, to taste. Add the optional chile oil too, if you'd like to give the dressing a Sichuanese slant (this is how the Bamboo Bar, one of my favorite Chengdu restaurants, used to make it).

Shortly before serving, add the dressing to the salad and mix together well. Pile up on a serving dish and garnish with the scallion greens.

*Dry-tossed three-sliver salad (ganban sansi 干拌三丝)*
*This is a completely different taste experience. Toss your three slivered ingredients with the following: ¼–½ tsp ground roasted Sichuan pepper or 1–1½ tsp Sichuan pepper oil, 2–3 tsp ground chiles, 2 tsp sesame oil, 4 tbsp thinly sliced scallion greens, and salt, to taste.*

*Mustardy dressing (jiemo wei 芥末味)*

*This is often made around the Chinese New Year. In a small bowl, combine ¼ tsp salt, ½ tsp superfine sugar, ½ tsp vinegar, 2 tsp light soy sauce and 1 tbsp water. Stir to dissolve the salt and sugar, then add hot smooth mustard or mustard oil to taste. Adjust the salt, if necessary. Some cooks add 2–3 tbsp chile oil as well. The sugar and vinegar soften the bitterness of the mustard. (Chengdu chef Lan Guijun makes his own mustard from freshly ground mustard seeds as follows: warm a bowl with hot water, then add 2 tsp ground mustard seeds and 2 tsp warm water—about 120°F (50°C)—and mix to a paste. Cover tightly to let the flavor develop.)*

*Sour-and-hot dressing (suanla wei 酸辣味)*

*In a small bowl, combine ½ tsp superfine sugar, 1 tbsp light soy sauce and 2 tbsp vinegar and stir to dissolve the sugar. Stir in 3 tbsp chile oil (with sediment, if you like).*

# "Old Arabian" Cold Beef with a Spicy Dressing

## tianfang ban niurou
## 天方拌牛肉

The Sichuanese provincial capital, Chengdu, has a Muslim population in the tens of thousands. Most are Hui people whose ancestors, from northern China, settled near the imperial heart of the city in the seventeenth century. Like Muslims in many parts of China, they developed their own version of the local cuisine, reinterpreting classic dishes along halal lines and serving them alongside recipes that spoke of their own northern gastronomic heritage. Until the 1990s, there was a small Muslim quarter around the Imperial City Mosque, a beautiful complex of buildings with tiled roofs and leafy courtyards in the center of town; unfortunately, despite local protests, the mosque was razed to the ground in 1998, along with the surrounding cluster of snack shops and restaurants, and replaced by a modern building. Happily, at least some of the old eateries have reappeared around the new mosque, so it's still possible to have a taste of halal Sichuanese cuisine, with its intriguing mix of northern and local influences. The most notable restaurant near the mosque is the "Old Arabian" (tianfanglou), whose name comes from an old Chinese word for the Arab world (tianfang). Here, amid Islamic arches and murals depicting Arab life, you can dine on halal versions of Sichuanese dishes such as twice-cooked pork and fish-fragrant pork slivers (both made with beef), as well as more classic Muslim fare like cumin-scented lamb. This is my attempt to re-create one of their signature appetizers, cold aromatic shin of beef in a glorious spicy dressing.  →

1½ lb (700g) beef shin, in one piece

For the marinade
2 tsp whole Sichuan pepper
2 tsp salt
2 tbsp Shaoxing wine
2½-inch piece (50g) ginger, unpeeled
2 scallions, trimmed

For the spiced broth
1¼-inch piece (25g) ginger, unpeeled
2 scallions
1 Chinese black cardamom pod
1 star anise
½ tsp whole Sichuan pepper
¼ tsp white or black peppercorns
1 bay leaf
2 slices sand ginger
2 slices licorice root
2 quarts (2 liters) stock
    (ideally made from beef bones and chicken)
2 tbsp Shaoxing wine or fermented
glutinous rice wine (see p. 460)
2 tbsp caramel coloring (see p. 458)
    and ½ tsp dark soy sauce (or 2½ tbsp dark soy sauce)
Salt

To serve
½ cucumber (about 5¼ oz/150g)
2 tsp superfine sugar
2 tsp Chinkiang vinegar
2 tbsp light soy sauce
¼ tsp ground roasted Sichuan pepper
4 tbsp chile oil, with sediment
2 tsp sesame oil
2 tbsp finely chopped garlic
3 tbsp (25g) roasted or deep-fried peanuts (see p. 458),
    coarsely chopped
A few sprigs of cilantro

If the meat is bloody, begin by soaking it in cold water for 1 hour, changing the water once halfway through. Drain well and pat dry with paper towels.  →

← Please note that the meat needs to be marinated overnight, so you'll need to start the day before. The spiced broth (*lushui*) can be strained and frozen for re-use the next time you wish to make this.

← Use a skewer or the point of a knife to stab the meat all over, to allow the marinade to penetrate, then place in a bowl. Toast the Sichuan pepper in a dry wok until aromatic. Add to the meat, along with the salt and Shaoxing wine. Lightly smack the ginger and scallions with the flat of a cleaver blade or a rolling pin to loosen them and add to the meat. Massage the marinade ingredients into the meat, then cover and refrigerate overnight.

Next make the spiced broth (*lushui*). Lightly smack the ginger, scallions and cardamom pod with the flat of cleaver blade or a rolling pin to loosen them. For best results, place these aromatics in a piece of muslin with the rest of the spices and tie into a bundle. Bring the stock to a boil, add the aromatics and spices, and simmer for about 30 minutes. While the broth is simmering, place the beef in a pot of cold water (discarding the solids from the marinade), bring to a boil and blanch for 1 minute. Transfer to a colander and rinse under cold water.

Add about 2½ tsp salt to the broth, to taste—it should taste just a little saltier than a dish where you would consume all the broth. Add the Shaoxing wine, caramel coloring and/or dark soy sauce and the blanched beef. Bring to a boil, then simmer for 1 hour. Switch off the heat, cover the pan and let steep for another hour. Remove the meat and chill, reserving the cooking liquid. (Alternatively, pressure cook the beef for 30 minutes, allow the pressure to release naturally and then let steep for 1 hour before chilling.)

To serve, remove the seeds from the cucumber and cut into thin slices; pile these up in a serving dish. Thinly slice the beef and arrange in a mound over the cucumber. Strain 4 tbsp cooking liquid into a bowl. Add the sugar, vinegar, light soy sauce, Sichuan pepper, chile oil, sesame oil and garlic and mix well. Pour this sauce over the beef, then garnish with the peanuts and cilantro.

Variation

*This gorgeous version of the sauce comes from another Hui Muslim restaurant, this one in the northern Sichuanese city of Langzhong, which also has a long-established Hui community. Strain ¾ cup plus 2 tbsp (200ml) cooking liquid into a bowl. Add 2½ tsp superfine sugar and salt to taste, and stir to dissolve. Stir in ¼ tsp ground roasted Sichuan pepper, 3–4 tbsp chile oil with sediment, 1 tsp sesame oil and 2 tbsp finely chopped garlic. Pour over the sliced beef. Garnish, as in the main recipe, with peanuts and cilantro.*

# "Man-and-wife" Offal Slices

## fuqi feipian
## 夫妻肺片

This gorgeous dish was originally a Chengdu street snack, sold in the Hui Muslim district near the old imperial palace in the heart of the city. There, among the halal restaurants and slaughterhouses, street vendors picked up cheap offcuts of beef, tossed them in spicy sauces and offered them to passers-by. In the 1930s, one particular vendor, Guo Chaohua, became known for his superb rendition, and the dish was eventually renamed in honor of him and his wife and business partner Zhang Tianzheng, with whom he had a famously harmonious relationship.

"Man-and-wife" offal slices consists of thinly sliced cold spiced beef and assorted beef offal (tripe, heart, tongue and head skin), dressed with a zingy numbing-and-hot mix of chile oil and Sichuan pepper, and then garnished with crunchy nuts and sprightly celery. Although its name literally means "man-and-wife *lung* slices," there is no beef lung in the dish. According to some local accounts, this is because of a confusion over similar-sounding Chinese characters: it was originally known as "discard slices" (*feipian* 废片) because it was made from cheap, rejected cuts of beef, but later people mistakenly started writing the word down as lung slices (*feipian* 肺片). Other accounts suggest that ox lung was at least one of the original ingredients. →

1 lb (450g) beef shin
5¼ oz (150g) beef honeycomb tripe

*For the spiced broth*
*2 quarts (2 liters) stock*
  *(ideally made from beef bones and chicken)*
*1¼-inch piece (25g) ginger, unpeeled*
*2 scallions, white parts only*
*1 Chinese black cardamom pod*
*1 star anise*
*½ tsp whole Sichuan pepper*
*½ tsp fennel seeds*
*¼ tsp white or black peppercorns*
*2 slices sand ginger*
*A small piece of cassia bark*
*2 tbsp Shaoxing wine*
*Salt*

*To serve*
*2 or 3 celery sticks (150g) or Chinese celery*
*1 tsp sesame seeds*
*½ tsp salt, or more to taste*
*½ tsp ground roasted Sichuan pepper*
*4 tbsp chile oil, plus 1 tbsp sediment*
*⅓ cup (50g) roasted or deep-fried peanuts (see p. 458)*
*Sprigs of cilantro, to garnish (optional)*

**First make the spiced broth.** Bring the stock to a boil in a large pan. Lightly smack the ginger, scallion whites and cardamom pod with the flat of a cleaver blade or a rolling pin to loosen them. Place them in a small piece of muslin with the other spices and tie up into a bundle with twine. (You can add the spices loose, but then you'll have to pick them out of the meat later.) Add this to the stock, return to a boil, then partially cover the pan, turn down the heat and simmer for about 30 minutes.

While the broth is simmering, place the beef and tripe in another pan, cover generously with cold water and bring to a boil over high heat. Blanch for 1 minute, then transfer to a colander and rinse thoroughly under cold water. →

Before it acquired its modern moniker, the dish was nicknamed *liang tou wang*, which might be translated as "frantic glances in both directions," because it was a cheap, somewhat disreputable street snack, but so delicious that well-to-do people couldn't resist stopping by to eat it, while looking around furtively to check they weren't being seen by anyone they knew.

At home, it's a little impractical to cook a whole tongue, heart and stomach with plenty of beef and head skin, which is why I have simplified the recipe, to give a more manageable amount of beef shin mixed with crisp, slithery tripe for texture. Please feel free to vary the ingredients as you please, bearing in mind that different kinds of offal may take more or less time to cook. If you're not mad about offal, it will work very well with beef shin alone.

As is typical of Chinese offal cooking, the ingredients are blanched and then simmered with spices to dispel any rankness of flavor, and celery is added to brighten and refine their tastes. The cooking liquid is known as a "white spiced broth" (*bailu*), because it is not colored with caramel, unlike the darker spiced broth more often used for this kind of dish (see next page).

When the spiced broth is ready, salt it: add about 2½ tsp—enough to make it taste just a little saltier than a dish where you would consume all the broth. Now add the blanched beef and tripe, with the Shaoxing wine, submerge them in the broth and bring to a boil. Turn down the heat and simmer for an hour. After this time, switch off the heat, cover the pan and let the shin and tripe steep for another hour or so, then drain and set aside. Chill the meats until needed. Reserve the cooking liquid for the dressing.

When the meats have cooled completely, thinly slice the shin. Then, holding your knife at a steep angle to the board, slice the tripe as thinly as possible: you should end up with thin, rectangular slices, each with a little frill of honeycomb along one side. Place the sliced meats in a bowl or arrange neatly on a serving dish.

Trim and remove any strings from the celery, and then finely chop. Toast the sesame seeds gently in a frying pan until pale golden. Dissolve the salt in 7 tbsp (100ml) of the spiced cooking liquid.

There are two ways to serve this dish. You can simply toss everything together and then serve (with a cilantro garnish, if you like). Alternatively—as shown in the photograph opposite—you can toss the meats with the salted cooking liquid, Sichuan pepper, chile oil and sediment until evenly coated, then pile the celery and any odd scraps of meat in the center of a serving dish and arrange the sliced shin and tripe in overlapping slices on top. Garnish with sesame seeds, peanuts and cilantro, if using.

## Spiced Chicken Hearts

lu jixin
卤鸡心

All over Sichuan there are street stalls and restaurants specializing in *lucai*: stewed meats and poultry, eggs and tofu, all cooked until tender in rich broths seasoned with salt, wine, aromatics and spices. The broth (*lushui*) is usually based on pork bones, but also absorbs the flavors of whichever meats are cooked in it.

The following recipe offers a taste of *lucai*, but feel free to scale up the broth, add a greater variety of spices—such as cloves, bay leaves, sand ginger, Indian black cardamom or Katsumade galangal seeds—and use it to flavor foods of your choice. Chicken drumsticks and wings, duck wings, pig's snouts and tails, fatty pork, duck's tongues and other poultry offal, goose and rabbit, firm tofu and hard-boiled eggs (rolled to crack them all over and then stewed in their shells) are all fair game. Cooked meats, sliced, can be served with a dash of the cooking liquid, a smidgeon of sesame oil and dips of ground chile and Sichuan pepper. The broth can be strained and refrigerated or frozen for later use; alternatively, boil it up every day and replenish with salt and spices. (Note that the "Old Arabian" cold beef on p. 94 and "man-and-wife" offal slices on p. 97 are also variations on the spiced-broth theme.)

Chicken (or duck) hearts can be bought in good Chinatown butchers. When I first cooked them for British friends in London, I wasn't sure how they would be received, but everyone loved them, and devoured the lot.

¾-inch piece (15g) ginger, unpeeled
1 scallion, white part only
¾ lb (350g) chicken hearts
1½ tbsp Shaoxing wine
Ground chiles and ground roasted
    Sichuan pepper, for dipping

*For the spiced broth*
2 cups (500ml) chicken or everyday stock (see p. 463)
¾-inch piece (15g) ginger, unpeeled
1 scallion, white part only
1 small Chinese black cardamom pod
½ star anise
¼ tsp whole Sichuan pepper
A thumbnail-sized piece of cassia bark
1 slice licorice root
¼ tsp fennel seeds
2 tsp caramel coloring (see p. 458) or ¾ tsp dark soy sauce
1 tbsp Shaoxing wine
Salt

**Lightly smack the ginger** and scallion white with a cleaver or rolling pin to loosen them. Bring a pot of water to a boil. Add the hearts, return to a boil and boil for 1 minute, then tip into a colander and rinse under cold water. Drain well, then place in a bowl with the ginger, scallion white and Shaoxing wine. Mix well and set aside for about 30 minutes.

Meanwhile, make the spiced broth. Bring the stock to a boil. Lightly smack the ginger, scallion white and cardamom pod with the flat of a cleaver blade or a rolling pin to loosen them. Add to the stock, along with all the other spices (tied up in a piece of muslin, if you have it). Simmer for 20 minutes, then add the caramel coloring or soy sauce, Shaoxing wine and salt to taste: the broth should taste a little saltier than you'd want it if you were going to consume it as a soup.

Discard the ginger and scallion white from the hearts, along with any juices. Add the hearts to the broth, bring to a boil and then simmer for 10 minutes. Switch off the heat, cover the pan and let steep for at least 30 minutes or until cool.

Place the drained hearts on a plate, with little heaps of ground chiles and ground roasted Sichuan pepper for dipping.

# Dry-tossed Beef

## ganban niurou
## 干拌牛肉

This is an extremely simple and delicious way to eat cold spiced beef—or poached chicken (it would probably also work well with the leftovers of a roast bird). The method is so straightforward that you barely need a recipe.

Because this is a dry dish, try to serve it alongside other dishes that have an element of sauce: a dressed salad, perhaps (in a non-Chinese context, a potato salad could be nice). This recipe is a homage to the delectable dry-tossed beef and chicken served by chef Yu Bo at Yu's Family Kitchen in Chengdu.

¾ lb (350g) cooked spiced beef, cooled
  (1 lb 2 oz/500g uncooked; cooked by the same
  method as the beef on p. 94)
Scant ½ tsp salt
Scant ½ tsp superfine sugar
½ tsp ground roasted Sichuan pepper
2–3 tsp ground chiles, to taste
5 tbsp thinly sliced scallion greens

Cut the beef into bite-sized slices or strips. Add the salt and sugar and mix well: taste and adjust the seasoning, if necessary. Add the Sichuan pepper and ground chiles. Finally, stir in the scallion greens.

Variation

Use cold, cooked chicken, on or off the bone, instead of beef.

# "Phoenix Tails" in Sesame Sauce

## majiang fengwei
## 麻酱凤尾

This simple, lovely dish is traditionally made with tender celtuce tips, little batons of crisp green flesh tufted with leaves that are named for their resemblance to the tails of the mythical bird. After peeling and trimming, they are sometimes briefly blanched in boiling water before being dressed, but may also be eaten raw. These days, many people prefer to use Indian lettuce or *youmaicai*, which is eaten raw and whose long, pointed, trailing leaves actually look more like feathered phoenix tails than celtuce. Both Indian lettuce and celtuce have a distinctive nutty note to their flavors that is perfectly complemented by the sesame sauce. Indian lettuce can be found in some Chinese supermarkets in the West (usually under its Cantonese name, *yau mak choi*, or *youmaicai* in Mandarin). If you can't find it, use the same sauce to dress a crisp lettuce such as romaine, or batons of cucumber. Some chefs add enough chile oil to lend the sauce a hint of spice and a reddish gleam.

In Chongqing, there's a trendy modern version of this dish with the unlikely name of "lettuce captured alive" (*huozhuo wosun*), in which the chile oil dressing is given a sweet-and-sour slant through the addition of sugar and vinegar and only a little sesame paste is used to give body to the sauce—see the variation to the right.

2 tsp sesame seeds
7 oz (200g) Indian lettuce (or use romaine)
1½ tsp light soy sauce
¾ tsp superfine sugar
2–3 tbsp cold stock or water
2–3 tbsp (40g) sesame paste
1 tsp sesame oil
1½ tbsp chile oil (optional)
Salt

Toast the sesame seeds in a wok or frying pan over gentle heat until golden, then set aside. Rinse and dry the lettuce, cut into chopstickable pieces and pile up on a serving dish.

Place the soy sauce and sugar in a bowl with 2 tbsp stock or water and stir to dissolve the sugar. Tip the sesame paste into another bowl with a little oil from the jar and smooth it with a spoon. Stir in the soy sauce mixture in a few stages, making sure each addition is emulsified into the sauce before adding more.

When you have a smooth sauce, stir in the sesame oil and chile oil, if using, and then, if you need it, add another tablespoon or so of stock or water until you have a sleek liquid with the consistency of half-and-half: it's important that the sauce is thick enough to cling to the lettuce, but thin enough to pour. Add a little salt, to taste, but take care not to overdo it, because this dish is best enjoyed as a refreshing contrast to more strongly flavored dishes.

Just before serving, pour the sauce over the lettuce, and garnish with the sesame seeds.

*"Lettuce captured alive"* (huozhuo wosun 活捉莴笋)
*Dilute 1 tbsp (15g) sesame paste with 1 tbsp water and stir until smooth. Add 2 tsp light soy sauce, 2 tsp superfine sugar, 1½ tsp Chinkiang vinegar and ¼ tsp ground roasted Sichuan pepper. Stir in 1 tsp sesame oil, 3–4 tbsp chile oil with sediment, and a couple of good pinches of salt, to taste. Use this to dress the lettuce, and omit the sesame seeds. With some versions of this dish, chefs will sizzle chiles and whole Sichuan pepper in oil, pour the hot oil over some chopped garlic to bring out its fragrance, and use this spicy oil instead of regular chile oil.*

# Rabbit with Peanuts in Hot Bean Sauce

## huaren ban tuding
## 花仁拌兔丁

This splendid autumn dish is typical of Sichuanese home cooking, but it would also work well with bread and salad as part of a Western-style lunch. The tender rabbit flesh contrasts nicely with the crisp peanuts and crunchy scallions; the sauce is a glossy dark red and robustly spicy.

The most famous version of this dish is the "second sister rabbit cubes" (*erjie tuding*), made by a skillful Chengdu woman named Chen Yonghui. Her dish was so delicious that it was even the subject of a poem written by a member of the local literati. Mrs. Chen's special extra touch, we're told, was to add a final sprinkling of ground, roasted Sichuan pepper, crushed peanuts and toasted sesame seeds.

In Sichuan, people make this dish with rabbit on the bone, with the disadvantage that sharp, jagged pieces of bone often remain in the finished dish. For this reason, I've suggested making it with boneless rabbit; if you like, you can then use the picked-clean rabbit carcass to make stock.

Chicken leg meat can also be used as a substitute (although I've never seen it prepared this way by Sichuanese cooks). For a vegetarian version, use cubes of firm spiced or smoked tofu instead.

1 farmed rabbit (about 3 lb/1.4kg with head and giblets, 2 lb 6 oz /1.1kg without)
1-inch piece (20g) ginger, unpeeled
1 whole scallion, plus 6 more, white parts only
½ cup (60g) roasted or deep-fried peanuts (see p. 458)

*For the sauce*
1 tbsp fermented black beans
2 tbsp cooking oil
4 tbsp Sichuan chile bean paste
½ tsp superfine sugar
2 tbsp light soy sauce
5–6 tbsp chile oil, plus 1 tbsp sediment
1 tsp sesame oil
½ tsp ground roasted Sichuan pepper (optional)

Cut the rabbit in half, to make it easier to handle, and rinse well with cold water. Place the two halves in a pan, cover with cold water and bring to a boil over medium heat. Lightly smack the ginger and whole scallion with the flat of a cleaver blade or a rolling pin to loosen them. When the water is boiling, add the smacked ginger and scallion. Turn the heat down to low and simmer gently for 15–20 minutes until the rabbit is cooked through (poke a skewer into the thickest part: the juices should run clear). Turn the heat off, then cover the pan and let rest for 10 minutes, before draining the rabbit and setting aside to cool completely. (This can be done the day before.)

When the rabbit has cooled completely, remove the meat from the carcass and cut as evenly as possible into ½–¾ inch (1–2cm) cubes.

Next make the sauce. Rinse the black beans and pound to a paste with a mortar and pestle. Heat the cooking oil in a seasoned wok over medium heat. Add the chile bean paste and stir-fry for a minute or so until the oil is red and fragrant, then stir in the black bean paste. When the whole lot is sizzly and delicious, transfer to a bowl. Stir in the sugar, soy sauce, chile oil and sediment, sesame oil and Sichuan pepper, if using.

Taste the scallion whites: if they have a harsh oniony taste, you can steam or microwave them briefly to soften their flavor. Cut them into ½ inch (1cm) slices and place in a bowl with the rabbit. Gradually stir in the sauce, tasting as you go, because the sauce is salty and you may not need it all. Finally, stir in the peanuts.

# Smacked Cucumber
# in Garlicky Sauce

liangban huanggua
凉拌黄瓜

In a glass cabinet by the entrance of the Bamboo Bar, one of my regular haunts when I was a student in Chengdu, there were bowls of spiced duck hearts and gizzards, fried peanuts and other tidbits, alongside all the seasonings for the cold dishes that would whet the appetites of the customers. Behind the counter, the serving girls would mix up their magical sauces for salads of fava beans, preserved eggs and cold chicken. One of my favorite dishes was also one of the simplest, a cucumber salad with the classic "garlic paste" (*suanni*) combination of flavors: mashed garlic, sweet soy sauce and chile oil.

At the Bamboo Bar, they used to chop up the cucumber, dress it and serve it immediately; if you wish, you can salt the cucumber first to draw out some liquid, which means the final dish won't become watery if you don't eat it at once. And if you don't want to make the sweet soy sauce for the dressing, just mix together 1½ tbsp light soy sauce and 1½ tsp superfine sugar and then combine this with the other ingredients.

A similar dressing is used for another local salad, composed of the sour, spicy leaves of *zhe'er gen* (also known as heartleaf, fish mint or *yuxing cao*, "fish-fragrant herb," and in Vietnamese as *diep ca*), slivers of celtuce and fava beans. Celtuce and *zhe'er gen* can sometimes be found outside China (try Vietnamese shops for the latter); in their absence, I often use this dressing for boiled fava beans—there is no need to peel them if they are young and tender.

1 cucumber (about 14 oz/400g)
½ tsp salt (optional, for pre-salting)

*For the dressing*
1½ tbsp sweet aromatic soy sauce
  (see p. 459)
1 tbsp crushed garlic
1 tbsp chile oil, with or without sediment
½ tsp sesame oil

Trim the ends off the cucumber, place it on a chopping board and smack it firmly a few times with the flat of a cleaver blade or a rolling pin, turning it once between smacks—the idea is to crack it open and loosen its flesh, not to send an explosion of cucumber fragments all over your kitchen! Cut the smacked cucumber into four lengths, then hold your knife at an angle to the board and cut the cucumber on the diagonal into ½–¾ inch (1–2cm) slices. (If you wish to pre-salt the cucumber, add the salt, mix well and set aside for at least 30 minutes: drain offthe water that emerges before dressing.)

Mix the dressing ingredients together in a small bowl. Just before serving, pour the dressing over the cucumber.

*Fava beans in garlicky sauce* (suanni hudou 蒜泥胡豆)
*Instead of the cucumber, use the dressing for 2 cups (250g) shelled fava beans, boiled until tender, cooled under cold water and drained. This is a gorgeous summer salad. (You can also make it with frozen fava beans.)*

# "Tragically Hot" Water Spinach Salad

## shangxin ban kongxincai
## 伤心拌空心菜

Over the last few years, Sichuanese chefs have developed a passion for the small, fiercely hot chiles known as "little rice chiles" (*xiaomila*), a type of bird's eye. In the past, cold dishes and snacks were normally seasoned with chile oil, ground chiles or pickled chiles, but these days, especially in southern Sichuan, they are often supplanted by fresh little rice chiles, red and green, which look gorgeous and can be fantastically spicy.

In particular, there's been a craze among young people for so-called *shangxin liangfen*: cool starch jelly in seasonings so hot they "cause damage" or "break your heart" (*shangxin*). I've taken the liberty of translating this phrase as "tragically hot," which I think conveys the appropriate meaning.

The following dish is my re-creation of one at the Bashu Weiyuan, a restaurant in Chengdu whose owner, Mr. Li, specializes in hearty rustic dishes. His blanched water spinach salad is dressed with seasonings similar to the famous starch jelly, so I've borrowed the name. You can step the heat up or down as you please by varying the amount of bird's eye chiles, or using milder chiles instead, but it's likely to be "tragically hot" whatever you do, so consider yourself warned! (I have a fairly high tolerance for chiles, but some of these southern salads challenge even my palate.)

*14 oz (400g) water spinach*
*1 long green Turkish pepper (about 1¾ oz/50g)*
*2½ tbsp light soy sauce*
*2½ tsp superfine sugar*
*2½ tsp Chinkiang vinegar*
*3 tbsp thinly sliced red bird's eye chile, to taste*
*2 tbsp finely chopped garlic*
*3 tbsp thinly sliced green bird's eye chile, to taste*

Bring a large pot of water to a boil. After washing the water spinach, place it on a board and cut to separate the stalks from the leafier parts.

When the water is boiling, add the stalks and blanch briefly until just cooked but still a little crisp; remove from the water with a slotted spoon and immediately refresh under cold water. Blanch the leafy parts until wilted; again, immediately refresh under cold water. Squeeze as much water as possible from stalks and leaves, cut into chopstickable lengths and then pile up in a serving dish.

Trim and remove the seeds from the green pepper, then chop finely. Combine the soy sauce, sugar and vinegar in a small bowl with 1 tbsp sliced red chile, and stir to dissolve the sugar.

Just before serving, pour the sauce over the water spinach. Scatter over the garlic, green pepper, sliced green chile and, finally, the remaining red chile.

Mix everything together before eating.

# Spiced Cucumber Salad

## qiang huanggua
## 炝黄瓜

1 cucumber (about 10 oz/300g)
½ tsp salt
8–10 dried chiles
2 tbsp cooking oil
½–1 tsp whole Sichuan pepper
1 tsp sesame oil

Stir-fried dishes are usually eaten hot, as part of a main meal. Many, however, taste delicious after cooling, and are eaten that way for more informal meals. Home cooks will often serve up leftovers from the previous night, either reheated or simply served cold, and cold stir-fried dishes are a major feature of *lengdanbei*, the casual, tapas-style eating enjoyed in the backstreets of Chengdu on sultry summer evenings. One *lengdanbei* restaurant whose menu I jotted down was serving a number of cold stir-fries, including green beans with chile and ginger, lotus root with chiles and green peppers, and pickled green beans with pork. Recipes for stir-fries like these are given in the Vegetables chapter, because they are mostly eaten hot—but, as a general rule, any stir-fry that doesn't involve animal fats or starch-thickened sauces can be cooled without spoiling.

This dish is unusual in that it is stir-fried with spices (a cooking method known as *qiang*), but invariably eaten cold. It is wonderfully simple to make—the only secret is to keep the cooking brief—and has the advantage that it can be prepared hours in advance. The slippery cucumber is permeated with an intriguing rumor of spice and sesame, and a scattering of red chiles and Sichuan pepper means it looks lovely too. In Sichuan you might find it on a mixed hors d'oeuvre platter at a banquet, perhaps with a selection of cold meats and peanuts or several different types of dumpling. I usually serve it as part of a Chinese meal or a simple salady lunch.

Cut the cucumber in half lengthwise and scoop out the pulp and seeds with a spoon (I usually eat these as I go along), then cut each half into three lengths and slice each one into thin strips. Place the cucumber in a bowl, sprinkle with the salt, mix well and set aside for at least 30 minutes.

Drain the cucumber and shake dry. Snip the dried chiles in half and shake out the seeds as much as possible.

Heat a seasoned wok over high heat. Pour in the cooking oil, quickly swirl it around, then add the chiles and Sichuan pepper. Stir-fry the spices until the chiles are darkening but not burned, then add the cucumber. Stir-fry very briefly to heat the surface of the cucumber and drive in the flavors of the oil. Remove from the heat, stir in the sesame oil and transfer to a serving dish.

*Spiced potato sliver salad (qiangban tudousi 炝拌土豆丝)*
*If you've never tasted a dish like this, prepare to be surprised. It's a simple concoction of potato slivers enlivened by scorched chiles and Sichuan pepper, but the potatoes are deliberately cooked fleetingly, so that they retain some of their raw crunchiness. Peel 10 oz (300g) potatoes (larger ones will be easier to cut). Cut them evenly into the thinnest-possible slices, and then into slivers; you can use a mandoline to slice them, if you have one. Place the slivers in a bowl of lightly salted cold water as you work, so they don't discolor.*

*Bring a pot of water to a boil and blanch the potato slivers for about 2 minutes—they should remain crisp. Tip them into a sieve, refresh under cold water and shake dry. Place in a bowl and add 1½ tbsp clear rice vinegar and salt to taste. Now make the spicy oil: snip 8 dried chiles in half and discard their seeds as much as possible. Heat 3 tbsp cooking oil in a wok over medium heat. Add the chiles and 1 tsp whole Sichuan pepper and sizzle gently until the chiles are darkening but not burned. Add the oil and spices to the potato with 2 tsp sesame oil, mix well, then serve.*

## North Sichuan
## Cool Starch Jelly

chuanbei liangfen
川北凉粉

Sichuanese people adore eating *liangfen*: cool jellies made from pea, mung bean, rice and sweet potato starches. The jellies are cut into cubes, ribbons or chunky strips, and served as snacks with spicy dressings. (Rice jelly, exceptionally, is eaten warm in various dishes.) The most famous *liangfen* comes from Nanchong in the north of the province, where people pride themselves on their slippery pea-starch jelly, with its refreshing sour-and-hot dressing and hit of pungent garlic. It feels cool and silken on the tongue, aromatic and slick with gleaming chile oil. Many snack-sellers use a gadget made from a.circle of metal punched with holes to scrape ribbony strands from a mound of *liangfen*; at home, it's easiest to cut the jelly with a knife.

A tiny amount of alum, a food additive that's also used in pickling and can be bought online or found in some Indian groceries, is added to the mix to give the finished jelly a slightly taut, tensile quality. You can make *liangfen* without it, but it will lack the slithery spring in its step that makes the real thing so delightful and refreshing. The jelly takes a while to cool and set, so is best made the day before you wish to serve it—this recipe makes about 1 lb 2 oz (500g).

In recent years, a fiercely hot version of this dish called "tragically hot" starch jelly (*shangxin liangfen*) has become popular in Sichuan: to make it, simply use the seasonings for "tragically hot" water spinach salad on p. 107.

⅓ cup plus 1 tbsp (50g) mung bean or pea starch
⅛ tsp powdered alum

*To serve*
¼ tsp salt
½ tsp superfine sugar
2 tsp light soy sauce
4 tsp Chinkiang vinegar
2½ tbsp chile oil, with sediment
About ¼ tsp ground roasted Sichuan
    pepper, to taste
1 tbsp finely chopped garlic
2 tbsp thinly sliced scallion greens

**To make the jelly,** place the starch in a bowl and gradually stir in ¾ cup plus 2 tbsp (200ml) cold water. Mix well until you have a smooth, lump-free liquid. Dissolve the alum in 1 tbsp hot water from the kettle and stir it into the starch mixture.

Bring 1⅔ cups(400ml) water to a boil in a saucepan. When the water is boiling, give the starch mixture a stir and add it gradually, in a steady stream, constantly stirring it into the simmering water: you must stir briskly as you add the starch, or the mixture will become lumpy. Bring back to a boil, then turn the heat down very low and stir constantly for another 3 minutes, scraping the base of the pan to avoid sticking. Pour the jelly mixture into a bowl and set aside to cool completely and set.

To serve, place all the remaining ingredients except the garlic and scallion greens in a serving bowl. Cut the jelly into thin strips and add to the bowl, then top with the garlic and scallion greens. Mix everything together before eating.

*Cool starch jelly with spicy black bean sauce*
*Rinse and strain 3 tbsp fermented black beans. Pound with a mortar and pestle to a coarse paste. Heat 4 tbsp cooking oil in a seasoned wok over medium heat. Add 3 tbsp Sichuan chile bean paste and stir-fry gently until the oil is red and fragrant. Next add the pounded black beans and stir until they are also fragrant. Off the heat, stir in ¼–½ tsp ground roasted Sichuan pepper and 2 tbsp chile oil. Pile strips of starch jelly on a serving dish and dress with the spicy, oily sauce to taste. Garnish with toasted sesame seeds and/or thinly sliced scallion greens. (Any leftover sauce makes a delicious relish with noodles or other dishes.)*

# "Lamp-shadow" Sweet Potato Chips

## dengying shaopian
## 灯影苕片

1–2 large (350–450g) orange-fleshed sweet potatoes
Cooking oil, for deep-frying
2 tsp superfine sugar
2–3 tbsp chile oil, without sediment
2–3 tsp sesame oil
Salt

Sweet potatoes are traditionally considered to be poor man's food, a substitute for rice in the mountains of western Sichuan, where rice cultivation is impossible and farmers rely on crops like this which cling more readily to the arid land. In times of famine during the twentieth century, the government sent relief supplies of sweet potato chips to rural areas when there was nothing else to eat. This, however, is a fancy banquet dish, an extravagance cooked up out of this most basic of foods, perhaps a symbol of better times. The crude potatoes are transformed into translucent wisps of crispness, piled delicately on a serving dish and dressed in a piquant red sauce.

If you don't plan to eat the chips immediately, store in an airtight jar, preferably with one of those desiccation sachets you find in packages of Japanese snacks and other foods (I always keep these, and add them to any jar of nuts, chips or crackers that I want to stay crisp). One large (350g) sweet potato will give you a good bowlful of chips, but it's worth making more than you need because you will find yourself eating at least some of them as soon as they come out of the wok.

Peel the sweet potatoes and cut them into the thinnest possible slices (a mandoline can be useful here). Traditionally, Sichuanese chefs trim the potatoes into neat rectangles if serving this as a banquet dish, but I take the slices as they come. Submerge in lightly salted cold water until you are ready to cook them.

Drain the sliced potatoes and pat dry with paper towels.

Heat the oil for deep-frying to 265°F (130°C) (hot enough to sizzle gently, not aggressively, around a test slice of sweet potato). Add the sweet potatoes, stirring with long cooking chopsticks or tongs to separate the slices (depending on the amount of oil you're using, you may want to cook them in batches). Fry for 7–10 minutes until they are slightly browned, then immediately remove with a slotted spoon and drain on paper towels. It's important to control the temperature and let the cooking take its time: if the oil is too hot, the slices will become puckered, and the outside will burn before the inside has dried out.

Transfer the chips to a large bowl. Add about ¼ tsp salt, to taste, and the sugar, then toss gently. Drizzle over the oils, turning the chips gently to coat. Pile up on a serving dish.

### Variation

For a numbing-and-hot (mala) flavor, use ¼–½ tsp ground roasted Sichuan pepper instead of the sugar.

# Firm Tofu with
# Celery and Peanuts

## liangban doufugan
## 凉拌豆腐干

This is a quick and easy relish that is perfect for "sending the rice down" (*xiafan*). It's also one example of a whole range of spicy tidbits sold by market stalls and deli-type shops across Sichuan. The basic seasonings of chile oil with its sediment, ground roasted Sichuan pepper, sesame oil, sugar, salt and (locally) MSG can be used to dress many types of tofu, including thin ribbons or rolls of tofu skin, as well as finely chopped pickles and salted, sun-dried vegetables; pickles and preserves don't usually need extra salt.

3½ oz (100g) spiced or smoked firm tofu
3 celery sticks (about 4½ oz/125g)
3 tbsp (30g) roasted or deep-fried peanuts (see p. 458)
1½ tbsp chile oil, plus ½ tbsp sediment,
   or more to taste
A good pinch of superfine sugar
Salt, to taste

**Cut the tofu into ½ in (1cm) cubes.** Remove any strings from the celery sticks, cut them lengthwise into ½ inch (1cm) strips, and then into cubes to match the tofu.

Bring a pot of water to a boil, add the celery and blanch for 30–60 seconds; it should remain a little crunchy. Tip into a colander and immediately rinse under cold water to arrest the cooking, then shake dry.

Combine all the ingredients in a bowl and mix well. Serve.

## Slivered Pig's Ear
## in Chile Oil Sauce

hongyou er si

红油耳丝

The Sichuanese have a genius for transforming odd bits of offal into irresistible delicacies, and this spicy pig's ear salad is one example. Locals love the crisp, slithery bite of the slivered ears, as well as the tingly, chile-laced dressing. If you want to be really Chinese about it, don't overcook the ears, which should be brisk and snappy, rather than soft and languid (incidentally, hen-pecked Sichuanese husbands are known dismissively as "soft ears," *pa'er duo*). If pig's ears sound a bit outré, it's worth remembering that they are actually one of the tamer varieties of offal enjoyed by the wildly omnivorous Sichuanese: the late-night snacks on display at one restaurant I visited recently in Chengdu included pig's snouts, tails and upper palates, duck gizzards and the heads of both ducks and rabbits.

This recipe is inspired by a fabulous version from a street stall in Luzhou, home of the famous Luzhou Laojiao distillery. Pig's ears can also be served with a classic "red-oil" sauce, made by mixing together 4 tsp superfine sugar, 3 tbsp light soy sauce, 4 tbsp chicken stock, 1 tsp sesame oil and 4 tbsp chile oil, with or without sediment. Either way, serve your ears with other cold dishes at the start of a meal, or nibble them as you knock back shots of hard liquor with friends, preferably at a table by the riverside on a hot summer's night.

2 nice clean pig's ears

1-inch piece (20g) ginger, unpeeled

2 scallions, white parts only

½ tsp whole Sichuan pepper

1 tbsp strong Chinese baijiu *grain liquor (optional)*

2 sticks celery (100g)

*For the sauce*

4 tbsp cold chicken stock

¾ tsp salt

2 tsp superfine sugar

4 tsp crushed garlic

½ tsp ground roasted Sichuan pepper

4–5 tbsp chile oil, with or without sediment

4–5 fresh red bird's eye chiles
  (optional—for chile fiends only)

*To finish*

3 tbsp chopped cilantro

4 tbsp roasted or deep-fried peanuts
  (see p. 458), coarsely crushed

1 tbsp toasted sesame seeds

4 tbsp thinly sliced scallion greens

1–2 fresh red chiles, thinly sliced

If there are any bristles on the pig's ears, scorch them with a flame and scrape off. Give the ears a good rinse and scrub. Cut open the base of each ear and cut out and discard the actual ear canal, along with any bits that won't come clean. Lightly smack the ginger and scallion whites with a cleaver or rolling pin to loosen them. Place the ears in a pan with water to cover and bring to a boil over high heat. Drain the ears, discarding the cooking water. Cover with fresh water and bring to a boil. Skim, if necessary, then add the ginger, scallion whites, whole Sichuan pepper and *baijiu* liquor, if using. Simmer for 10 minutes, then remove the ears and let cool: for maximum crispness, immediately plunge them into a bowlful of ice water. (If you'd prefer them to be more tender, simmer the ears for the same length of time but let them steep in the cooking liquid, lid on, for another 20 minutes or so.)

When the ears are cool, slice them very thinly. Remove any strings from the celery and cut into thin strips (if you are using slender Chinese celery, simply cut it into 2½ inch/6cm lengths). Blanch briefly in boiling water, refresh under cold water and drain.

Now make the sauce. Mix the stock, salt and sugar together in a small bowl, and stir to dissolve the sugar. Add the garlic, Sichuan pepper and chile oil and mix well. For extra heat, coarsely chop some bird's eye chiles and stir into the sauce.

Place the slivered ears and celery in a large bowl. Sprinkle over the cilantro and peanuts, add the sauce and toss everything together. Pile onto a serving dish, then sprinkle with the sesame seeds, scallion greens and chile slices.

# "Rabbit Eaten Cold"

## leng chi tu
## 冷吃兔

"Water-boiled beef" (see p. 161) may
be the best-known dish of Zigong, the
old salt-mining capital of Sichuan, but
Zigong people themselves consider
this delectable rabbit concoction to be
their most notable culinary specialty.
It's a gorgeous tumble of small chunks
of rabbit and scorched chiles in spicy,
aromatic oil, with a gently rising heat
and fragrance. It's made by almost every
household in Zigong, and served for
every special occasion. (In Chengdu,
a similar dish is known as rabbit cubes
with Sichuan pepper, *huajiao tuding*.)

The Sichuanese taste for rabbit meat
is a relic of the socialist planned economy.
Until the 1950s, farmers occasionally
ate wild rabbits, but otherwise there
was little rabbit meat around. In the
1950s, however, during the American-
led trade embargo on China, the Beijing
government, desperate for foreign
currency, commanded Sichuan to develop
a rabbit industry so that pelts and meat
could be exported to the Soviet Union.
Rabbit farming took off, and the furs and
finer cuts of rabbit meat were exported—
leaving locals with the heads, kidneys and
stomachs, all of which became much-
loved delicacies. The stomachs, prized
for their slippery-crisp texture, are known
as "crisp in the mouth" (*koukoucui*), the
kidneys are often strung on skewers and
cooked in spicy hotpots, and the heads
(*tu naoke* in local dialect) are stewed in a
spiced broth and guzzled as a late-night
street snack. (Eating the heads is an
absorbing, intricate business, which is
why the Sichuanese jokingly call French
kissing "eating rabbit heads.")

2½-inch piece (50g) ginger, unpeeled
3 scallions, white parts only
1½ lb (650–750g) lean, boneless rabbit meat
   (1 farmed rabbit)
1½ tbsp Shaoxing wine
Scant 1 oz (25g) dried chiles
Cooking oil, for deep-frying
2½ tsp whole Sichuan pepper
1⅔ cups (400ml) everyday stock (see p. 463)
1 tsp dark soy sauce
2 tbsp light soy sauce
2½ tbsp superfine sugar
1 tbsp Chinkiang vinegar
2 tsp sesame oil
Salt

*To finish*
1 tsp sesame seeds
2 tbsp thinly sliced scallion greens

**Lightly smack the ginger** and scallion whites with the flat of a
cleaver blade or a rolling pin to loosen them. Cut the rabbit meat
as evenly as possible into ¾-inch (2cm) cubes and place in a
bowl. Add half the ginger, 2 scallion whites, ½ tsp salt and the
Shaoxing wine and mix well. Set aside to marinate for at least 30
minutes, or several hours in the fridge. Snip the chiles into ¾-
inch (2cm) sections and shake out the seeds.

Heat the oil for deep-frying in a wok to 375°F (190°C). Remove
the ginger and scallion whites from the marinade, then deep-fry
the rabbit for 1–2 minutes until tinged with gold, stirring gently
to prevent the pieces from sticking together (depending on the
amount of oil you are using, you may want to do this in a couple
of batches). Drain on paper towels and set aside.

Carefully strain the deep-frying oil and wipe or brush the wok
clean. Return 4 tbsp oil to the wok and place over medium
heat. Add the chiles, and as soon as they begin to sizzle, tip in
the Sichuan pepper and stir-fry until the chiles are beginning
to darken—take great care not to burn them. Tip in the stock,
along with the remaining ginger and scallion whites, the rabbit,
dark soy sauce and ½ tsp salt.

Bring to a boil and simmer, stirring occasionally, for about
5 minutes, until the liquid has reduced by about two thirds.

I first cooked this for a discerning group of Chinese friends, and it was their favorite dish of the night, even in competition with mapo tofu. I hope you'll agree that rabbit, like revenge, is perhaps best served cold. Be aware that boning a raw rabbit is a fiddly business: take your time with a sharp knife. Alternatively, use boned chicken thighs or lean pork.

Add the light soy sauce, sugar and vinegar, and keep stirring until the liquid has almost disappeared. Turn off the heat, stir in the sesame oil and set aside to cool. Remove and discard the ginger and scallion whites before serving.

Toast the sesame seeds over very gentle heat until fragrant and tinged with gold. Serve the rabbit with a sprinkling of sesame seeds and scallion greens. (If not serving straight away, the dish keeps well for a few days in the fridge.)

# Tea-smoked Duck

## zhang cha yazi
樟茶鸭子

Smoked duck is one of Sichuan's most-lauded delicacies. At its best it is juicy, rich, and infused with the delicate aromas of jasmine tea, camphor leaves, cypress twigs and wood shavings. In Chengdu, it will forever be associated with an alley that was famous in the early days of Republican China for its lively teahouses and wine shops; because of its narrow, inconspicuous entrance and capacious interior, it was nicknamed "the mousehole." In 1928, a man named Zhang Guoliang set up a duck stall near the entrance which soon became known for its exquisite smoked duck. There's still a restaurant in Chengdu called Mr. Zhang's Mousehole Duck, which specializes in smoked duck and other traditional Sichuanese dishes. The duck here, which can be eaten in or taken out, is exceptionally fine. In the 1990s, there were still old smokehouses in the backstreets of Chengdu, where golden ducks hung above smoldering piles of tea and camphor leaves: sadly, they have all now disappeared.

Sichuanese cookbooks call this dish "camphor- and tea-smoked duck" (*zhang cha yazi*), and suggest using camphor (*zhang* 樟) leaves as smoking material. However, according to some experts, this is based on a confusion over Chinese characters, and the dish derives its name not from any connection with camphor, but because it was originally smoked over tea leaves from Zhangzhou, in Fujian province.

The cooking method was invented by a man named Huang Jinlin, one-time

1 young duck (3¾ lb/1.75kg)
Cooking oil, for deep-frying
  (enough to half-submerge the duck)
2 tsp sesame oil

*For the curing*
2 tbsp (35g) salt (or continental curing salts
  with 0.4% sodium nitrite)
1 tsp whole Sichuan pepper
¼ tsp ground white pepper
2 tbsp Shaoxing wine
3 tbsp fermented glutinous rice wine
  (or another 2 tbsp Shaoxing wine)

*For the smoking*
3½ oz (100g) nutshells (I used almond shells)
2½ oz (75g) peanut shells or sunflower seed husks
¾ oz (20g) cypress clippings
  (a handful, if you can get them)
⅔ cup (20g) jasmine tea

*For the steaming*
1½-inch piece (30g) ginger, unpeeled
2 scallions, white parts only

First cure the duck. Place the salt, Sichuan pepper and white pepper in a mortar and pound with a pestle. Mix together the two wines. Tip the salt mixture into the duck's body cavity and rub it into the interior walls. Then rub some wine mixture all over the skin; tip the rest into the body cavity and rub it in. Cover the duck and let rest, breast-side down, in the fridge for 12 hours or overnight.

Place the duck in a colander in the sink. Bring a kettleful of water to a boil and pour all over the duck to tighten the skin, carefully turning the duck halfway through. Hang the duck in a cool, shady, well-ventilated place for several hours, until the skin is dry to the touch.

Line a dry wok with two layers of foil, pressing them against the metal. Scatter over the nutshells, the peanut shells or sunflower seed husks, then the cypress clippings (if using), and finally the tea. Place a metal trivet in the base of the wok. Place over it a steaming rack and set the duck on this, breast-side down. Place the wok over very high heat (and turn your exhaust fan

118

manager of the Dowager Empress Cixi's kitchens in Beijing, who brought the dish to Sichuan when he opened the famous Auntie's Feast (gugu ting) restaurant in Chengdu.

Tea-smoked duck is not a dish that is normally attempted at home, because the recipe is complicated: even restaurants buy it from specialty vendors. I have found it hard to re-create in my simple wok the depth of flavor I've enjoyed in real Sichuanese duck, which is cold-smoked over wood-shavings and fragrant leaves of cypress, camphor and tea to exquisite effect. However, it is possible to make a pretty tasty imitation. Be warned, though, that smoking food in a wok will make your home smell like a bonfire! (If you do have access to outdoor space, cypress twigs and camphor leaves, please see the note below the main recipe for the full traditional method.)

To make this dish you will need a smoking rack that fits into your wok and a steamer that is big enough to fit the whole duck in a deep bowl. Use 2% salt, by weight, to cure the duck—and if you want to give the meat a pretty pink color, use curing salts that include saltpeter, or the sodium nitrite recommended in some Sichuanese recipes for this dish, which can be bought from specialty suppliers. The same method can also be used to smoke whole geese, squab pigeons and quail.

It's much easier to smoke individual duck breasts, however, with fantastic results (slices of tea-smoked duck breast are shown in the photograph on p. 65). Simply salt at 2% by weight, as in the main recipe, and reduce the other ingredients proportionally. Reduce the smoking materials by half and smoke for 15 minutes only, turning halfway through.

up to maximum power). When the tea leaves are beginning to smoke merrily, cover the wok with a lid and smoke the bird for 30 minutes, turning it after 15. You can turn the heat down to medium when everything is smoldering, but make sure smoke continues to emerge. After 30 minutes the bird should be a light golden yellow.

Discard the smoking materials, and place the duck in a bowl that will fit into your steamer. Lightly smack the ginger and scallion whites with the flat of a cleaver blade or a rolling pin to loosen, then place them in the bowl too. Now steam the duck over high heat until tender: this will take up to 1 hour, depending on the heat of the smoking (when it's done, you should be able to poke a chopstick easily into the thickest part).

Remove the duck from the bowl, reserving the delicious juices (which can be used in a soup or soupy noodle dish), and drain well, patting it dry with paper towels.

Half-fill a wok with the deep-frying oil and heat to 390°F (200°C). Place the duck in a fine-mesh strainer and hold it above the surface of the oil, then ladle hot oil over the skin. When the skin starts to brown, move the strainer away from the stove and carefully turn the duck over, then repeat the oil-basting process for the other side, only lowering the duck into the hot oil once the worst of the spitting is over. When all the skin is a rich caramel brown, carefully lift out the duck and switch off the heat. While the duck is still warm, brush its skin sparingly with sesame oil to enhance its gloss and fragrance. Carve the duck, or chop into pieces, Chinese-style, and reassemble on a serving dish.

### Traditional smoking method
*One old Sichuanese cookbook in my collection gives this method: mix together 7 oz (200g) wood shavings and 7 oz (200g) cypress twigs, then stir in 1½ cups (50g) jasmine tea and 1¾ oz (50g) camphor leaves. Place a large wooden pail on the ground. Place a third of the smoking materials in a clay bowl. Add a glowing ember from the fire to get them smoking. Place a rack over the pail, lay the prepared duck on the rack and cover with another wooden pail. Smoke for 10 minutes, then add another third of the smoking materials and another glowing ember, turn the duck and smoke for 7 minutes. Finally, with the palest side of the duck facing downward, smoke over the remaining smoking materials for 5 minutes, by which time the bird should be a deep yellow color.*

## Numbing-and-hot
## Dried Beef

mala niurou gan
麻辣牛肉干

These dark, chewy strips of beef, made by the *zhashou* method (see pp. 62–63), are delicious, bursting with the flavors of Sichuan. They can be served as a starter, or eaten as a very casual snack, perhaps with drinks. For me, they bring back memories of hard but spectacular journeys into the mountains of western Sichuan, when my friends and I used to buy them in packets and munch them with peanuts whenever the bus broke down. They will keep for several days in the fridge.

1 small Chinese black cardamom pod
2lb 2 oz (1kg) lean beef (stew meat will do)
1 star anise
4 scallions, white parts only
2-inch piece (40g) ginger, unpeeled
2 tbsp Shaoxing wine
Cooking oil, for deep-frying
3 tbsp superfine sugar
Salt

*To finish*
About 1 tsp ground roasted Sichuan pepper, to taste
About 1 tbsp ground chiles, to taste
3–4 tbsp chile oil, to taste
2 tsp sesame oil
2 tsp sesame seeds

**Smack the cardamom pod** with the flat of a cleaver blade or a rolling pin to crack it open. Place the beef in a pan, cover with cold water and bring to a boil. Blanch the beef for a minute or so, then drain and rinse under cold water before returning to the pan. Cover with fresh water and bring to a boil, then skim. Add the star anise and cardamom, then simmer for 30 minutes, until the beef is cooked through (it doesn't need to be tender). Remove and let cool, reserving the cooking liquid.

Smack the scallion whites and ginger with the flat of a cleaver blade or a rolling pin to loosen them, then chop into a few large pieces. Cut the beef along the grain into ½ inch (1cm) slices and then across the grain into ½ inch (1cm) wide, bite-sized strips. Place in a bowl with half the scallion whites and ginger, 1 tsp salt and the Shaoxing wine. Mix well, then marinate for 30 minutes.

Remove and discard the scallion whites and ginger from the marinade. Heat the deep-frying oil in a wok to 355°F (180°C). Add the beef and deep-fry for about 4 minutes until browned. (You may wish to cook it in batches, depending on the amount of oil you're using.) Remove with a slotted spoon and drain.

Carefully strain the deep-frying oil and wipe or brush the wok clean. Return 2 tbsp oil to the wok and place over high heat. Add the remaining scallion whites and ginger and stir-fry until fragrant and tinged with gold. Add 3 cups (700ml) reserved cooking liquid, along with the sugar and 1 tsp salt, then fish out and discard the scallion whites and ginger. Add the beef and bring to a boil, then simmer over gentle heat for about 20 minutes, until the liquid has mostly evaporated, leaving only a little glossy, delicious oil; stir occasionally to begin with, then constantly as the liquid dries up. Off the heat, stir in the ground Sichuan pepper and chiles to taste, then add the chile and sesame oils and mix well.

Toast the sesame seeds in a dry wok or frying pan over very gentle heat until fragrant and tinged with gold. Scatter over the beef before serving.

# Fragrant Deep-fried Peanuts

## yousu huaren
## 油酥花仁

I have enjoyed this nibble or appetizer so many times: with drinks on the Chengdu riverside on balmy summer evenings, as a side dish in homes and restaurants, even with a hasty breakfast of rice porridge and pickled vegetables on my way to classes at the Sichuan cooking school. The peanuts are dark red and glossy, crisp and fragrant. They should be served on a small plate, topped with salt and ground roasted Sichuan pepper, which are mixed in with chopsticks at the table. Do resist the temptation to be impatient and deep-fry at too high a temperature—the nuts can easily burn and develop a bitter taste. And remember that fried peanuts keep cooking when they are taken off the heat, so spread them out quickly to let them cool down. (In Sichuan, chefs often assess the progress of frying peanuts by lifting a few out of the oil in a slotted spoon and tossing them an inch (a few centimeters) into the air: when they hit the metal of the spoon again, cooked peanuts make a more ringing sound than when they are raw.)

*1⅓ cups (200g) raw peanuts*
*Cooking oil, for deep-frying*
*Salt and ground roasted*
   *Sichuan pepper, to serve*

**Tip the peanuts into a wok** and cover with oil. Heat slowly to 250–265°F (120–130°C), by which point the oil should be sizzling gently around the peanuts. Fry them at this temperature for about 20 minutes, taking care not to let the oil overheat. By this time, the nuts should be crisp and fragrant: if you taste one, you will notice that it has lost its hint of raw moistness and has a faintly golden color and a toasty flavor. Remove the nuts from the oil with a slotted spoon, drain well, and spread out on paper towels to cool completely.

To serve, pile the nuts onto a small plate, season to taste with salt and Sichuan pepper and mix well before eating.

# "Strange Flavor" Peanuts

guaiwei huaren
怪味花仁

*1⅓ cups (200g) raw peanuts*
*¼ tsp salt*
*1½ tbsp ground chiles*
*½ tsp ground roasted Sichuan pepper*
*¾ cup (150g) superfine sugar*

Like "strange flavor" chicken (see p. 70), this concoction is named for its weird combination of several different flavors, although the two dishes bear no further resemblance. The crisp peanuts (shown in the photograph on p. 121) are encrusted in a delicious fudgy paste that is unexpectedly spiced with chile and Sichuan pepper. They are eaten as part of a cold course at a banquet and also sold on the streets with other snack foods. The recipe is a sort of Sichuanese version of the caramelized peanuts occasionally encountered on Western city streets. Please feel free to vary the amount of spices used, depending on your taste and the zing of your ground chiles and Sichuan pepper. If you'd like something even "stranger," you can add a small amount of very finely chopped ginger, garlic and scallion along with the other flavorings; and if you don't fancy the idea of chile-hot confections, just omit the spices and use toasted sesame seeds instead. Deep-fried or toasted walnuts or cashews can also be prepared in this manner—cashews are fabulous.

Traditionally in China, where most kitchens lacked ovens until recently, peanuts are roasted by covering them in salt and then "stir-frying" them gently in a wok. The salt acts as a conductor and guarantees an even roasting. It is later sifted away from the peanuts and set aside for the next batch of roasting. The peanut skins are rubbed off with the fingertips and then gently blown out of a nearby door or window.

Preheat the oven to 300°F (150°C). Place the peanuts on a rimmed baking sheet and roast for about 20 minutes until crisp and pale golden. Keep a close eye on them, as they can easily become too dark. Remove from the oven and cool completely. When the peanuts are cool, gently massage off their skins with your fingers. If possible, go and stand outdoors and blow over the peanuts as you shake them about: the feather-light skins will blow away.

Combine the salt, ground chiles and Sichuan pepper in a dish.

Put the sugar and about 5 tbsp (75ml) water into a clean wok and heat gently, stirring to dissolve the sugar. When the sugar has dissolved, turn up the heat and boil to the hard-ball stage, about 257°F (125°C) (the syrupy bubbles that keep rising to the surface are known as "fish-eye bubbles"—you will be able to see exactly why). If you don't have a thermometer, keep lifting your wok scoop from the syrup: initially the syrup will fall off the scoop in droplets, then in a thin stream, and finally it will start trailing, in the hair-like strands the Chinese call "flying silks" (*feisi*). When the syrup reaches this stage, turn off the heat and let cool for about 30 seconds. Swiftly stir in the spice mixture, and then the peanuts. Keep stirring as the syrup cools and sets to a fudgy frosting, taking care to separate the nuts into single nuts or small clusters.

Let cool completely, then store in an airtight jar. (I always add to the jar one of those desiccation sachets that often come with packaged Japanese snacks, for maximum crispness.)

# Meat

"The Chinese probably have the most adventurous approach to meat eating that the world has ever seen; ancient gastronomic texts and modern culinary encyclopedias read like a Noah's Ark of extraordinary and exotic creatures"

# Meat 肉食类

The Chinese probably have the most adventurous approach to meat eating that the world has ever seen; ancient gastronomic texts and modern culinary encyclopedias read like a Noah's Ark of extraordinary and exotic creatures. Bear's paw, which for more than 2,000 years was considered one of the most exalted of culinary exotica, appeared in recipes published up until the 1980s. Such delicacies were beyond the reach of all but the extremely rich or well connected, but they were part of a culture largely uninhibited by food taboos. These days, over-exploitation and environmental degradation have removed most wild and exotic creatures from banquet menus and made many of them illegal. Most people in China, anyway, eat mainly pork, with some beef, goat, lamb and—particularly in southern Sichuan—rabbit. The exceptions to this are, of course, Chinese Muslims, who eat only beef, goat and lamb or mutton.

But if the range of creatures eaten by the wealthy has shrunk, the old habit of adventurousness is still in spectacular evidence in Sichuan, in the form of a kind of "nose-to-tail" eating that leaves Westerners in the dust. The Chinese in general, and the Sichuanese in particular, have a genius for creating exquisite dishes from the parts of animals most Westerners never touch—not only the obvious offal like hearts and livers, but also tripe, intestines, ears and tendons. In Yibin I once tasted a New Year's soup made from pig's lung, intestine, liver, heart and jellied blood, all stewed in stock with daikon and sweet potato noodles. A Chongqing hotpot feast can involve esoteric animal parts such as gristly ox or pig aorta, rabbit kidneys and goose intestines. Incredibly, the resourceful cooks of Chengdu have even found a use for the chewy upper palate of the pig, which is dressed in spicy oil and eaten as a midnight snack known as "paradise" (*tiantang*).

A cultural predilection for savoring the textures of food partly explains this enthusiastic omnivorousness. From a Western point of view, eating a goose intestine is pointless because of its rubberiness and lack of flavor; from a Sichuanese point of view, its slithery, snappy mouthfeel is something to be enjoyed. Similarly, a rabbit head or a duck neck is so fiddly and scarce of actual meat that for most Westerners it's not worth the effort of dissection; for someone Sichuanese, this "high grapple factor" is part of the fun.

The Chinese also have a rather philosophically enlightened and open-minded approach to their ingredients. Instead of ruling anything specifically edible or inedible, the accomplished Chinese cook will examine an ingredient, assess its strengths and weaknesses, and then use culinary technique to enhance those strengths and overcome those weaknesses. A tendon, for example, has a thrilling texture but little flavor, so a good cook will braise it in a rich stock so the final dish is both sumptuous on the lips and profoundly delicious. Kidneys are delicate and nourishing but have an unclean aroma and become leathery when overcooked, so a skilled cook will marinate them in rice wine to purify their flavor and then cut them intricately to maximize surface area, so they can be fast-fried over very high heat.

Esoteric offal is traditionally associated with both extremes of the social scale: the rich with their shark's fins and bear's paws, the poor with their duck's blood boiled up in a potful of chiles. Pork is the middle ground and the meat of the majority: in fact, when the Chinese talk of "meat" (*rou*), they normally mean pork unless otherwise specified. Pork is the meat of everyday life, so ubiquitous that most local butchers' stalls sell nothing else. It can be stir-fried, braised, steamed, deep-fried, stewed, roasted, boiled, salt-cured or smoked. It can be cooked on its own, tossed in a wok with plenty of vegetables or made into stocks. Its sweet, delicate lard can add magic to meat or vegetable dishes; its fat can be cooked to slow, tender perfection. For if pork is ordinary, it is by no means inferior, and it is relished for its tenderness and its sweet, fresh taste.

In one of his poems, "Eating pork" (*shi zhurou*), the great Song-dynasty poet Su Dongpo ridiculed those who looked down on this most humble of meats:

*The good pork of Huangzhou,*
*It's as cheap as dirt,*
*The rich disdain it,*
*The poor have no idea how to cook it,*
*But with a slow flame, and just a little water,*
*When it's cooked just right it's certainly delicious.*
*Have a bowlful every morning*
*And you'll feel as though you haven't a care*
 *in the world.*

Archeological evidence from northern China suggests that the Chinese were rearing pigs around the fifth or sixth millennium BC; by the third century BC they had become one of the main kinds of livestock, and were also used in sacrifices. Written sources from that period refer to various ways of cooking pork, including roasting, boiling and steaming it, and making it into thick soupy stews (geng). These days, pork still accounts for the vast majority of meat consumption in China, and it's typically the only meat on the Sichuanese dinner table at home.

At the Chinese New Year, pork comes into its own as the centerpiece of the feast. Farmers traditionally fatten up a pig before the festival. In the last month of the lunar year (*layue*, the month of winter sacrifices), they cook up and devour the offal and then cure the rest of the meat. In most places, people salt-cure the meat and then give it a long, cool smoking or paint it with sweet flour sauce and hang it under the eaves to wind-dry.

Many people still make their own sausages, the fatty stuffing jazzed up with ground chiles and Sichuan pepper. In mountainous Hanyuan county, they confit great chunks of fatty pork in its own lard and then stow it in earthenware jars: on winter evenings, late in the year, great cauldrons of fat bubble away over the orange glow of wood fires in every courtyard (this "clay jar pork," tanzi rou, is incredibly delicious after a quick stir-frying with black beans and green garlic).

In the past, the New Year was also the time to make complex meat dishes with many elements, like the "head bowl" (*touwan*) of Li Zhuang, the historic Yangtze river port. People here would coat slices of pork in eggy batter and deep-fry them to make "crisp pork" (*surou*); and steam, deep-fry and then slice meatloaf (*baba rou*) made from fatty rib meat. They would then assemble them prettily in a large bowl with wood ear mushrooms, day-lily flowers and other luxuries, and steam everything together before serving. In other parts of rural Sichuan, people would place slices of prized belly meat in a shallow bowl with a topping of preserved vegetable or sweet glutinous rice and steam them until gorgeously yielding. At one memorable family lunch I attended near Chengdu in the festive season, we were honored with home-made bacon, pork cured in sweet flour sauce, wind-dried sausages, stewed chicken with mushrooms and a ravishing array of vegetables.

The Chinese particularly appreciate cuts of pork with a generous proportion of fat, and are masters of the arts of cooking it so that the fat becomes fragrant and meltingly tender without being cloying (*fei er bu ni*, as they say: "richly fat but not greasy"). For this reason, dishes such as twice-cooked pork, bowl-steamed pork belly with preserved vegetable and—especially—"sweet white" rice pudding are best made with very fatty pork: either the piece of rump known as "second-cut pork" (see p. 132) or belly with a good layering of fat. (In London, once, I was delighted to find an extremely fatty piece of belly that I knew would be perfect for my rice pudding: the European butcher was so apologetic about the high proportion of fat that he sold it to me at half price!) Similarly, when making dumplings and meat sauces, the Chinese generally favor ground pork that is three parts fat to seven parts lean.

In Chinese antiquity, oxen appear to have been as important as pigs in Chinese food culture; they were also used in ritual sacrifices and are often mentioned in ancient texts, including the *Book of Rites* (*liji*). With the development of agriculture, however, the ox came to be seen primarily as a farm animal, employed for ploughing fields and carrying heavy loads, and many imperial governments passed decrees banning its slaughter for food.

From the Han dynasty (206 BC–220 AD) onward,

beef was rarely mentioned in texts discussing food and seldom won the praise of poets or gourmets. Some of the herding peoples on the fringes of China, like the Tibetans, continued to view beef as an important foodstuff; elsewhere, its consumption was limited to the meat of working beasts that had perished in the harsh winter months.

These days beef is still less common than pork, and has to be hunted down in Sichuanese markets (though it is currently enjoying a renaissance as part of a fashion for Western-style grilled steaks). There is, however, a fascinating local tradition of beef-eating around the salt-mining areas of southern Sichuan, where oxen once drove the machinery used to draw the brine from the bowels of the earth. Local people would eat the meat of expired working oxen: the origin, they say, of the famous Zigong dish, "water-boiled beef" (shuizhu niurou). Zigong, the "salt capital," is also known for a kind of beef jerky, "fireside beef" (huobianzi niurou), made from enormous, extremely thin slices of beef that were dried around the edges of the simmering salt pans until they were chewy and almost transparent.

Beef does play a starring role in some notable Sichuanese dishes, including mapo tofu (see p. 245), which is properly made with ground beef (though many people use pork instead), and "man-and-wife" offal slices (see p. 97). A famous restaurant in Chongqing, the Old Sichuan, which was established in 1930, has long been renowned for its beef specialties, including clear-simmered oxtail soup (see p. 313). Beef is also eaten by Sichuanese Hui Muslims, who use it to make halal versions of classic local dishes like twice-cooked pork and fish-fragrant pork slivers.

Lamb or goat (the same word, yangrou, is used for both) is a rarity on conventional Sichuanese menus. It is generally associated with the food of the northern provinces, where the culinary legacy of China's conquest by sheep-eating Mongols in the thirteenth century and the proximity of nomadic cultures are more keenly felt. Lamb or goat is, however, served in local halal restaurants, and is a particular specialty of the town of Jianyang: a few Jianyang restaurants in Chengdu serve goat soup, along with preparations made of every part of the

beast, from blood to hoof. Goat soup is regarded as particularly "heating" in traditional medicinal terms, and many Sichuanese people drink it as a tonic around the time of the winter solstice. Rabbit has been popular in Sichuan since the 1950s (the introduction to the recipe for "rabbit eaten cold," on p. 116, explains why).

The following chapter contains some of the classic meat dishes of Sichuan.

A "village cook" (*xiang chuzi*)
preparing a funeral feast
in a village near Li Zhuang,
Yibin, southern Sichuan

# Twice-cooked Pork

## hui guo rou
## 回锅肉

*Hui guo rou*—literally, "back-in-the-pot meat"—is the most profoundly loved of all local dishes. A ravishing combination of fragrant pork, intensely savory seasonings and sprightly vegetables, it's the focus of great nostalgia and often tied up with childhood memories. One elderly roast-duck vendor in Chengdu told me that in pre-industrial days, when all pork came from free-range pigs, a whole neighborhood would know if someone was cooking the dish, so captivating was its aroma. The dish is said to have been eaten at meetings of Sichuan's notorious secret societies, before the communists wiped them out, and is still nicknamed "secret society meat" (*paoge rou*) in some parts of western Sichuan.

Twice-cooked pork derives its name from the fact that the pork is first boiled and then stir-fried. In the hot oil, the thin slices of meat curl into what chefs call "lamp-dish shapes" (*dengzhanwo xing*), resembling the tiny oil-filled dishes used as lamps in pre-revolutionary China. The main ingredient is a cut of pork rump known as "second-cut pork" (*erdao rou*), a boned-out upper back leg with trimmed edges (the "second cut")—a tidy square that is half fat, half lean. This luxurious morsel, cooked, is sometimes laid on an altar for ancestral sacrifices, after which it can be put to other uses: this, some say, is how twice-cooked pork came about.

Fatty pork is essential. If you can, use rump or leg with a good 1 inch (2–3cm) layer of fat; failing that, belly meat is excellent. To make the slicing easier, start with a larger piece of pork than you need and use the scraps for other dishes.

1½-inch piece (30g) ginger, unpeeled
1 scallion, white part only
¾ lb (350g) fatty pork rump, leg or belly,
    in one piece, with skin
3¼ oz (90g) Chinese green garlic (or baby leeks,
    red onions or green and/or red peppers)
2 tbsp lard or cooking oil
A pinch of salt
1½ tbsp Sichuan chile bean paste
1½ tsp sweet flour sauce
2 tsp fermented black beans,
    rinsed and drained
¼ tsp dark soy sauce

Lightly smack the ginger and scallion white with the flat of a cleaver blade or a rolling pin to loosen them. Bring a large pot of water to a boil. Add the pork and return to a boil. Add the ginger and scallion white, turn the heat down and simmer until the pork is barely cooked: about 10–20 minutes, depending on the thickness of the piece. Remove from the water and set aside for a few hours to cool completely; refrigerate until needed (the pork can be cooked a day ahead).

When you are ready to make the dish, slice the pork as thinly as possible, making sure each piece has skin, fat and lean meat. Cut the green garlic at a steep angle into long, thin "horse ear" slices (baby leeks can be cut in the same way, onions or peppers into bite-sized slices).

Heat the lard or oil in a seasoned wok over medium heat. Add the pork and stir-fry, with a pinch of salt, until the pieces have curled up and released some of their oils, and smell delicious. Tilt the wok, push the pork up one side and add the chile bean paste to the oil that pools in the base; stir-fry until it smells wonderful and has reddened the oil. Add the sweet flour sauce and black beans and stir briefly, then tilt the wok back and mix everything together. Finally, add the soy sauce and green garlic (or other vegetable) and stir-fry until just cooked.

### Variation

*The green shoots that sprout out of forgotten heads of garlic can be used instead of the leeks in this dish.*

# Pork Slivers
# with Yellow Chives

## jiuhuang rousi
韭黄肉丝

Yellow chives (*jiuhuang,* Latin name
*Allium tuberosum*), which can sometimes
be found at Chinese food shops in the
West, are ordinary Chinese chives that
have been grown in hothouses and
deprived of sunlight. The darkness steals
their greenness, leaving their leaves a
pale, shy, delicate yellow. These chives
have a powerful aroma that will fill your
shopping bag and your kitchen. When
cooked they are silky and succulent, a
real treat. The technique of blanching
chives in hothouses has been known
since the Han dynasty, and those grown
near Chengdu were praised by the
twelfth-century poet Lu You. These days
yellow chives are a Sichuanese specialty,
although not exclusive to the region. For
an older Sichuanese generation, chives
were always on the New Year's Eve
menu because their name, *jiu,* is a pun
on "long-lasting" (*changjiu*)—a good
augury for the coming year.

This recipe is a common home-
cooked dish, either eaten with rice or
wrapped in fresh spring roll pancakes
(see p. 399). It's just one of a whole genre
of recipes for pork slivers fried with one
vegetable or another (see the variations).
Pork is the most commonly used meat,
although Chinese Muslims might use
beef or lamb; chicken or turkey can also
be cooked this way. Yellow chives are
fragile and are best eaten soon after
purchase, although they should keep for
a couple of days if wrapped in paper and
refrigerated. Feel free to add a few slivers
of ginger, red pepper or chile to the wok
with the chives, if you wish.

*5¼ oz (150g) lean pork leg meat*
*5¼ oz (150g) Chinese yellow chives*
*3 tbsp cooking oil*

*For the marinade*
*¼ tsp salt*
*1 tsp Shaoxing wine*
*2 tsp potato starch*

*For the sauce*
*⅛ tsp salt*
*¼ tsp potato starch*
*½ tsp Shaoxing wine*
*¾ tsp Chinkiang vinegar*
*¼ tsp light soy sauce*
*1½ tbsp stock or water*

**Cut the pork as evenly as possible** into thin slices, and then
into very fine slivers. Place in a bowl, add the marinade
ingredients, along with 1½ tbsp water, and stir in one direction
to mix. Set aside while you prepare the other ingredients.

Trim the chives and cut them into 2-inch (5cm) lengths.
Combine the sauce ingredients in a small bowl.

Heat the oil in a seasoned wok over high heat. Add the pork
slivers and stir briskly. As soon as the slivers have separated,
toss in the chives. Continue to stir-fry until the chives are hot
(make sure the pork is just cooked), then give the sauce a stir
and add it to the wok. Stir as the sauce thickens, then serve.

## Variations

*Instead of yellow chives, feel free to use green Chinese chives,
celery, red or green peppers or other vegetables, all cut evenly
into thin slivers. Fleshy vegetables are best stir-fried in advance
for 1–2 minutes over moderate heat to "break their rawness,"
then set aside and returned to the wok after you have separated
the pork slivers (if you don't pre-fry them, the pork may be
overdone by the time the vegetables are ready).*

*Vegetarians can use strips of smoked or spiced firm tofu instead
of the pork (omitting the marinade and frying the tofu directly).*

# Bowl-steamed Pork in Ricemeal with Peas

## fenzheng rou
## 粉蒸肉

This is one of the magnificent bowl-steamed dishes that were traditionally served at Sichuanese rural feasts and celebrations (see p. 137). Slices of pork belly are marinated and then clothed in crumbs of rice that swell during cooking to create a soft, huggy coating, and the pork ends up melting dreamily into the peas. The dish is closely related to spicy steamed beef with ricemeal (see p. 165), which was originally a Muslim specialty. In Chongqing and other parts of southern Sichuan, it is known by the name zharou, a reference to an ancient method of pickling involving pounded rice, which is known in these areas as zha powder.

This dish is easy to make but takes 2 hours to steam, so you have to keep an eye on it to make sure it doesn't boil dry; it can, however, be steamed in a pressure cooker in 30 minutes. You may be able to find the ricemeal (usually sold as "steam powder," zhengroufen) in a Chinese supermarket; alternatively, make your own (see p. 454). You will also need a bowl about 7 inches (18cm) in diameter and 2 inches (5cm) deep that will fit in your steamer, some foil and some twine (made from natural fiber). The dish can be made in advance, then refrigerated and heated through in a steamer or microwave before serving.

Meaty pork ribs can also be cooked this way. Instead of peas, try using green soy beans (edamame) or chunks of peeled pumpkin or sweet potato. In Yibin, I once had a sweet version, with orange-fleshed sweet potato clothed in ricemeal and brown sugar syrup, then mixed with fatty pork and steamed: delicious.

1 cup (150g) fresh peas (about 1 lb/450g in the pod)
   or frozen peas
5 tbsp ricemeal
7 tbsp (100ml) stock
1 tbsp cooking oil
1½ tbsp Sichuan chile bean paste
¾ lb (350g) pork belly, with skin
2 tsp white or red fermented tofu, mashed with its brine
2 tsp Shaoxing wine
1 tsp finely chopped ginger
¼ tsp dark soy sauce
½ tsp superfine sugar
⅛ tsp ground white pepper
1–2 tbsp thinly sliced scallion greens
Salt

**Place the peas in a bowl** and add ¼ tsp salt, 1 tbsp ricemeal and 2 tbsp stock. Mix well. Heat the oil in a seasoned wok over medium heat; add the chile bean paste and stir-fry gently until the oil is red and fragrant. Remove from the wok and set aside.

Cut the pork into slices like thickly cut bacon, about 4 inches (10cm) long and ⅛ inch (3–4mm) thick, with an edge of skin. Place in a bowl and add the fermented tofu, Shaoxing wine, ginger, soy sauce, sugar and pepper, together with the chile bean paste and its cooking oil. Stir in the remaining ricemeal and stock, plus ¼ tsp salt, and mix well.

Arrange the pork slices over the sides and base of your steaming bowl in an overlapping pattern, leaving no holes, with the strip of skin on each piece of meat resting on the bowl (as in the photograph on p. 136). Fill the bowl with the peas, spreading them out evenly so the top layer is fairly flat. Cover the bowl with foil and, for easy removal from the steamer, tie up like a parcel with a piece of twine. Bring plenty of water to a boil in your wok or steamer, set the bowl on the rack, cover with a lid and steam over medium heat for 2 hours, topping up the water as needed. (Alternatively, pressure cook at high pressure for 30 minutes, then allow the pressure to reduce naturally.)

When you wish to serve the pork, remove the bowl from the steamer. Cover with a deep plate and swiftly invert. Remove the bowl, leaving a bowl-shaped mound of meat and peas. If the meat subsides slightly in its tenderness, don't worry—it'll still taste fantastic. Sprinkle with the scallion greens.

# Bowl-steamed Pork Belly with Preserved Vegetable

han shaobai

咸烧白

For old-fashioned rural weddings, families traditionally hire a "village chef" (*xiang chuzi*) to create a feast. The chef, often a local farmer with special cooking skills, arrives with his equipment and helpers, and caters for the many dozens of guests who will eat at makeshift tables set up in the courtyards of the house. *Han shaobai*—literally "salty cooked white [pork]"—is almost always on the menu. It's also indispensable for the ritual New Year's Eve dinner. Slices of pork belly are placed in a bowl and steamed until the fat is exquisitely tender: the sharp saltiness of preserved vegetable perfectly complements the meat. A Sichuanese cousin of similar versions found in Hakka communities and the Cantonese south, the dish is, as the Chinese say, "richly fat without being greasy" (*fei er bu ni*).

Bowl-steamed dishes like this are the stars of what are known as "field feasts" (*tianxi*) or "farmyard feasts" (*babaxi*) because they can be made in advance and left to steam gently until needed: a boon when feeding hordes of people. Often, the feasts themselves are simply called "nine big bowls" (*jiu dawan*) or "three steamed dishes and nine steamed bowls" (*sanzheng jiukou*).

At one wedding lunch I attended, a makeshift stove had been built in the courtyard from bricks and clay, and a team of helpers spent two days preparing the food. By the time the guests arrived, a dozen round tables were already laden with cold appetizers; later, bowl after bowl of hot dishes were unloaded from a towering stack of bamboo steamers.

*1 lb (450g) pork belly, in one piece, with skin*

*1¾ tsp dark soy sauce*

*7 tbsp (100ml) cooking oil*

*3 Sichuan pickled chiles (optional)*

*1 tbsp fermented black beans*

*1 cup (150g) Yibin yacai or Tianjin preserved vegetable, rinsed and squeezed dry*

Bring a large pot of water to a boil, add the pork and boil for about 10 minutes. Remove the pork, reserving the cooking water, and rinse in cold water. While the meat is still warm, pat it completely dry with paper towels or a clean dish towel, then smear the skin with ¼ tsp soy sauce. Set aside on paper towels for a few minutes to dry (and so minimize spitting when you place it in the hot oil).

Heat the oil in a seasoned wok over high heat to about 320°F (160°C) (hot enough to sizzle vigorously around a test piece of the pork). Add the pork, skin side down, and fry for about 2 minutes until the skin has puckered into little bubbles and is rich red-brown all over, taking care not to burn it. Remove the meat from the wok and return it to the reserved cooking water to soak for 5–10 minutes, until the skin is again supple, then remove from the liquid and set aside to cool completely.

When the pork is cold, cut it as evenly as possible into ¼-inch (5mm) slices, each with a strip of skin along the top. If the slices are very wide, cut them in half across the grain of the meat (ideally the pieces should be about 3¼ inches × 1½ inches/8cm × 4cm). Reserve any offcuts. Trim off the tops of the pickled chiles, if using, and gently scrape along them with your knife to squeeze out as many seeds as possible; cut each chile into three sections.

In a heatproof bowl about 8¼ inches (21cm) in diameter and 1½ inches (4cm) deep (and that will fit in your steamer or pressure cooker), lay two slices of pork along opposite sides, with their lines of skin facing the center. Then arrange about eight more slices in a tidy row across the base: each slice should overlap the last, and the strip of skin on each piece should be in contact with the surface of the bowl. Place any offcuts on top (or reserve them to use in other dishes), then sprinkle 1½ tsp soy sauce all over the meat. Add the fermented beans and pickled chiles, then fill the bowl with the preserved vegetable, pressing down gently with your hands. Cover the bowl with foil and, for easy removal from the steamer, tie up like a parcel with twine (made from natural fiber).  →

← Place the bowl in your steamer, cover with the lid, and steam over energetically boiling water for about 2 hours, replenishing the water as necessary. (Alternatively, steam in a pressure cooker at high pressure for 30 minutes, then allow the pressure to release naturally.) This step can be done a day or two ahead.

To serve, reheat if necessary, then discard the foil and twine. Cover the bowl with a deep serving dish and swiftly invert, to turn out the bowl's contents in a domed shape.

*"Dragon-eye" steamed pork with preserved vegetable
(longyan han shaobai 龙眼咸烧白)*
*To make this grander version of the dish, stuff a single fermented black bean into a section of pickled red chile, then wrap a slice of pork around each chile section. Stack these tubes upright, with the skin side of each pork slice facing down, in the center of your heatproof bowl, building a surrounding "wall" of preserved vegetable to keep them in place. Steam as for the main recipe. When the bowl is turned out onto the serving dish, the tops of the tubes stare up like a dozen beady red dragon's eyes with black pupils.*

# Pork in "Lychee" Sauce with Crispy Rice

guoba roupian
锅巴肉片

This dish is quite a party piece. A steaming hot bowl of soupy sauce is taken to the table, along with a deep platter piled with shards of crisp rice crust. As the guests sit back in their seats, the sauce is poured over the rice to explosive effect—not for nothing is the dish known in some places as "a sudden clap of thunder" (*pingdi yi sheng lei*). (When we learned this dish at the Sichuan cooking school I attended, my classmates snickered at its somewhat tasteless alternative name: "bombing Tokyo.") It's not just dramatic, however, but a delightful mixture of tastes, colors and textures. The rice crust soaks up the sauce in a gorgeous half-juicy, half-crunchy way.

As you will notice, there are no lychees in the dish. The name refers to the Sichuanese sauce known as "lychee flavor": a lighter version of sweet-and-sour, in which the sour notes stand out a little more than the sweet, rather like the fruit. The rice crust (*guoba*) is traditionally the toasty layer that sticks to the bottom of the pot when rice is cooked over a fire. Sprinkled with salt and spices, it's a favorite children's snack and can be bought in packets like potato chips.

When I was a student in Chengdu, *guoba* was sold in every market: it was made in enormous woks, and the crusts, as large as satellite dishes, were then sun-dried before being broken into pieces for sale. Happily, this crispy rice is easy to make at home in an oven, and can be prepared in advance and kept in an airtight jar until needed. →

4 dried shiitake mushrooms

A few pieces of dried wood ear mushroom

½ cup (60g) bamboo shoot, fresh or canned

2 scallions, white parts only

2 Sichuan pickled chiles or 1 ripe tomato

7 oz (200g) boneless pork loin or tenderloin

3 tbsp cooking oil

2 garlic cloves, peeled and thinly sliced

An equivalent amount of ginger,
   peeled and thinly sliced

2 cups (500ml) everyday stock (see p. 463)

A handful of small leafy greens

2 tbsp potato starch, mixed with
   3 tbsp cold water

### For the rice crust

1 cup (200g) Thai jasmine rice

Cooking oil, for deep-frying

### For the marinade

¼ tsp salt

2 tsp Shaoxing wine

2 tsp potato starch

### For the sauce

3 tbsp superfine sugar

3 tbsp Chinkiang vinegar

1½ tbsp light soy sauce

¾ tsp salt

**First make the rice crust** (this should be done in advance). Preheat the oven to 400°F (200°C). Cook the rice as normal, and then spread it out on a baking sheet lined with parchment paper, in a layer about ¼ inch (6mm) thick—tidy up the edges so the thickness is as even as possible. Bake the rice for about 30 minutes, until it is dry, crisp and faintly golden at the edges. Remove and allow to cool and dry completely. Then break into rough 2½-inch (6–7cm) squares and store in an airtight jar.

Cover both kinds of mushroom with hot water from the kettle and let soak for 30 minutes. Squeeze out excess water, then thinly slice the shiitake caps, discarding the stalks, and break the wood ears into bite-sized pieces, removing any knobbly bits. →

← To make this dish, you will need one wok for the pork, and another wok or deep-fryer for the rice crust. For safety's sake, if you are frying the crust in a wok, I advise enlisting another person to keep an eye on the oil so it doesn't overheat while you're cooking the pork and making the sauce. You will also need a wide serving dish and a deep bowl that you can cover with a lid or small plate to keep the sauce warm.

← Cut the bamboo shoot into thin slices and blanch for a minute or two in boiling water, then drain. Cut the scallion whites at a steep angle into "horse ear" slices; do the same with the pickled chiles, if using (alternatively, slice the tomato).

Thinly slice the pork, add the marinade ingredients and 1 tbsp cold water and mix well.

Combine the sauce ingredients in a small bowl.

When you are ready to cook, start heating the deep-frying oil on a second burner: you want it to be 390°F (200°C) for frying the rice crust (but make sure it does not overheat while you concentrate on the pork and the sauce).

Heat the 3 tbsp oil in a seasoned wok over high heat. Add the pork and stir to separate the slices. When the pork has become pale, tip in the garlic, ginger, scallion whites and pickled chiles, if using, and stir-fry until they smell wonderful. Add both kinds of mushroom, the bamboo shoot and tomato, if using, and stir until piping hot. Pour in the stock and bring to a boil. Skim. Give the sauce a stir and add to the wok, followed by the greens. Give the potato starch mixture a quick stir, then add it to the wok in a couple of stages, stirring as the liquid thickens into a lazy gravy (do not use more than you need). Pour the contents of the wok into a deep bowl and cover to keep warm.

Check that the temperature of the deep-frying oil has reached 390°F (200°C), then add the rice crust and fry for a minute or two until puffy and golden. Drain well on paper towels, then pile up in a serving dish. Moving quickly, take both serving dish and sauce bowl to the table, and pour the sauce over the crispy rice in front of your guests.

Variations

*Some restaurants use squid instead of pork; chicken is also a fine substitute, and vegetarians will enjoy using a selection of fresh mushrooms instead of any kind of meat. The garlic, ginger and scallions are essential flavorings, but you can vary the vegetable ingredients at will—just aim for an attractive variety of colors.*

# Stir-fried Pork Slivers with Sweet Flour Sauce

## jingjiang rousi
## 京酱肉丝

Wandering around an old riverside town near Zigong, my friends and I came across a pickle shop that belonged to the fourth generation of a family fermentation business. In the backyard were jars of fermenting sweet flour sauce (*tianmianjiang*), a flavoring that dates back to at least the Yuan dynasty (1279–1368). Although this condiment is sold in every corner shop, it's rare to witness artisanal production. Behind his shop, Mr. Fan showed us a room whose entire floor area was covered with clumps of steamed wheat dough that were quietly growing a coat of mold under their paper shroud. After two weeks, they would be transferred to jars, covered in brine, and left to bake in the sun (covered only at night and during rainfall) until they had been transformed into a dark, earthy paste with a heady aroma and rich flavor. Thick fermented sauces (*jiang*) made by this basic method, from soy beans and other grains as well as wheat flour, were the most important savory condiments in Chinese cooking for about two millennia, until they were displaced by the modern upstart known as soy sauce.

In this dish, which was on every restaurant menu in Chengdu in the 1990s, *tianmianjiang* is the principal seasoning. Its Chinese name translates as "pork slivers in Beijing sauce," which suggests the recipe was inspired by similar versions found in northern China. The dark, glossy mound of pork slivers is topped with a pile of crisp, white scallion or leek, a refreshing contrast to the richness of the meat.

9 oz (250g) pork leg or shoulder meat
4 scallions, white parts only,
    or 1 white Beijing leek
1½ tbsp sweet flour sauce
5 tbsp cooking oil

### For the marinade
¼ tsp salt
1 tbsp potato starch
½ tbsp Shaoxing wine

### For the sauce
1 tsp superfine sugar
¼ tsp potato starch
1½ tsp light soy sauce
½ tsp dark soy sauce
1 tbsp stock or water

**Cut the pork into very thin,** even slices and then into long, thin slivers, ideally about ⅛ inch (3mm) thick—this way they will cook quickly and simultaneously, and will therefore be tender. Place in a bowl, then add the marinade ingredients, along with 1½ tbsp cold water, and stir in one direction to combine. Set aside while you prepare the other ingredients.

Cut the scallion whites or leek into 4-inch (10cm) lengths, and then lengthwise into fine slivers. Let soak in a bowl of cold water until needed. Dilute the sweet flour sauce with 1 tbsp cold water, to give a runny consistency.

Combine the sauce ingredients in a small bowl.

When you are ready to cook, drain the scallion or leek slivers and set aside. Heat the oil in a seasoned wok over high heat. Add the pork slivers and stir-fry briskly until they have separated and are nearly cooked. Tilt the wok, push the pork slivers up one side and add the diluted sweet flour sauce to the oil that pools at the base. Stir-fry for 10–20 seconds until it is fragrant, then tilt the wok back and mix the pork back in, making sure the meat is cooked through.

Now, working swiftly, give the prepared sauce a stir and pour it into the wok. Stir as the sauce thickens, then turn out onto a serving dish. Top with the scallion or leek slivers and serve.

# Red-braised Pork

## hongshao rou
## 红烧肉

This dish is made with streaky pork belly, which is known poetically in Chinese as "five-flower meat" (*wuhua rou*) because of its layers of fat and lean. The meat and fat are braised to slow, tender perfection in a sauce that finally reduces to a dark, syrupy glaze, delicately flavored with star anise. It's extremely easy to make and tastes sensational.

The Sichuanese version of this universally popular Chinese dish is less dark and treacly than the Shanghainese. It's often served alongside other braised dishes (shaocai) at casual "fly" restaurants, where you can assemble your meal from a gorgeous display of cold dishes, bubbling stews, jars of pickles and a great potful of rice.

It's always best to make this dish a day in advance if you can: the flavor and texture of the meat seem to improve overnight, and once it is chilled, you can remove the fat that solidifies on the surface before serving (use it to add delicious umami flavors to stir-fried vegetables or noodle soups).

*1 lb 10 oz (750g) boneless pork belly, with skin*
*1½-inch piece (30g) ginger, unpeeled*
*2 scallions, white parts only*
*2 tbsp cooking oil*
*3 cups (700ml) everyday stock (see p. 463)*
*About 1 tbsp dark soy sauce or 1½ tbsp*
*    caramel coloring (see p. 458)*
*2½ tbsp Shaoxing wine*
*About ¾ tsp salt*
*3 tbsp brown sugar or rock sugar*
*½ star anise*

Bring a large pot of water to a boil. Add the pork and blanch for 4–5 minutes; remove, rinse in cold water and cut into 1¼-inch (3–4cm) chunks. Lightly smack the ginger and scallion whites with the flat of a cleaver blade or a rolling pin to loosen them.

Heat the oil in a heavy-bottomed pan until just beginning to smoke. Add the pork chunks and fry for a couple of minutes until the meat has "tightened." If you wish, you can pour off any excess fat at this stage.

Stir in all the other ingredients and bring to a boil. Simmer, half-covered or uncovered, over gentle heat for about 2 hours, stirring from time to time, until the meat is tender. Remove and discard the ginger and scallion whites.

Before serving, adjust the seasoning and, if you wish, add a little extra soy sauce or caramel to deepen the color. You may also turn the heat up high to reduce and thicken the sauce.

## Variations

*You can use the same method to cook spare ribs, rabbit or beef and some offal, although beef is more commonly red-braised by an alternative method that involves Sichuan chile bean paste (see p. 168).*

# Fish-fragrant Pork Slivers

yuxiang rousi
鱼香肉丝

The so-called "fish-fragrant" flavor is one of Sichuan's most famous culinary creations and epitomizes the Sichuanese love of audacious combinations of flavors. It is spicy, sweet, sour and salty, and infused with the heady tastes of garlic, ginger and scallions. The mellow heat comes from pickled chiles, which also color the cooking oil a brilliant orange-red. Fish-fragrant dishes have been one of Sichuan's most successful culinary exports, but the strangeness of the term has led to a great variety of translations on English-language menus: "mock-fish," "sea-spice" and "fish-flavored" among them. The two Chinese characters literally mean "fish" and "fragrant," which is why I prefer the translation given above (see p. 24 for an explanation of the term).

    Fish-fragrant pork slivers is the most famous of Sichuan's fish-fragrant dishes. Sichuanese chefs tend to use fine strips of winter bamboo shoot or celtuce as a crunchy element in the dish, but you can also use celery. This dish should be cooked quickly to preserve the tenderness of the pork. In Sichuan, the pickled chiles give the oil a wonderful orange color; sambal oelek tends to give a paler tint, which is why I sometimes add a little extra chile oil to achieve the traditional red luster.

4–5 dried wood ear mushrooms
2–3 celery sticks (125g) or celtuce
7 oz (200g) trimmed pork leg or loin
4 tbsp cooking oil
4 tsp Sichuan pickled chile paste (or sambal oelek)
2 tsp finely chopped garlic
1½ tsp finely chopped ginger
2 tbsp thinly sliced scallion greens
2–3 tbsp chile oil, without sediment (optional)

*For the marinade*
¼ tsp salt
1 tsp Shaoxing wine
1 tbsp potato starch
1 tsp cooking oil

*For the sauce*
¾ tsp potato starch
3 tsp superfine sugar
2 tsp Chinkiang vinegar
2 tsp light soy sauce
2 tbsp cold stock or water

**Place the wood ears in a bowl,** cover with hot water from the kettle and let soak for 30 minutes. Discard any knobbly bits, then cut into ⅛-inch (3mm) slivers (you want to end up with 1¾ oz/50g). Peel and trim the celery or celtuce and cut into ⅛-inch (3mm) slivers. Cut the pork into slices about ¼ inch (5mm) thick, and then into slivers. Place in a bowl, then add all the marinade ingredients except the 1 tsp oil, along with 1 tbsp water. Stir in one direction to combine, then mix in the oil.

Combine the sauce ingredients in a small bowl.

Heat a seasoned wok over high heat and add the 4 tbsp cooking oil. When it is hot, add the pork and stir-fry swiftly to separate the slivers. As soon as they have changed color, tilt the wok, push the pork up the side and add the chile paste, ginger and garlic to the oil that pools in the base. Stir-fry until they are fragrant and the oil has reddened, then tilt the wok back and stir the pork slivers into the paste. Tip in the wood ears and celery or celtuce and swiftly mix everything together. Give the sauce a stir and pour into the center of the wok, stirring to incorporate. Finally, stir in the scallion greens—and the chile oil, if using. Serve immediately.

# Sweet-and-sour Pork

## tangcu liji
## 糖醋里脊

In the smoky kitchen of the Bamboo Bar, one of my favorite Chengdu restaurants, a desperate pandemonium reigns. The place is always filled with guests demanding long lists of complicated dishes, but most of the cooking is done in a single wok. The head chef stands over the coal-fired stove stirring and tossing, flinging spices and sauces into the wok with wild abandon. His three assistants rush around the tiny kitchen, mincing garlic and ginger, chopping meat into slices, dices and slivers, washing dishes. The kitchen seems precariously balanced on the brink of chaos. Bamboo baskets, overflowing with scallions, celery and Chinese cabbage, stand on every surface in riotous disorder. Huge tubs of soaking dried squid and mushrooms obstruct the floor.

But, miraculously, out of this mad mess comes some of the best Sichuanese food in the district, authentically spiced, precisely cooked and served with a complete lack of pretension.

One of the dishes the Bamboo Bar does best is sweet-and-sour pork. Deep-fried strips of tender pork are dressed in a dark, tangy sauce that is light years away from the synthetic-looking confections typically served under the same name in the West.

9 oz (250g) pork tenderloin
2 tsp Shaoxing wine
1 large egg
⅔ cup (75g) potato starch
At least 2 cups (500ml) cooking oil,
  for deep-frying
1 tbsp finely chopped garlic
1 tbsp finely chopped ginger
3 tbsp thinly sliced scallion greens
2 scallion whites, cut into very
  fine slivers (optional)
A few very fine slivers of fresh red
  chile (optional)
Salt

_For the sauce_
5 tbsp superfine sugar
2 tbsp Chinkiang vinegar
½ tbsp light soy sauce
1¼ tsp potato starch
5 tbsp stock or water

**Cut the pork into slices** about ½ inch (1cm) thick, and then into bite-sized ½-inch (1cm) strips. Place in a bowl. Add the Shaoxing wine and ¼ tsp salt and mix well. In another bowl, beat the egg and then gradually stir in the potato starch to make a thick, custardy batter. Add to the pork and mix to coat all the pieces.

Combine the sauce ingredients, along with ¾ tsp salt, in a bowl.

Heat the deep-frying oil in a wok to 300°F (150°C) (hot enough to sizzle gently around a test piece of pork). Working swiftly, drop about half the pork strips into the oil, adding them individually to prevent them sticking together, and nudge with long cooking chopsticks or tongs to separate. Fry the strips for a minute or two until pale and nearly cooked through. Remove from the oil with a slotted spoon. Repeat with the rest of the pork strips.

Reheat the oil to 375°F (190°C) (hot enough to sizzle vigorously around a test piece of pork). Add all the pork strips and deep-fry until they are crisp and golden: make sure they are cooked through by removing and cutting open one of the larger pieces. Remove from the wok with a slotted spoon, draining off as much oil as possible, and pile up on a serving dish.

146

Carefully pour off all but about 3 tbsp oil from the wok and return to high heat. Add the garlic and ginger and stir-fry briefly until they smell wonderful. Give the sauce a stir and pour it in, stirring to dissolve the sugar. When the sauce has thickened and is full of bubbles, quickly stir in the scallion greens and then pour over the pork strips. Garnish with the slivered scallion whites and chile, if using, and serve immediately.

*Deep-fried pork with salt and Sichuan pepper*
*(jiaoyan liji 椒盐里脊)*
*Omit the sauce, and serve the deep-fried pork strips piping hot, with a dip of salt and ground roasted Sichuan pepper (see p. 456).*

*Deep-fried pork with fish-fragrant sauce (yuxiang liji 鱼香里脊)*
*Instead of the sweet-and-sour sauce in the main recipe, use the fish-fragrant sauce on p. 145. This is delicious too.*

# Li Zhuang "Head Bowl" Meatloaf Stew

## li zhuang touwan
李庄头碗

Li Zhuang is one of the best-preserved old towns of southern Sichuan. In the days when the Yangtze River was China's most important transport artery, it was a busy port and a wealthy regional center, but with the advent of the railways it slipped into obscurity. These days, Li Zhuang is a picturesque backwater on an unspoiled stretch of the Yangtze, its old lanes lined with wooden houses and open shopfronts where locals laze around drinking tea, gossiping and playing cards or mahjong. There are makers of traditional straw sandals and bamboo chairs, and sweet shops specializing in crumbly rice cakes and puffed rice in syrup. On market days the streets fill with traders, including elderly farmers bearing baskets of eggs or vegetables, and barbers who hang a mirror on a nearby wall and proceed to shave and trim their customers in full view of the street.

This delectable dish is traditionally eaten at weddings and for the Chinese New Year and other celebrations. Known in Chinese simply as "head bowl" (*touwan*) because of its status as a celebratory dish, it consists of slices of steamed meatloaf (*baba rou*), whole yellow peas, wood ear mushrooms, day-lily flowers and other adornments in a bowlful of broth. The meatloaf should be made in advance and allowed to cool before slicing. You will need a square or rectangular heatproof vessel to cook it in: I use a glass food storage container about 6½ inches by 4¼ inches (17cm by 11cm) and 2 inches (5cm) deep. I learned how to make this dish from two Li Zhuang chefs, Ren Qiang and Zhang Yong.

A small handful of dried day-lily flowers
A small handful of dried wood ear mushrooms
A few heads of green bok choy
1 cup (150g) cooked yellow peas
   or chickpeas
2 cups (500ml) clear superior stock (see p. 464)
A small handful of thinly sliced scallion greens (optional)
Salt and ground white pepper

*For the meatloaf*
9 oz (250g) fatty ground pork
2 small eggs
½ cup (60g) potato starch
1½ tbsp finely chopped ginger
1½ tsp salt
¾ tsp ground roasted Sichuan pepper
A little cooking oil

**First make the meatloaf.** Place the pork in a bowl. Separate the eggs and add one of the whites to the pork, along with the potato starch, ginger, salt, Sichuan pepper and 6 tbsp (90ml) cold water. Mix well.

Brush your cooking container with oil. Tip in the pork mixture and spread it out so that the top is flat and even. Beat the egg yolks with the remaining white and brush over the surface of the pork, then cover with foil. Place in a steamer and steam over high heat for 30 minutes. Remove from the steamer and allow to cool completely.

Cover the day-lily flowers in cold water and let soak for at least an hour to soften. Cover the wood ears with hot water from the kettle and let soak for at least 30 minutes to soften, then break into bite-sized pieces, discarding any knobbly bits, and return to the water until needed. Cut the bok choy lengthwise into halves or quarters and then, if large, into bite-sized pieces. Blanch briefly in boiling water, then rinse under cold water. Cover with cold water and set aside until needed.

Turn the meatloaf out of its container and cut into slices about ¼ inch (5mm) thick. Layer them, egg side down, in the base of a bowl that will fit into your steamer. Scatter the yellow peas or chickpeas on top, and tuck the drained wood ears and day-lily flowers around the sides. Place the bowl in a steamer and steam over high heat for 20–30 minutes, to heat through.

Meanwhile, bring the stock to a boil, season with salt and white pepper to taste and keep warm.

Remove the bowl from your steamer. Hold a deep soup bowl upside-down over it, swiftly invert and then gently remove the steaming bowl. Quickly dunk the bok choy into the hot stock, just to reheat, then nestle it around the meatloaf. Pour the hot stock around the sides of the bowl and garnish with scallion greens, if you wish. Serve.

## Pork Slivers with Preserved Mustard Tuber

zhacai rousi
榨菜肉丝

This simple, home-style dish is most delicious, a gentle entwining of pale pork slivers, salty pickled vegetable and fresh scallions. It's also quick and easy to prepare. The preserved vegetable *zhacai*, whose name literally means "pressed vegetable," is made from the tuber of a type of mustard green. It was originally eaten fresh or pickled in spicy brine, but in the late nineteenth century an enterprising farmer from Fuling, near Chongqing, tried dry-salting it as a way of preserving an unusually abundant harvest. The result was so good that, with the encouragement of his brother, the farmer went into business, and within a few decades he and his imitators were producing *zhacai* all over the province. To make *zhacai*, the swollen mustard stems are first semi-dried on wooden frames in the gentle winds of the Yangtze Valley; they are then salted and pressed to extract some of their water content, before being mixed with ground chiles, Sichuan pepper and a selection of other spices and sealed into earthenware jars to ferment. The final product is sour, salty, aromatic and slightly crunchy.

Preserved mustard tuber is often eaten as a relish, or chopped up and scattered over noodle or tofu dishes, but it's particularly delicious in the following stir-fry. Chinese cooks often use lard to make this dish, for an extra layer of umami richness: feel free to use lard, cooking oil or a mixture of both.

7 oz (200g) pork tenderloin
1¾ oz (50g) preserved mustard tuber
2 scallions
4 tbsp cooking oil or lard

*For the marinade*
1½ tsp Shaoxing wine
1½ tsp potato starch
⅛ tsp salt
2 tsp cooking oil

*For the sauce*
¼ tsp superfine sugar
½ tsp potato starch

**Cut the pork into very thin slices** and then cut evenly into thin strips, ideally 1¼ inches (3–4mm) thick (you can chill the pork for an hour or so in the freezer beforehand to make cutting easier). Place the strips in a bowl, add 1 tbsp cold water and all the marinade ingredients except the oil. Stir in one direction to combine, then set aside while you prepare the other ingredients.

Rinse the preserved mustard tuber thoroughly and cut it into very thin slices to match the pork. If it is extremely salty, blanch it for 10 seconds in boiling water, then drain. Cut the scallions into 2½-inch (6cm) lengths and then lengthwise into fine slivers. Combine the sauce ingredients with 2 tbsp cold water in a bowl.

Add the 2 tsp oil to the marinating pork and mix well, then heat the 4 tbsp oil or lard in a seasoned wok over high heat. Add the pork slivers and stir-fry until they have separated and are turning pale, then add the preserved vegetable and continue to stir-fry until the pork is just cooked and the preserved vegetable is fragrant. Give the sauce a stir and add to the wok, stirring swiftly as it thickens. Finally, add the scallions and stir once or twice to give them a lick of heat. Serve.

*Stir-fried ground pork with preserved mustard tuber*
*(zhacai roumo 榨菜肉末)*
*Instead of pork slivers, use ground pork, and finely chop the preserved mustard tuber to match it. Omit the marinade: simply stir-fry the pork until nearly cooked, then add the preserved vegetable. When both are cooked and fragrant, stir in some thinly sliced scallions and serve. This is a quick, easy supper dish that is perfect for "sending the rice down" (xiafan).*

# Sichuanese
# Stir-fried Bacon

huiguo larou
回锅腊肉

One of the best ways to eat Sichuanese bacon, or pork cured with sweet flour sauce, is to steam it, slice it and then stir-fry it with a fragrant vegetable to balance its oily luxuriance and salty flavor. Around the Qingcheng Mountain near Chengdu, a place of Daoist pilgrimage, cooks often stir-fry the famed local bacon, which is almost black after its long smoking, with nothing but slices of green garlic. Thin-skinned green peppers are another delectable accompaniment, and baby leeks would also work well.

This very simple recipe is extremely delicious, but you may jazz it up further if you wish by adding a little dried chile and Sichuan pepper to the wok just before you add the green peppers, and also perhaps some sliced ginger and garlic, giving them a lick of heat to release their aromas. If you are not making your own cured meats, you can use exactly the same method for the gorgeous Cantonese soy-sauce-cured pork or wind-dried sausage you may find in your local Chinatown.

5¼ oz (150g) Sichuanese bacon (see p. 424)
   or pork cured with sweet flour sauce
   (see p. 427)
¾ lb (350g) long green Turkish peppers
   or Chinese green garlic
   (or a mix of the two)
1 tbsp cooking oil
Salt

Place the bacon or cured pork in a steamer basket and steam over high heat for around 20 minutes, until cooked through. Allow to cool, then slice thinly. Trim the green peppers and/or green garlic, and cut both diagonally into ½-inch (1cm) "horse ear" slices.

Heat the oil in a seasoned wok over high heat. Add the bacon or cured pork and stir-fry until the fat has released some of its oil. Tip in the peppers and/or green garlic and stir-fry until they are just cooked and fragrant, and the bacon is tinged with gold, adding salt to taste if needed (remember the bacon will already be quite salty).

## Salt-fried Pork

## shengbao yanjian rou
生爆盐煎肉

This dish, like the more famous twice-cooked pork (see p. 132), is an example of "home-style" flavor: salty, rich with savory fermented tastes and just a little hot. The difference between the two dishes is that raw pork is used here, so it ends up with a very different mouthfeel from the pre-boiled, twice-cooked version. Salt-fried pork is just the kind of dish you might find on a dinner table at home in Sichuan, with a few stir-fried vegetables, a simple soup and plenty of rice to set off its vibrant flavors.

The pork is often stir-fried with Chinese green garlic, but baby leeks, garlic stems, celery, young ginger and even strips of firm tofu may be used instead; I've chosen green bell pepper for the following recipe. A pinch of salt is added as the pork is tossed in the wok to help it yield up its moisture, hence the name of the dish. Its full title is actually "raw-exploded salt-fried pork," because of the high temperature at which the raw pork is first fried, although people tend to use the simpler version of the name.

*9 oz (250g) pork rump or leg,*
  *with a good layer of fat*
*1 green bell pepper (about 7 oz/200g)*
*3 tbsp lard, cooking oil or*
  *a mixture of the two*
*A good pinch of salt*
*1½ tbsp Sichuan chile bean paste*
*½ tbsp fermented black beans*
*¼ tsp dark soy sauce*

Slice the pork as thinly as possible, making sure each slice has some fat and some lean.

Core and trim the green bell pepper and cut as evenly as possible into bite-sized squares.

Heat the lard and/or cooking oil in a seasoned wok over high heat. Tip in the pork and stir-fry, adding the salt as the slices separate. Fry for a minute or so until the meat smells delicious and has given up some of its fat. Turn the heat down to medium. Tilt the wok, push the pork up one side and add the chile bean paste and black beans to the oil that pools in the base. Stir-fry until they smell wonderful and the oil is red. Tilt the wok back and mix everything together, then add the soy sauce and green bell pepper and stir until everything is piping hot. Serve immediately.

# Stir-fried Pig's Liver

## baiyou ganpian
## 白油肝片

Liver, like kidneys, is best cooked swiftly, which makes it particularly well suited to the Chinese stir-fry. This dish is everyday fare, but has a lightness and delicacy that is rare in Western liver dishes. For best results, use a sharp knife and cut the liver slices as thinly and evenly as possible (these tapered slices, following the natural shape of the liver, are known as "willow-leaf" slices).

One of my sources for this recipe was a 1980s cookbook which, amazingly, was once treated as classified information in China. On its back cover it bears the tell-tale phrase *neibu faxing*, "for internal circulation only," which is most commonly associated with political documents. The book appears to be a simple collection of recipes, and so far I've been unable to find any atomic formulae or coded maps hidden among its lists of ingredients for twice-cooked pork and dry-fried eels. Did someone think the United States might use China's culinary secrets to subvert its political system? Or are "pork" and "bamboo shoots" part of some complex food-related cipher? The mind boggles.

A few dried wood ear mushrooms
9 oz (250g) pig's liver
2 celery sticks (about 2½ oz/75g)
3 Sichuan pickled chiles or ½ red bell pepper
2 scallions, white parts only
10 tbsp (150ml) cooking oil
2 garlic cloves, peeled and sliced
An equivalent amount of ginger, peeled and sliced

For the marinade
¼ tsp salt
1 tsp Shaoxing wine
2 tsp potato starch

For the sauce
¼ tsp salt
¾ tsp superfine sugar
¾ tsp potato starch
A couple of pinches of ground white pepper
1 tsp Shaoxing wine
1 tsp light soy sauce
2 tbsp stock or water
1 tsp sesame oil

Soak the wood ears in hot water from the kettle for 30 minutes. Discard any knobbly bits, then cut into thick strips. Peel the outer membrane from the liver. If it is still in one piece, cut in half lengthwise, then slice as thinly as possible, discarding any gristly bits. Put the liver into a bowl, add the marinade ingredients and mix well. Cut the celery into strips 2 inches (5cm) long, about the thickness of chopsticks. Do the same with the red bell pepper, if using. Cut the scallion whites (and the pickled chiles, if using) at a steep angle into "horse ear" slices. Combine the sauce ingredients in a small bowl.

Heat the oil in a seasoned wok over high heat. Add the liver and stir-fry until the slices have separated and are turning pale—take care not to overcook it—then remove with a slotted spoon. Carefully pour off all but 2 tbsp of the oil from the wok and return to high heat. Add the garlic, ginger and scallion whites (and the pickled chiles, if using) and stir-fry briefly until they smell delicious. Add the celery and wood ears (and the red bell pepper, if using) and stir until piping hot. Return the liver to the wok and stir-fry until it is just cooked. Give the sauce a stir, add it to the wok and stir-fry for a few seconds before serving.

# Fire-exploded
Kidney "Flowers"

## huobao yaohua
## 火爆腰花

The first time I visited Chengdu, my friend Zhou Yu offered me this dish in a restaurant and, as I savored it, challenged me to guess what I was eating. I looked at the pinkish, frilly morsels tossed with celtuce and pickled chiles in a honey-colored sauce, and had no idea at all.

*Huobao yaohua* is kidneys as you have never seen or tasted them before: crisp, dainty and quite delicious. The dish is, for me, a perfect example of the ability of Sichuanese cooks to transform the most clumsy offal into unexpected delicacies. It is also an illustration of that old truism that Chinese cooking is all in the preparation. The kidneys must be cut carefully in a special manner, the vegetables chopped and arranged neatly on a plate, the sauce ingredients blended in a bowl. The actual cooking takes very little time. *Huobao*, which literally means "fire-exploded," is a method that involves stir-frying briefly at a very high temperature. It is superb for preserving the delicate crisp-tenderness of ingredients which, like kidney and liver, become "old" (*lao*) if overcooked. The *hua* in the name of the dish means "flower," a term often used to describe meat that is cross-cut so it unfolds like a blossom during cooking. Don't be put off by the tricky cutting method—if you have a sharp knife it's not as complicated as it sounds. As far as the cooking is concerned, the crux is to turn the heat up high and work swiftly.

2 pig's kidneys (10–12 oz/300–350g)
1 celery stick (about 1¾ oz/50g) or
    1¾ oz (50g) peeled celtuce
2 scallions, white parts only
2 Sichuan pickled chiles or ¼ red bell pepper
7 tbsp (100ml) cooking oil
2 garlic cloves, peeled and sliced
An equivalent amount of ginger,
    peeled and sliced
Salt

*For the marinade*
1½ tsp Shaoxing wine
¼ tsp salt
1½ tsp potato starch

*For the sauce*
¾ tsp potato starch
⅛ tsp ground white pepper
1 tsp light soy sauce
1 tsp Shaoxing wine
1½ tbsp stock

**Place the kidneys flat on a chopping board,** and use a cleaver or sharp knife to cut them in half, parallel to the board. Place each half, skin side down, on the board. Use the knife, again held parallel to the board, to slice away the core of each kidney, leaving only the pale pink-brown kidney flesh. You may need to make several delicate cuts to do this.

Now hold the knife at a 30° angle to the board and make little cuts across the entire inner surface of each kidney, ⅛–¼ inch (3–5mm) apart, taking care not to cut all the way through. Then, with the knife held at a right angle to the board, make similar cuts perpendicular to the original cuts, again taking care not to cut right through. The entire inner surface of each kidney should now be cross-hatched with little lines.

Finally, cut each kidney into bite-sized rectangular or diamond-shaped pieces. Don't worry if these are a bit uneven—they will curl up during the cooking. (For alternative, even more intricate ways of cutting, see variations on next page.) Put the kidney pieces into a bowl, add the marinade ingredients and mix well. Set aside while you prepare the other ingredients. →

←    Remove any strings from the celery sticks and cut them (or the celtuce) into 1½–2-inch (4–5cm) strips about the thickness of chopstick handles. Cut the scallion whites and pickled chiles at a steep angle into "horse ear" slices. If you are using red bell pepper, cut it into thin strips to match the celery.

Combine the sauce ingredients in a small bowl.

Heat the oil in a seasoned wok over high heat until smoke starts to rise from the sides of the wok. Add the kidneys and stir-fry briefly until they have separated and are beginning to turn pale. Carefully pour off all but about 2 tbsp of the oil from the wok and return to high heat. Add the garlic, ginger and scallion whites (and the pickled chiles, if using). Stir just once or twice, then add the celery or celtuce (and the red bell pepper, if using). Continue to stir-fry until the kidneys are just cooked. Give the sauce a stir and add to the wok, stirring as it thickens and coats the kidneys. Serve immediately.

### Variations

*If you want to try your hand at some even fancier cutting, you can cut the kidneys into the following shapes.*

#### "Eyebrows" (meimao yaohua 眉毛腰花, as shown in the photograph on p. 156)
Make the 30° cuts in the kidney flesh as described above, then make the perpendicular cuts in the same manner, but cut all the way through to the board on every third cut. Trim any very long pieces to make them about 3¼ inches (8cm) in length. You will end up with frilly strips of kidney which do look like very hairy eyebrows when cooked.

#### "Phoenix tails" (fengwei yaohua 凤尾腰花)
*Prepare as for "eyebrows," except that you should cut right through to the board for part of each perpendicular cut, and then sever the piece completely for every third cut. This way, one end of each piece will have three fronds branching out like the tail of the mythical bird.*

## Stewed Pork with Carrots

### huluobo shao rou
### 胡萝卜烧肉

In the backstreets of Chengdu, the cheap, casual eateries known affectionately as "fly" restaurants (*cangying guanzi*) because of their supposed—but usually not actual!—lack of hygiene, often try to tempt passers-by with rows of stew-pots, simmering away in full view and wafting their seductive aromas into the street.

If you decide to stop, you sit down at a makeshift table and order a bowlful of your favored stew, along with your selection from another ravishing display of pre-made dishes, steamed rice and pickles. At one typical restaurant (now vanished) in an old wooden building near the Yuelai opera teahouse, the stewed dishes (*shaocai*) included pig's trotters stewed with white beans, red-braised pork, beef with bamboo shoot, pork ribs with potatoes, daikon with pig's intestines, pork ribs with lotus root, chicken with taro, red-braised pork knuckle, chicken with shiitake mushrooms, and fiery duck-blood stew.

The following recipe is based on a specific stew served at the Rice Apocalypse "fly" restaurant in Chengdu (see p. 193 for an explanation of this curious restaurant name). It can be made in advance and reheated; you can also cook the meat a day or two ahead, and then reheat to cook the carrots shortly before you want to serve the dish. Green beans or potatoes and other root vegetables may be used instead of carrots, if you wish.

1 lb (450g) pork belly or shoulder, with or without skin
1¼-inch piece (25g) ginger, unpeeled
2 scallions, white parts only
4 tbsp cooking oil
2 tbsp Shaoxing wine
3 tbsp Sichuan chile bean paste
1 star anise
A small piece of cassia bark or cinnamon stick
5½ cups (1.3 liters) everyday stock (see p. 463)
2 tsp superfine sugar
½ tsp dark soy sauce
14 oz (400g) carrots (about 5 large)
Salt and ground white pepper

Cut the pork into 1¼-inch (3cm) chunks. Bring a pot of water to a boil. Add the meat and blanch for a minute or so, then rinse in a colander under cold water. Drain well. Lightly smack the ginger and scallion whites with the flat of a cleaver blade or a rolling pin to loosen them.

Heat a seasoned wok over high heat. Add the oil and swirl it around, then add the meat and fry until lightly browned, moving it around for even coloring. Splash in the Shaoxing wine and stir as the liquid evaporates. Tilt the wok, push the meat up one side and add the ginger and scallion whites to the oil that pools in the base; stir-fry until aromatic and tinged with gold. Add the chile bean paste, star anise and cassia or cinnamon and stir-fry until the oil is red and wonderfully fragrant. Tilt the wok back and mix everything together, then pour in the stock and bring to a boil. Skim off any froth from the surface, then add the sugar and soy sauce, along with salt to taste.

Turn down the heat and simmer gently for about 1 hour, until the pork is tender; alternatively, pressure cook for 20 minutes, then allow the pressure to release naturally. (I normally transfer the contents of the wok to a saucepan for the simmering, so that I can use the wok for other dishes.)

Peel the carrots and roll-cut into chunks to match the meat. Add them to the pork, topping up with a little stock or water if necessary, then return to a boil and simmer for 30 minutes or so, until they are completely tender. Season with salt and pepper to taste before serving.

# Sliced Pork with Black Wood Ear Mushrooms

mu'er roupian
木耳肉片

At the age of nearly 80, my friend Deng Hong's mother is still a dynamo of energy and hilarious humor. She grows some of her own vegetables in flower-pots and a rooftop garden, pickles her own ginger and chiles, and dries nuts and seeds in bamboo trays spread out next to a sunny window. One day, she whipped up a beautiful lunch for us: cold chicken in a chile oil sauce, spiced goose feet and pork skin, home-made tofu with a piquant dip, braised beef with potatoes, a rich soup of chicken and Chinese yam, and this simple yet colorful and delicious stir-fry, which is typical of local home cooking.

The pale pork slices are tossed in a wok with bright red pickled chiles, slithery black mushrooms and slices of crisp green celtuce. The sauce is the kind described as "white-flavored" (*baiwei*) because it is seasoned only with salt and white pepper, rather than deeply colored flavorings such as soy sauce. If you can lay your hands on celtuce, a variety of lettuce with thick, truncheon-like stems and a most exquisite flavor, please use it. Otherwise, sliced celery makes a delicious substitute.

⅓ oz (10g) dried wood ear mushrooms
  (around 3 oz/80g after soaking)
7 oz (200g) lean pork tenderloin
7 oz (200g) celtuce or celery (2–3 sticks)
1 scallion
2–3 Sichuan pickled chiles or ¼ red bell pepper
4 tbsp cooking oil
2 garlic cloves, peeled and sliced
An equivalent amount of ginger, peeled and sliced

### For the marinade
¼ tsp salt
½ tbsp Shaoxing wine
4 tsp potato starch

### For the sauce
½ tsp salt
A couple of pinches of ground white pepper
½ tsp potato starch
3 tbsp cold stock or water

**Soak the wood ears in hot water** from the kettle for about 15 minutes to soften. Slice the pork as thinly as possible, ideally into pieces about 1½ × 1¼ inches (4cm × 3cm). Place in a bowl, along with the marinade ingredients and 4 tsp cold water, and mix well.

Cut or tear the drained wood ears into bite-sized pieces, discarding any knobbly bits. If you are using celtuce, peel off the coarse skin to leave only the delicate green flesh. Slice at an angle into ¾-inch (2cm) chunks, then place flat on the board and cut into thin diamond-shaped slices. If using celery, remove any strings and thinly slice at an angle. Cut the scallion and pickled chiles or red bell pepper at a steep angle into very thin slices.

Mix the sauce ingredients together in a small bowl.

Stir 1 tbsp oil into the marinating pork. Heat the remaining oil in a seasoned wok over high heat, add the meat and stir-fry briskly. When the pork slices have separated and are turning pale, add the garlic, ginger, scallion and pickled chiles or red bell pepper. Stir-fry until the garlic and ginger smell wonderful. Add the celtuce or celery and the wood ears, and stir-fry until everything is piping hot. Finally, give the sauce a stir and add it to the wok. Stir as the sauce thickens, then serve.

# Boiled Beef Slices in a Fiery Sauce

## shuizhu niurou
## 水煮牛肉

This dish, known in Chinese simply as "water-boiled beef," comes from Zigong, the city poetically referred to as Sichuan's "salt capital," because it was the center of a salt-mining industry that flourished from the Han dynasty until the 1960s. Salt-traders from different provinces built their own guild headquarters in Zigong; one of them, a splendid eighteenth-century complex of buildings with a magnificent, many-horned gatehouse, remains, and now houses a local salt industry museum. In a timber-framed building nearby, bare-chested laborers work in a sauna-like atmosphere, tending simmering salt pans that are fueled, as they have been for centuries, by natural gas. The pans are encrusted with salt crystals; salt drifts across the floor like snowfall.

In the past, oxen drove the wooden machinery that drew the salty bittern from deep within the Earth; when they died, miners bought the meat cheaply and boiled it up for their suppers, originally with Sichuan pepper and ginger, later with chiles. The name of the dish is humorously misleading, because although the beef slices are indeed boiled, the final dish is covered in an electrifying sizzle of chiles and Sichuan pepper. It's a perfect dish for a cold winter's day when you need firing up with energy and warmth; as they say in Sichuan, it'll make you pour with sweat, even on the coldest days of the year.

The beef is served on a bed of crisp vegetables—typically a mix of green garlic, celtuce tips and Chinese celery.

*9 oz (250g) beef tenderloin*
*1 tbsp Shaoxing wine*
*¾ cup (180ml) cooking oil*
*7 oz (200g) Napa cabbage*
   *(preferably the white crunchy parts)*
*2 celery sticks (about 3½ oz/100g)*
*10–12 dried chiles*
*2 tsp whole Sichuan pepper*
*1 tbsp potato starch*
*2½ tbsp Sichuan chile bean paste*
*2 tsp ground chiles*
*1 tbsp finely chopped garlic*
*1 tbsp finely chopped ginger*
*1½ cups (350ml) stock*
*¼ tsp dark soy sauce*
*A few sprigs of cilantro or 2 tbsp*
   *thinly sliced scallion greens*
*Salt*

**Cut the beef across the grain** into thin, broad slices. Place in a bowl with ¼ tsp salt, the Shaoxing wine and 1 tbsp oil. Mix well and set aside while you prepare the other ingredients.

Place the Napa cabbage on a chopping board. Cut lengthwise into finger-thick slices, and then into 2-inch (5cm) pieces. Remove any strings from the celery, cut into 2-inch (5cm) lengths, and then into thin batons.

Prepare the "knife-mouth chiles." Snip the chiles in half or into ¾-inch (2cm) sections and shake out the seeds as much as possible. Heat 3 tbsp oil in a wok over high heat. Before the oil gets too hot, add the chiles and stir. When they begin to sizzle, add the Sichuan pepper and stir until the chiles begin to darken, then quickly remove the spices from the wok with a slotted spoon or fine-mesh strainer, letting any excess oil drain back into the wok. Turn the spices out onto a chopping board and finely chop (or pound with a mortar and pestle). Set aside until needed.

Add the potato starch and 1 tbsp cold water to the beef and mix well to coat all the slices.

Return the oily wok to high heat and, when it's hot, tip in the vegetables and stir-fry until hot and barely cooked, seasoning with about ¼ tsp salt. Pile the vegetables in the center of a large, deep serving bowl. →

← Add 3 tbsp oil to the wok and heat over medium heat. Add the chile bean paste and stir-fry gently until the oil is red and fragrant. Add the ground chiles and stir a couple of times, then tip in the garlic and ginger and continue to stir-fry until they smell wonderful. Pour in the stock and soy sauce and bring to a boil. Scatter the beef slices into the boiling liquid, nudging them so they don't stick together. When the beef is just cooked, pour the contents of the wok over the waiting vegetables.

Rinse and dry the wok, then return to high heat and add 5 tbsp oil. Stir until the oil is sizzling hot (test the temperature by dripping some onto some scallion or vegetable offcuts in a heatproof bowl: it should produce a sudden, dramatic sizzle). When the oil is ready, quickly tip the reserved spices into the center of the serving bowl and ladle over the hot oil. Scatter over the cilantro or scallion greens and rush the bowl to the table before the sizzling stops!

Variations

*The same method can be used for all kinds of other ingredients, including thick slices of plain white tofu (which don't need a marinade), sliced pork (in which case, add 1 tbsp chopped garlic with the chopped spices before you ladle over the hot oil, and omit the cilantro), and squid, cut into frilly slices (again, no need for a marinade).*

*The dish is traditionally finished off with a scattering of what they call "knife-mouth chiles" (daokou haijiao)—dried chiles and Sichuan pepper that are fried and then chopped—but if you'd prefer a shortcut, you can use 1 tbsp coarsely ground chiles and ¼ tsp ground roasted Sichuan pepper instead.*

# Spicy Steamed Beef
## with Ricemeal

### xiaolong fenzheng niurou
### 小笼粉蒸牛肉

In the narrow backstreets of the now-vanished old Manchu district of Chengdu, the tiny snack shops and restaurants were open to the street. Often, under the eaves of the timber-framed buildings, towering stacks of tiny bamboo steamers would be steaming away over a great wokful of boiling water. If you lifted their lids, you would be assailed by the scent of rich, aromatic chunks of beef that had been steamed to melting tenderness, languidly embraced by a soft, comforting layer of ricemeal.

This halal dish was originally associated with the Hui Muslims who migrated to Chengdu from northern China during the early Qing dynasty, as part of the effort to repopulate Sichuan after the devastation of dynastic war (see p. 13). A snack shop on Changshun Street in central Chengdu is said to have made it popular in the 1920s. The Chinese name for the dish literally translates as "meat steamed in powder," and the northern Hui still eat a version of it, but made with spiced wheat flour rather than ground rice. Perhaps their ancestors started using ricemeal instead of wheat after their migration south.

You can either steam the beef in a bowl that fits in your steamer basket, or on a piece of lotus leaf placed directly in the basket (dried lotus leaves should be soaked briefly in hot water from the kettle to soften and then cut to fit the steamer, making sure they extend up the sides to hold the juices). The beef can be served with lotus-leaf buns (see p. 392).

¾ lb (350g) beef tenderloin
2 tsp crushed garlic,
    mixed with 1 tbsp cold water
½–1 tsp ground chiles, to taste
¼ tsp ground roasted Sichuan pepper
1 tsp sesame oil
1½ tbsp thinly sliced scallion greens
2 tbsp chopped cilantro

_For the marinade_
1 tbsp Sichuan chile bean paste
1 tsp fermented black beans
2½ tbsp cooking oil
1–2 cubes white fermented tofu,
    with some of the juices from the jar
2 tsp finely chopped ginger
½ tsp dark soy sauce
2 tbsp fermented glutinous rice wine
    or 1 tbsp Shaoxing wine
½–⅔ cup (3½ oz/100g) ricemeal (see p. 454)

Cut the beef across the grain into thin, bite-sized slices and place in a bowl. Place the chile bean paste and black beans on a chopping board and finely chop them together with a knife. Heat 1 tbsp cooking oil in a seasoned wok over medium heat and gently stir-fry the bean paste mixture until the oil is red and fragrant; set aside to cool. Mash the fermented tofu with a little of its juices to make about 1 tbsp creamy paste, then add this to the beef, along with the bean paste mixture (and its oil), ginger, soy sauce and whichever wine you are using, and mix well. Stir in the remaining cooking oil. Finally, add the ricemeal and mix to coat all the beef. Set aside to marinate for at least 30 minutes.

In a wok, bring some water to a boil for steaming. Place the beef slices in a shallow bowl or on a piece of soaked lotus leaf that will fit in your steamer basket, then steam over high heat for 30 minutes until beautifully tender.

When the beef is ready, sprinkle over the garlic and water mixture, followed by the ground chiles, Sichuan pepper and sesame oil, and finally the scallion greens and cilantro. Serve in the steamer.

# Dry-fried Beef Slivers

## ganbian niurou si
## 干煸牛肉丝

The following dish is a common variation of the famous Sichuanese dish of dry-fried eel slivers, which is made with fresh paddy eels (*shanyu* or *huangshan*). The dry-frying method itself is a Sichuanese invention. It involves neither marinade nor sauce, and traditionally relied on the gradual drying out of the main ingredient over moderate heat, with the subsequent addition of spices and flavorings; these days many cooks speed the process up by deep-frying. The principal ingredient, which is usually cut into strips or fine slivers, ends up slightly crisp and chewy, with a delicious toasty fragrance and a dry, spicy taste.

Eels, beef, pork and dried squid can all be dry-fried, as can some vegetables, such as green beans, eggplant and bitter melon. If you can lay your hands on paddy eels, they should be killed and gutted just before use, and cut into strips about ½ inch (1cm) wide. The cooking method is the same as that described here (please note that the larger eels eaten in the West are not a suitable substitute).

15 oz (425g) beef tenderloin
3–4 celery sticks (about 7¾ oz/220g)
1-inch piece (20g) ginger
2 scallions, white parts only
7 tbsp (100ml) cooking oil
1 tbsp Shaoxing wine
2 tbsp Sichuan chile bean paste
¼ tsp dark soy sauce
½ tsp sesame oil
1–2 tbsp chile oil, with sediment (optional)
¼ tsp ground roasted Sichuan pepper (optional)
Salt

**Cut the beef evenly into thin slices** and then across the grain into ¼-inch (5mm) slivers. Discard any fat or gristly bits. Remove any strings from the celery, cut crosswise into 2½-inch (6cm) lengths and then lengthwise into thin strips to match the beef. Mix the celery with a little salt to draw out some of its water. Peel the ginger, then cut it into fine slivers. Cut the scallion whites into fine slivers to match the ginger.

Heat the cooking oil in a seasoned wok over high heat until very hot, then add the beef and stir-fry. The oil will initially become cloudy as the beef releases its juices. Stir constantly until the oil has cleared, the beef has lost most of its water content and is beginning to color and smell deliciously fragrant—this will take about 10 minutes, depending on the beef you use (you will notice that the beef starts sizzling as the water disappears). As the meat dries out, splash the Shaoxing wine around the edges of the wok and let it sizzle.

When the oil is clear, turn the heat down to medium. Tilt the wok, push the beef up one side and add the chile bean paste to the oil that pools in the base; stir-fry until the oil is red and fragrant. Tilt the wok back and add the ginger and scallion whites. Mix everything together and continue to stir-fry for another 10 seconds or so until you can smell the ginger. Finally, add the celery strips and soy sauce, and continue to stir-fry until the celery is heated through.

Remove the wok from the heat, stir in the sesame oil—and the chile oil, if using—and tip onto a serving plate. If you wish, sprinkle with the Sichuan pepper.

# Red-braised Beef
with Daikon

## hongshao niurou
## 红烧牛肉

Red-braising is a cooking method used all over China that generally involves slow cooking with soy sauce, which gives the dish its "red" color (a "white" dish is one made without soy sauce). In Sichuan, however, the main flavoring used to red-braise beef is not soy sauce but chile bean paste, which gives the gravy a glorious chestnut color and a deep chile kick. The daikon, which is added toward the end of the cooking time, remains clear and crisp, in delightful contrast to the rich and tender beef.

In Sichuanese restaurants, stews like this are often put into tall, glazed pots and left to simmer by the entrance, in the hope of luring potential customers.

If you want to serve this dish Sichuan-style, with rice and a few stir-fried dishes, it has the advantage that you can make it in advance and just reheat it when you want to eat. The dish also works very well as a Western-style stew, served perhaps with mashed potato. (I have actually used Sichuan chile bean paste in the same way to create new and exciting versions of traditional Western stews involving lamb and root vegetables—the chile taste makes them even more warming and comforting.)

2 lb 2 oz (1kg) beef brisket or stew meat
1-inch piece (20g) ginger, unpeeled
1 Chinese black cardamom pod
2 scallions, white parts only
1 quart (1 liter) beef or everyday stock (see p. 463)
4 tbsp cooking oil
4 tbsp Shaoxing wine
4 tbsp Sichuan chile bean paste
1 tsp whole Sichuan pepper
1 star anise
1 tsp dark soy sauce
1 lb 5 oz (600g) daikon (1 medium)
A few sprigs of cilantro, to garnish
Salt

Cut the beef into 1¼-inch (3cm) chunks. Lightly smack the ginger, cardamom and scallion whites with the flat of a cleaver blade or a rolling pin to loosen them. Bring a pot of water to a boil. Add the beef and return to a boil, then blanch for a minute or so. Tip the meat into a colander and rinse under cold water, then let drain for a few minutes.

Bring the stock to a boil and keep warm. Heat 1 tbsp oil in a seasoned wok over high heat, then add the beef and brown in the hot oil. Toward the end of the browning, splash in the Shaoxing wine and stir as it evaporates, then tip the beef into a heavy-bottomed saucepan or casserole.

Add 3 tbsp oil to the wok and tip in the ginger, chile bean paste, cardamom, Sichuan pepper and star anise. Turn down the heat to medium and stir-fry until the oil is red and wonderfully fragrant. Stir in about half of the stock and mix everything together, then pour over the beef. Add the rest of the stock to the beef, along with the soy sauce and scallion whites, and bring to a boil. Season with salt to taste. Half-cover the pan, turn down the heat and simmer gently for 2 hours (or pressure cook for 30 minutes, then allow the pressure to release naturally).

Meanwhile, peel and trim the daikon, then cut into 1¼-inch (3cm) chunks. About 20 minutes before the end of the cooking time, add the daikon. Bring to a boil, then turn down the heat and simmer for the remaining time. (If you've used a pressure cooker, bring to a boil, add the daikon and simmer for about 20 minutes, until it is tender.) Pick out the ginger, scallion whites and whole spices before serving, garnished with cilantro sprigs.

# Spicy Blood Stew

## mao xue wang

## 毛血旺

Our table was a riot of oil and offal, flushed faces and red chiles, zinging Sichuan pepper and loud, outrageous laughter and conversation. Two of my chef friends knocked back competitive shots of *baijiu* as they argued over how to make cat's ear pasta. Around us the decibels soared as people teased each other, boasted and laughed, nose-deep in chiles.

The food in this old-school Chongqing restaurant was everything I'd hoped for: cured pig's face dressed lavishly in chile oil, eyebrow-shaped slices of ox cartilage covered in sliced green chiles, pork intestines in thick pea soup, frilly ox tripe with ground chiles for dipping, crunchy morsels of deep-fried duck carcass buried in a mound of dried chiles, rustic tofu sizzling in a skillet—and the pièce de résistance, a magnificent *mao xue wang* or spicy blood stew.

I'd had this dish countless times before, but always gussied up for a Chengdu audience, the blood and lunch meat arranged in prissy slices. Here, it was a true *jianghu* dish, a riverside laborer's delight of humble ingredients and abundant spices, joyfully thrown together. The blackened iron cauldron contained chunks of jellied duck's blood, ribbons of tofu and slabs of Spam on a bed of bean sprouts, all but submerged in an oily sea of scorched chiles and Sichuan pepper.

This recipe is my homage to that ultimate *mao xue wang*, the memory of which still makes my mouth water.

*1 stick dried tofu "bamboo" (about 1 oz/30g)*
*1 section lotus root (5¼–6¼ oz/150–175g)*
*A big handful of dried chiles (about ¾ oz/20g)*
*2 scallions*
*3 tbsp Sichuan chile bean paste*
*2 tsp fermented black beans*
*5¼ oz (150g) canned lunch meat, such as Spam (about half a can)*
*7 oz (200g) jellied pig's or duck's blood*
*1½ cups (150g) bean sprouts*
*10 tbsp (175ml) red spicy infused oil (see p. 461)*
*1 tbsp finely chopped ginger*
*2 tsp finely chopped garlic*
*3 cups (700ml) everyday stock (see p. 463)*
*2 tbsp Shaoxing wine*
*2 tbsp whole green or red Sichuan pepper*
*Salt and ground white pepper*

Soak the tofu "bamboo" in cold water for at least an hour, until softened. Remove and trim off any hard ends and cut into 1¼-inch (3cm) lengths, then return to its soaking water until needed. Trim off the ends of the lotus root, then peel and cut into ⅛-inch (3mm) slices. Set aside in a separate bowl of cold, lightly salted water.

Snip the chiles into ¾-inch (2cm) sections and shake out the seeds as much as possible. Trim the scallions and cut into 2-inch (5cm) lengths. Place the chile bean paste and black beans on a board and finely chop together, then set aside. Cut the lunch meat and blood into bite-sized slices (about 2 inches x 1¼ inches/5cm x 3cm), ¼ inch (5mm) thick.

Bring a big pot of water to a boil. Add the bean sprouts and blanch briefly, then rinse under cold water and pile up in a large, deep serving bowl. Drain the tofu and lotus slices. Blanch them for about 30 seconds in the boiling water, then drain and set aside. Do the same with the lunch meat and the blood (it's best to blanch the blood after the vegetables, because it will slightly discolor the water).

Heat 4 tbsp infused oil in a seasoned wok over medium heat. Add the chile bean paste and black bean mixture and stir-fry gently until the oil is red and fragrant. Tip in the ginger, garlic

The curious name of the dish is said to be a composite of "raw" (*mao*), "blood" (*xue*) and a dialect version of an old word for blood (*huang*). According to local sources, it was invented by a butcher's daughter-in-law in Ciqikou, an old town near Chongqing. She had a street stall selling offcuts of meat warmed in broth, and one day added some jellied pig's blood to the mix, to wide acclaim. The dish can be made with jellied pig's or duck's blood (the raw blood is mixed with salt and set to a curd that's often known as blood "tofu"); jellied pig's blood can be found in some Asian supermarkets, but duck's blood is hard to find outside China. Please note that you will need to prepare the infused oil in advance: if you make the dish with plain cooking oil, it will taste flat and dull.

and scallions and stir-fry until they smell wonderful too. Pour in the stock and bring to a boil, then turn the heat down and simmer for 5 minutes. Add the lunch meat, blood, tofu and lotus slices to the wok, then return to a boil and add the Shaoxing wine, salt and white pepper to taste: this dish should be on the salty side, to balance the oiliness. Simmer for 1–2 minutes to "send the flavors into" the ingredients (*ruwei*), then ladle and pour the contents of the wok over the bean sprouts in your serving bowl. Cover to keep warm.

Rinse and dry the wok, then return to high heat and add the remaining infused oil. When the oil is hot but not smoking, add the chiles and stir-fry as they become fragrant and start to change color. Tip in the Sichuan pepper and sizzle the spices until the chiles are deep red-brown but not yet black: make sure you don't burn them. Immediately ladle the hot oil over the food in the bowl and take it, still sizzling, to the table.

Variations

*You can use this basic template and vary the main ingredients as you please: feel free to add slices of pork, oyster or enoki mushrooms or slices of plain white tofu. Many Sichuanese cooks add slices of frilly ox tripe too.*

## Scalded Kidneys
## with Fresh Chile

xianjiao yaopian
鲜椒腰片

The last decade has seen a craze across Sichuan for fresh red and green chiles, which add a vibrant color (and sometimes a searing heat) to contemporary Sichuanese dishes. Often, handfuls of chopped bird's eye chiles ("little rice chiles" in Chinese) are given just a lick of heat from sizzling-hot oil before they are scattered over a dish.

This particular dish is one I enjoyed at the Cherry Garden rooftop restaurant in Chengdu, and I'm grateful to chef Zhang Wei for explaining the method to me. The kidneys are thinly sliced to maintain their delicate texture, briefly blanched and then bathed in delicious seasonings. The level of fieriness will, of course, depend on the kind of chiles you use: I prefer to use those with a kick of heat but without the overwhelming spiciness of bird's eyes. Do make sure you assess the hotness of your chiles before judging how many to use.

2 pig's kidneys (10–12 oz/300–350g)
3–4 fresh red and green chiles, to taste
2 tbsp cooking oil
1½ tbsp finely chopped garlic
½ cup (125ml) chicken stock
2 tsp light soy sauce
½–1 tsp green Sichuan pepper oil
Salt

_For the marinade_
¼ tsp salt
A pinch of ground white pepper
2 tsp Shaoxing wine
2 tsp potato starch

**Place the kidneys flat on a chopping board,** and use a cleaver or sharp knife to cut them in half, parallel to the board. Place each half, skin side down, on the board. Then use the knife, again held parallel to the board, to slice away the core of each kidney, leaving only the pink-brown kidney flesh. You may need to make several delicate cuts to do this. Now, holding the knife at a close angle to the board, cut each piece of kidney into the thinnest-possible slices. Place the kidneys in a bowl, then add the marinade ingredients and mix well.

Thinly slice or finely chop the fresh chiles. Bring a pot of salted water to a boil, add the kidneys and blanch very briefly, until just cooked through (about 30 seconds). Drain well and transfer to a serving dish.

Heat the cooking oil in a seasoned wok over high heat. Add the chiles and garlic and stir-fry briefly until the garlic smells wonderful (do not let the garlic color). Add the stock, soy sauce and salt to taste. Bring to a boil, then switch off the heat, stir in the Sichuan pepper oil and pour over the kidneys. Serve immediately.

# Dry-braised Beef Tendons

## ganshao niujin
干烧牛筋

The Sichuanese have, in their own inimitable fashion, invented dazzling local ways of cooking traditional banquet delicacies such as dried squid and sea cucumber. Often, they favor the classic dry-braising method combined with the hearty "home-style" flavors. One example is the magnificent "dry-braised sea cucumber" I learned to make at cooking school in Chengdu. Unfortunately, sea cucumbers are hard to find outside China and, anyway, are exorbitantly expensive. Happily, one can achieve a very similar effect with beef tendons.

While banquet chefs in China traditionally cook with the reconstituted dried tendons of pigs or deer (the latter a rare and expensive luxury), Chinese chefs abroad use fresh beef tendons instead. In terms of Western tastes, these may sound gristly and unappetizing, but when they are slow-cooked into soft, quivering submission, as in this recipe, few people, in my experience, can resist their charms. They go blissfully with a bowlful of plain rice and a simple green vegetable, and the sauce is so luscious it will make you lick your lips.

You must pre-cook the tendons and let them steep overnight until they are meltingly soft. A pressure cooker, if you have one, makes relatively short work of the initial cooking. If you wish to present the dish in banquet style, garnish the plate with a few pieces of quartered, blanched green bok choy.

Chef Zhang Xiaozhong kindly showed me how to cook this dish.

4 scallions
4 Sichuan pickled chiles
   (or ½ red bell pepper and 1 tbsp sambal oelek)
3 tbsp cooking oil
3½ oz (100g) ground pork
1 tsp dark soy sauce
1½ tbsp Sichuan chile bean paste
1½ tbsp finely chopped garlic
1½ tbsp finely chopped ginger
4 tbsp Yibin yacai or Tianjin preserved vegetable,
   rinsed and squeezed dry
1 tsp sesame oil
Salt

*For the pre-cooking*
1 lb 2 oz (500g) fresh or defrosted beef tendons
1-inch piece (20g) ginger, unpeeled
2 scallions, white parts only
5½ cups (1.3 liters) everyday stock (see p. 463)
   (or 1 quart/1 liter, if using a pressure cooker)
3 tbsp Shaoxing wine
1 small piece of cassia bark or ½ cinnamon stick
1 star anise
½ tsp whole Sichuan pepper

To pre-cook the tendons, bring a large pot of water to a boil. Add the tendons and blanch for a minute or two, then drain and rinse well in cold water. Lightly smack the ginger and scallion whites with the flat of a cleaver blade or a rolling pin to loosen them.

Place the drained tendons in a saucepan or pressure cooker and add the stock (noting that you will only need 1 quart/1 liter if using a pressure cooker). Bring to a boil, then add all the other pre-cooking ingredients, along with ¼ tsp salt, and simmer over very low heat for 2 hours. (If you are using a pressure cooker, cook at high pressure for 30 minutes, then allow the pressure to release naturally.)

Remove from the heat, cover with a lid and let the tendons steep in a cool place overnight (if they have cooled down enough by the time you go to bed, you can put them in the fridge). They must remain submerged in the liquid, so you may need to weigh them down with a small plate. →

← On the following day, extract the tendons from the jellied stock and set aside (or freeze for later cooking); reserve the stock. Cut the scallions into 2½-inch (6cm) lengths, keeping white and green parts separate. Cut off the tops of the pickled chiles, then place them on a board and scrape along them with your knife to squeeze out the seeds; cut each chile into three lengths. (If using red bell pepper, cut into 2½-inch/6cm lengths to match the scallions.)

Cut the tendons into batons about 2 inches (6cm) long and ½–¾ inch (1–2cm) thick: they will be bouncy and slippery, so do this carefully. Reheat the jellied stock in a small pan.

Heat 1 tbsp cooking oil in a seasoned wok over high heat. Add the ground pork and stir-fry. As the pork changes color, stir in ¼ tsp soy sauce. When the pork is cooked and fragrant, remove from the wok and set aside.

Rinse and dry the wok if necessary, then return to high heat. Add 2 tbsp cooking oil and the scallion whites and stir-fry until they smell wonderful. Add the chile bean paste, turn the heat down to medium and stir-fry until the oil is red and fragrant. Then turn the heat up high, add the garlic, ginger, preserved vegetable, pickled chiles (or red bell pepper and sambal oelek), and stir-fry until you can smell them too.

Pour in ¾ cup plus 2 tbsp (200ml) of the reheated stock, together with the tendons and the pork, and bring to a boil. Simmer over medium heat for a few minutes, stirring constantly, to allow the tendons to absorb the flavors of the sauce, then add ¾ tsp soy sauce. When the sauce has reduced to a small pool of liquid, taste for salt and adjust if necessary, then add the scallion greens and stir to give them a lick of heat. Turn off the heat, stir in the sesame oil and serve while piping hot.

# Poultry & Eggs

"The chicken has a place at the heart of Chinese gastronomy: not only is its meat enjoyed in countless dishes, but its natural juices are thought to possess the very essence of flavor"

# Poultry & Eggs 禽蛋类

The chicken has a place at the heart of Chinese gastronomy: not only is its meat enjoyed in countless dishes, but its natural juices, extracted by gentle stewing, are thought to possess the very essence of flavor. For rich, dense chicken stock is the embodiment of *xianwei*, that elusive, delicious, savory taste that is in many ways the inspiration for the Chinese culinary arts (and which is now commonly known in the West by its Japanese name, umami). This is why chicken, and stock made from chicken, are crucial ingredients in so many of China's most celebrated dishes—especially those made with the rarefied ingredients like sea cucumber and bamboo pith fungus that are known collectively as "treasures from the mountains and flavors of the seas" (*shanzhen haiwei*). This is also why you'll find chicken added to dishes made with other meats, such as the oxtail soup on p. 313, where the fowl is invisible in the final dish, but its juices enhance and refine the coarser natural flavors of the beef.

The Chinese, like many others, also see chicken soup as a tonic and a particularly vital source of nourishment. The finest chicken soups—the most *xian*, the most nutritious—are made from mature hens, birds that are what English-speakers would now call "organic" and the Chinese "rustic, earthy, farmyard chickens" (*tuji*). Younger male chickens often provide the tender flesh for stir-fried dishes. There are several notable breeds of chicken in China, and the Sichuanese specialty is the "black-boned chicken" (*wuguji*), a black-skinned fowl with a froth of fluffy white feathers. The ancestors of the Chinese were among the earliest people to domesticate chickens, and they have been bred in the Sichuan region since about the third century BC.

The chicken's poetic alter ego is the phoenix, a gorgeously plumed mythical bird that was a symbol of the empress in imperial China. The phoenix, along with the emperor's symbol, the dragon, is a common decorative motif, and you still see images of the two creatures on the lacquered hors d'oeuvre boxes offered at banquets in Sichuan (see p. 64).

The phoenix also lends its name to some chicken dishes—so you know what to expect when you find "phoenix claws" on a Chinese restaurant menu.

In the countryside, chicken is mainly a dish for special occasions: a free-range bird will be caught, killed and plucked before it graces the festive table. Even in Chengdu, until recently, chickens were almost always chosen from a clucking pen in the market and killed and cleaned to order. Those market birds were leaner and more muscular than what my classmates at cooking school dismissively referred to as "Western chickens" (*ouzhou ji*): plump, lazy birds with an abundance of smooth but less flavorful flesh. Many Chinese people still have a preference for the tenser meat of the hard-working legs and wings (known as "live" meat, *huorou*) over insipid breast meat (known as "dead" meat, *sirou*), because of its superior bite and flavor. And although many elegant banquet dishes are made with boneless chicken meat, the bird is commonly chopped on the bone for everyday cooking and eating.

Aside from recognizable chicken dishes, the Sichuanese have a penchant for whipping the breast meat with egg whites into a light paste that can be transformed into silken sheets, a cloud-like custard or even a facsimile of tofu. Such dishes are often served at old-school banquets: one extraordinary New Year's feast I attended in Chengdu included a dish of "snowflake chicken custard" (*xuehua jinao*) topped with morsels of gelatinous fish lip that was so ambrosial that even now, years later, just thinking of it makes me sigh. "Hibiscus-blossom chicken slices" (*furong jipian*) comprises folds of tender, yet slightly taut, sheets of poached chicken served in a pool of golden chicken stock. And what could be more lyrical than *jimeng kuicai*, a clear broth afloat with tender shoots of Chinese mallow, that ancient local green, each one dipped in a delicate chicken paste? However, in the riotous, spice-crazed contemporary era of Sichuanese cooking, you're more likely to come across fried chicken buried in an avalanche of chiles than these quieter, more refined creations.

Duck is the other main cooking fowl in Sichuan, although eaten less than chicken. While its flavor is not as exquisitely umami-savory (*xian*) as chicken, it is prized for the special fragrance (*xiang*) of its meat, which is often coaxed out by roasting or deep-frying the bird whole. Perhaps because some of the most famous Sichuanese duck recipes demand extravagant amounts of cooking oil or the use of an oven (an extreme rarity in traditional kitchens), duck cooking is often left to professionals. The finished dishes, however, such as tea-smoked and roasted duck, may be bought and served alongside home-cooked food on dinner tables.

In the 1990s, there were still artisanal duck roasters in Chengdu. In the former Manchu quarter, I befriended one of them, a man named Mr. Li, whose tiny shop stood in an alley flanked by sprawling courtyard houses. He stuffed his ducks with salty preserved vegetable, pickled chiles, ginger, scallions, fermented black beans and Shaoxing wine, with perhaps a few spices, chosen according to his mood. Then he scalded the ducks in boiling water to tighten their skins, painted them with malt sugar syrup and hung them up outside the shop until their skin was paper-dry. Finally, he roasted them in a domed oven made from bricks and clay, hanging them in the intense heat of the smoldering embers of oriental white oak wood. As they roasted, their fragrant juices dripped into earthenware pots below.

When the ducks were ready, they were strung up in a row under the eaves, shining like lacquer and steaming in the open air. Customers queued up to buy them, fresh from the oven. Mr. Li would neatly chop the birds on a slab of tree trunk and put the pieces into customers' bowls before spooning over some gravy from a simmering pot, augmented by the roasting juices, an array of spices and a final sprinkling of salt, pepper and sesame oil. According to Liu Xuezhi, of the Sichuan Institute of Higher Cuisine, this Sichuanese version of roast duck was developed, like its more illustrious Peking relative, from the techniques used to roast suckling pigs in the emperor's kitchens.

Needless to say, no edible parts of the bird are wasted. At the famous purveyor of tea-smoked duck in Chengdu, Mr. Zhang's Mousehole Duck restaurant (see p. 118), they serve dishes made from intestines, tongues and gizzards, while jellied duck's blood may be savored in a fiery Chongqing stew (see p. 170). Late-night drinkers often drop by a snack shop when they're out partying, for strongly flavored nibbles like duck feet and beaky heads cleft down the middle, all slathered in chile and Sichuan pepper oil.

Frogs are neither fowl nor fish, but one of their Chinese names is "field chicken" (*tianji*), so they perhaps deserve separate mention here. Succulent frogs legs are a rustic delicacy, often served with an abundance of chiles and ginger to dispel their "fishiness," and complemented by a final sizzling of hot oil, ladled over fruity green Sichuan pepper. In Zigong, guests might be feted with a glorious stew of frogs, young ginger and fresh red chile.

Eggs are also important in Sichuanese cuisine. Hen eggs are, of course, the most common, and may be steamed into delicate custards, hard-boiled and stewed with stock or tea and spices, or scrambled with different vegetables, particularly tomatoes. In country cooking, they are often beaten with chopped wild greens (such as purslane or toon shoots) and then poured into very hot oil to make a golden, fluffy omelet. Hard-boiled eggs dyed red are traditionally sent as a gift to new parents: an odd number of eggs for a boy, even for a girl.

Duck eggs are occasionally eaten fresh, but are more typically cured with lime to make the alkaline delicacy known in the West as "thousand-year-old eggs," salted eggs or—most fascinatingly—"boozy" eggs, preserved in liquor (see p. 431). Quail eggs are also popular: they are usually hard-boiled, shelled and then added to soups and stews, but may also be lime-cured like duck eggs.

As I've mentioned, many traditional Sichuanese dishes are made with whole chickens chopped into pieces on the bone. Chopping the large birds commonly available in the West requires a heavy cleaver and high degree of skill. Because of this, and the preference of many for boneless meat, I have suggested using boneless thigh meat instead in several recipes. For stocks, of course, you will need a whole fowl: a mature hen if you can find one, or at least a free-range bird (see pp. 463–465 for more information on stocks).

# Gong Bao Chicken with Peanuts

## gongbao jiding
宫保鸡丁

This dish, also known as Kung Pao chicken, is named after a nineteenth-century governor-general of Sichuan, Ding Baozhen, who is said to have enjoyed eating it. Ding was born in Guizhou province and, before moving to Sichuan in 1876, served as tutor to the imperial princes in Shandong—an honorary role for which he was known as "Palace Guardian" (*gongbao*). Guizhou, Shandong and Sichuan all lay claim to versions of Ding's famous dish, but the Sichuanese is the most renowned. No one can quite agree on the details of its origins. Some say Ding Baozhen brought it with him from Guizhou to Sichuan; others that he ate it at a modest restaurant when he went out in disguise to observe the real lives of the people. Whatever the truth of its origins, its association with an imperial bureaucrat was enough to provoke the wrath of the Cultural Revolution radicals, and it was renamed "fast-fried chicken cubes" (*hongbao jiding*) or "chicken cubes with seared chiles" (*hula jiding*) until its political rehabilitation in the 1980s.

Gong Bao chicken is a glorious medley of succulent chicken, golden peanuts and dark red chiles. The "lychee-flavored" sauce is pepped up with a scorched-chile spiciness and a trace of Sichuan pepper that will make your lips tingle pleasantly. Although the classic dish is made with peanuts, cashew nuts are even more delicious.

10 oz (300g) boneless chicken breast
5 scallions, white parts only
A good handful of dried chiles (at least 12)
4 tbsp cooking oil
1 tsp whole Sichuan pepper
3 garlic cloves, peeled and sliced
An equivalent amount of ginger, peeled and sliced
½ cup (75g) roasted or fried peanuts (or cashews)

### For the marinade
½ tsp salt
2 tsp light soy sauce
1 tsp Shaoxing wine
1½ tbsp potato starch

### For the sauce
2 tbsp superfine sugar
¾ tsp potato starch
¾ tsp dark soy sauce
1 tsp light soy sauce
2 tbsp Chinkiang vinegar
1½ tbsp chicken stock or water
1 tsp sesame oil

Cut the chicken breasts as evenly as possible into ½-inch (1.5cm) cubes. Place in a bowl, add the marinade ingredients and 1½ tbsp cold water, and mix well. Cut the scallion whites into small chunks to match the chicken cubes. Snip the chiles in half or into ¾-inch (2cm) sections and shake out the seeds.

Combine the sauce ingredients in a small bowl—if you dip your finger in you should be able to taste the light sweet-and-sour or "lychee" base flavor of the dish.

Pour the cooking oil into a seasoned wok over high heat. Quickly add the chiles and Sichuan pepper and stir-fry briefly until the chiles are fragrant and darkening but not burned. Tip in the chicken and stir to separate. As soon as the pieces have separated, add the garlic, ginger and scallion whites and stir-fry until they smell delicious and the chicken is just cooked (you may test a piece by cutting it in half to make sure).

Give the sauce a stir and pour into the center of the wok. Wait for a second or two, then stir as the sauce thickens and coats the chicken pieces. Mix in the peanuts (or cashews) and serve.

# Zigong "Small-fried" Chicken

## zigong xiaojian ji
## 自贡小煎鸡

In the past, the salt trade was one of the pillars of the Chinese economy, and the salt-mining city of Zigong in southern Sichuan grew rich on its profits. These days, Zigong is still best known locally for its salt—and abroad for its dinosaur museum—but local food people are keen to promote it as a center of what they call "salt gang" or "salt clique" cooking (*yanbang cai*). Like people across southern Sichuan, Zigong folk insist on eating masses of chiles and ginger to drive out the intense humidity of their climate, so *yanbang* cooking is a riot of spice and color. "Small-fried" chicken is a particular local favorite. I have a high tolerance for chiles, but the first time I tasted this dish, made with black-skinned silkie chicken and blazing with ludicrous amounts of fresh chiles, red and green, I was in such pain I could barely speak. Happily, you can tone down the heat without losing the lively spirit of the dish.

In the following recipe, I've suggested using a mix of fresh red chile, chopped salted chiles (but feel free to use Sichuan pickled chiles if you can get them) and green and red bell peppers. If that seems like a cop-out, by all means substitute some or all of the green and red bell pepper with fresh green and red chiles, at your peril. If you can find it, you might wish to add a couple of tablespoons of chopped young ginger too. Zigong chef Chen Weihua, of A Xi restaurant, showed me how to make this dish; the method, called "small-frying" (*xiaojian*) is typical of Zigong cooking (see p. 475 for more on this technique).

10 oz (300g) boneless chicken thighs, with skin
2 fresh red chiles (scant 1 oz/25g)
3½ oz (100g) long green Turkish peppers
3½ oz (100g) celery (1–2 sticks)
¼ red bell pepper (about 1½ oz/40g)
4 tbsp cooking oil
1 tsp whole green or red Sichuan pepper
2 tbsp chopped salted chiles
1½ tbsp finely chopped ginger
1 tbsp finely chopped garlic
1 tsp Chinkiang vinegar

### For the marinade
¼ tsp salt
2 tsp Shaoxing wine
1½ tsp potato starch

### For the sauce
½ tsp superfine sugar
½ tsp dark soy sauce
1 tsp light soy sauce

**Place the chicken thighs on a chopping board,** skin side down. Make shallow, parallel cuts into the flesh at ¼-inch (5mm) intervals, then make similar cuts at right angles (this will help the flavors to penetrate the chicken). Cut the chicken into ½–¾-inch (1–2cm) cubes, place in a bowl, and add the marinade ingredients and 1 tbsp cold water and mix well. Set aside.

Combine the sauce ingredients with 1 tbsp cold water in a bowl. Trim the fresh chiles and thinly slice (with the seeds). Do the same with the Turkish peppers, but scrape out the seeds and then cut into slightly thicker slices. Remove any strings from the celery and cut it and the red bell pepper into squares to match the chicken.

Heat the oil in a seasoned wok over high heat until smoke starts to rise from the sides of the wok. Add the chicken and stir-fry until the pieces have separated. Add the Sichuan pepper and stir-fry briefly until you can smell it, then add the fresh and salted chiles, ginger and garlic and stir-fry until wonderfully fragrant. Add the green and red bell peppers and stir-fry for a minute or two until piping hot. Give the sauce a stir and add it to the wok, followed by the celery. When everything is hot and fragrant, and the sauce has mostly evaporated, stir in the vinegar and then turn out onto a serving dish.

# Taibai Chicken

## taibai ji
## 太白鸡

This delectable dish consists of golden chicken pieces, mixed with green scallion and red pickled chiles, in a fragrant, spicy, orange-tinted oil. It is named in honor of the illustrious Tang-dynasty poet Li Bai, who lived in the eighth century and upon reaching adulthood, following Chinese custom, was given the courtesy name Great Purity (*taibai*—also the name given to the star Westerners call Venus).

Li Bai was born in northern China, but moved to Sichuan in his childhood. Later he led a wandering life, spurned by the decadent political circles he tried to enter and seeking refuge in wine and poetry. In one of his most famous works, "The Sichuan Road," he wrote of the perils of traveling to Sichuan, that green, fertile basin ringed by forbidding mountains. He described a path flanked by towering peaks, plunging chasms and thundering river torrents, with the strange cries of wild birds emanating from the trees, and the constant threat of snakes and tigers. He finished with a warning:

*The City of Brocade [Chengdu]*
*    may be a pleasant place,*
*But it is best to seek your home.*
*For it is easier to climb to Heaven*
*Than to take the Sichuan road.*
*I gaze into the west, and sigh.*

These days, in the City of Brocade, you may still find the following dish, Li Bai's namesake.

*A small handful of dried chiles*
*5 scallions*
*14 oz (400g) boneless chicken thighs,*
*    preferably with skin*
*3 tbsp cooking oil*
*1 tsp whole Sichuan pepper*
*4 Sichuan pickled chiles, cut into 2½-inch (6cm) strips*
*    (or 3 tbsp chopped salted chiles and*
*    a few 2½-inch/6cm strips of red bell pepper)*
*1 tbsp Shaoxing wine*
*10 tbsp (150ml) chicken or everyday stock (see p. 463)*
*1½ tsp dark soy sauce*
*1¼ tsp superfine sugar*
*¾ tsp salt*
*2 pinches of ground white pepper*
*1–2 tsp sesame oil*

Snip the dried chiles in half and shake out the seeds as much as possible. Cut both the white and green parts of the scallions into 2½-inch (6cm) lengths, but keep them separate.

Chop the chicken into 1¼-inch (3cm) chunks. Heat the cooking oil in a seasoned wok over high heat. Add the chicken and stir-fry until it has become pale but is not crisp or fully cooked through. Remove and set aside, leaving as much oil as possible in the wok. Turn the heat down to medium, add the dried chiles and Sichuan pepper and stir-fry until the chiles are darkening but not burned. Swiftly add the pickled chiles (or chopped salted chiles, is using) and stir-fry until they smell good too. Add the scallion whites (and red bell pepper, if using) and stir-fry until you can smell the scallions.

Return the chicken to the wok and stir in the Shaoxing wine. Pour in the stock and season with the soy sauce, sugar, salt and white pepper. Bring to a boil, then turn down the heat and simmer gently for 5–10 minutes, stirring often. As the liquid evaporates, remove the dried chiles and scallion whites with long cooking chopsticks or tongs and discard them.

When the stock has almost all evaporated, leaving just the spicy oil, add the scallion greens and give them a lick of heat. Remove the wok from the heat, stir in the sesame oil and spoon everything out onto a serving dish.

# Dry-fried Chicken

## ganbian ji
干煸鸡

While the Chengdu I knew as a student has largely disappeared, its atmosphere lingers in some of the quieter backstreets, including one where people play mahjong under the trees and sun-dry cabbage leaves on chairs and motorbikes, ready to make their winter preserves. Halfway down, there's a tiny restaurant whose flavors evoke, for me, the magic of my old student haunts. The dining room, open to the street, is white-tiled and has just a handful of tables. Out the back, chef Zhang Guobin conjures up the most beautiful dishes in his tiny kitchen, while the owner, Li Qi, chats with customers in the front. Thanks to the kindness of Mr. Li and Chef Zhang, I'm able to bring you a couple of their recipes, like this delectable version of dry-fried chicken.

In this dish, the chunks of chicken are delightfully toasty and flavorful, and are complemented by the freshness of the green pepper. The dish has a deep, gentle chile hotness, and looks extremely appetizing in its chile-reddened oil. As with all dry-fried dishes, there is no starch, marinade or sauce. You can vary the vegetables as you please—for this version, I recommend the long, thin-skinned peppers sold in Turkish shops, but you can use squares of regular green bell pepper if you prefer.

14 oz (400g) boneless chicken thighs,
  with skin
5 scallions, white parts only
6–8 dried chiles
7 oz (200g) long green Turkish peppers
2 tbsp cooking oil
1 tsp whole Sichuan pepper
1½ tbsp Sichuan chile bean paste
3 garlic cloves, peeled and sliced
An equivalent amount of ginger,
  peeled and sliced
½ tsp dark soy sauce
A good pinch of superfine sugar
1 tbsp chile oil,
  with or without sediment
Salt

Cut the chicken thighs into ¾-inch (2cm) cubes. Cut the scallion whites into ½-inch (1cm) lengths. Snip the chiles in half or into ¾-inch (2cm) sections and shake out the seeds as much as possible. Trim off the stem ends of each green pepper and make a slit down its side so you can pull out and discard most of the seeds, then cut at a steep angle into ½-inch (1cm) "horse ear" slices.

Heat the cooking oil in a seasoned wok over high heat. Add the chicken and fry for about 4 minutes, until it is fragrant and tinged with gold. You can encourage it to color by leaving it in a single layer on the base of the wok and only stirring intermittently. Add the chiles and Sichuan pepper and stir-fry until they are fragrant and the chiles are beginning to darken.

Tilt the wok, push the chicken up one side and turn the heat down to medium. Add the chile bean paste to the oil that pools in the base and stir-fry until the oil is red and fragrant, then tilt the wok back, turn the heat up high and mix everything together. Add the garlic, ginger and scallion whites and stir-fry briefly until fragrant.

Stir in the soy sauce and sugar, followed by the green peppers, and continue to fry for another minute or two until the peppers are hot and sizzly, adding salt to taste.

Finally, stir in the chile oil and serve.

## Braised Chicken with Chestnuts

banli shaoji
板栗烧鸡

As the Sichuanese summer fades and damp winter nights draw in, chestnut sellers begin to appear on the streets. These itinerant vendors roast chestnuts in their shells in enormous woks full of charcoal, then wrap them in cloths and tuck them snugly into baskets to keep them warm. The hot nuts are the perfect snack to placate your hunger in a streetside teahouse, where you might stop for an hour before lunch.

Chestnuts have been cultivated in China since antiquity: the character for chestnut appears on the Shang-dynasty oracle bones, the earliest examples of the Chinese script, and they are also mentioned in the ancient *Book of Songs*. The great Qing-dynasty gourmet Yuan Mei left behind notes for his own recipe for chicken stewed with chestnuts, while the following dish is based on a contemporary Sichuanese version that is widely enjoyed during chestnut season.

The dish can be made in advance and reheated. In the first edition of this book, I gave a recipe for a whole chicken; this one is a more manageable version made with boneless chicken thighs.

*4 boneless chicken thighs (about ¾ lb/350g),*
*preferably with skin*
*1-inch piece (20g) ginger, unpeeled*
*2 scallions, white and green*
*parts separated*
*3 tbsp cooking oil*
*1½ tbsp Shaoxing wine*
*1¼ cups (300ml) chicken stock or water*
*1 tbsp brown or superfine sugar*
*1½ tsp dark soy sauce*
*1⅓ cups (200g) cooked, peeled chestnuts*
*(canned or vacuum-packed)*
*Salt*

Cut the chicken into bite-sized chunks. Lightly smack the ginger and scallion whites with the flat of a cleaver blade or a rolling pin to loosen them, then cut each scallion white into a couple of pieces. Cut the scallion greens into neat 1½-inch (4cm) lengths.

Heat the oil in a seasoned wok over high heat. When it is hot, add the ginger and scallion whites and stir-fry until you can smell their fragrances. Add the chicken pieces and fry until they are lightly browned: don't move them around too much, but let them rest against the base of the wok so they take on a little color. Drain off some of the excess oil at this stage, if you wish.

Splash the Shaoxing wine into the wok and stir well, then tip in the stock or water. Bring to a boil, then add the sugar, soy sauce and chestnuts, along with salt to taste (¾ tsp should do). Turn down the heat, cover and simmer for about 15 minutes to allow the chicken to cook through and the chestnuts to absorb some of the flavors of the sauce, stirring from time to time.

At the end of the cooking time, increase the heat to reduce the liquid, if you wish, and adjust the seasoning as needed. At the last minute, add the scallion greens, cover for just a moment to let them feel the heat, then serve.

*If you wish to use a whole chicken*
*For a chicken weighing 2–3 lb (1–1.5 kg), you will need 3½ cups (500g) chestnuts, 1½-inch piece (30g) ginger, 2 scallions, 4 tbsp Shaoxing wine, 3 cups (700ml) stock, 4 tsp brown or superfine sugar, 4 tsp dark soy sauce and salt to taste. Chop the chicken into bite-sized chunks, as for the main recipe, and proceed as above.*

## Chicken in a Delicate Vinegar Sauce

culiu ji
醋熘鸡

The chicken in this dish is beautifully pale and tender, lolling in a pool of red oil. Its succulent flesh is complemented by the refreshing crunch of the celery. The sauce is gently vinegar-sour, with a deep, lingering spiciness from the pickled chiles. In Sichuan the vegetable ingredient is usually winter bamboo shoot or tender celtuce: at home I use celery instead. The initial frying of the chicken in its protective clothing of starch and egg white, in fairly cool oil, keeps it beautifully succulent, ready to receive a delicious draping of sauce. The key to this dish is to avoid overcooking the chicken—but do check one of the larger pieces to make sure it's just cooked through before serving. This recipe is based on a method taught by chef Gong Xingde of the Sichuan Provincial Business and Services School.

Incidentally, many of my Chinese friends associate vinegar with betrayal in love: "eating vinegar" (*chi cu*) is a common phrase which means to be cuckolded or to feel amorous jealousy.

2 boneless chicken breasts (about 10 oz/300g),
   with or without skin
¼ tsp salt
1½ tsp Shaoxing wine
2 tbsp potato starch
2 tbsp egg white (from 1–2 eggs)
5¼ oz (150g) celery (about 3 sticks)
1⅔ cups (400ml) cooking oil, for deep-frying
2 tbsp Sichuan pickled chile paste
   or sambal oelek
1 tbsp finely chopped ginger
1 tbsp finely chopped garlic
3 tbsp thinly sliced scallion greens
2 tsp Chinkiang vinegar

For the sauce
1½ tsp superfine sugar
¼ tsp salt
1 tsp potato starch
2 tsp Chinkiang vinegar
1 tsp Shaoxing wine
3 tbsp stock or water

Cut the chicken breasts as evenly as possible into ½-inch (1.5cm) strips and then diagonally into small lozenge shapes. Place in a bowl with the salt and Shaoxing wine and mix.

In another bowl, gradually stir the potato starch into the egg white to make a smooth, runny batter. Add the batter to the chicken and mix well.

Remove any strings from the celery sticks, cut them in half lengthwise, and then into lozenge shapes to match the chicken. Mix the sauce ingredients together in a small bowl.

Heat the deep-frying oil in a wok over high heat to about 265°F (130°C) (hot enough to sizzle gently, not violently, around a test piece of chicken). Add the chicken and celery, and nudge gently with long cooking chopsticks or tongs to separate the pieces. Stir gently until the pieces of chicken have separated and are turning white, then immediately remove from the wok with a slotted spoon. (The chicken will still be half-raw—resist the temptation to cook it through at this stage or you'll find the finished dish less than succulent.) →

←   Carefully pour off all but about 3 tbsp oil from the wok
and return to medium heat. Add the pickled chile paste or
sambal oelek and stir-fry gently until the oil is a rich, deep red.
Add the ginger and garlic and continue to stir-fry until they
smell wonderful.

Return the chicken and celery to the wok and stir in quickly.
Still working swiftly, give the sauce a stir and add to the wok,
stirring as it thickens.

Finally, add the scallion greens and the vinegar and
stir to give them a lick of heat before turning everything out
onto a serving dish. (The chicken should be just cooked
and very tender—test the largest piece to make sure it's cooked
through.)

# Stir-fried Chicken with Preserved Vegetable

## jimi yacai
## 鸡米芽菜

This is a quick dish that is perfect for "sending the rice down" (*xiafan*), meaning that it's saltily flavorful enough to season bowlfuls of plain rice. It's from a restaurant in Chengdu that is named, amusingly, something that might be translated as "Rice Apocalypse" (*fan zaiyang*). Apparently this is because the restaurant owner reckons his dishes are so tasty you will demolish enormous piles of rice when eating them—clearly a disaster for the rice!

Judging by the quality of the meals I've enjoyed there, I think he may have a point. The morsels of chicken, tossed in a wok with the intensely savory preserved vegetable, green pepper and other aromatics, are irresistible. I ate this dish alongside other, equally perilous (for the rice) dishes that included eggplant fritters in a fish-fragrant sauce, spicy stewed pork with potatoes and green beans, and stir-fried celtuce tips with chile and Sichuan pepper.

If you don't have Yibin *yacai*, you could make this with another classic Sichuanese salty pickle, such as preserved mustard tuber (*zhacai*) or "big-headed vegetable" (*datoucai*), both finely chopped.

At the Rice Apocalypse restaurant, they use thinly sliced fresh red and green chiles so the dish is pretty hot: I've suggested using a mix of hot chile and mild pepper, but please do vary the proportions as you please. This dish is lovely served with wraps of crisp lettuce (although I've not had it served that way in Chengdu).

9 oz (250g) skinless, boneless chicken thigh
    or breast meat
2 tsp Shaoxing wine
2 tsp potato starch
1 fresh red chile
2½ oz (75g) long green Turkish pepper
1 iceberg lettuce (optional)
2 tbsp cooking oil
2½ oz (75g) Yibin yacai (or other) preserved vegetable,
    rinsed and squeezed dry
2 tsp finely chopped garlic
2 tsp finely chopped ginger

Cut the chicken meat into slices, then into strips, and finally into tiny morsels (ideally around ¼ inch (5mm) thick—these are known as *jimi* or "chicken rice-grains" because they are small). Place in a bowl and add the Shaoxing wine and potato starch, along with 2 tsp cold water. Mix well.

Cut the red chile and green pepper into tiny morsels to match the chicken. If you wish to serve the dish with lettuce cups, cut the lettuce in half, then use scissors to cut circles from the outer leaves.

Heat the oil in a seasoned wok over high heat. Add the chicken and stir-fry until the pieces have become pale and are nearly cooked. Tip in the preserved vegetable, along with the garlic and ginger, and stir-fry until they smell wonderful. Add the red chile and green pepper and continue to stir-fry until everything is piping hot, then serve.

# Braised Chicken with Baby Taro

## yu'er shao ji
## 芋儿烧鸡

In the late 1990s, my Chengdu friends started driving out of town on the weekends for a taste of *nongjiale* ("the happiness of rural homes"). Farmers around the city were opening "rustic" restaurants where city-dwellers could dabble in country life, playing mahjong and nibbling watermelon seeds in bamboo sheds, catching their own fish for dinner and tucking into feasts of spicy braised rabbit and other hearty dishes. One particular county town just south of the city, Huayang, became known for its riotously spicy and oily chicken stewed with taro. One evening a couple of chef friends and I drove out to try it. We were presented with a glorious hotpot in which chunks of chicken and taro bobbed around in an oily broth.

This is my version, scaled down for home cooking but still a delicious and heart-warming stew, perfect for a winter's evening. In Sichuan, people like to make it with chunks of whole chicken, on the bone, but I've suggested using boneless thigh meat and chicken stock (if you wish to use chicken on the bone, increase the cooking time to allow the chicken to become tender); I've also used less oil than in many local versions. The taro has a silky, comforting texture that goes beautifully with the chicken, but you can use potato or carrot if you prefer.

The same method can be used for pork ribs or shoulder; ribs will take a little longer to cook.

1 lb 2 oz (500g) boneless chicken thighs, with skin
½ tsp dark soy sauce
1 tbsp Shaoxing wine
1 lb 2 oz (500g) baby taro
6 dried chiles
2 scallions, white parts only
1 small Chinese black cardamom pod
6 tbsp cooking oil
About 3 cups (750ml) chicken stock
3½ tbsp Sichuan chile bean paste
½ star anise
A small piece of cassia bark
1 tbsp finely chopped garlic
1 tbsp finely chopped ginger
1 tbsp ground chiles
1 tsp whole Sichuan pepper
A small handful of cilantro, to garnish
Salt

Cut the chicken into 1¼-inch (3–4 cm) cubes and place in a bowl. Add the soy sauce and Shaoxing wine and mix well. Put on rubber gloves and peel the taro (the raw skin contains an irritant that can make your hands itch), then cut each one into 2–3 pieces (ideally, turn the taro between cuts for "roll-cut" chunks). Snip the chiles in half and shake out the seeds as much as possible. Lightly smack the scallion whites and cardamom with the flat of a cleaver blade or a rolling pin to loosen them.

Heat 2 tbsp oil in a seasoned wok over high heat. Add the chicken pieces, spreading them out across the base of the wok, and fry for a minute or two until pale and slightly tinged with gold, turning them a few times during cooking. Remove from the wok and set aside. Rinse and dry the wok if necessary. Bring the stock to a boil in a separate pan.

Heat 4 tbsp oil in the wok over gentle heat. Add the chile bean paste, cardamom, star anise and cassia bark and stir-fry until the oil is red and wonderfully fragrant. Do not hurry this step: take a few minutes to allow the flavors to develop. Add the garlic, ginger and scallion whites and stir-fry until they smell wonderful too. Tip in the dried chiles, ground chiles and Sichuan pepper and continue to stir-fry until beautifully aromatic. (This is like conducting an orchestra, letting each set of ingredients express themselves before calling on the next, building up to a grand crescendo of flavors.)

Next add the chicken, taro and a little of the stock to the wok. Stir well, then transfer to a saucepan. Add enough stock to cover, bring to a boil and season with a little salt to taste. Cover and simmer for 30 minutes. At this stage you can remove and discard the cardamom, star anise and cassia, if you like.

At the end of the cooking time, if you wish to reduce the liquid, turn the heat up and boil for about 5 minutes. Taste for salt, adding a little more if necessary, and then serve with sprigs of cilantro to garnish.

# Chongqing Chicken with Chiles

lazi ji
辣子鸡

The first time you encounter this dish, it appears terrifyingly spicy, the cubes of chicken peeking out from a vast pile of blood-red chiles. But it's not, in fact, as extreme as it looks. The chiles that give the dish its visual drama are used to lend fragrance and a gentle heat to the cooking oil and are not usually eaten: you just use your chopsticks to extract delectable morsels of deep-fried chicken, leaving the chiles on the plate.

Anyway, if you think this version involves an excessive amount of chiles, you should see the one served in its place of origin, the scenic Gele Mountain near Chongqing. At the famed "Happiness in the Woods" restaurant, each portion is made with a whole chicken buried in eye-popping quantities of chiles, served on a tray as wide as a satellite dish. When I visited recently, ten enormous sacks of chiles were piled outside the kitchen: the owner, Xia Jun, told me they got through that amount every Saturday.

Xia Jun kindly allowed me into the small kitchen dedicated to this single dish. Inside, four chefs were engaged in relentless lazi ji production. Two of them stood at wooden chopping blocks, reducing chicken after chicken to bite-sized chunks. I watched, mesmerized, as the other two, a man and a woman, commanded their woks. They tipped bucketfuls of dried chiles into their cauldrons of oil and then added handfuls of Sichuan pepper. They stirred and stirred in the fiendish heat as the spices sizzled, before chucking in the chicken, followed by a glug of soy sauce and, →

1 young chicken (about 1 lb/450g) or 1 lb (450g) boneless chicken thighs, with skin
1¾ oz (50g) medium-hot dried chiles
½ tsp sesame seeds (optional)
2 garlic cloves
½-inch piece (10g) ginger
2 scallions, white parts only
About 2 cups (500ml) cooking oil
½ tbsp Sichuan chile bean paste
2 tsp whole Sichuan pepper
Dash of Shaoxing wine
¼ tsp salt
½ tsp superfine sugar
1 tsp sesame oil
2 tbsp thinly sliced scallion greens (optional)

*For the marinade*
1-inch piece (20g) ginger, unpeeled
1 scallion, white part only
2 tsp Shaoxing wine
½ tsp salt

**If using a young chicken,** pull out the leg and wing joints and cut the legs and wings away from the body. Chop off and discard the wing and drumsticks tips. Cut down to the bone along each leg, and wiggle and cut out the thick leg bones. Cut each wing into two joints. Chop the legs and wings into ½–¾-inch (1–2cm) chunks. Cut the bird in half crosswise to separate breast and back. Place the back flat and chop lengthwise along both sides of the backbone, so you can discard the backbone. Cut the rest of the back into ¾-inch (2cm) chunks. Cut the breasts away from the breastbone and chop the meat into ¾-inch (2cm) chunks. Keep any fragments of skin, which will be particularly delicious.

If using chicken thighs, simply cut into ¾-inch (2cm) chunks. Place the chicken pieces in a bowl.

Next make the marinade. Lightly smack the ginger and scallion white with the flat of a cleaver blade or a rolling pin to loosen them, then add to the bowl of chicken, along with the Shaoxing wine and salt. Mix well, then let the chicken marinate for 10–15 minutes. →

← later, a scattering of MSG. Then they scooped the whole lot onto a tray and sprinkled over a few sesame seeds.

The following recipe is easier to make at home. I suggest you use either a young chicken weighing 14–16 oz (400–450g)—a reasonable size to chop and cook in a home wok—or boneless chicken thigh meat (be sure to include the skin, which is fantastically delicious). If you choose a whole young chicken, you will need a heavy chopping knife or cleaver to cut it into small pieces. Do make sure you use only medium-hot chiles of the kind you can buy in enormous bags in good Chinese supermarkets: you may be able to find them pre-cut into sections, which saves time in the kitchen. The key to cooking this dish is not to burn the chiles, which should end up scorched but still gloriously red.

← Meanwhile, snip the chiles into ½–¾-inch (1–2 cm) sections and shake out the seeds as much as possible. Toast the sesame seeds, if using, in a small frying pan over very gentle heat until fragrant and tinged with gold. Peel and slice the garlic and ginger. Lightly smack the scallion whites with the flat of a cleaver blade or a rolling pin to loosen them.

Remove and discard the ginger and scallion white from the marinade. Heat 1⅔ cups (400ml) cooking oil in a seasoned wok over high heat to 375°F (190°C). Add the chicken, stirring to separate the pieces, and deep-fry for 4 minutes until slightly golden. Remove from the oil with a slotted spoon. Reheat the oil to 375°F (190°C), return the chicken to the wok and fry for another 3–4 minutes until golden and crisp. Remove from the wok with a slotted spoon and set aside.

Carefully pour off the oil and wipe or brush out the wok if necessary. Return 3½ tbsp oil to the wok and place over medium heat. Add the chile bean paste and stir until the oil is red, then add the garlic, ginger and scallion whites and stir-fry briefly until they smell delicious. Add the chiles and Sichuan pepper and stir until slightly scorched and aromatic, taking great care not to burn them. (If the chiles are in danger of burning, remove the wok from the stove for a moment.)

Return the fried chicken to the wok and stir briskly to coat in the fragrant oil. Add the Shaoxing wine, together with the salt and sugar. Finally, off the heat, stir in the sesame oil. Turn out onto a serving dish and scatter with the sesame seeds and scallion greens, if using.

# Stir-fried Chicken Hodgepodge

chao jiza
炒鸡杂

My Sichuanese chef friends might be surprised to see me include the following recipe in this book—it's not a fancy dish and is rarely seen on restaurant menus. It is, though, extraordinarily delicious and a perfect illustration of the resourcefulness of Sichuanese cooking. My friend Feng Rui had invited me to spend a day cooking (and eating) with a couple of his friends, both former chefs at two of Chengdu's best hotels. In the morning we went to the local market to buy ingredients. The chickens, of course, weren't just raw, but were still clucking around in their pen. Feng Rui chose a fowl with a scarcely developed thumb, a sign that it was young and tender. It was duly dispatched, plucked and dressed, and we took it home. Almost nothing of that bird was wasted. We ate the meat cold with a chile oil dressing, the bones made the stock base for our winter melon soup, and all the innards (except the bitter gall bladder) went into the following dish, including intestines, heart and blood. It was an enticing mix of strong flavors and different textures, all set off by the crunchy celery and a delicate assortment of seasonings.

The following is a re-creation of the dish, which can be made with chicken livers and/or hearts. I have reworked the method with some tips from restaurateur Li Qi and his chef Zhang Guobing, who serve a particularly gorgeous version.

7 oz (200g) chicken livers and/or hearts
9 oz (250g) celery (about 4 sticks)
2 Sichuan pickled chiles
  (or 2 tsp sambal oelek and ¼ red bell pepper)
6 scallions, white parts only
3 tbsp cooking oil
½ tbsp Sichuan chile bean paste
A few slices of peeled pickled or fresh ginger
1 tbsp chile oil

## For the marinade
¼ tsp salt
2 tsp Shaoxing wine
1½ tsp potato starch

## For the sauce
2 tsp light soy sauce
½ tsp superfine sugar
½ tsp Chinkiang vinegar
¼ tsp potato starch
1 tbsp stock or water

**Thinly slice the chicken offal.** Place in a bowl, then add the marinade ingredients, mix well and set aside.

Remove any strings from the celery, then cut into narrow batons about 2 inches (5cm) long. If you are using Sichuan pickled chiles, trim off the stem ends, then squeeze out the seeds as much as possible and cut at an angle into "horse ear" slices. (If you are using red bell pepper, cut into batons to match the celery.) Cut the scallion whites into ½-inch (1cm) slices. Combine the sauce ingredients in a small bowl.

Heat the cooking oil in a seasoned wok over high heat, add the chicken offal and stir-fry until pale in color. Tilt the wok, push the offal up one side and tip the chile bean paste (and sambal oelek, if using) into the oil that pools in the base. Stir-fry until the oil is red and fragrant: the oil should sizzle gently around the paste; turn down the heat if necessary. Tilt the wok back, add the pickled chiles (or red bell pepper, if using), scallion whites and ginger and mix everything together. Stir-fry over high heat until the scallion whites and ginger smell wonderful, then add the celery and stir-fry until piping hot. Give the sauce a stir and add it to the wok, stirring as it thickens. Finally, stir in the chile oil and serve.

# Fish-fragrant
# Fried Chicken

## yuxiang bakuai ji
## 鱼香八块鸡

The fish-fragrant combination of pickled chiles, ginger, garlic and scallions with a good dash of sweet-and-sour flavor is one of Sichuan's most brilliant inventions. And while fish-fragrant pork slivers (see p. 145) and fish-fragrant eggplants (see p. 266) may be its best-known standard-bearers, this chicken version deserves more acclaim. Deep-fried chicken nuggets in one of the world's most delicious sauces: who could resist? In Sichuan, cooks would normally use a paste made from freshly chopped local pickled chiles, but a younger, brighter-red chile bean paste also gives delectable results. The same sauce is spectacular with deep-fried shrimp or other seafood.

10 oz (300g) skinless, boneless chicken thighs
¼ tsp salt
2 tsp Shaoxing wine
About ½ cup (60g) potato starch
1 large egg white
At least 2 cups (500ml) cooking oil, for deep-frying
1½ tbsp Sichuan chile bean paste or pickled chile paste
1 tbsp finely chopped garlic
1 tbsp finely chopped ginger
4 tbsp thinly sliced scallion greens

_For the sauce_
2 tsp superfine sugar
½ tsp potato starch
1 tsp light soy sauce
1 tbsp Chinkiang vinegar
3 tbsp stock or water

**Place the chicken thighs on a chopping board.** Use a knife to make shallow, parallel cuts into the flesh at ¼-inch (5mm) intervals, then make similar cuts at right angles to the first ones (this cross-hatching will help the flavors to penetrate the chicken and speed up the cooking). Cut the chicken into bite-sized pieces about ¾ inch (2cm) square and place in a bowl. Add the salt and Shaoxing wine and mix well. In a separate bowl, gradually stir the potato starch into the egg white until you have a thick batter—you may not need all of it. Add the batter to the chicken and mix well to coat all the pieces.

Combine the sauce ingredients in a small bowl.

Heat the deep-frying oil in a wok to 355°F (180°C) (hot enough to sizzle vigorously around a test piece of chicken). Using long cooking chopsticks or tongs, carefully drop about half the chicken pieces into the hot oil, adding them individually to minimize sticking, and using a slotted spoon to nudge apart any pieces that do stick together. Deep-fry the chicken for 1–2 minutes, until faintly golden, then remove and drain on paper towels. Repeat with the rest of the chicken.

Reheat the oil to 355°F (180°C). Return all the chicken pieces to the hot oil and fry for another 1–2 minutes until beautifully golden. Remove from the wok and let drain on paper towels. (Do make sure the chicken is cooked through: cut into one of the thickest pieces to test.)

Carefully pour off the oil and wipe or brush out the wok if necessary. Return about 3 tbsp oil to the wok and place over medium heat. Add the chile bean paste and stir-fry until the oil is red and fragrant. Tip in the garlic and ginger and stir-fry until they smell amazing.

Give the sauce a stir and pour into the wok, turning the heat up high. Immediately add the chicken and stir rapidly as the sauce thickens and coats the pieces. Finally, stir in the scallion greens and serve.

# Chicken "Tofu"

## ji douhua
## 鸡豆花

The elaborate culinary joke has long been part of Chinese food culture, and is a measure of the sophistication of the cuisine. Vegetarian dishes that look and taste like meat or fish are a notable feature of cooking in Buddhist monastery restaurants, while in the following Sichuanese specialty, an apparently plain vegetarian dish turns out to be made from expensive chicken breast and a luxurious stock. The chicken flesh is pummeled to a paste with egg white, and then set into a kind of curd that looks exactly like "flower" tofu, a cheap and popular snack. As they say, it's "flower tofu without the beans; chicken without the appearance of chicken" (douhua buyong dou, chi ji bujian ji). Apart from being witty, this gentle soup is most delicious, with its cloud-like mouthfeel, fine stock and dainty garnish of green leaves and deep-pink ham or goji berries. The quality of the dish depends on the quality of your stock and careful control of heat. Chicken "tofu" has been eaten in Chengdu for at least a century: it is one of the dishes mentioned in Fu Chongju's 1909 survey of the city.

Do remember to thoroughly clean any surfaces and implements that come into contact with the raw chicken mixture.

1-inch piece (20g) ginger, unpeeled
2 scallions, white parts only
1 skinless, boneless chicken breast (about 5¾ oz/160g)
A handful of baby choy sum or pea shoots
½ cup (125ml) egg white (from about 4 large eggs)
½ tbsp Shaoxing wine
1½ tbsp potato starch, mixed with 1 tbsp cold water
1 quart (1 liter) chicken stock (see p. 463) or clear superior stock (see p. 464)
A few goji berries or 2 tbsp very finely chopped cooked ham, to garnish
Salt and ground white pepper

Lightly smack the ginger and scallion whites with the flat of a cleaver blade or a rolling pin to loosen them. Place in a bowl with 1¼ cups (300ml) cold water and let infuse for a few minutes. Place the chicken breasts on a chopping board and trim off every last morsel of fat, gristle or tendon, then cut the meat into small chunks. Bring a small pot of water to a boil, add the choy sum or pea shoots and blanch for just long enough to wilt, then rinse under cold water and set aside in a bowl of cold water.

Place the chicken meat in a blender. Add about half the strained soaking water from the ginger and scallion whites and blitz until smooth. Gradually add the rest of the soaking water, then the egg whites, and blitz again until evenly blended. Add the Shaoxing wine, ¾ tsp salt, a pinch of pepper and the potato starch mixture. You should end up with a pale chicken "smoothie." For perfect results, strain the mixture through a conical chinois strainer.

Pour the stock into a saucepan and bring to a boil over high heat. Season to taste with salt and pepper. Now give the stock a good stir to make it circulate, and quickly pour in the chicken mixture, which will rise to the surface in fluffy clouds. As soon as the stock has returned to a boil, turn the heat down very low, cover the pan and cook for 10–20 minutes until the chicken "tofu" has completely set to a white curd (the exact time will depend on the size of your pan and the thickness of the chicken mixture). Do make sure it is fully cooked: if you're not sure, scoop some "tofu" out from the center of the mass to check.

Scoop the chicken "tofu" into four or six bowls and strain over enough stock to nearly cover. Place a piece of choy sum in each bowl and garnish with the goji berries or chopped ham.

## "One Tender Bite," from Qiaotou, Zigong

qiaotou yi nen

桥头一嫩

One day, Chen Weihua, the chef of A Xi restaurant in Zigong, took me for a drive into the countryside. We drove past broad ponds where men in wooden punts were fishing, past gleaming paddy fields and shady bamboo groves, to the county town of Qiaotou, where a small family restaurant had become known for its "three tender bites" (*san nen*). The restaurant had no menu: everyone just ordered the "three tender bites"—three separate dishes of fast-fried pig's liver, kidneys and stomach—with a few sides. The offal was as tender as promised because of the swift, precise cooking.

With just a few core seasonings, chef Xie Xinyuan, a veteran with thirty years' experience, whipped up his famous *xiaochao* ("small stir-fries") with almost inconceivable speed. He piled all the seasonings together in a big bowl, scooped one of the chopped "tender bites" into another bowl, heated an improbable amount of oil in a wok over a volcano-like flame, tossed in the "tender" ingredient, stirring like a maniac, followed by all the seasonings, and then, in a flash, removed the wok from the heat and kept stirring its contents in the fiery oil until they were just done.

The recipe here follows exactly his method, but slightly adapted for a home stove, and with chicken; feel free to use offal if you prefer. Mr. Xie used a mixture of lard and rapeseed oil for cooking, which gives a particularly delicious result.

10 oz (300g) boneless chicken thigh
    or breast meat, preferably with skin
2 tsp potato starch
1 tsp whole Sichuan pepper
6–8 scallions, white parts only
1 tsp finely chopped ginger
2 tsp Sichuan chile bean paste
1 tbsp chopped salted chiles
    or coarsely chopped Sichuan pickled chiles
1½ tbsp ground chiles
¼ tsp salt
6 tbsp cooking oil (ideally a mix of half lard
    and half rapeseed oil)

**Place the chicken on a chopping board,** skin side down. Use a knife to make shallow, parallel cuts into the flesh at ¼-inch (5mm) intervals, then make similar cuts at right angles to the first ones (this cross-hatching will help the flavors to penetrate the chicken and speed up the cooking). Cut the chicken into ½–¾-inch (1–2cm) cubes. Place in a bowl, add the potato starch and Sichuan pepper, along with 1½ tbsp cold water, and mix well.

Cut the scallion whites into ¾-inch (2cm) lengths. Place in a bowl and add the ginger, chile bean paste, chopped chiles, ground chiles, salt and 1 tbsp oil.

Heat the rest of the oil in a seasoned wok over high heat. When the oil is sizzling hot, add the chicken and stir-fry. As soon as the pieces have separated, add the bowlful of aromatics. Continue to stir-fry until the oil is gorgeously orange in color and the chicken is just cooked (test one of the larger pieces by cutting it in half to make sure). Serve immediately.

Please note that the finished dish will be pretty oily: do not spoon the oil over your rice, but use chopsticks to help yourself to pieces of chicken, leaving the oil behind. Alternatively, strain off some of the oil before serving; this amount of oil is, however, necessary for the cooking method, to keep the chicken exquisitely tender.

# Fragrant and Crispy Duck

## xiangsu quan ya
## 香酥全鸭

A version of Sichuanese crispy duck has become de rigueur in Chinese restaurants in London. The duck flesh is tender and succulent, the skin marvelously crisp and golden. Most Chinese restaurants in the UK serve it like Peking duck, with Mandarin pancakes, hoisin sauce and strips of crunchy vegetables such as scallion and cucumber—but in Sichuan it may be served on its own, perhaps with a dip of salt and Sichuan pepper, or accompanied by fluffy steamed buns and shards of white Beijing leek (*jingcong*, which is like a leek-sized scallion but with a milder flavor) with sweet flour sauce on the side.

The recipe has several stages but is not particularly difficult, and the duck can be marinated and steamed in advance, and then simply deep-fried when you want to eat it. (If you do wish to serve the duck in the British Chinese-restaurant style, you can buy frozen Peking duck pancakes and hoisin sauce in most Chinese food shops.) I've suggested toasting your own whole spices, but feel free to use 1 tsp five-spice powder instead, if you prefer.

1 young duck (4½–5½ lb/2–2.5kg)
Cooking oil, for deep-frying
  (enough to at least half-submerge the duck)
1 tbsp sesame oil

*For the marinade*
1 tsp whole Sichuan pepper
A piece of cassia bark
1 star anise
2 cloves, with their powdery heads
  pinched off and discarded
½ tsp fennel seeds
½ Chinese black cardamom pod
1–2 slices sand ginger
3 tsp salt
3 tbsp Shaoxing wine
1½-inch piece (30g) ginger, unpeeled
2 scallions

*Optional trimmings*
Steamed lotus-leaf buns (see p. 392)
Dip of sweet flour sauce
Slivers of white Beijing leek or scallion
Thin strips of cucumber
Salt and Sichuan pepper dip (see p. 456)

**First marinate the duck.** Toast the spices with the salt in a wok over gentle heat until wonderfully aromatic, then roughly crush with a mortar and pestle. Prick the duck all over with a skewer, and then rub it, inside and out, with the spice mixture and the Shaoxing wine. Place it in a good-sized bowl that will fit into your steamer. Lightly smack the ginger and scallions with the flat of a cleaver blade or a rolling pin to loosen them, then roughly chop into a few lengths. Put some of the ginger and scallions into the duck's cavity, and tuck the rest around it in the bowl. Let marinate in a cool place for several hours, or in the fridge overnight.

Drain off any juices that have emerged from the duck. Place the bowl in a steamer, cover with foil and steam the duck over high heat for about 2 hours, until it is completely tender. Remove the duck from the bowl, draining any steaming juices from its cavity into the bowl, and set aside to cool and dry out slightly. Remove and discard the ginger and scallions.  →

← (The reserved juices make the most delicious base for a noodle broth or other soup, although they will be salty and may need diluting.) At this point, the duck can be chilled until needed.

To minimize oil-spitting during the deep-frying, pat the duck dry with paper towels.

Heat the deep-frying oil to 390°F (200°C). If you are using a wok, make sure it is absolutely stable.

Use a large fine-mesh strainer to carefully lower the duck into the hot oil and deep-fry for several minutes, turning it halfway through, until the skin is beginning to turn golden. Carefully remove the duck from the wok. Reheat the oil to 390°F (200°C), return the duck to the wok and deep-fry until it is crisp and golden brown on all sides, and wonderfully aromatic. Remove and drain well, then brush the duck sparingly all over with the sesame oil.

If you wish, you can cut the duck into small pieces and pile them up, breast pieces on top, in something resembling its original shape. Otherwise, set the whole bird on a big serving platter and let your guests pluck at it with their chopsticks. Either way, the duck should be served piping hot.

*Fragrant and crispy duck legs*
*Deep-frying a whole duck can be quite unwieldy and requires a lot of oil, so it's worth remembering that the method works brilliantly with duck legs alone. If you use 2 duck legs (about 14 oz/400g in total), you will need to make a marinade of 1½ tsp salt, 1 tsp whole Sichuan pepper, 1 star anise, a small piece of cassia bark or cinnamon stick, 1-inch piece (20g) ginger, 2 scallion whites and 1 tbsp Shaoxing wine. You should only need 1⅔–2 cups (400–500ml) oil for deep-frying in a round-bottomed wok stabilized on a wok stand.*

# Duck Braised with Konnyaku "Tofu"

moyu shaoya
魔芋烧鸭

Known as devil's tongue in English and "magical taro" (*moyu*) in Chinese, konnyaku, or konjac (*Amorphophallus konjac*), has eerie-looking purple flowers, each one enclosing a huge phallic spadix, and a famously offensive stink. The yam-like corms of the plant are, however, edible after processing, and are usually dried, ground and made into a kind of jelly, which is why it is sometimes referred to as konnyaku "tofu." Konnyaku tofu is well known in Japan; it is also a Sichuanese specialty, widely used in the imitation meats and seafood of Buddhist vegetarian cooking and sold in markets alongside tofu and other jellies made from rice and pulses. On Emei Shan, Sichuan's great Buddhist mountain, monks traditionally make a variety of konnyaku tofu called "snow konnyaku" (*xue moyu*), which is frozen to give it a porous, honeycombed texture.

In the following dish, long strips of konnyaku tofu are added to a rich, spicy duck stew. It's a classic Sichuanese dish that was popular when I was a student in Chengdu in the 1990s but is rarely seen on menus these days. It is thought to be of value in treating many diseases. The soft brown, translucent konnyaku can be found in the refrigerated section of Japanese food shops. Please be forewarned that it will have an arrestingly weird smell when you open the package: this is why it is blanched and soaked before cooking. Sichuanese cooks would use a whole duck; I've suggested an easier version that requires only a couple of duck legs and breasts.

2 duck legs (about 1 lb 6 oz/650g)
¾-inch piece (15g) ginger, unpeeled
1 scallion, white part only
2 duck breasts (about ¾ lb/325g), with skin
10 oz (300g) konnyaku jelly
3 tbsp cooking oil
3½ tbsp Sichuan chile bean paste
½ tsp whole Sichuan pepper
¾-inch piece (15g) pickled or fresh ginger, sliced
1 tbsp Shaoxing wine
1 tsp dark soy sauce
2 scallions, green parts only,
    or Chinese green garlic
2 tsp potato starch, mixed with 2 tbsp cold water
Salt and ground white pepper

Remove the bones from the duck legs (don't worry if you only manage to do this roughly and leave some meat on the bone: it will contribute to the flavor of the stock). Lightly smack the ginger and scallion white with the flat of a cleaver blade or a rolling pin to loosen them. Place in a saucepan, along with the duck bones, and cover with about 6¼ cups (1.5 liters) of water. Bring to a boil, skim, then turn down the heat and simmer for 1–2 hours until you have a flavorful stock. Strain the duck stock, discarding the solid ingredients.

Place the boned duck legs and the breasts, skin side down, on a chopping board and cut into strips about as wide as a finger.

Open the package of konnyaku jelly and cut into strips of a similar size. Bring some water to a boil in a kettle. Separately, bring a pot of lightly salted water to a boil and blanch the konnyaku pieces for 1 minute, then remove with a slotted spoon, transfer to a bowl and cover with boiling water from the kettle. Set aside to soak until needed.

Heat the oil in a seasoned wok over high heat. Add the duck and fry for about 4 minutes, until it is tinged with gold and smells delicious. Remove from the wok and set aside.

Carefully strain off the oil. Rinse and dry the wok, then return to medium heat with 3 tbsp oil (any leftover oil will contribute to excellent roast potatoes). Add the chile bean paste and Sichuan pepper and stir-fry gently until the oil is red and richly fragrant, taking care not to burn the seasonings.

Pour in about 2½ cups (600ml) duck stock—you can top it up with water, if necessary—and bring to a boil. Fish out and discard the solids from the chile bean paste and the Sichuan pepper with a slotted spoon or fine-mesh strainer (these will have now yielded up their flavors). Add the duck, ginger, Shaoxing wine and soy sauce. Return to a boil, skim any froth from the surface, then turn the heat down low and simmer for about 30 minutes, until the duck is tender, topping up with a little stock or water as needed.

When the duck is done, add the drained konnyaku strips and return to a boil, then turn the heat down to low. Simmer for about 5 minutes, to allow the konnyaku to absorb the flavors of the sauce (the konnyaku can become tough if boiled, which is why it should be simmered gently).

Meanwhile, cut the scallion greens or green garlic into 2-inch (5cm) lengths. When the konnyaku is ready, adjust the seasoning to taste with salt and white pepper. Add the scallion greens or green garlic and give them a lick of heat.

Finally, give the potato starch mixture a stir and add it in stages, stirring in between each addition, and adding just enough to give the liquid a nice gravy-like consistency. Serve.

# Steamed Egg Custard with Ground Pork Topping

saozi zheng dan
臊子蒸蛋

This simple dish makes a particularly lovely breakfast, perhaps alongside a bowlful of noodles, but can also be served as part of a main meal. You can jazz it up for a special occasion: the Chengdu master chef Yu Bo sometimes infuses his custard with matsutake mushrooms, and replaces the pork in the topping with ground rabbit.

You can steam the custard in two or three individual rice bowls for a breakfast dish, or in a larger, shallower bowl if you want to serve it alongside other dishes as part of a main meal, with rice. Do make sure you control the heat as you steam the eggs: if the heat is too intense they will become frothy rather than custardy. The ground pork topping can be prepared in advance.

3 large eggs
About 1 cup (225ml) hot stock or water
1 tbsp Shaoxing wine
1 tsp sesame oil
Salt

*For the topping*
2 tbsp cooking oil
2½ oz (75g) ground pork
½ tbsp Shaoxing wine
1 tsp sweet flour sauce

**First make the topping.** Heat the oil in a seasoned wok over high heat. Tip in the pork and stir-fry until it turns pale, then add the Shaoxing wine and sweet flour sauce and stir briefly until fragrant. Season with salt to taste, then set aside.

Break the eggs into a liquid measuring cup, beat until evenly mixed and note the volume, then add 1½ times as much stock or water and mix well (the stock or water should be hot, but not boiling: ideally 160–175°F [70–80°C], if you have a thermometer). Stir in the Shaoxing wine and ½ tsp salt. Use a spoon to skim off any froth from the surface, then pour into two or three rice bowls and cover with foil or small saucers.

Place the bowls in a bamboo steamer over boiling water. Cover and steam over high heat for 5 minutes, then keep the lid slightly ajar and steam over gentle heat for another 10 minutes or so, until the eggs have set to a delicate custard.

While the custard is cooking, reheat the pork topping in a small saucepan, with a little water if necessary.

When the custard is ready, spoon over the topping, drizzle with sesame oil and serve.

# Fish & Seafood

"Freshwater fish has always been a vital part of the local cuisine in this region threaded by rivers and streams"

# Fish & Seafood 鱼虾类

Because Sichuan is a landlocked province, far from the Chinese coast, saltwater fish scarcely featured in its traditional cooking. The only exception was dried seafood, such as mussels, shrimp and, for special occasions, the more exotic squid and sea cucumber. Freshwater fish, however, has always been a vital part of the local cuisine in this region threaded by rivers and streams. The Yangtze River thunders down from its source on the Tibetan plateau, circles Chongqing and then courses on toward the wetlands of the east coast and Shanghai. The Brocade River (*jinjiang*), named because Sichuan's famous woven silks were once washed in its waters, flows through Chengdu, and the Min River swirls around the feet of the giant stone Buddha at Leshan.

Over the centuries, the Sichuan region developed a reputation for the excellence of its fish. The poet Zuo Si, in his third-century ode to the ancient Shu capital (the antecedent of today's Chengdu), recalled "tasting precious fish" in the city; centuries later, the Tang-dynasty poet Du Fu said the local fish were "a pleasure to be seized." There are several notable local breeds, most famously rock carp (*yanli*), Ya'an snowtrout (*yayu*), large jiangtuan catfish, shipayu catfish and Yangtze sturgeon (*changjiang xun*), most of which are now scarce in the wild. Sichuanese cooks also use more common fish like carp (*liyu*), grass carp (*caoyu*), Chinese perch or mandarin fish (*guiyu*), catfish (*nianyu*) and crucian carp (*jiyu*), as well as paddy eels (*huangshan*) and loaches (*niqiu*). The crucian carp, although small and relatively bony, has a particularly delicious flavor and is often used to make milky-white soups and stocks. Eels and loaches, once the harvest of waterways and ponds amid the rice paddies, feature more in rustic cooking than on banquet tables. According to one of my sources, Sichuan is home to more than 120 breeds of freshwater fish.

The finest flavors come from wild river fish: those bred in lakes or paddy fields are darker in color, their flavors muted by the muddy, still waters in which they live. Some Chengdu residents remember the not-so-distant days when people bathed in the Brocade River, and when the clear waters were alive with fish and other wildlife. When I was a student in Chengdu, I did once see a cormorant fisher drifting by with his punt full of great black birds. His long-necked cormorants were fitted with tight collars so they couldn't swallow the fish they caught, but would give them up to the fisherman in exchange for tiny fish from his own supply. But this scene was a rarity, even then: pollution has wiped out most of the wildlife in the Brocade River, and those in search of unfarmed fish have to head west to the edges of the Tibetan plateau. Even there, stocks are low, and several species of fish are now officially protected.

In Sichuanese markets, fish are still leaping, living things when you buy them, and they are almost always eaten fresh. Many restaurants will bring a wriggling fish to the table in a net before they cook it—a guarantee of freshness. Sichuanese fish cooking makes much use of pickled chiles, ginger, scallions and garlic: this is said to be the origin of the famous "fish-fragrant" style of flavoring. But some Sichuanese fish dishes are also gentle and delicate, and there's a Sichuanese version of that universal Chinese treat, sweet-and-sour crispy fish.

Crazes for particular fish dishes sweep the region from time to time. In the early 2000s, Chengdu people liked to drive out of town to feast on whole, enormous bighead carp, which were presented live and then whisked away to the kitchen, to reappear a short time later in succulent chunks in a capacious enameled basin, covered in a sea of sizzling chiles and Sichuan pepper.

Like people all over China, the Sichuanese insist on serving a whole fish on New Year's Eve because the phrase "every year a fish" sounds the same as "every year a year of plenty" (*niannian you yu*). In one farmhouse I visited just after the New Year, the owners had stuck the tail of their festive fish on the kitchen wall for good luck: they told me that in the past, prosperous people liked to cover their kitchen walls in fishtails to show that they could afford to eat fish frequently.

As China has grown more prosperous and Sichuanese cuisine has begun to flourish all over the world, Sichuanese cooks have become adept at applying their genius flavoring techniques to saltwater fish and other seafood, creating popular modern dishes such as fragrant-and-hot crab and Gong Bao shrimp.

The varieties of carp and catfish used most commonly in Sichuanese cooking can be hard to find abroad, which is why I often make Sichuanese recipes with sea bream or sea bass. It's worth remembering that the keys to many of the dishes in this chapter are the seasonings and cooking method, which can work well with many different kinds of fish, including, for example, grey mullet. In general, try to choose varieties of fish with pale, silky flesh, rather than the more oily, meaty kinds of fish like salmon and tuna: I do, however, make an exception for fish braised in chile bean sauce, which works particularly well with trout.

Some Sichuanese dishes are harder to re-create outside the region, like the scrumptious barbecued fish with "flower" tofu served every evening on the streets of the Yangtze town of Luzhou. At night, the riverside district comes alive with food stalls that spill onto the streets around the White Pagoda, an ancient monument to filial piety. Many of them specialize in this particular fish dish. Carp are split open, spiced and grilled over charcoal. They are then placed with clumps of fresh white tofu on a bed of heartleaf roots in a vessel that resembles a paella pan. Finally, they are dressed with rapeseed oil, chile oil and beany seasonings, brought to a sizzling boil and served on a table-top burner with a crown of fresh herbs.

As in other parts of China, Sichuanese cooks take care to refine the flavors of fish and seafood, dispelling unpleasantly "fishy" tastes (*xingwei*) by using salt, Shaoxing wine, ginger and scallions in marinades to allow the natural savoriness of the ingredients to shine through.

# Fish Braised in Chile Bean Sauce

douban xianyu
豆瓣鲜鱼

This recipe showcases the famous Sichuan chile bean paste, made in the county town of Pixian from local *erjingtiao* chiles and fava beans, and typical of Sichuanese home cooking. The fish is clothed in a rich, ruddy sauce, flecked with green scallion and morsels of garlic and ginger. The flavor is dominated by the intensity of the chile bean paste, but the addition of a little vinegar at the end makes it sing. Sichuanese cooks typically use carp, but many different kinds of fish work well. This is the first Sichuanese dish I ever made, from a version in Yan-kit So's *Classic Chinese Cookbook*.

A common Sichuanese practice is to return any leftover sauce to the wok after the fish is eaten, add some tofu, heat it through and then continue the meal. To do this, cut some tofu into thick slices or cubes, let it sit in lightly salted water for a few minutes over very gentle heat, and then add to the reheated sauce. Simmer for a few minutes to allow the tofu to absorb the flavors, then serve.

1 whole sea bass, carp, trout or other fish (about 1½ lb/700g), scaled and cleaned, but with head and tail intact
1 tbsp Shaoxing wine
2–3 tbsp potato starch
About 7 tbsp (100ml) cooking oil
4 tbsp Sichuan chile bean paste
1½ tbsp finely chopped garlic
1 tbsp finely chopped ginger
1¼ cups (300ml) stock
½ tsp superfine sugar
1 tsp light soy sauce, or to taste (optional)
4 tbsp thinly sliced scallion greens
½ tsp Chinkiang vinegar
1 tsp sesame oil
Salt

**Make three or four diagonal cuts** into the thickest part of each side of the fish, to allow the flavors to penetrate. Rub the fish inside and out with a little salt, then rub the Shaoxing wine into its belly cavity and let rest for 10–15 minutes. Drain off any liquid and pat the fish dry. Rub 1–2 tbsp potato starch into the skin and slashes (this helps to prevent the fish from sticking as it cooks). In a small bowl, mix 1 tbsp potato starch with 2 tbsp cold water.

Add the cooking oil to a seasoned wok over high heat. When the oil is hot, slide the fish into the wok and fry on both sides until the skin is a little golden (it won't be cooked through). Don't move it around too much at the beginning, or the skin may disintegrate. Carefully turn the fish, and tilt the wok so the hot oil comes into contact with every part. When the fish is golden all over, carefully strain off the oil from the wok and slide the fish onto a plate.

Rinse the wok, scrubbing it clean if needed, then dry it. Return 4 tbsp cooking oil to the wok and place over high heat. When the oil is hot, turn down the heat to medium, add the chile bean paste and stir-fry until the oil is red and smells delicious. Add the garlic and ginger, and continue to stir-fry until you can also smell their fragrances. Pour in the stock, add the sugar and bring to a boil.

Slide the fish back into the wok and cook it for 5 minutes or so, turning it once halfway through, and seasoning with soy sauce to taste, if desired. Keep spooning the sauce over the fish as it cooks, and tilting the wok so the whole of the fish gets cooked.

Using a wok scoop and a fish spatula, carefully lift the fish out of the sauce and place it as neatly as possible on a serving dish.

Turn the heat up, stir the potato starch mixture and add just enough of it to thicken the sauce to a rich, clingy consistency (add it in a couple of stages to avoid the risk of over-thickening). Throw in the scallion greens and vinegar, stir two or three times and then switch off the heat. Finally, stir in the sesame oil and ladle the sauce over the waiting fish. Serve.

# Fish Stew with Pickled Mustard Greens

suancai yu
酸菜鱼

This delectable fish stew, said to be a 1980s innovation, became all the rage in urban Chongqing, and later in Chengdu, in the 1990s. Some say the dish was created by a humble restaurateur in the Chongqing countryside; others, more romantically, that it was invented by the wife of an elderly fisherman who accidentally dropped her husband's catch into a simmering soup of pickled greens. Whichever, it's a wonderful, hearty dish, and easy to make.

Grass carp is the favored fish, although grey mullet or sea bream work beautifully too (skinned plaice, sole and other flat fish would likely also be delicious). The mustard greens, which the Sichuanese pluck out of earthenware pickling jars as clusters of whole, long green leaves, lend the soup a delicately sour, salty flavor. Many chefs finish the dish with a dramatic sizzle of spices and oil. When I was a student in Sichuan, people used dried red chiles and red Sichuan pepper; these days, they often use green Sichuan pepper, which has a fresh, citrusy flavor that is particularly marvelous with fish. Dried green Sichuan pepper is good, while sprigs of fresh green Sichuan pepper (which you may be able to find refrigerated and vacuum-packed in Chinese shops) are even better. The Sichuanese often serve a huge fish in a vast bowlful of soup, glistening with oil and chiles—the following version is on a more modest scale.

1 whole grass carp, grey mullet or sea bream (about 1 lb 10 oz/750g), scaled and cleaned
1 tbsp Shaoxing wine
1 tbsp potato starch
1 tbsp egg white
1 scallion, white part only
2 garlic cloves
An equivalent amount of ginger
5¼ oz (150g) pickled mustard greens
2 red Sichuan pickled chiles (or 4–5 small green pickled chiles)
5 tbsp cooking oil (or a mixture of lard and cooking oil)

_To finish_
2 sprigs vacuum-packed fresh green Sichuan pepper or 2 tsp dried green Sichuan pepper
A few slices of fresh red and green chile
1–2 tbsp thinly sliced scallion greens
Salt and ground white pepper

Cut away the flesh from each side of the fish to give you two fillets, reserving the head, tail and bones (you can ask your fishmonger to do this). Use the heel of your cleaver or knife to crack the head of the fish—this will allow its flavors to emerge—and cut the backbone into about three pieces. Place the head, tail and bones in a bowl with ½ tsp salt and ½ tbsp Shaoxing wine, then mix and set aside.

Place one of the fish fillets, skin side down, on your chopping board. Starting at the tail end, and holding your knife at an angle to the board, cut the fillet into slices a little more than ¼ inch (5mm) thick, each with a piece of skin. Repeat with the other fillet. Place the fish in another bowl, add ½ tbsp Shaoxing wine, ¼ tsp salt and the starch and egg white, then mix well.

Lightly smack the scallion white with the flat of a cleaver blade or a rolling pin to loosen it. Peel and slice the garlic and ginger. Chop the pickled mustard greens at an angle into slices to match the fish. If using Sichuan pickled chiles, trim off the stem ends and gently squeeze out and discard the seeds, then cut at an angle into slices. (If using small green chiles, slice in half at an angle.) Bring 6¼ cups (1.5 liters) of water to a boil in a kettle. →

←    Heat 2 tbsp oil in a seasoned wok over high heat. Add the scallion white, ginger, garlic and chiles and stir-fry briefly until they are fragrant but not colored. Add the pickled mustard greens and stir-fry until they too are piping hot and fragrant. Pour in the hot water from the kettle and return to a vigorous boil, then add the fish head, tail and bones and fast-boil for 5–10 minutes until the stock is rich and slightly opaque. Fish out and discard the head, tail and bones.

Season the soup with salt and white pepper to taste. Then drop in all the fish slices, one by one so they don't stick together. When they are just cooked (this should take less than a minute), pour the fish stew into a serving bowl.

Place the Sichuan pepper and sliced chile in a small saucepan. In another pan or a wok, heat 3 tbsp oil over high heat until sizzling hot, then carefully pour the oil over the spices—make sure it is hot enough to produce a vigorous, fragrant sizzle (the reason for doing this in a separate pan is that green Sichuan pepper is easy to burn if you fry it directly). Immediately pour the oil, pepper and chile over the fish stew, garnish with the scallion greens and serve.

### Variation

_Dried chile and red Sichuan pepper garnish_
_Before you start cooking the fish soup, snip a handful of dried chiles in half and shake out their seeds as much as possible. Heat 3 tbsp cooking oil in a wok over medium heat until hot but not yet smoking. Add the chiles and 2 tsp whole Sichuan pepper and stir-fry until they are fragrant, and the chiles are darkening but not burned. Remove the spices with a slotted spoon or fine-mesh strainer, let cool and then finely chop them together, to make what's known as "knife-mouth" chiles (daokou haijiao). When the fish soup is ready, rinse and dry the wok, add another 3 tbsp cooking oil and heat until sizzling hot. Sprinkle the chopped chiles and pepper over the soup, and immediately pour over the hot oil, which will sizzle and fizz. Garnish with the scallion greens and serve immediately._

# Boiled Fish in a Seething Sea of Chiles

## shuizhu yu
水煮鱼

This dish, perhaps more than any other, embodies the dramatic numbing-and-hot (*mala*) excesses of chiles, Sichuan pepper and oil with which Sichuanese cuisine has taken China and the world by storm. Apparently a modern take on the classic Zigong dish of "water-boiled beef" (see p. 161), this "boiled fish" strutted onto the Sichuan dining scene in the 1990s and lured Chengdu people out of town to specialty restaurants where waiters would bring giant carp, still flapping, in nets to the table for approval. Shortly afterward, the waiters would reappear with huge enamel basins laden with fizzing oil, red chiles, Sichuan pepper and slippery chunks of fish for the customers to devour.

This version is scaled down for the home kitchen, but it's still a fabulous centerpiece for a feast, especially if brought to the table while the oil is still bubbling away like a witch's cauldron. The fish slices should be beautifully tender and the chiles should be fragrant but not burned, retaining most of their red color. The oil and chiles themselves are not supposed to be eaten: just pluck out the sliced fish and bean sprouts with chopsticks or a slotted spoon.

You must make the fragrant infused oil a day or two in advance (if you use plain cooking oil, the dish will seem greasy). The recipe leaves you with more of this than you need, but the strained oil keeps well for use in other dishes. Ask your fishmonger to fillet the fish, but make sure you get the head, tail and bones as well as the fillets.

1 whole sea bream, grass carp or sea bass
   (1 lb 10 oz–1¾ lb/750–800g),
   scaled, cleaned and filleted
1½ oz (40g) dried chiles
2 tbsp whole Sichuan pepper
1 tbsp cooking oil
2 cups (200g) bean sprouts
1 cup plus 1 tbsp (250ml) clear spicy infused oil
   (see p. 461)
Salt and ground white pepper

*For the marinade*
½ tsp salt
1 tbsp Shaoxing wine
1 tbsp egg white
1½ tbsp potato starch

*For the broth*
Head, tail and bones from the fish
1 scallion, white part only
2 tbsp cooking oil
3 garlic cloves, peeled and sliced
An equivalent amount of ginger,
   peeled and sliced
1 tbsp Shaoxing wine

**Place one of the fish fillets on a chopping board,** skin side down. Holding your knife at an angle and cutting toward the tail, cut the fillet into slices ⅛–¼ inch (3–5mm) thick. Repeat with the other fillet. Place the fish in a bowl, then add the marinade ingredients and mix well.

Snip the chiles in half or into ¾-inch (2cm) sections and shake out the seeds as much as possible, then place in a small saucepan, along with the Sichuan pepper.

Heat the cooking oil in a seasoned wok. Add the bean sprouts and stir-fry until piping hot, seasoning with salt to taste. Pile them up in a deep serving bowl.

Next make the broth. Use the corner of a cleaver blade or the tip of a sturdy knife to make a crack in the fish head. Cut the bones into a few chunks and set aside. Lightly smack the scallion white with the flat of a cleaver blade or a rolling pin to loosen it. Put the kettle on to boil. →

← Rinse and dry the wok if necessary and return to high heat. Add the cooking oil and, when it is hot, add the scallion white, garlic and ginger and stir-fry until they smell delicious.

Pour in 3¾ cups (900ml) hot water from the kettle, along with the Shaoxing wine and the fish head, tail and bones. Bring to a boil and then let it bubble away for about 7 minutes, until the liquid is milky and flavorful. Strain out and discard the solid ingredients, skim off any foam from the surface and then season with salt and white pepper to taste.

Drop the fish slices into the broth, separating them gently with long cooking chopsticks or tongs. When the slices are just cooked, which will take around a minute, scoop them out with a slotted spoon and pile them on top of the bean sprouts in the serving bowl. Pour over the broth.

Give the wok a quick rinse and dry, then return to high heat. Add the infused oil and heat until a few drops dripped onto the dried chiles and Sichuan pepper in the saucepan produce a fizzing sound. Working quickly, pour the oil over the chiles and Sichuan pepper. Let them fizz for a few seconds until they are darkening slightly, and then swiftly pour over the fish. Rush the dish to the table before the fizzing stops!

Variation

*You can make this with fillets only, if you prefer, substituting 2½ cups (600ml) everyday stock (see p. 463) for the stock made from the fish head and bones.*

# Dry-braised Fish with Pork in Spicy Sauce

## ganshao xianyu
## 干烧鲜鱼

Dry-braising is a distinctively Sichuanese version of a cooking method used all over China. All braised dishes involve heating ingredients over high heat before simmering them gently in liquid, which is then reduced or thickened with a mixture of starch and water. With dry-braising, however, the liquid is allowed to evaporate completely, until all the seasonings have been absorbed by the main ingredient or cling to it in a delicious glaze. Starch is never added to thicken the sauce. The following is a Sichuanese specialty and one of my favorite local dishes. By the time you serve the fish, the braising liquid has entirely disappeared, and the fish relaxes in a pool of glossy red oil, with a scattering of scarlet chiles, pale scallions, crisp pork and dark salted mustard greens. It is not excessively hot. The classic version is made with rock carp (*yanli*), one of the most esteemed local river fish, but grey mullet works well too, and sea bass is sensational. Pescetarians may omit the pork and use vegetable stock.

The fish tends to disintegrate slightly with the lengthy cooking, so a little care is needed when transferring it to the serving dish. If you follow Sichuanese practice and let your guests use their chopsticks to help themselves to pieces of fish, most of the oil will be left on the plate, but it's still a rich dish and is best served with plain rice and one or two simple stir-fried vegetables. I honed the details of this recipe with the help of Chengdu chef Zhang Xiaozhong.

*1 whole rainbow trout, sea bream, grey mullet or sea bass (about 1 lb 5 oz/600g), scaled and cleaned*

*1-inch piece (20g) piece of ginger, unpeeled, plus 1 tbsp finely chopped ginger*

*2 tbsp Shaoxing wine*

*4 scallions, white parts only*

*½ red bell pepper or 3 Sichuan pickled chiles*

*7 tbsp cooking oil*

*2½ oz (75g) ground or finely chopped skinless pork belly*

*2 tsp potato starch*

*1½ tbsp Sichuan chile bean paste*

*1 tbsp finely chopped garlic*

*2 tbsp finely chopped Yibin yacai preserved vegetable or preserved mustard tuber (zhacai), rinsed and squeezed dry*

*1 cup plus 1 tbsp (250ml) stock*

*1 tsp superfine sugar*

*¼ tsp dark soy sauce*

*1 tsp sesame oil*

*Salt*

**Make four or five diagonal cuts** into the thickest part of the fish, and then four or five diagonal cuts in the opposite direction, so you end up with a criss-cross pattern. Repeat on the other side.

Lightly smack the piece of ginger with the flat of a cleaver blade or a rolling pin to loosen it. Rub both sides of the fish with ½ tsp salt and 1 tbsp Shaoxing wine, then tuck the smacked ginger into its belly cavity.

Cut four 2–2½-inch (5–6 cm) lengths of scallion white, and then cut three strips of red bell pepper of a similar size; if using Sichuan pickled chiles, cut into 2–2½-inch (5–6 cm) lengths, discarding the seeds.

Heat 1 tbsp cooking oil in a seasoned wok over high heat and stir-fry the pork until pale and cooked through. Set aside.

Rinse, dry and re-season the wok if necessary. Discard the ginger from the fish's belly and pat the fish dry. Rub the potato starch into the cuts on both of its sides. Heat 2 tbsp oil in the wok over high heat, and sprinkle a little salt around the base of the wok to help prevent sticking.  →

←    When the oil is hot, slide in the fish and fry until golden on both sides, tilting the wok so you brown the base of the tail too. (In restaurants, the fish would be deep-fried, but home-cooks normally fry in shallow oil.) Slide the fish onto a plate and set aside.

Rinse, dry and re-season the wok if necessary, then heat over high heat with 4 tbsp oil. When the oil is hot, turn down the heat to medium, add the chile bean paste and stir-fry until the oil is red and fragrant. Add the chopped ginger, garlic, preserved vegetable, scallion whites, red bell pepper or pickled chiles and cooked pork, and stir-fry until they all smell delicious.

Pour in the stock and bring to a boil. Add the sugar, soy sauce and 1 tbsp Shaoxing wine, then slide the fish back into the wok. Simmer over gentle heat for 8–10 minutes, basting the fish in the sauce, and shaking the wok gently from time to time to prevent sticking. Tilt the wok to make sure the head and tail also absorb the flavors of the sauce, and carefully turn the fish over halfway through the cooking time.

By the end, the fish should be cooked through, and the sauce reduced to a wonderful sticky glaze. Sprinkle in the sesame oil, then ease the fish onto a serving dish and pour over the sauce. Arrange the scallion whites alternately with the strips of red bell pepper or pickled chile on top of the fish.

# Dry-braised Shrimp

## ganshao xia
## 干烧虾

This dish is based on my memory of a version that was served at banquets at the Dragon Wonton restaurant in Chengdu. Like other Sichuanese dishes made with fresh seafood, this is a relatively recent invention, in which the classic "dry-braising" method is applied to shrimp.

You may keep the shrimp whole, or remove their heads and legs, but do leave the shells and tails intact—and remember to use a thin skewer or a darning needle to poke out the dark thread of intestine that runs down the back of each shrimp.

By the end of the cooking, the shrimp will be coated in a luscious mess of ginger, garlic, chile and pickles. Put them in your mouth whole and suck off the sauce, then extract the meat with your teeth and tongue, removing the remains of the shells from your mouth with chopsticks.

1 lb 5 oz (600g) shell-on tiger shrimp, fresh or frozen
3 scallions, white and green parts separated
2 Sichuan pickled chiles or ¼ red bell pepper
3 tbsp Yibin yacai preserved vegetable
At least 1⅔ cups (400ml) cooking oil, for deep-frying,
      plus 1 tbsp more
1 tbsp Sichuan chile bean paste
1 tsp finely chopped garlic
1 tsp finely chopped ginger
10 tbsp (150ml) everyday stock (see p. 463)
½ tsp superfine sugar
1 tsp light soy sauce
1 tsp dark soy sauce

### For the marinade
1-inch piece (20g) ginger, unpeeled
2 scallions, white parts only
½ tsp salt
1½ tbsp Shaoxing wine

Rinse the shrimp, then drain well and place in a bowl. For the marinade, lightly smack the ginger and scallion whites with the flat of a cleaver or a rolling pin to loosen them. Add to the shrimp with the salt and Shaoxing wine. Let rest for 15 minutes.

Cut the scallion whites at a steep angle into "horse ear" slices, and cut the greens into 2-inch (5cm) lengths. Cut the pickled chiles into "horse ears," or the red bell pepper into thin strips about the length of the shrimp. Rinse the preserved vegetable and squeeze dry, then stir-fry briefly in 1 tbsp oil until fragrant.

Remove the shrimp from the marinade and shake dry. Heat the deep-frying oil in a wok to 355°F (180°C), add the shrimp and fry briefly until they curl and change color. Remove from the oil with a slotted spoon. Reheat the oil to 355°F (180°C), add the shrimp and fry for a minute or two until crisp. Remove from the oil and drain on paper towels. Carefully pour off all but 3 tbsp oil from the wok and return to medium heat. Add the chile bean paste and stir-fry gently until the oil is red and fragrant. Tip in the scallion whites, pickled chiles or red bell pepper, garlic and ginger and stir-fry until you can smell them too. Add the shrimp, stock, sugar and both soy sauces, then bring to a boil. Let it bubble away, stirring constantly and spooning the sauce over the shrimp, until the liquid has mostly evaporated. Add the preserved vegetable and stir until all that is left of the sauce is fragrant oil and a sticky glaze. Stir in the scallion greens and serve.

# Sweet-and-sour Crispy Fish

tangcu cuipi yu
糖醋脆皮鱼

This dish is a real party piece—a whole, delectably crunchy fish draped in sweet-and-sour sauce and scattered with slivers of brilliant red and white garnishes. It's a popular banquet delicacy in Sichuan and often the centerpiece of a dinner out with friends. Sichuanese cooks usually make it with grass carp or mandarin fish, but I've successfully used the more readily available sea bass and also grey mullet. The dish looks most splendid when a whole fish is used, but you do need a wok or deep-fryer large enough to hold it. If this isn't feasible, cut the fish in half and reassemble it on the serving plate, or use large boneless chunks of firm, white-fleshed fish (these can be simply dusted with dry potato starch just before frying). Please note that this is one of the more challenging dishes in this book.

Do make sure you deep-fry the fish twice, as the recipe advises; otherwise it may become crisp and golden before the flesh is cooked through.

1 whole sea bass, grass carp or grey mullet
  (1 lb 6 oz–1½ lbs/650–700g), scaled and cleaned
About 1¾ cup (200g) potato starch
Cooking oil, for deep-frying, plus 1 tbsp more
3 scallions, white parts only
3 Sichuan pickled chiles or ¼ red bell pepper
Salt

For the marinade
1 tbsp Shaoxing wine
2 whole scallions
1–1½-inch piece (20–30g) ginger, unpeeled

For the sauce
1 tbsp light soy sauce
6 tbsp superfine sugar
3 tsp finely chopped garlic
3 tsp finely chopped ginger
4 scallions, white parts only, thinly sliced
1¼ cups (300ml) everyday stock (see p. 463)
1 tbsp potato starch, mixed with 3 tbsp cold water
3 tbsp Chinkiang vinegar
½ tsp sesame oil

**Place the fish on its side.** Using a sharp knife or cleaver, cut down into the thickest part of the fish near the backbone, about 2 inches (5cm) from the base of the fish head and at right angles to the backbone itself. When the knife touches the backbone, swivel the blade inside the flesh to face the head and continue cutting parallel to the backbone and toward the head for another 1¼ inches (3cm). This will create a thick flap of fish flesh. Make further, similar cuts at 2-inch (5cm) intervals until you reach the thinner tail flesh, and then repeat on the other side of the fish, again cutting down to the spine and back toward the head. (When you have finished, if you hold the fish by its tail, the flaps should hang outward slightly.) Use the back corner of a cleaver or the tip of a sturdy knife to pierce the head of the fish, making a gash, to allow its flavors to emerge. Trim the tail into a tidy shape, if desired.

Rub the fish, inside and out, with ¾ tsp salt and the Shaoxing wine. Lightly smack the whole scallions and ginger with the flat of a cleaver blade or a rolling pin to loosen them, roughly chop, then stuff into the belly cavity and flaps in the fish. Let marinate for about 30 minutes. →

←   In a bowl, mix ¾ cup plus 2 tbsp (100g) potato starch with enough water (a bit less than 7 tbsp/100ml) to make a fairly thick but still drippy paste, then stir in 1 tbsp cooking oil.

Cut the scallion whites and pickled chiles or red bell pepper into very fine slivers and let rest in a bowl of cold water until needed. Assemble the other ingredients near the stove, and make sure your serving dish is on hand.

Heat the deep-frying oil to 390°F (200°C). Discard the scallions and ginger from the fish and pat it dry with paper towels. Dust all over, including into the flaps, with the remaining, dry potato starch. When the oil has reached temperature, hold the fish by its tail and coat with the potato starch paste, using your fingers to push it into all the crevices. The flaps of flesh should hang outward slightly, laden with paste. Still holding the fish by its tail, lower the head into the oil and allow it to fry for a couple of minutes as you ladle hot oil over the body of the fish and into the flaps. When the oil has fixed the flaps in their open position, standing stiffly out from the body, submerge the fish completely in the oil and fry for another minute or two until the flesh is just cooked. If your wok isn't large enough to fully submerge the fish, keep ladling over the hot oil, and turn it over halfway through. Carefully lift the fish out of the wok and onto your serving dish.

Reheat the oil to 390°F (200°C). Submerge the fish in the hot oil and fry for a few minutes until the coating is crisp and golden, ladling oil over the fish if it is not fully submerged. Carefully remove it and place it belly-down on your serving dish. Cover your hand with a clean dish towel and gently squash the fish—this will help the flavors of the sauce to penetrate. Keep the fish warm.

For the sauce, combine the soy sauce, sugar and 1 tsp salt in a bowl. Carefully strain off the deep-frying oil and wipe or brush the wok clean. Return about 3 tbsp oil to the wok and place over high heat. When the oil is hot, add the garlic, ginger and scallion whites and stir-fry briefly until they are richly fragrant but not colored. Pour half the stock into the wok. Stir the rest of the stock into the bowl of seasoned soy sauce, then add to the wok. Bring to a boil. Give the potato starch mixture a stir and add to the wok in two or three stages, stirring as the sauce thickens. Stir in the vinegar and give it a lick of heat.

Finally, off the heat, stir in the sesame oil and ladle the sauce over the fish. Garnish with the slivers of scallion and pickled chile or red bell pepper and serve.

# Numbing-and-hot Tiny Fish

## mala ziyu
麻辣仔鱼

At many riverside towns and villages in the Sichuanese countryside, tiny fish and freshwater shrimp are deep-fried, spiced and then sold as a delicious, crunchy snack. In Leshan, where the world's largest statue of the Buddha presides over the sweeping brown waters of the Min River, I remember buying them from a tiny stall on the riverbank. Fresh and crisp, they left the tingling traces of chile and Sichuan pepper on my lips.

This recipe is splendidly easy and, served hot, makes a wonderful snack for a cocktail party. I've suggested using frozen whitebait as the fish, because they are relatively easy to find, but you can also use the tiny frozen shrimp sold in some Asian supermarkets or the more familiar large shrimp; the advantage of the tiny fish and shrimp is that you can eat them whole. You could add salt to the final seasoning if you wish, but I don't find it necessary with whitebait.

1 lb 2 oz (500g) frozen whitebait, defrosted
½ tsp salt
1 tbsp Shaoxing wine
1½-inch piece (30g) ginger, unpeeled
2 scallions
Cooking oil, for deep-frying
⅔ cup (75g) potato starch

### For the seasoning
1–3 tsp ground chiles, to taste
½–1½ tsp ground roasted Sichuan pepper

**Place the fish in a bowl,** add the salt and Shaoxing wine and mix well. Lightly smack the ginger and scallions with the flat of a cleaver blade or a rolling pin to loosen them, and then roughly chop. Add to the fish and set aside for about 15 minutes.

Heat the deep-frying oil in a wok to 375°F (190°C). Remove the ginger and scallions from the bowl of fish. Shake the fish dry in a colander and then toss them in the potato starch, making sure they are evenly coated.

Fry the fish in two or three batches until they are crisp—about 2–3 minutes per batch. Remove and drain on paper towels.

When the fish are all done, carefully strain off the deep-frying oil and wipe or brush the wok clean. Return 2 tbsp oil to the wok and place over medium heat. Add the ground chiles and stir-fry briefly, until the oil is red and fragrant, taking great care not to let them burn. Add the Sichuan pepper and mix well, then tip in the fish and toss briskly to distribute the spices evenly. Serve immediately.

### Variation

You can use the same method to make delicious potato fries: deep-fry them as normal, then toss in a hot wok with oil, ground chiles, ground roasted Sichuan pepper and salt to taste.

# Gong Bao Shrimp
# with Cashews

gongbao xiaqiu
宫保虾球

As recently as the 1990s, very little
fresh seafood was eaten in Chengdu.
Although the markets were full of paddy
eels, loaches and freshwater fish, fresh
seafood could be found only at the Green
Stone Bridge (*qingshiqiao*) wholesale
market and a few fabulously expensive
Cantonese restaurants. These days,
seafood is more widely available, and
Sichuanese chefs at home and abroad
have been giving it the Sichuanese flavor
treatment. One of my favorites among the
new-wave Sichuanese seafood dishes is
Gong Bao shrimp, a luxurious version of
the popular chicken dish. Fresh shrimp
are poached in oil to keep them silky-
soft and then wokked with the traditional
Gong Bao seasonings: chiles, Sichuan
pepper and a delicate "lychee" sauce
(see p. 473). For an extra burst of heat,
stir in about1 tbsp chile oil just before
serving.

9 oz (250g) peeled raw shrimp, fresh or defrosted
10 dried chiles
5 scallions, white parts only
1 celery stick
1¼ cups (300ml) cooking oil
½ tsp whole Sichuan pepper
2 garlic cloves, peeled and thinly sliced
An equivalent amount of ginger, peeled and thinly sliced
½ cup (75g) fried or roasted cashews

*For the marinade*
¼ tsp salt
1 tsp Shaoxing wine
2 tbsp potato starch
1 tbsp egg white

*For the sauce*
3 tsp superfine sugar
¼ tsp potato starch
1 tsp Shaoxing wine
1 tsp light soy sauce
2½ tsp Chinkiang vinegar

**With a sharp knife,** make a slit lengthwise down the back of
each shrimp, through the thickest part. Place in a bowl, add the
marinade ingredients and refrigerate, preferably for a few hours.
Snip the chiles in half or into ¾-inch (2cm) sections and shake
out the seeds. Cut the scallion whites into ½-inch (1cm) slices.
Cut the celery at an angle into diamond shapes. Combine the
sauce ingredients with 1½ tbsp cold water in a small bowl.

Heat the oil in a seasoned wok to 300°F (150°C) (hot enough to
produce a notable, though not violent, sizzle around a test shrimp).
Add the shrimp, separating them with long cooking chopsticks
or tongs, then add the celery. When the shrimp are half-cooked,
remove them and the celery with a slotted spoon and set aside.

Carefully pour off all but about 3 tbsp of the oil from the wok and
return to high heat. Add the chiles and Sichuan pepper and stir-
fry briefly until the chiles are fragrant. Add the garlic, ginger
and scallion whites and stir-fry until you can smell them. Tip
in the shrimp and celery and stir-fry until just cooked (test a
shrimp to make sure). Give the sauce a stir, pour into the wok
and stir as the sauce thickens and coats the shrimp. Finally, stir
in the cashews and serve.

# Fish with Fresh Chile and Green Sichuan Pepper

tengjiao yu

藤椒鱼

Since green Sichuan pepper burst onto the Sichuan culinary scene in the early twenty-first century, its zingy, fruity flavor has inspired a whole host of new dishes. This recipe is based on one I enjoyed at the Taolin restaurant in Chengdu, a gorgeous assembly of slippery fish with bright red and green chiles and lavish amounts of fresh green Sichuan pepper, which I've attempted to re-create with the advice of the restaurant's Chef Yu.

If you can find it, use fresh vacuum-packed Sichuan pepper; otherwise, dried green Sichuan pepper is fine. The level of heat will depend on the kind of chiles you use: I prefer to use mild chiles that provide a splash of color with heat that is not overwhelming. This recipe is similar to that for boiled fish in a seething sea of chiles (see p. 223), but here I've suggested using fish fillets rather than a whole fish. Note that the infused oil must be made at least 24 hours in advance.

¾ lb (325g) fillets of sea bream,
  sea bass or grass carp
2¼ oz (60g) red chiles, or to taste
2¼ oz (60g) green chiles, or to taste
2 scallions
2 tbsp dried green Sichuan pepper
  or a few sprigs of fresh green Sichuan pepper
1 tbsp cooking oil
2 cups (200g) bean sprouts
¾ cup plus 2 tbsp (200ml) clear spicy infused oil (see p. 461)
Salt and ground white pepper

For the marinade
½ tsp salt
1 tbsp Shaoxing wine
1 tbsp egg white
1½ tbsp potato starch

For the broth
2 cups (500ml) everyday stock (see p. 463)
1 scallion, white part only
2 tbsp cooking oil
3 garlic cloves, peeled and sliced
An equivalent amount of ginger, peeled and sliced
2 tsp light soy sauce

**Place each fish fillet on a chopping board,** skin side down. Holding your knife at an angle and cutting toward the tail, cut the fish into slices ⅛–¼ inch (3–5mm) thick. Place all the fish slices in a bowl, add the marinade ingredients and mix well. Set aside while you prepare the other ingredients.

Thinly slice the red and green chiles, discarding their stems and any loose seeds. Separate the green and white parts of the scallions, then cut the whites into ¼-inch (5mm) slices and thinly slice the greens. Place all the chiles in a small saucepan with the green Sichuan pepper and the scallion whites.

Heat the cooking oil in a seasoned wok. Add the bean sprouts and stir-fry briefly, just until piping hot, seasoning with salt to taste. Pile them up in a deep serving bowl.

Next make the broth. Bring the stock to a boil and keep it warm. Lightly smack the scallion white with the flat of a cleaver blade or a rolling pin to loosen it. Rinse and dry the wok if necessary, then return to high heat and add the cooking oil. When the oil is hot, add the scallion white, garlic and ginger and stir-fry until they smell delicious. Pour in the hot stock and bring back to a boil, then add the soy sauce and season with salt and ground white pepper to taste.

Drop the marinated fish slices into the broth, gently separating them with long cooking chopsticks or tongs. When they are just cooked, which will take around a minute, scoop out with a slotted spoon and pile on top of the bean sprouts, then pour over the broth.

Give the wok a quick rinse and dry, then return it to high heat. Add the infused oil and heat until a few drops dripped onto the chiles in the saucepan produces a loud, dramatic fizz. Carefully pour the hot oil over the chiles and other aromatics and let them fizz for a few seconds until they smell wonderful, then swiftly pour over the fish. Serve immediately.

# Tofu

"Tofu is one of the most nutritious and versatile of all Chinese foods and, in Sichuanese hands, one of the most gorgeously satisfying"

# Tofu 豆腐类

Tofu (*doufu*) is one of the most nutritious and versatile of all Chinese foods and, in Sichuanese hands, one of the most gorgeously satisfying. In the West, tofu is often seen as a poor substitute for meat, but while it is a vital food for vegetarians in China, it's also an integral part of mainstream diets. Sichuanese tofu comes in many forms: not only plain white tofu, but thin, golden slabs of smoked tofu (*doufu gan*); glossy chunks of firm tofu that have been simmered in five-spice broth (*wuxiang doufu*); sheets of leather-thin "tofu skin" (*doufu pi*); sausage-shaped rolls of tofu (*suji*, "vegetarian chicken"); tender silken or "flower" tofu (*douhua*); and ripe-smelling fermented tofu in aromatic chile oil (*doufu ru*).

Tofu can be eaten in many different ways. Smoked or spiced tofu can be sliced, dressed in a spicy sauce and consumed directly as a snack, or stir-fried with other ingredients. Fermented tofu, the Chinese equivalent of ripe blue cheese, is eaten as a relish with rice or used in marinades. Plain white tofu can be braised in a wok, directly or after deep-frying, or added to soups. Before it is cooked, this kind of tofu is usually left to soak for a few minutes in very hot, lightly salted water, which heats the curd and removes any lingering taste of the coagulant, refreshing its flavor.

Tofu is made from soy beans, the richest of all plant protein sources. The raw beans are not easily digestible, so they are normally fermented, sprouted or transformed into tofu before they are eaten. To make tofu, dried soy beans are soaked in cold water for several hours or overnight. They are then ground with fresh water to make "bean-milk" (*dounai*) and strained through muslin to remove the solid beany residue—this residue (*douzha*) may be used as animal feed, but can also be cooked in various ways, for example in the Sichuanese dish of duck with tofu residue (*douzha yazi*). The strained soy milk is boiled and simmered, and then a coagulant is added, either gypsum or mineral salts (typically known in English by their Japanese name, nigari). When nigari is used, a salt solution is gradually stirred into a potful of heated soy milk until curds start to form; gypsum may be added off the heat.

The fresh, unpressed curds are known as silken or "flower" tofu (*douhua*, literally "bean flower"). For firmer tofu that can be cut with a knife and holds its shape, the curdled liquid is poured into a mold lined with muslin and pressed in a vice to expel water. The final consistency of the tofu depends on the amount of water squeezed out: the plain white tofu used to make mapo tofu, for example, remains wobbly and tender, while firm tofu (literally "dry tofu," *doufugan*) is pressed to the consistency of Edam cheese. Firm tofu may subsequently be simmered in a spiced broth or smoked on a rack over the embers of a wood fire.

Chinese legend has it that tofu was the invention of a second-century king of Huainan, Liu An, but the earliest known written reference to it isn't until much later, in a tenth-century work by Tao Gu, and its historical origins are mysterious. There are striking similarities in method between the manufacture of tofu and simple cheeses, which has led to some fascinating conjecture about whether tofu was developed in China through contact with nomadic cheese-making peoples. All that is known for certain is that by the time of the Song dynasty (960–1279 AD) it had become a popular Chinese food.

Gourmets insist that the quality of the water used to make tofu is a crucial determinant of its quality and flavor. For this reason, some places in Sichuan with particularly fine water sources are celebrated for their tofu, like Xiba, in the south of the province. In nearby Leshan, where the giant Buddha draws many visitors, there are specialty Xiba tofu restaurants that offer thirty or forty different dishes made with fresh Xiba tofu. In particular, southeastern Sichuanese "flower" tofu is often known as "running water" tofu (*huoshui douhua*), apparently because it was traditionally made with fresh spring water.

Even this "flower" or silken tofu has many distinct types. In southern Sichuan, the milk is usually set with bittern or mineral salts (*yanlu* or *danba*), a by-product of the local salt-mining industry; in other places, including Chengdu, gypsum is commonly used. The texture of the tofu depends on the coagulant: tofu made with gypsum is custard-like and reminiscent of Italian panna cotta, while tofu made with nigari has a slightly elastic quality, which means that clumps of it can be picked up with chopsticks and dipped in a sauce—the way it is normally eaten in southern Sichuan. Silken tofu so tender that it can only be scooped up with a spoon is known as tofu "brain" (*doufu nao*), and is often consumed in a porridgy, starch-thickened liquid with spicy seasonings and crunchy garnishes.

In some parts of Sichuan, they stir finely chopped sweet potato leaves or other greens into the soy milk to make vegetable "flower" tofu (*cai douhua*). In Luzhou, I even managed to track down pork "flower" tofu (*rou douhua*), for which morsels of cooked ground pork were added to the soy milk just before coagulation; the meat-speckled tofu was simmered in chicken stock and served with a gorgeous dip made from roasted green chiles. The most extraordinary variety of "flower" tofu I've ever tasted, however, was in Hejiang, in southeastern Sichuan. This black "flower" tofu (*hei douhua*), a local specialty, was made from black soy beans and was a stunning, purplish-gray color. We ate it for breakfast with spicy dips and plain steamed rice. (I have tried making this at home, but only achieved a very pale purple tint: perhaps because, as one friend suggested, locals use a variety of beans with more deeply colored skins.)

Fermented tofu is a wonderful product that is largely ignored in the West, but which, in my opinion, should be adopted immediately by vegetarians, vegans and anyone trying to reduce the amount of meat in their diet. It is made by encouraging cubes of fairly firm tofu to grow a thick coat of fluffy white mold. The traditional method involves placing the tofu in bamboo baskets and leaving it in a shady place, covered with pumpkin leaves, until ambient molds do their work; these days, specialty makers inoculate the tofu with a mix of suitable microorganisms. The tofu is then packed into jars with salt-brine, liquor and spices and left to ferment. In Sichuan, naturally, they like to add chile to their fermented tofu. Sometimes the tofu is matured in jars full of rapeseed oil laced with ground chile, Sichuan pepper and spices. Alternatively, the cubes can be dipped into strong liquor, then salt and finally ground chiles and Sichuan pepper before being packed into jars. Fermented tofu of all kinds can be used in sauces and marinades, but is often eaten straight from the jar with rice or congee: just serve a cube in a dipping dish with your rice, and pluck a morsel with your chopsticks to eat with each mouthful of rice (it's also delicious on hot toast).

One other, intriguing Sichuanese variety of tofu goes by the name of tofu "curtains" (*doufu lianzi*), one of the so-called "three matchless delicacies" of Huaiyuan, just outside Chengdu—the other two, in case you're interested, are steamed rice cakes (*donggao*) and leaf-wrapped glutinous rice dumplings (*ye'er ba*). Tofu "curtains" are made by placing rolls of tofu skin on bamboo slats until they are covered in snow-white mold. The fermentation gives the tofu a deliciously rich, slightly cheesy flavor. At one memorable lunch in Huaiyuan, local chef Fu Qiang served some of my friends and me braised sliced tofu "curtains" in a fabulous "home-style" sauce that was lavish with chile bean paste, garlic, ginger and scallion.

Clay pots of soy sauce maturing
on the banks of the Yangtze River
at the Xianshi Soy Sauce Factory
in Hejiang, southern Sichuan

TOFU

# Mapo Tofu

## mapo doufu
## 麻婆豆腐

This glorious dish, sometimes known in English as pock-marked old woman's tofu, is named after the smallpox-scarred wife of a restaurateur. In the late nineteenth century, "old mother Chen" (*chen mapo*) is said to have cooked this up near the Bridge of Ten Thousand Blessings in the north of Chengdu for passing laborers, who would lay down their loads of cooking oil to eat lunch before continuing on their way to the city's markets.

Heartwarming, homely and utterly delicious, it's one of the most famous Sichuanese dishes, and epitomizes the spicy generosity of the folk cooking of the region. The Sichuan pepper will make your lips tingle pleasantly, and the tender tofu will slip smoothly down your throat.

Mapo tofu makes the perfect riposte to those who consider tofu boring, and tends to seduce meat-eaters and—if you omit the meat and use a vegetable stock—vegetarians alike. I probably cook it more frequently than any other Sichuanese dish.

Traditionally, the tofu is cooked with ground beef, but many restaurants, even in Chengdu, use pork instead. I often make a vegetarian version: the rich, savory chile bean paste and fermented beans mean the meat is rarely missed. In Sydney, I once made it with ground wallaby: stunningly good!

If you can find it, use Chinese green garlic instead of the scallions; alternatively, use sliced baby leeks or the green shoots that emerge from forgotten garlic bulbs in your kitchen. →

1 lb 2 oz (500g) plain white tofu
2 scallions or 2 stalks Chinese green garlic
6 tbsp cooking oil
3½ oz (100g) ground beef
2½ tbsp Sichuan chile bean paste
1 tbsp fermented black beans
2 tsp ground chiles
1 tbsp finely chopped garlic
1 tbsp finely chopped ginger
¾ cup (175ml) stock or water
¼ tsp ground white pepper
1 tbsp potato starch,
    mixed with 2½ tbsp cold water
¼–1 tsp ground roasted Sichuan pepper

Cut the tofu into ¾-inch (2cm) cubes and let steep in very hot, lightly salted water while you prepare the other ingredients. Cut the scallions or green garlic into ¾-inch (2cm) lengths.

Heat a seasoned wok over high heat. Pour in 1 tbsp cooking oil and heat until the sides of the wok have begun to smoke. Add the beef and stir-fry until it is fully cooked and fragrant, breaking the clumps of meat into tiny pieces as you go. Remove from the wok with a slotted spoon and set aside.

Rinse and dry the wok if necessary, then re-season it and return to medium heat. Pour in 5 tbsp cooking oil and swirl it around. Add the chile bean paste and stir-fry until the oil is a rich red color and smells delicious. Next add the black beans and ground chiles and stir-fry for a few seconds more until you can smell them too, then do the same with the garlic and ginger. Take care not to overheat the aromatics—you want to end up with a thick, fragrant sauce, and the secret is to let them sizzle gently, allowing the oil to coax out their flavors.

Remove the tofu from the hot water with a perforated ladle, shaking off any excess liquid, and place it gently into the wok. Sprinkle over the beef, then add the stock or water and white pepper. Nudge the tofu tenderly into the sauce with the back of your ladle or wok scoop to avoid breaking up the cubes.

Bring to a boil, then simmer for a couple of minutes to allow the tofu to absorb the flavors of the seasonings. If you're using green garlic (or baby leeks or garlic sprouts), stir them in now. →

← This dish is most delicious when made with mature Pixian chile bean paste, with its deep chestnut color and ripe savory flavor. Adjust the final sprinkling of Sichuan pepper according to your guests' tastes (Sichuanese people can take about four times as much pepper as outsiders, in my experience).

← When they are just cooked, add a little of the potato starch mixture and stir gently as the liquid thickens. Repeat this twice more, until the sauce clings deliciously to the seasonings and tofu (don't add more than you need). If you're using scallions, add them now, nudging them gently into the sauce.

Pour everything into a deep serving bowl. Sprinkle with the ground roasted Sichuan pepper and serve.

# Home-made Nigari "Flower" Tofu

## huoshui douhua
## 活水豆花

It was a gorgeous spring day, and we'd stopped off at an old town in southern Sichuan. In teahouses along the meandering main street, elderly people gossiped over their playing cards, smoking tobacco in bamboo pipes. An artisan was crafting parasols from bamboo splints and oiled paper painted with colored flowers. In a small restaurant open to the street, noisy with laughter and conversation, we lunched on fish-fragrant pork, yard-long beans stir-fried with chile, leaf-wrapped cones of glutinous rice (zongzi) and bowlfuls of fresh "flower" tofu (douhua).

Freshly made "flower" tofu, served warm with a spicy dip, is one of the joys of eating in southern Sichuan. It is just fresh soy-milk curds that have not been pressed to make firmer tofu. The soy beans must be soaked overnight before you make the tofu, and you'll need a piece of muslin large enough to gather into a bundle around the soy milk, and a thermometer. The coagulant, nigari, can be bought online; you'll also need a wok or saucepan sufficiently deep that the head of froth created as the milk boils does not overflow. This recipe makes about 4 servings.

The tofu is served with glorious dips made from chiles, oil, soy sauce, salt, crushed nuts, chopped herbs and other ingredients. Many cooks add scallions or spearmint; some stir in chopped peanuts or pumpkin seeds for crunch; others include morsels of datoucai preserved vegetable or preserved duck egg for extra flavor. →

1¼ cups (250g) dried yellow soy beans
½ tsp cooking oil
1¼ tsp nigari (coagulant mineral salts)
A dip of your choice (see next page)

**Place the soy beans in a bowl,** cover generously with cold water and let soak overnight in a cool place. If possible, change the water once or twice during the soaking.

The following day, rinse and drain the beans, then place in a blender with 3⅓ cups (800ml) cold water and ¼ tsp cooking oil. Blitz at full power until you have a smooth soy milk.

Place a sieve above your wok or saucepan, and line it with a large piece of muslin. Pour the soy milk into the muslin-lined sieve, then rinse out the blender with 1⅔ cups (400ml) cold water and tip this milky water into the sieve too. Now gather up the edges of the muslin to make a bundle, twisting them together at the top so the soy milk cannot escape, and squeeze out as much milk as possible into the wok or pan.

When you have extracted all the milk you can, set aside the soy-bean dregs (these have other culinary uses in Chinese and Japanese cooking; some Chinese cooks stir them into the dough for making steamed buns). Place the soy milk over medium heat and bring slowly to a boil. Keep an eye on it: as soon as the milk boils, a huge head of foam will try to erupt: at this point, turn the heat down very low, very quickly. Now keep the milk at a bare simmer, just murmuring at the edges, for 8 minutes.

Now switch off the heat and allow the milk to cool to 175°F (80°C). Bring a little water to a boil in a kettle, then use 3–4 tbsp of it to dissolve the nigari. As the milk simmers and then cools, skins will form on the surface: remove these with a chopstick and hang them up to dry (after a quick soaking in water, they make a delicious, protein-rich addition to soups and stir-fried greens).

When the milk has reached 175°F (80°C), stir in the nigari solution in a few stages. As soon as you see cloud-like curds forming in the milk, stop adding the nigari, cover the pan and leave the tofu undisturbed for 5 minutes to set. (You won't need all the nigari solution.) After this, you can firm up the texture a little by placing a sieve on the surface, pressing gently and scooping out the water that pools in the sieve with a rice bowl. →

← Other possible ingredients include chopped cilantro, *mujiangcai* (Latin name *Elsholtzia souliei*, a variety of mint) or *zhe'er gen* (Latin name *Houttuynia cordata*, also called heartleaf or fish mint); chopped garlic; sesame or Sichuan pepper oil, chopped roasted green chiles, ground pork—and, of course, MSG. I've included a few examples of these dips below the main recipe.

← If you wish, you can gently reheat the tofu before serving. Scoop portions into bowls, and serve with little dishes of a spicy dip.

**Some dips for tofu**

<u>Chile bean paste dip</u>
*This is my favorite dip for tofu. Take 6 tbsp (100g) Sichuan chile bean paste, and finely chop if it is chunky. Rinse about 2 tbsp fermented black beans, then pound to a paste with a mortar and pestle; stir in the chile bean paste. Heat 4 tbsp cooking oil in a seasoned wok over medium heat. Add the mixed bean paste and stir-fry slowly and gently until the oil is red and the paste smells cooked. Then turn it out into a bowl and stir in ½–1 tsp ground roasted Sichuan pepper. This is fantastically delicious.*

<u>Chile oil dip</u>
*Mix 3 tbsp chile oil or cold-pressed rapeseed oil with 3 tbsp chile oil sediment. Add 3 tbsp light soy sauce, or salt to taste, followed by 3 tbsp thinly sliced scallion greens. If you can get it, add a few drops of lemony litsea oil, a local ingredient in Guizhou province and the neighboring part of Sichuan.*

<u>Pounded ciba chile dip</u>
*This version is extremely typical of southern Sichuan. Snip 10 dried chiles in half or into ¾-inch (2cm) sections and shake out the seeds as much as possible, then place in a small bowl with 1½ tsp whole green or red Sichuan pepper. Cover with hot water from the kettle and let soak for 5 minutes. Drain the spices, then place in a mortar with ¼ tsp salt and pound to a paste. Heat 3 tbsp cooking oil in a seasoned wok until hot enough to sizzle vigorously when dripped onto the chile paste. Pour the hot oil over the chiles and stir, then add 3 tbsp light soy sauce and 3 tbsp finely chopped spearmint or scallion greens.*

<u>Ground chile dip</u>
*For a simple dip that's quick to make, mix together 2 tbsp ground chiles, ½ tsp ground roasted Sichuan pepper, 2 tbsp thinly sliced scallion greens, 3 tbsp light soy sauce and 1–2 tbsp cold-pressed rapeseed oil.*

# Home-style Tofu

## jiachang doufu
## 家常豆腐

"Home-style" is the name given to a particular Sichuanese flavor type, which is salt-savory and moderately hot, with sometimes a hint of sweetness in the sauce. It is usually based on Sichuan chile bean paste, with variations in the additional flavorings used. Some recipes call for fermented black beans or sweet flour sauce, others pickled chiles. As the name suggests, this style of cooking is inspired by the hearty simplicity of Sichuanese home cooking, although it may also be used to cook extravagant ingredients such as sea cucumber. In this recipe, the puffy tofu becomes juicy and flavorful in the hot, beany sauce, and the vegetables add an attractive splash of green. Although Sichuanese restaurants generally cook this dish with meat, the pork can easily be omitted to give a delicious vegetarian dish (I almost always cook the vegetarian version myself). If you fry the tofu in advance, it is extremely quick to make.

Another version of this dish is called "bear's paw" tofu, named because the tofu is not deep-fried but pan-fried in a little oil on the hot surface of the wok until it is toasty and golden in places, lending it a puckered appearance like a bear's paw (bear's paw is a famous Chinese delicacy, now frowned upon for conservation reasons). Cooking the tofu this way takes longer than deep-frying, unless you do it in a very wide frying pan.

*1 lb (450g) plain white tofu*
*3½ oz (100g) pork tenderloin or leg (optional)*
*3 baby leeks or scallions*
*¾ cup plus 2 tbsp (200ml) cooking oil*
*2 tbsp chile bean paste*
*3 garlic cloves, peeled and sliced*
*An equivalent amount of ginger,*
*    peeled and sliced*
*¾ cup plus 2 tbsp (200ml) 200ml stock*
*½ tsp superfine sugar*
*½–1 tsp light soy sauce, to taste*
*1 tsp potato starch,*
*    mixed with 4 tsp cold water*

Cut the tofu into 1½–2-inch (4–5cm) squares or rectangles, about ½ inch (1cm) thick. Thinly slice the pork, if using. Cut the baby leeks or scallions into lengths, keeping the white and green parts separate.

Heat the oil in a seasoned wok over high heat until sizzling hot, then fry the tofu slices in a few batches until golden. Remove and drain on paper towels.

Carefully pour off all but 3 tbsp of the oil from the wok and return to high heat. Add the pork, if using, and stir briskly to separate the slices. Turn down the heat to medium, then add the chile bean paste and stir-fry until the oil is red and richly fragrant. Add the garlic and ginger, along with the leek or scallion whites, and fry until they, too, are fragrant.

Tip in the stock and tofu and bring to a boil. Turn down the heat slightly, season with the sugar and soy sauce and simmer for 3–4 minutes, until the liquid has reduced and the tofu has absorbed some of the flavors of the sauce.

Add the leek or scallion greens and stir briefly until just cooked. Give the potato starch mixture a stir and add to the wok in a couple of stages, adding just enough to thicken the sauce to a glossy gravy that clings to the slices of tofu. Serve.

# Tofu with Ground Meat in Fermented Sauce

jiang shao dou fu

酱烧豆腐

Given the chance to eat mapo tofu, it's hard to see why anyone would desire an alternative, but sometimes people do have their reasons for avoiding spicy flavors, which is why the famous Pockmarked Mother Chen's Tofu restaurant in Chengdu offers this dish too, like a shy younger sister to the classic version.

The cooking method is the same, but with sweet flour sauce rather than Sichuan chile bean paste as the principal flavoring. While less electrifying, obviously, than Mrs. Chen's famous dish, it is extremely delicious and satisfying, and another of those Chinese dishes that is ideal for those who would like to eat less meat without any sacrifice of gastronomic pleasure.

1 lb 2 oz (500g) plain white tofu
4 scallions or baby leeks
1½ tbsp fermented black beans
3 tbsp cooking oil
3½ oz (100g) ground beef or pork
½ tsp dark soy sauce
1 tbsp sweet flour sauce
7 tbsp (100ml) stock or water
1 tbsp light soy sauce
1 tbsp potato starch,
    mixed with 2½ tbsp cold water
Salt

Cut the tofu into ¾-inch (2cm) cubes and let steep in very hot, lightly salted water while you prepare the other ingredients. Slice the scallions or baby leeks at a steep angle into thin "horse ears." Rinse the black beans under cold water.

Heat the oil in a seasoned wok over high heat. Add the ground meat and stir-fry, breaking it into little morsels—the oil will initially become cloudy as the meat releases its juices. When the meat has become pale and the oil has cleared, stir in the dark soy sauce. Add the black beans and sweet flour sauce and stir-fry briefly until they smell delicious, then pour in the stock or water and mix well.

Use a slotted spoon to transfer the tofu from its soaking water into the wok. Nudge the tofu tenderly with the back of your ladle or wok scoop to mix it into the sauce without breaking up the cubes. Add the light soy sauce and salt to taste. Simmer the tofu for a few minutes to allow it to absorb the flavors of the sauce, then stir in the scallions or leeks: if using leeks, let them simmer for a moment to become tender.

Give the potato starch mixture a stir, then add it to the wok in three stages, stirring the sauce as it thickens between each addition—and adding just enough of the starch mixture to reduce the sauce to a thick gravy that clings to the tofu.

Tip the tofu into a bowl and serve.

# Leshan "Bear's Paw" Tofu

## xiongzhang doufu
## 熊掌豆腐

The pace of life in Leshan, home of the giant stone Buddha, is gentle and relaxed. In the afternoons, the markets dwindle and the restaurants quieten, and practically everyone seems to settle down to a good game of cards or mahjong. As one taxi driver explained to me: "Everyone goes on about the leisurely tempo of life in Chengdu, but it's frenetic compared to Leshan."

The sleepy streets down by the river in the old part of town are wonderful hunting grounds for traditional snacks and dishes, including the local Xiba tofu, which comes from a town just downriver. Made with water that flows through limestone cliffs, Xiba tofu is showcased in many Leshan restaurants. One I visited recently, Eighth Sister Dai's restaurant, is run, as you might guess, by a woman named Dai who was the eighth child in her family. The last time I was there I lunched with friends on bowlfuls of hot silken tofu with ground pork, crunchy pickles, fried peanuts and croutons, and plenty of chile oil; "strange flavor" tofu; cylinders of "lantern" tofu stuffed with ground pork and bathed in a sweet-and-sour sauce; and this delicious "bear's paw" tofu in a glossy red sauce. The name "bear's paw" derives from the fact that the tofu is traditionally pan-fried until the surface of each slice is puckered like a paw, although in this case the tofu is deep-fried instead.

*1 lb (450g) plain white tofu*
*⅓ cup plus 1 tbsp (50g) potato starch*
*At least ¾ cup plus 2 tbsp (200ml) cooking oil,*
*    for deep-frying*
*1 tbsp Sichuan chile bean paste*
*1 tbsp Sichuan pickled chile paste*
*    or sambal oelek*
*2 tsp finely chopped ginger*
*2 tsp finely chopped garlic*
*1¼ cups (300ml) stock*
*5 tbsp superfine sugar*
*2 tsp light soy sauce*
*1 tsp potato starch,*
*    mixed with 1 tbsp cold water*
*2 tsp Chinkiang vinegar*
*2 tbsp thinly sliced scallion greens*

**Cut the tofu into 1½–2-inch (4–5cm) squares** or rectangles, about ½ inch (1cm) thick, and drain well. Place the potato starch on a plate.

Heat the deep-frying oil in a wok to 355–375°F (180–190°C). Dredge the tofu slices in the potato starch and drop about half of them, one at a time, into the hot oil, using long cooking chopsticks or a wok scoop to nudge them apart. Deep-fry until puffy and golden. Drain well on paper towels and set aside. Repeat with the rest of the tofu.

Carefully pour off all but 3 tbsp of the oil from the wok, then return the wok to medium heat. Add the chile bean paste and stir-fry gently until the oil is red and fragrant. Add the pickled chile paste or sambal oelek and stir-fry until fragrant, then add the ginger and garlic and continue to stir-fry until they also smell delicious. Pour in the stock and bring to a boil. Use a slotted spoon or fine-mesh strainer to scoop out and discard the solid remnants of the aromatics, then stir in the sugar and soy sauce. Add the tofu, stir gently, and let it simmer in the sauce for a minute or two to allow it to absorb the flavors, spooning over the liquid from time to time.

Give the potato starch mixture a stir, then add it to the wok in stages, stirring in between each addition and adding just enough to give you a luxurious gravy that clings to the tofu. Stir in the vinegar, then transfer to a serving dish and sprinkle with the scallion greens.

# Mount Emei Spicy Silken Tofu

## emei doufu nao
## 峨眉豆腐脑

It was a cold, dim morning just after the Lunar New Year, and I was on my way to the Wenshu Monastery in Chengdu to burn some incense offerings, when I came across a tiny tofu shop run by a friendly young woman from Leshan. The star attraction in her shop was the spicy silken tofu, which she said was made from a recipe that had been in her family for three generations. So I sat there on a stool in the open-fronted shop and ate a bowlful of the spicy, custardy porridge, which filled me with warmth and energy and drove away the winter chill. This is my attempt to re-create her recipe. Her full version includes a scattering of spicy steamed beef (see p. 165) and some of the pork cracklings left over from rendering lard, but it's also stunningly delicious without them.

In most of Sichuan, silken tofu is known as "flower" tofu (*douhua*), but in the south, especially around the Buddhist pilgrimage sites of Leshan and Mount Emei, where they break up the tofu into fragments and serve it in a starch-thickened liquid, they call it tofu "brain" (*doufu nao*). It's a favorite snack, especially for breakfast. This recipe makes enough for 2 decent servings, or for 4 as a snack.

Don't fret if you don't have all the topping ingredients: the preserved vegetable is essential; otherwise, just try to include at least one fresh green element and one that is dry and crunchy.

4 tbsp potato or sweet potato starch
10 oz (300g) silken tofu
1 tbsp light soy sauce
2 tbsp chile oil, with sediment
¼ tsp ground roasted Sichuan pepper
4 tbsp finely chopped celery or Chinese celery
2 tbsp chopped cilantro
2 tbsp thinly sliced scallion greens
4 tbsp finely chopped preserved mustard tuber (zhacai) or "big-headed vegetable" (datoucai)
2 tbsp roasted or deep-fried peanuts (see p. 458)
2 small handfuls of Bombay mix

Mix the starch with 5 tbsp cold water in a small bowl. Run a fork through the silken tofu to break it up into smallish pieces. Divide the soy sauce, chile oil and Sichuan pepper between two serving bowls (or four smaller bowls).

Bring 1¼ cups (300ml) water to a boil in a small saucepan. When the water is boiling, gradually stir in the starch mixture, adding just enough to thicken the liquid to a viscous, lazy consistency. Add the tofu and stir to distribute the fragments evenly.

Divide the tofu mixture between the bowls. Scatter over all the remaining ingredients and serve. Mix everything together before eating with spoons.

# Sour-and-hot "Flower" Tofu

## suanla douhua
## 酸辣豆花

It's a sleepy, sunny afternoon in one of Chengdu's teahouses, tucked away down a back alley near Sichuan University. The owner of the teahouse wanders around among the tables with her copper kettle, refilling the lidded tea bowls, stopping here and there for a chat with the regulars. Then a call goes up in the street outside, slowly approaching: *"Dou hua'er! Dou hua'er!"* A few minutes later, the tofu vendor walks into the courtyard and sets down the pair of red-and-black barrels hung from his bamboo shoulder-pole. For a small sum, he scoops some of his home-made silken or "flower" tofu into a bowl, drizzles it with seasonings, and then scatters over finely chopped preserved vegetable, scallions and crunchy fried soy beans, finishing each bowl with a sprinkling of ground, roasted Sichuan pepper. The tofu is still warm and meltingly tender, the dressing piquant and richly satisfying.

This popular Chengdu street snack is one of the few still encountered in the lanes and alleys of the changing city, but its most famous purveyor is Mr. Tan's Flower Tofu (*tan douhua*), a specialist in all kinds of Chengdu "small eats" with branches across the city. It's also quick and easy to make, using a pack of pre-made silken tofu; this makes two servings. At home, I use Bombay mix for the requisite crunch, in place of the usual Chengdu finishing touch of fried peanuts and deep-fried soy beans.

10 oz (300g) silken tofu
1 tbsp Chinkiang vinegar
2 tsp light soy sauce
1½ tbsp chile oil, plus ½–1 tbsp sediment
½ tsp sesame oil
A couple of good pinches of ground roasted Sichuan pepper (optional)
Salt

### To serve
1 tbsp finely chopped preserved mustard tuber (zhacai)
2 tbsp thinly sliced scallion greens
A small handful of Bombay mix

**Bring a pot of lightly salted water** to a boil. Use a spoon to scoop large pieces of the tofu into the water, then simmer it very gently for about 5 minutes, just to warm it through.

Meanwhile, prepare the other ingredients. Divide the vinegar, soy sauce, chile and sesame oils—and the Sichuan pepper, if using—between two individual serving bowls, and then give them a stir.

When the tofu is ready, use a slotted spoon to divide it between the two bowls. Scatter over the preserved mustard tuber, scallion greens and Bombay mix, then serve. Mix everything together before eating.

# Xiba Tofu

## xiba doufu
## 西坝豆腐

In the West, tofu has traditionally been viewed as a vegetarian substitute for meat, but in China it is an essential part of most people's diets, which is why you needn't be surprised to find many dishes that incorporate both meat and tofu. The following recipe is based on one I tasted in a backstreet restaurant in Leshan, and it's pure comfort food: little cubes of tender tofu in a luxurious stock enlivened by morsels of chicken, ham, tomato and pork. It's named after Xiba, a town near Leshan that is renowned for the flavor and quality of its tofu.

The success of this dish depends entirely on the richness of your stock. The manager of the Kaishuiji restaurant, where I lapped up the version upon which this recipe is based, explained that they use a reduced milky stock made from whole chickens and pork knuckles. This dish will be most delicious with tofu that is just firm enough to hold its shape when cut into little cubes.

*2½ oz (70g) cooked chicken*
*1¾ oz (50g) cooked ham*
*1 medium tomato*
*1 tbsp cooking oil or lard*
*2½ oz (75g) ground pork*
*14 oz (400g) plain white tofu*
*1¼ cups (300ml) rich milky stock (see p. 465)*
*1½ tbsp potato starch,*
   *mixed with 4 tbsp cold water*
*2 tbsp thinly sliced scallion greens*
*Salt and ground white pepper*

Cut the chicken, ham and tomato into ½-inch (1cm) cubes (for best results, discard the tomato seeds). Heat the cooking oil or lard in a seasoned wok over high heat, add the ground pork and stir-fry until cooked through, breaking the meat into tiny morsels as you go. Set aside.

Bring a pot of lightly salted water to a boil. Cut the tofu into ½-inch (1cm) cubes and submerge it in the water, then simmer very gently for a few minutes, just to warm it through.

Bring the stock to a boil. Remove the tofu from the water with a slotted spoon, drain well and then add to the stock, along with the chicken, ham, tomato and pork. Season with salt and pepper to taste, stirring very gently so you don't break up the tofu. Simmer for a few minutes to allow the flavors to mingle.

Give the potato starch mixture a stir and add it in stages to the wok, stirring in between each addition, and adding just enough to thicken the stock to a lazy, gravy-like consistency. Adjust the seasoning if necessary, then ladle into a serving bowl. Scatter over the scallion greens.

# Vegetables

"The markets of Sichuan, a region known since ancient times as a land of plenty, overflow with fresh vegetables all year round; each season brings new delights"

# Vegetables 蔬菜类

Although the most renowned Sichuanese dishes are virtually all made with meat, fish or poultry, many local people still favor a traditional diet dominated by pulses, grains and vegetables. In the past, this was an economic necessity, but it is also related to ideas about health and longevity in traditional Chinese culture. Ancient medical texts described the health benefits of largely vegetarian eating, and many members of the ruling classes and literati have throughout history expressed a preference for frugal living and the simple peasant diet. These days, discerning people still eat very little meat at home, and everyone knows that it's better to "eat more vegetables, eat less meat" (*duo chi shucai, shao chi rou*). A typical home-cooked dinner in Sichuan might consist of a few dishes of vegetables stir-fried with morsels of meat, some tofu, a simple stock-based soup and plenty of rice: extravagant consumption of meat and fish is usually associated with dining out and entertaining.

Despite the widespread acceptance of a diet based largely on grains and vegetables, total vegetarianism is still rare in China, and most people find it hard to imagine abstaining from meat all the time. In some of the more cosmopolitan cities, a small but growing minority are shunning meat altogether, but otherwise strict vegetarianism is largely confined to Buddhist monasteries. One of the central precepts of Buddhism is a ban on killing, although the religion doesn't explicitly forbid the consumption of meat. In the original Indian form of Buddhism, monks were expected to eat almost all the food that was placed in their begging bowls: this included meat, as long as they didn't suspect that an animal had been killed specifically for their benefit.

After Buddhism entered China during the early Han period, however, a distinct tradition of vegetarian eating developed, partly because begging was never culturally acceptable in China, so Chinese Buddhist monasteries had to produce their own food. The idea of vegetarian eating wasn't completely alien: periods of abstention from meat had been part of Chinese ritual life since ancient times. But the establishment of the tradition is credited to one Chinese emperor, Wu Di, of the Liang dynasty (sixth century AD), whose own conversion to Buddhism led him to adopt a vegetarian diet on compassionate grounds. He banned the use of meat in sacrifices, and enforced a practice of strict vegetarian eating in Buddhist monasteries all over the lower Yangtze region.

The daily diet of Buddhist monks is typically a simple affair of grains, vegetables and tofu, but in the centuries since the reign of Emperor Wu Di, when monasteries began to hold feasts, Buddhist vegetarian cooking has become extraordinarily sophisticated. In the larger monasteries, the need to entertain guests and patrons led to the creation of banqueting halls where people could dine on grand dishes of "shark's fin," "abalone" and other delicacies cunningly fashioned from vegetable ingredients. This tradition of imitation meat dishes (*fanghun cai*) dates back to at least the Song dynasty (960–1279); more recently, its development was fostered by specialty Buddhist restaurants that grew out of the lay Buddhist associations of the 1920s and 1930s, like the famous Gongdelin restaurant in Shanghai, which was founded in 1922.

One of the most fascinating aspects of Chinese Buddhist vegetarian cooking is the development of parallel cuisines that mirror the classic dishes of each Chinese regional style. In Shanghai, you can eat stir-fried "crabmeat" made from mashed potato and carrot, while in Sichuan you can eat "twice-cooked pork," "Gong Bao chicken" and "fish-fragrant pork slivers": these are all made without a scrap of meat, fish or poultry. They are also free from the pungent seasonings that strict Buddhists avoid because they are thought to inflame the carnal passions: known collectively as the "five pungents" (*wuhun*), these include garlic, scallions and other alliums (fortunately for Sichuanese Buddhists, chiles and Sichuan pepper are allowed).

Until recently, the ancient Wenshu Monastery in Chengdu had a restaurant where inexpensive vegetarian dishes could be ordered from a hatch downstairs, while vegetarian feasts of stunning artistry were served in the banqueting rooms on the upper floor. The "beef slivers with sesame seeds" were made from shiitake mushroom stalks, chosen for their chewy, meaty texture and rich taste—the finished dish, drizzled in chile oil and scattered with seeds, looked and tasted remarkably like the real thing. The "spare ribs" were puffs of gluten impaled on lotus root "bones"; the "fish in chile bean sauce" was a fish-shaped mass of mashed potato wrapped in tofu skin, deep-fried and then draped in a lustrous red sauce; and the "twice-cooked pork" was made from sweet potato slices. Many of the "meat," "poultry" and "seafood" products were concocted from wheat gluten, various bean and tofu preparations and konnyaku "tofu" (*moyu*), a Sichuanese specialty.

Ordinary Sichuanese vegetable cooking may not be this elaborate, but it is also colorful, exciting and richly varied. The markets of Sichuan, a region known since ancient times as a "land of plenty" (*tianfu zhi guo*), overflow with fresh vegetables all year round; each season brings new delights. Some of the local produce will be familiar to outsiders, such as tomatoes, potatoes, onions and peppers. Likewise certain East Asian varietals of common vegetables: long, thin, sweet-fleshed eggplants; pink-skinned radishes the size of parsnips; tight-fleshed, prickly cucumbers; and loosely gathered heads of slender, fragrant Chinese celery. You'll also find the produce strongly associated with Chinese cooking: winter melons, silk gourds and bitter melons; lotus roots or rhizomes; green, yellow and flowering chives; fresh ginger and garlic; long green Chinese onions; shelled green soy beans and yard-long beans. Fresh bamboo shoots, quite unlike the dried or canned versions sold abroad, come in several varieties, including spring bamboo shoots (chunsun), winter bamboo shoots (dongsun) and the local specialty, bitter bamboo shoots (kusun), with their delicate and refreshing bitterness, which are only available in spring. Slices of the tender winter shoots of one variety of bamboo (nanzhu or maozhu) are boiled and dried

for long storage; known as jade magnolia slices (yulan pian), they were one of the key ingredients of old-fashioned banquet dishes. In southern Sichuan, people produce smoked, dried bamboo shoots that are treacle-dark and add a fabulous flavor to slow-cooked stews made with pork or beef.

The famous "Bamboo Sea" (*shunan zhuhai*), near Yibin, in southern Sichuan, is known for its feasts of bamboo shoots and other wild delicacies of the bamboo forest. Here, the landscape is miraculous, beautiful. The bamboo grows lavishly and intensely green, arching over isolated farmhouses, quivering in the gentle breeze. Within the forest, thin, smoke-green bamboo trunks rise smooth and unadorned, exploding overhead into a lushness of leaves. Cataracts spill down rocky hillsides, over red earth and boulders. The air buzzes with the chatter of birds and insects. Everything is damp and moss-grown, moist and oozing.

Aside from bamboo shoots, local restaurants serve dishes made with the bamboo flower lichen (*zhuhua*), which grows on the bamboo itself; tender bamboo frogs, which are delicious braised with wild mountain chiles; a frilly fungus known as "bamboo bird's nest" (*zhu yanwo*); the famous "ox-liver" mushroom (*niuganjun*), a type of Boletus, with its heavy, gelatinous texture and rich taste; and numerous other wild fungi. Bamboo leaves are used to smoke bacon and bamboo shoots, and hollow sections of bamboo may be used as vessels for steaming glutinous rice or setting tofu, to both of which it lends a delicate bamboo fragrance.

According to Sichuanese gourmets, however, the "king of mountain treasures" and the "empress of all the fungi," is the magnificent bamboo pith fungus (*zhusun*), which grows on the leafy floor of the forest. Its Latin name is Phallus indusiatus, for reasons that quickly become obvious when you see its shape. The mushroom has a phallic central section topped by a darker cap with a forbidding smell. From beneath the cap extends a delicate, lacy white parasol that gives it an extraordinary, otherworldly appearance. The sought-after main part, including the parasol, is usually dried before it is eaten. It's most commonly served in clear broths so that its slithery, faintly crunchy texture and lovely appearance can be appreciated, but I've also enjoyed it stir-fried with chiles and Sichuan pepper, to delicious effect. The cap of the fungus, with its tripe-like patterning, is known as "vegetarian tripe." If you visit the Bamboo Sea in springtime, you can sample the extraordinary volvae of the unripe fungus, known as its "eggs" (zhusundan). These plump mushroom balls, through which the mature fungus eventually bursts, are a pale pink-brown, and usually the size of a small tangerine. When sliced, they reveal a rainbow of layers of pink, white and gray flesh, with a lacy, embryonic fungus curled up within. The outer membranes of the "eggs," translucent and slippery, are known as the "placenta" and can also be eaten. Bamboo pith fungus has been eaten in China since at least the time of the Tang dynasty (618–906 AD).

Returning to more everyday vegetables, the Sichuanese varieties of cabbage and mustard (the Brassica family) deserve special mention. Aside from the familiar Chinese leaf cabbage (known in Chinese as "big cabbage," da baicai), the Sichuanese eat various smaller, loose-leafed cabbage or bok choy varieties ("green vegetables," qingcai), as well as the huge, tight cabbages known as lianhuabai. Tender, juicy rape shoots, either green or purple, are a delicacy of early spring, faintly bitter and exquisitely delicious (in local parlance, they are known as bai caitai, "white" rape shoots, or hong caitai, "red" rape shoots). They are often stir-fried and served with a spicy dip that always includes a little vinegar, but may also be served in a fish-fragrant sauce. Amid tough competition, they are probably my favorite Sichuanese vegetable.

Large, loose heads of mustard greens are normally pickled to make the "sour greens" (suancai) typically used in soups. Swollen mustard stems are semi-dried, spiced and salt-cured to make the famous Sichuan preserved vegetable (zhacai). Fleshy mustard tubers (qingcaitou, or mustard "heads") may be eaten fresh or pickled, while the charmingly named "sons vegetable" (ercai), a cluster of tiny cabbages on a thick stalk, is the local equivalent of Brussels sprouts, but far more delicate and delectable. The tender sprouts of one variety of mustard are treated to

make "mustardy greens" (chongcai), a pungent, refreshing winter treat, while the stems of another variety are preserved with salt, brown sugar and spices to make the celebrated pickle of Yibin—yacai, a vital ingredient in dandan noodles and dry-fried green beans.

Aside from the mustards, the Sichuanese enjoy a variety of other greens, including spinach, water spinach and chard (the latter known as ox-leather vegetable, niupicai, because of its thick, broad leaves). Purple amaranth leaves (hancai in local dialect, xiancai in Mandarin) are wonderful stir-fried with garlic; another popular vegetable is heartleaf or fish mint (zhe'er gen, Latin name Houttuynia cordata), whose green, purple-tinged leaves and pallid, pinkish root stalks are used in soups and salads. Delicate pea shoots (doumiao), sometimes known as "dragon's whiskers" because of their curling tendrils, are sometimes added to elegant banquet soups. Westerners often think of "eating their greens" as a dull dietary duty; in Sichuan, green vegetables are cooked so beautifully that they are eaten as much for pleasure as for nutrition, and are served at almost every meal.

Green garlic or "Chinese leeks" (suanmiao locally; qingsuan or dasuan in other parts of China), which are longer, thinner and more tender than Western leeks, are widely used in Sichuanese cuisine, for example to bring a flash of green pungency to twice-cooked pork or mapo tofu. Another ubiquitous vegetable is celtuce, also known as stem lettuce (wosun or qingsun). This marvelous vegetable has swollen stems the size of truncheons, and scanty leaves. The leaves are usually stir-fried, while the peeled stems have a beautiful green color, a delicately crisp texture and a gorgeous nutty flavor, and are used in all kinds of salads, stir-fries and braised dishes. Day-lily flowers (huanghua) are sometimes added to soups and stir-fries, and you can also find seasonal delicacies such as the purplish spring shoots of the Chinese toon tree (chunya, Latin name Toona sinensis), which are often added to salads or chopped and made into omelets with an intriguing herby taste.

One local specialty, known as the cluster mallow (donghancai or kuicai, Latin name Malva *verticillata*) has been revered in China since the dawn of history and mentioned in the ancient Book of Songs; it is still eaten in Sichuan, and can often be found in local markets. Sometimes called "duck's feet" because of the shape of its leaves, it is used in soups and stir-fries, and has a slippery, mucilaginous texture. Its tender leaf-tips, coated in a fluffy chicken-breast paste, are served in clear broth as a classic banquet dish (*jimeng kuicai*). The Sichuanese also enjoy Malabar spinach (*Basella alba*), known locally as "wood ear vegetable" (*mu'er cai*) or "tofu vegetable" (*doufu cai*) because of its fleshy, slippery leaves.

Wild vegetables have a curious status in Chinese culinary culture. For centuries, they have been praised by literary men besotted with the idea of the simple, rustic life. For many rural people, however, they are associated with hard times when crops failed and they were driven to foraging by sheer hunger. In contemporary China, they are prized by wealthy urbanites in search of healthy, "green" ingredients and exotic tastes.

Day-trippers visiting the ancient irrigation works at Dujiangyan and nearby Qingcheng Mountain, not far from Chengdu, often order specialties such as purple fiddlehead ferns (*juecai*), which are fabulous stir-fried with the treacle-black local bacon, stir-fried fat hen or lamb's quarters (*huihuicai*, Latin name *Chenopodium album*) or winter vetch (*shaocai*, Latin name *Vicia hirsuta*).

In general, vegetables are just as likely to be made into vegetarian dishes as they are to be cooked with small pieces of meat, stock, lard or other non-vegetarian ingredients, a practice known as "vegetable ingredients cooked meatily" (*sucai hunzuo*). Many cooks swear that vegetables are most delicious when stir-fried in either lard or a mixture of lard and vegetable oil.

The following chapter contains a selection of my favorite Sichuanese vegetable dishes. Not all are entirely vegetarian, although those that do contain meat can easily be adapted for vegetarians by the simple omission of meat and the substitution of vegetable stock or oil for any animal stock or fat. Many of them are simple home-cooked dishes that don't usually appear in serious cookbooks and aren't taught in cooking schools. They are, however, quick to make, delicious to eat, and very healthy when served with a bowlful of rice.

The range of Chinese vegetables available in good Chinese shops in the West is expanding all the time, and some are even beginning to appear in mainstream supermarkets. I live in hope that celtuce, garlic stems and Chinese chives, in particular, will become more widely available as more people outside China come to understand how delicious and versatile they are. In the meantime, it's worth remembering that many of the cooking methods described in this chapter can be applied to a wide variety of different vegetables, depending on what you have on hand. The qiang method, which involves stir-frying with dried chiles and Sichuan pepper, for example, is delicious with water spinach, bok choy, slivered potatoes, lotus root and many other ingredients, so please regard these recipes as a template and a guide rather than culinary dogma.

# Fish-fragrant Eggplants

## yuxiang qiezi
## 鱼香茄子

The following recipe is a local classic, and one of my all-time favorite dishes of any cuisine. More than any other dish, for me it sums up the luxuriant pleasures of Sichuanese food: the warm colors and tastes, the subtlety of complex flavors. Like other fish-fragrant dishes, it is made with the seasonings of traditional fish dishes: pickled chiles, garlic, ginger and scallions. But unlike the more illustrious fish-fragrant pork slivers, it derives its color not from pickled chiles alone, but from pickled chiles combined with fava beans in chile bean paste. The sauce is sweet, sour and spicy, with a reddish hue and a visible scattering of chopped ginger, garlic and scallion.

The dish is equally delicious hot or cold. I usually serve it with a meat or tofu dish and a stir-fried green vegetable, but it makes a fine lunch simply eaten with brown rice and a salad. The eggplants, deep-fried to a buttery tenderness, are delectable. I have eaten this dish in restaurants all over Sichuan, and recorded numerous different versions of the recipe. The following one will, I hope, make you sigh with delight.

If you want to scale up this recipe for a party, rinse and dry the salted eggplants, toss in a little cooking oil and then roast for 15–20 minutes in a 425°F (220°C) oven until golden. Make the sauce, but don't thicken it with starch; instead, pour it over the roasted eggplants and set aside to allow the flavors to mingle. Serve at room temperature.

*1 lb 5 oz (600g) eggplants (1–2 large)*
*Cooking oil, for deep-frying*
*1½ tbsp Sichuan chile bean paste*
*1½ tbsp finely chopped garlic*
*1 tbsp finely chopped ginger*
*10 tbsp (150ml) hot stock or water*
*4 tsp superfine sugar*
*1 tsp light soy sauce*
*¾ tsp potato starch, mixed with 1 tbsp cold water*
*1 tbsp Chinkiang vinegar*
*6 tbsp thinly sliced scallion greens*
*Salt*

Cut the eggplants into batons about ¾ inch (2cm) thick and 2¾ inches (7cm) long. Sprinkle with salt, mix well and set aside for at least 30 minutes.

Rinse the eggplant, drain well and pat dry with paper towels. Heat the deep-frying oil to around 390°F (200°C) (hot enough to sizzle vigorously around a test piece of eggplant). Add the eggplant, in two or three batches, and deep-fry for about 3 minutes, until tender and a little golden. Drain well on paper towels and set aside.

Carefully pour off all but 3 tbsp oil from the wok and return to medium heat. Add the chile bean paste and stir-fry until the oil is red and fragrant: take care not to burn the paste (move the wok away from the burner if you think it might be overheating). Add the garlic and ginger and stir-fry until they smell delicious.

Tip in the stock or water, sugar and soy sauce. Bring to a boil, then add the eggplant, nudging the batons gently into the sauce so they do not break apart. Simmer for a minute or so to allow the eggplant to absorb the flavors.

Give the potato starch mixture a stir and add it gradually, in about three stages, adding just enough to thicken the sauce to a luxurious gravy (you probably won't need it all). Tip in the vinegar and all but 1 tbsp of the scallion greens, then stir for a few seconds to fuse the flavors.

Turn out onto a serving dish, scatter over the remaining scallion greens and serve.

# Dry-fried Eggplants

## ganbian qiezi
## 干煸茄子

*14 oz (400g) eggplants (2 small or 1 medium)*
*2½ oz (75g) long green Turkish peppers*
*2–3 tbsp cooking oil*
*1 tsp sesame oil*
*Salt*

This simple recipe is typical of much Sichuanese home cooking, and a classic example of the local "dry-frying" method, which brings out the fragrance of the ingredients and gives them a slightly toasty taste, rather like Western grilled or roasted vegetables. It's often used for eggplants, bamboo shoots and bitter melon. You can vary the proportions of eggplant and green pepper as you please, but don't overload the wok or they won't cook evenly. The bright green peppers should taste fresh and slightly crunchy, livening up the languid flesh of the eggplants. I like to use thin-skinned Turkish peppers for this dish.

Cut the eggplants in half lengthwise, then slice thinly at an angle (ideally the slices should be ⅛ inch/3–4mm thick). Sprinkle with salt, mix well and set aside for at least 30 minutes.

Trim the peppers and slice thinly. Rinse the eggplant, drain well and pat dry with paper towels.

Use a paper towel to lightly smear a seasoned wok with cooking oil, then heat over high heat. Add the eggplant and stir and toss for about 3 minutes until it is floppy and fragrant. Add the pepper slices and 1–2 tbsp cooking oil, and continue to stir-fry for another 2 minutes or so until the pepper is just cooked. Season with salt to taste.

Finally, remove from the heat, stir in the sesame oil and serve.

# Stuffed Eggplant Fritters with Sichuan Pepper Dip

jiaoyan qiebing

椒盐茄饼

These extremely moreish snacks offer a tantalizing combination of textures: crisp batter and buttery eggplant surrounding a succulent heart of meat. They are sometimes served with a fish-fragrant sauce, but here I've suggested an easier version, offered simply with a dip of salt and ground roasted Sichuan pepper. The recipe can be prepared a few hours in advance, right up to the final frying. The fritters are made with long, thin oriental eggplant, which is peeled, then chopped into linked slices (*liandaopian*), where the knife blade stops short of the chopping board on alternate cuts, so the final result is lots of pairs of slices that are still joined together at one end. The filling is then simply stuffed into what I like to think of as "sandwich slices" before they are dipped into the batter.

Vegetarians can stuff their fritters with a good handful of very finely chopped mushrooms of any type mixed with 1 tsp light soy sauce, 1 tsp potato starch, 2 tsp cold water and salt to taste. The first time I made this version, for some friends in Chengdu, they were so popular that I never managed to sample them—by the time I emerged from the kitchen my greedy friends had devoured the lot! Even meat-eaters insisted they were as good as, if not better than, the real thing.

1 Chinese eggplant (about 6¼ oz/175g)
Cooking oil, for deep-frying
1 tbsp salt and Sichuan pepper dip
  (see p. 456)

*For the stuffing*
1¾ oz (50g) ground pork
A couple of good pinches of salt
1 tsp Shaoxing wine
2 tbsp cold stock or water

*For the batter*
1 large egg
⅓ cup plus 1 tbsp (50g) potato starch

**First make the stuffing.** Place the ground pork in a small bowl. Add the remaining ingredients and mix well to give a soft paste.

For the batter, beat the egg in a bowl, then gradually stir in the potato starch to make a thick but runny batter, with a consistency like cream.

Peel the eggplant and thinly slice it at ⅛-inch (3–4mm) intervals, but only cut through to the board on alternate slices, so you are left with "sandwich slices" that can be stuffed.

Stuff a small amount of pork into each eggplant "sandwich," squeezing the two halves gently together (try not to leave any stuffing hanging out of the sides).

Heat the deep-frying oil to 320°F (160°C) (hot enough to produce a gentle sizzle around a test piece of eggplant). Then, working swiftly with long cooking chopsticks or tongs, dip each eggplant sandwich into the batter, turning to cover completely, and then drop into the hot oil. Fry the fritters until the pork is cooked through: this will probably take 3–4 minutes from when you start battering the eggplant (cut a slice in half to make sure the meat is cooked). Remove with a slotted spoon.

Reheat the oil to 355°F (180°C). Add all the fritters and fry them for a second time until crisp and golden. Remove with a slotted spoon and drain well on paper towels, then pile up on a serving plate. Serve hot, with the salt and Sichuan pepper dip.

# Stir-fried Water Spinach with Chiles and Sichuan Pepper

qiang kongxincai

炝空心菜

7 oz (200g) water spinach
5–6 dried chiles
3 tbsp cooking oil
½ tsp whole Sichuan pepper
1 tsp sesame oil
Salt

Water spinach is grown in most parts of Sichuan and is usually eaten stir-fried. After cooking it has a wonderfully juicy texture. There are two main varieties of the plant, with different-shaped leaves, but both have the same round, hollow stems, which is why the Sichuanese call it "hollow-heart vegetable" (*kongxincai*). Water spinach is known in Mandarin Chinese as *wengcai* and *tongcai*; in Cantonese supermarkets, it is sold as *ong choy* or *tong choy*. Its Latin name is *Ipomoea aquatica*.

The key to the cooking method, *qiang*, is to coax the wonderful aromas of the chiles and Sichuan pepper into the cooking oil without burning the spices: to achieve this, it's essential to add them before the oil is smoking-hot, and then to tip in the vegetables as soon as the chiles have begun to darken, stirring and tossing them into the oil. If you accidentally burn the spices, it's best to start again with fresh oil and spices.

Rinse the water spinach, discarding any wilted leaves and coarser stalks, then shake dry. Cut into chopstickable sections, keeping the stalks and leaves roughly separate.

Snip the chiles in half or into ¾-inch (2cm) sections and shake out the seeds as much as possible.

Heat the cooking oil in a seasoned wok over high heat. Before the oil gets really hot, add the chiles and stir-fry briefly until aromatic and beginning to darken, Quickly add the Sichuan pepper, stir a couple of times, then tip in the water spinach stalks and stir and toss in the fragrant oil. When the stalks are hot, add the leaves and continue to stir-fry until everything is piping hot and the leaves have wilted. Season with salt to taste. Turn off the heat, stir in the sesame oil and then serve.

Variation

*Water spinach is also delicious stir-fried with just garlic and seasoned with a little salt. Simply substitute about 1 tbsp finely chopped garlic for the spices in the recipe above.*

# Stir-fried Mashed Fava Beans with Scallion

## huiguo hudou
## 回锅胡豆

The fava bean is native to western Asia and North Africa, but has been cultivated in China since ancient times. It is thought to have reached China during the Han dynasty, at around the time of Christ, and its Sichuanese dialect name is still *hudou* ("barbarian bean"), a sign that it belongs to a family of Han-dynasty imports that share the same prefix, including black pepper and cucumber. (The character *hu*, which originally referred to the non-Chinese people living to the north and west of China, also appears in all kinds of phrases meaning to talk nonsense, to rave like a madman or to really mess things up—which gives you some idea of what the ancient Chinese thought of foreigners.) The fava bean's more common Chinese name is *candou* ("silkworm bean"), because its pod is thought to resemble the adult silkworm. Sichuan is China's center of fava bean cultivation, and the fresh beans often crop up on local seasonal menus. The dried beans are also, most famously, one of the key ingredients of chile bean paste.

This simple supper dish, known literally as "back-in-the-pot fava beans," is easy to make and extremely delicious. It's important to boil the beans until they are tender enough to rupture (*kaihua*, "burst into flower") when you give them a squeeze; the finished dish should be soft and comforting. Sichuanese people insist that the beans are fried in lard, for maximum fragrance. Fava beans and scallions are a classic combination across southern China.

2½ cups (300g) shelled fava beans (frozen or fresh, around 1¾ lb/800g in their pods)
1¾ oz (50g) scallions
3–4 tbsp (30g) lard
Salt

Bring a pot of water to a boil. Add the fava beans and boil for 10 minutes, until completely tender. Drain and then return to the pan. While the beans are still hot, mash them with a fork, a big pestle or a potato masher: the idea is to split them all open so that some of the flesh spills out. This step can be done in advance.

Thinly slice the scallions, keeping the white and green parts separate. Put the kettle on to boil.

Melt the lard in a seasoned wok over medium heat. Turn the heat to high, add the scallion whites and stir-fry briefly until they sizzle. Add the fava beans, scraping out the pan so you include all the bits. Stir the beans into the hot lard, then pour in ½ cup (125ml) hot water from the kettle, stirring constantly. Season with salt to taste. When the liquid has reduced to a thick coating, stir in the scallion greens, then serve.

# Pickled Yard-long Beans with Ground Pork

## pao jiangdou chao roumo
## 泡豇豆炒肉末

This simple dish is typical of Sichuanese home cooking, and is sometimes also served in restaurants. It's the epitome of what people call a "dish to send the rice down" (*xiafan cai*), because its punchy pickle sourness and appetizing saltiness are the perfect foil to a bowlful of plain white rice: for this reason, it is often served with the rice, toward the end of a meal. The yard-long beans are steeped briefly in brine, which gives them a gentle salty sourness and preserves their crunchy texture. They are then stir-fried with just a little meat and a few spices.

Because of the pickling, you must start preparations a day or two beforehand—and you do need to have a Sichuanese pickle jar filled with brine in order to make this dish.

7 oz (200g) yard-long beans
Enough Sichuanese pickling solution
    (see p. 420) to submerge the beans
2½ oz (75g) ground pork
1 tsp Shaoxing wine
4 dried chiles
2 tbsp cooking oil
½ tsp whole Sichuan pepper
Salt

**Rinse the beans** and spread them out on a clean dish towel or paper towel to dry thoroughly. Submerge them in the pickling solution for 1–3 days, until they are refreshingly sour.

When you're ready to cook the dish, place the pork in a bowl with the Shaoxing wine and a couple of good pinches of salt and mix well.

Drain the beans and cut into ½-inch (1cm) slices. Snip the chiles into ¾-inch (2cm) sections and shake out the seeds as much as possible.

Heat the oil in a seasoned wok over high heat. Quickly add the chiles and Sichuan pepper and stir-fry very briefly until the chiles are fragrant but not burned. Add the ground pork and continue to stir-fry until pale and fragrant, using your wok scoop to break it into tiny morsels.

Add the beans and stir-fry until piping hot. Serve hot or cold, with rice.

# Dry-fried Green Beans

## ganbian sijidou
干煸四季豆

My first experience of Sichuanese home cooking was at the home of the grandmother of my friend Tao Ping. This eighty-year-old lady lived on the seventh floor of a block of apartments without an elevator, and was lively and fit enough to cook us a lavish feast that I've never forgotten. Dry-fried green beans was one of the dishes she prepared: we also ate stewed beans with bacon, egg-flower soup, braised duck with konnyaku "tofu," stir-fried pork with bamboo shoots and fish in chile bean paste with whole cloves of garlic ("sensational," I wrote in my diary that night).

A Sichuanese classic, this dish is now famous all over the world. Officially, the beans should be "dry-fried" (*ganbian*) in a wok with minimal oil, over moderate heat, until wrinkled and tender, but in fact everyone I've ever met prefers to deep-fry them for speed. If you'd rather not deep-fry, you can also roast the beans before stir-frying them: place them in a single layer on a baking sheet and roast for about 15 minutes at 475°F (250°C), until just tender and tinged with brown (turn them halfway through the cooking). I'm grateful to my friend Rose Leng for this suggestion. Some people add a few dried chiles and some whole Sichuan pepper to this dish: if you do, fry them very briefly in the lard or oil before adding the ground pork.

14 oz (400g) green beans
Cooking oil, for deep-frying
3 tbsp lard (optional)
2½ oz (75g) ground pork (fatty is most delicious)
½ tbsp Shaoxing wine
4½ tbsp finely chopped Yibin yacai
   or Tianjin preserved vegetable
2 tsp light soy sauce
1 tsp sesame oil

**Remove any strings from the beans,** and top and tail them. Cut them into bite-sized lengths.

Heat the deep-frying oil to 355°F (180°C) (hot enough to sizzle vigorously around a test piece of bean). Add the beans and deep-fry until they are tender and a little wrinkled. Remove from the wok and drain well.

Carefully pour off all but 3 tbsp oil from the wok, then return to high heat (if using lard, pour off all of the oil and heat the lard in the wok instead). Add the pork and stir-fry until cooked and fragrant, splashing in the Shaoxing wine as the meat becomes pale. Add the beans and toss together. When the beans are piping hot again, add the preserved vegetable and soy sauce. (You can add extra salt or soy sauce, if you like, but you probably won't need to.)

Off the heat, stir in the sesame oil and serve.

### Vegetarian dry-fried green beans
*Prepare 14 oz (400g) green beans as above. Cut the white parts of 2 scallions into thin "horse ear" slices. Snip 8 dried chiles in half or into ¾-inch (2cm) sections and shake out the seeds as much as possible. Peel and slice 3 garlic cloves and an equivalent amount of ginger. Deep-fry the beans as in the main recipe. Return the wok to high heat with 3 tbsp of the deep-frying oil. Add the dried chiles, stir a couple of times, then add ½ tsp whole Sichuan pepper and the ginger, garlic and scallion whites. Stir-fry briefly until they smell wonderful. Add the beans—along with 4 tbsp finely chopped preserved vegetable, if you like—then toss everything together, adding salt to taste. Stir in 1 tsp sesame oil and serve.*

# Stir-fried Lotus Root with Chiles and Sichuan Pepper

## qiangchao oukuai
炝炒藕块

*1 lb (475g) lotus root (about 3 sections)*
*8 dried chiles*
*3 tbsp cooking oil*
*1 tsp whole Sichuan pepper*
*1 tsp sesame oil*
*Salt*

This is one of those utterly simple yet enchanting Sichuanese dishes: a swift stir-fry of lotus root that can be eaten either hot or cold. It's often found among the pre-made dishes on display outside "fly" restaurants in Chengdu, where you can lunch on your choice of a few dishes with steamed rice, or at places specializing in *lengdanbei*, the local equivalent of tapas.

Often, lotus root is served in thin slices that highlight its extraordinary internal structure; here, it's simply cubed, which makes the most of its delicately nutty flavor and exquisite crunch. A rumor of scorched chile and Sichuan pepper make it truly delectable.

**Trim off and discard the ends** of each section of lotus root, and then peel. Cut into ½–¾-inch (1–2cm) cubes. Let soak in a bowl of lightly salted cold water until you wish to cook them.

Snip the chiles into ¾-inch (2cm) sections and shake out the seeds as much as possible.

When you are ready to cook, drain the lotus root. Heat the cooking oil in a seasoned wok, and add the dried chiles before it gets too hot. Stir as the chiles begin to sizzle, then add the Sichuan pepper. When the chiles are darkening but not burned, add the drained lotus root and stir-fry for a few minutes until piping hot, seasoning with salt to taste.

Finally, off the heat, stir in the sesame oil. Serve hot or cold.

### Variations

*Many other vegetables can be cooked like this, by the method known as* qiang *or* qiangchao *in Chinese—a quick stir-fry with dried chiles and Sichuan pepper, with no sauce or starch thickener added. Water spinach is a classic example (see p. 271), as are potato slivers (see p. 287), but you can also use peas, green soy beans (edamame) and all kinds of leafy greens, or whatever else takes your fancy.*

# Tender Boiled Vegetables with a Spicy Dip

papa cai
炮炮菜

The following is an old-fashioned rustic, healthy dish that involves no oil and is beautifully simple. Assorted vegetables are just boiled in stock or water until tender (*pa* in local dialect, hence the name of the dish), and then served with a dip. The vegetables may be given extra flavor by dipping, but the broth is often no more than water that has absorbed some of the taste of the vegetables. In the past, the vegetables were often cooked in the water under the rice steamer, or the milky "rice broth" (*mitang*) left after parboiling the grains.

A seasonal version of this dish is made with "sons vegetable" or *ercai* (tiny cabbage-like greens that grow on a "mother" stalk like Brussels sprouts), and served with a small dish of ground chiles and Sichuan pepper, mixed with a little of the cooking liquid, for dipping. The vegetables taste a bit like broccoli stalks, and the broth ends up tinted a soft limpid green. Other vegetables I've eaten this way include daikon, Malabar spinach, yard-long beans, carrots, pumpkin, eggplants, cabbage and choy sum; kohlrabi and small potatoes are also very good.

If you wish, you can make a slightly richer dipping sauce (see the variations to the right), but I usually prefer to keep things plain, and eat papa cai as a remedy after a few days of gluttonous eating!

*Selection of fresh vegetables of your choice*
*Stock, "rice broth" (see p. 327) or water*
*Salt*
*Ground chiles*
*Ground roasted Sichuan pepper*
*Thinly sliced scallion greens*
*Toasted sesame seeds (optional)*

**Cut the vegetables evenly** into bite-sized pieces. Pour enough stock, broth or water to cover the vegetables into a saucepan and bring to a boil. Add the vegetables and simmer until tender: it's best to add vegetables that take longer to cook, such as potatoes, at the beginning, and vegetables that don't take as long, like leafy greens, later on.

Give each person a dipping dish and invite them to add salt, ground chiles, Sichuan pepper, scallion greens—and sesame seeds, if using—to taste.

Serve the vegetables in the pan or transfer to a serving bowl with their cooking liquid. Spoon a little of the cooking liquid into the dipping dishes to make a sauce. Use your chopsticks to dip the vegetables into the dipping sauce before eating, and then drink the rest of the liquid as a broth.

Variations

*Traditionally, in the countryside, the dip is often made with* cuo chiles: *dried chiles that have been roasted in the embers of the cooking stove, dusted off and then rubbed between the hands into flakes (they can also be dry-fried in a wok until crisp and bronzed).*

*For a richer dip, gently stir-fry about 3 tbsp Sichuan chile bean paste in 1–2 tbsp oil (per serving) until the oil is red and fragrant. Transfer the oil and paste to a bowl, then add ground chiles, soy sauce, ground roasted Sichuan pepper, thinly sliced scallion greens and chopped cilantro to taste. This is also delicious.*

# Dry-fried "Eels"
## (Shiitake Mushrooms)

ganbian shanyu
干煸鳝鱼

This delicious example of Buddhist trompe l'oeil cooking is based on a memorable version I enjoyed in the restaurant at the Temple of Divine Light, near Chengdu. The "eels," made from dried shiitake mushrooms, look strikingly similar to the real paddy eels used in the classic Sichuanese recipe. The original dish did not include garlic, which strict Buddhists avoid as one of the pungent vegetables thought to inflame carnal passions, but I've added it here for extra deliciousness. Dried mushrooms are particularly important in Chinese vegetarian cooking because of their enticing savory flavors and satisfyingly meaty textures. I like to use long, thin-skinned Turkish peppers, for their more delicate texture and milder taste.

*10–12 dried shiitake mushrooms (9 oz/250g after soaking)*
*⅔ cup (75g) potato starch*
*8 dried chiles*
*6¼ oz (175g) long green Turkish peppers*
*Cooking oil, for deep-frying*
*1 tsp whole Sichuan pepper*
*1½ tbsp Sichuan chile bean paste*
*3 garlic cloves, peeled and sliced*
*An equivalent amount of ginger, peeled and sliced*
*1 tsp sesame oil*

*For the sauce*
*¾ tsp potato starch*
*½ tsp superfine sugar*
*1 tsp light soy sauce*
*¼ tsp dark soy sauce*

Place the dried mushrooms in a saucepan, cover with hot water from the kettle and leave to soften for at least 30 minutes. Bring to a boil, season lightly with salt and simmer the mushrooms for 20 minutes, then drain. When they are cool enough to handle, squeeze out as much water as possible, then cut into strips about ½ inch (1.5cm) wide. Place in a bowl with the potato starch and mix until evenly coated. Snip the chiles in half or into ¾-inch (2cm) sections and shake out the seeds as much as possible. Cut the green peppers into bite-sized pieces. In a small bowl, combine the sauce ingredients with 4 tbsp cold water and mix well.

Heat the deep-frying oil in a wok over high heat to about 375°F (190°C) (hot enough to sizzle vigorously around a test piece of mushroom). Working in two or three batches, carefully slip the mushrooms into the hot oil, adding them individually so they don't stick together. Fry for a minute or so until crisp and a little golden, then remove with a slotted spoon and drain well.

Carefully pour off all but 3 tbsp oil from the wok, and return to high heat. Add the chiles and Sichuan pepper and stir-fry briefly until the chiles are aromatic, but not burned. Immediately move the wok away from the heat and add the chile bean paste, stirring as it sizzles, until the oil has reddened. Add the garlic, ginger and green pepper and return the wok to the stove, stir-frying until everything is piping hot and smells delicious. Swiftly stir in the mushrooms, then give the sauce a stir and pour it into the center of the wok. Mix quickly to allow the sauce to coat the mushrooms as it thickens. Stir in the sesame oil and serve.

# Stir-fried Cabbage with Chile

## qiang lianhuabai
## 炝莲花白

The Chinese understand how to make the cheap, healthy greens of the cabbage or Brassica family taste irresistible, and this quick dish is a prime example. Hand-torn cabbage is stir-fried with a rumor of dried chile and Sichuan pepper and seasoned with a dash of sweet-and-sour flavorings. In China, they make it with large, flattish and somewhat loosely-leaved white cabbage (*lianhuabai,* Latin name *Brassica oleracea* var. *capitata*); at home I've made it with the pointy "sweetheart" cabbage the Chinese sometimes call a "chicken-heart cabbage" because of its shape.

¾ lb (350g) pointy "sweetheart" cabbage
(minus its dark outer leaves)
6 dried chiles
1½ tsp superfine sugar
½ tsp salt
2 tsp light soy sauce
1½ tbsp Chinkiang vinegar
3 tbsp cooking oil
2 tsp whole Sichuan pepper

Tear the cabbage leaves into chopstickable pieces (do not include the thick central stem in this dish). Snip the chiles in half or into ¾-inch (2cm) sections and shake out the seeds as much as possible. Combine the sugar, salt, soy sauce and vinegar in a small bowl with 1 tbsp cold water, and mix well.

Heat the oil in a seasoned wok over high heat, and quickly add the chiles and Sichuan pepper. Stir-fry until the spices smell wonderful and the chiles are darkening but not burned, then swiftly add the cabbage and toss everything together. Stir-fry until the cabbage is piping hot and barely cooked. (At the beginning you will appear to have an unfeasibly large amount of cabbage in the wok, but it will settle down as you turn it in the wok.) Add a tablespoon or so of water to the wok if the cabbage starts to stick.

Finally, give the contents of the bowl a stir and add to the wok. Stir briefly to allow some of the liquid to evaporate and the flavors to fuse, and then serve.

# Stir-fried Cabbage with Pork Cracklings

youzha lianbai

油渣莲白

If you render your own lard, you will end up with the most delicious pork cracklings, which can be added to soups, noodles and stir-fries like this one, for a bit of crunch and savor. Even if you don't make your own lard, you might like to try this recipe, in which small morsels of fragrant pork fat, sizzled until crisp in the same way, make a wokful of cabbage irresistible. A good butcher should be able to supply the back fat; if you can't get it, use fatty pork belly instead. The method is based on a recipe explained to me by the manager of the People's Commune restaurant in Chengdu.

¾ lb (350g) pointy "sweetheart" cabbage
  (minus the dark outer leaves)
2½ oz (75g) pork back fat
6 dried chiles
3 garlic cloves
1 tbsp cooking oil
3½ tsp light soy sauce

Tear the cabbage into bite-sized pieces. Cut the pork fat into ½-inch (1cm) dice. Snip the chiles in half or into ¾-inch (2cm) sections and shake out the seeds as much as possible. Peel and slice the garlic.

Heat the oil in a seasoned wok over medium heat. Add the diced pork fat and stir-fry until every piece is crisp, golden and fragrant. Remove the pork cracklings with a slotted spoon and set aside.

Carefully pour off all but 1 tbsp of the oil and rendered fat from the wok and return to medium heat. Add the chiles and Sichuan pepper and stir-fry until they are fragrant and the chiles are darkening but not burned. Add the garlic and pork cracklings and stir-fry briefly, until you can smell the garlic. Add the cabbage, turn the heat up high and stir and toss until the cabbage is just cooked (add a tablespoon of water if at any point the wok seems too dry and scorchy). Finally, add the soy sauce, mix well and serve.

# Cauliflower
# with Smoked Bacon

## larou shao huacai
## 腊肉烧花菜

Cauliflower is thought to be native to the eastern Mediterranean, and has only been used in China for a couple of hundred years. In Sichuan you occasionally see it blanched and cold-dressed in stock and sesame oil, but it's more commonly cooked with a little smoked bacon, as in the following recipe, which was one I often ate in the 1990s at the Bamboo Bar restaurant in Chengdu. The dish is typical of everyday Chinese cooking in the way that a little meat is used to lend delicious umami flavors to a pale-tasting vegetable; if you use lard rather than vegetable oil, the flavors will be further intensified.

*1 small cauliflower (about 1 lb/450g)*
*2½–3½ oz (75–100g) smoked bacon slices*
*3 tbsp cooking oil or lard*
*3 garlic cloves, peeled and sliced*
*1¼ cups (300ml) stock*
*1½ tsp potato starch,*
*    mixed with 2 tbsp cold water*
*Salt and ground white pepper*

**Break or cut the cauliflower** into bite-sized, chopstickable florets. Thinly slice the stem. Trim off and reserve the bacon rinds, then cut the bacon into bite-sized pieces.

Heat the oil or lard in a seasoned wok over high heat. Add the bacon and the rinds and stir-fry until wonderfully fragrant and tinged with gold. Remove and discard the rinds, then add the sliced garlic and stir-fry until it smells delicious. Tip the cauliflower into the wok and turn in the fragrant oil, then add the stock and salt to taste. Nudge the pieces of cauliflower sitting around the edges of the wok into the liquid so they are not touching the bare metal (top up with a small amount of stock or hot water if necessary). When the liquid has come to a boil, cover the wok and simmer for about 5 minutes, removing the lid briefly to stir once or twice, until the cauliflower is tender.

When the cauliflower is ready, remove the lid and turn up the heat. Season to taste with pepper and a little more salt if necessary. Give the potato starch mixture a stir and gradually add it to the wok, stirring as the sauce thickens. Serve.

# Stir-fried Garlic Stems with Smoked Bacon

larou chao suantai
腊肉炒蒜薹

9 oz (250g) garlic stems
3 slices smoked bacon,
  thickly cut if possible
3 tbsp cooking oil
½ tsp sesame oil
Salt

One of my favorite Sichuanese stir-fries is a simple mix of garlic stems or scapes (*suantai* or *suanhao*) and thin strips of smoked bacon. The stems have a juicy texture, reminiscent of asparagus, and a wonderful garlicky taste that softens and sweetens with cooking; they are perfectly complemented by the umami flavor of the bacon. In Sichuan, the long garlic stems are sold doubled up into skeins with their tiny bulbs still attached; abroad, they can often be found in good Chinese supermarkets—usually shorn of their bulbs and tied into bunched lengths of about 12 inches (30cm). Most Sichuanese cooks steam the bacon before cutting it, but I don't usually bother. Instead of smoked bacon, feel free to use Chinese wind-dried sausage or Cantonese soy-sauce-cured pork, both of which are delicious.

If the bases of the garlic stems are a little fibrous, cut them off and discard them, then cut the stems into 2-inch (5cm) lengths. Slice off the bacon rinds, reserving them to flavor the cooking oil, and cut the bacon across the grain into thin lardons.

Heat a seasoned wok over high heat. Add the cooking oil and swirl it around, then add the bacon and its rinds and stir a few times to separate the pieces. Add the garlic stems and stir-fry until they are just tender and starting to wrinkle, seasoning with salt to taste.

Off the heat, remove and discard the bacon rinds, stir in the sesame oil and serve.

*Stir-fried flowering chives with smoked bacon*
*(larou chao jiucaihua 腊肉炒韭菜花)*
*Instead of garlic stems, use Chinese flowering chives, which are lovely cooked this way, but have a coarser texture than garlic stems. You can recognize flowering chives by their thin, angular green stems, each topped by a papery little bud. They are normally sold in bunches—just snip off the bulbs before you begin.*

# Dry-fried Bitter Melon

## ganbian kugua
## 干煸苦瓜

In Chinese, bitterness (*ku*) is the universal metaphor for suffering. Chinese people remember the famine years of the late 1950s and the grim banishments of the Cultural Revolution as a time when they "ate bitterness," *chiku*. But despite its association with sorrow, bitterness also has its benefits. Bitter words spoken by an emperor's adviser could be seen as a token of loyalty, and bitterness in food can be efficacious according to traditional Chinese medicine. In Sichuan, during the sultry summer months, bitter foods are thought to cool the body and drive out perspiration.

The undisputed queen of bitter foods is the bitter melon or gourd (*kugua*, Latin name *Momordica charantia*), a long, gnarled, bright green vegetable with a withering bite. It's a common feature on Sichuanese dinner tables whenever the weather's hot and humid, particularly prepared according to the following dry-frying method, which is a local specialty. The extremely bitter flavor of the vegetable is definitely an acquired taste, but one adored by those who grow to like it.

*1 bitter melon (about 1 lb 2 oz/525g)*
*5 dried chiles*
*3 tbsp cooking oil*
*½ tsp whole Sichuan pepper*
*1 tbsp finely chopped garlic*
*4 tbsp finely chopped Yibin yacai*
*    preserved vegetable, rinsed*
*    and squeezed dry*
*1 tsp sesame oil*
*Salt*

Trim the ends off the bitter melon and cut it in half lengthwise, then cut each half crosswise into fairly thin slices. Snip the dried chiles into ¾-inch (2cm) sections and shake out the seeds as much as possible.

Heat a seasoned wok over medium heat. Add the sliced melon and stir-fry with no oil for a few minutes, until it is piping hot and reduced in volume, looks wet and has caught the fragrance of the wok.

Push the melon slices up one side of the wok and pour the cooking oil into the base. Add the chiles and Sichuan pepper and stir-fry in the small pool of oil until the chiles smell wonderful and are beginning to darken. Add the garlic to the oil, stir a couple of times until you can smell it, then tip in the preserved vegetable and give it a stir or two in the oil. Toss everything in the wok together, seasoning with salt to taste.

Off the heat, stir in the sesame oil and then serve.

*Dry-fried bitter melon with ground pork*
*Before you fry the melon, stir-fry 1¾ oz (50g) ground pork in a little oil with a dash of soy sauce until cooked and fragrant, then set aside; rinse and dry the wok if necessary. Add the cooked pork to the wok with the preserved vegetable in the above recipe.*

*Classic dry-fried bitter melon*
*Instead of using chiles, Sichuan pepper, garlic and preserved vegetable, you can simply dry-fry the sliced melon with a thinly sliced green pepper (hot or not), and season with salt alone, as in the dry-fried eggplants recipe on p. 268. This is the most common version of dry-fried bitter melon.*

# Stir-fried Potato Slivers with Chiles and Sichuan Pepper

qiang tudou si
炝土豆丝

14 oz (400g) potatoes
6 dried chiles
2 tbsp cooking oil
½ tsp whole Sichuan pepper
1 tsp sesame oil
Salt

The Chinese attitude to potatoes is radically different from the Western one. They're not seen as a staple food, but as a vegetable to be cooked and eaten as an accompaniment to rice. In Chinese, they are known as "earth beans" (*tudou*) or as "foreign taro" (*yangyu*), the latter a reference to their New World origins and comparatively recent introduction into China. Sometimes potato chunks are simmered with beef or pork in slow-cooked stews. More often in Sichuan they are cut into fine slivers and stir-fried. This cooking method keeps them crunchy, and lends them a very different character from mashed, boiled, deep-fried and roasted potatoes. (If you cut the potatoes slightly more thickly, don't rinse away the starch and extend the cooking time a little, the result will have a stickier, more "potatoey" mouthfeel.)

You can make this with any kind of potato, but it works best with waxy rather than baking varieties. The tastier the potatoes, the better, obviously: I find yellow potatoes such as Yukon Gold work well. The finer and more even your chopping, the better the result—good Sichuanese cooks slice their potatoes so finely that they look almost like skeins of wool when cooked and languidly entwined on the plate. Some Sichuanese friends of mine jokingly call this dish *yangyu chao tudou*, which can be roughly translated as "spud-fried potatoes"—a way of sending up a cheap and humble dish by giving it a fancier name.

Peel the potatoes and cut them, as evenly as possible, into very thin slices. Then cut them into very fine slivers. Soak for a few minutes in cold, lightly salted water to remove excess starch. Just before cooking, drain the potatoes in a colander, shaking out as much water as possible. Snip the chiles in half or into ¾-inch (2cm) sections and shake out the seeds as much as possible.

Heat the cooking oil in a seasoned wok over high heat. Before the oil gets really hot, add the chiles and stir-fry briefly until aromatic and beginning to darken. Quickly add the Sichuan pepper, stir a couple of times, and then tip in the potato slivers. (The key here is to scorch the chiles without burning them.)

Stir-fry briskly until the potatoes are piping hot and have lost their starchy raw taste, but are still a little crisp, seasoning with salt to taste. Finally, off the heat, stir in the sesame oil and serve.

*Stir-fried potato slivers with scallion*
*(cong chao tudousi 葱炒土豆丝)*
*Omit the chile and Sichuan pepper and stir-fry the potato slivers, adding salt to taste and a small handful of thinly sliced scallion greens just before you take the wok off the heat; the scallions only need to be stir-fried for a few seconds, just until you can smell them. Add the sesame oil and serve.*

*Stir-fried potato slivers with green bell pepper*
*(qingjiao tudousi 青椒土豆丝)*
*Omit the chile and Sichuan pepper and stir-fry the potato slivers with a handful of green bell pepper slivers (aim for about one-fifth of the amount of potato slivers), adding salt to taste and a small handful of thinly sliced scallion greens just before you take the wok off the heat.*

*Stir-fried potato slivers with vinegar (culiu tudousi 醋溜土豆丝)*
*Stir-fry the potato slivers with a few slivers of green bell pepper, for color. Season with salt and a little light soy sauce and add 2 tsp Chinkiang vinegar toward the end of the cooking time.*

# "Crossing-the-river" Choy Sum

## guojiang caixin
## 过江菜心

The southern Sichuanese have a particular predilection for serving food with dips—poached rabbit, cold cuts of meat and offal, fresh silken tofu and vegetables. Many are based on soy sauce laced with chile oil or ground chiles, fresh bird's eye chiles, chopped herbs and garlic, sometimes with a dash of vinegar. In particular, when they serve leafy greens that must be picked up with chopsticks and then dipped in a sauce, this is described as "crossing-the-river" and is included in the name of the dish. The greens may be simply stir-fried, blanched and drained, or boiled and served in their cooking water. At one dinner in Hejiang, my friends and I were served stir-fried amaranth in a pool of its own magenta juices, and a bowlful of tender water spinach in hot water, both with a single, spicy dip.

The following recipe suggests using choy sum, but you could instead use water spinach, amaranth, chard or bunched spinach. And please treat the sauce recipe as a series of hints rather than strict instructions: you might want to add a little chopped ginger, a pinch of superfine sugar or some thinly sliced scallions to the mix. As long as the vegetable is served with a separate dip, it will still be "crossing-the-river."

10 oz (300g) choy sum (or other leafy greens)

*For the dipping sauce*
*2 tbsp light soy sauce*
*1 tsp Chinkiang vinegar*
*1 tbsp finely chopped garlic*
*2 tsp ground chiles*
*¼ tsp ground roasted Sichuan pepper*

**Rinse the greens thoroughly,** trim if necessary, and then cut into long sections that can be picked up with chopsticks.

Combine all the ingredients for the sauce in a small bowl.

Bring a pot of water to a boil. Add the greens and boil briefly until the leaves are wilted and the stems tender. Drain and pile up on a serving dish, or serve in a bowl with the cooking liquid. Dip the vegetables into the sauce before eating.

# Green Soy Beans with "Golden Hooks"

## jingou qingdou
## 金钩青豆

This gentle dish, soothing to the eye and palate, is a lovely contrast to the more dramatic Sichuanese dishes. It's a classic combination of fresh beans and "golden hooks" (*jingou*), as the Sichuanese call dried shrimp. When we were taught this at my Sichuan cooking school, the teacher recommended using a rich milky stock, though an ordinary stock will suffice. At a banquet, the dish would be finished with a dash of chicken oil, but you can use sesame oil for everyday eating. If you're using frozen green soy beans, defrost them before cooking.

3 tbsp dried shrimp

1 tbsp Shaoxing wine

¾-inch piece (15g) ginger, unpeeled

2 scallions, white parts only

2 tbsp lard or cooking oil

1 cup plus 1 tbsp (250ml) milky stock (see p. 465) or everyday stock (see p. 463)

2 cups (300g) shelled green soy beans (edamame)

2 tsp potato starch, mixed with 1½ tbsp cold water

1½ tsp chicken oil (see p. 462) or sesame oil

Salt and ground white pepper

**Place the dried shrimp in a small bowl** with the Shaoxing wine. Add enough hot water from the kettle to cover, and let soak for at least 30 minutes. Lightly smack the ginger and scallion whites with the flat of a cleaver blade or a rolling pin to loosen them.

Heat the lard or oil in a seasoned wok over high heat. Add the ginger and scallion whites and stir-fry until wonderfully fragrant. Tip in the stock and bring to a boil, then strain out and discard the ginger and scallion whites. Add the soy beans and the drained shrimp. Return to a boil, season with salt and white pepper to taste, and then simmer for a couple of minutes to let the flavors mingle.

When the liquid has reduced by about a third, give the potato starch mixture a stir and gradually add it to the wok, stirring as you go, and adding just enough to give the liquid a lazy, gravy-like consistency. Stir in the chicken oil or sesame oil and serve.

### Variations

*The same method can be used to cook other vegetables, including green bok choy, chunks or balls of peeled winter melon and shelled peas. If using green bok choy, blanch to "break its rawness" before adding to the flavored stock, then remove the bok choy to a serving dish before thickening the sauce, adding the chicken or sesame oil and then pouring it over the vegetables. If using winter melon, add a little more stock and simmer until the melon is tender before thickening the sauce.*

# "Ants Climbing a Tree" (Bean-thread Noodles with Ground Pork)

mayi shangshu
蚂蚁上树

If you dangle a few strands of these noodles from your chopsticks, tiny morsels of meat will cling to them "like ants climbing a tree," hence the name. This cheap and hearty dish was typical of Sichuanese home cooking and modest restaurants in the 1990s, but now rarely appears in cookbooks or on menus.

It is, however, delicious: a snaking mound of glassy noodles, dotted with morsels of ground meat, scarlet chile and green scallion. Some cooks deep-fry the dried noodles instead of soaking them; the noodles do, however, tend to disintegrate with this method. Bean-thread noodles, which are enjoyed for their strandy, slippery mouthfeel, are not considered a staple food; "ants climbing a tree" is always served with plain white rice and other dishes. Sometimes the dish is made with sweet potato noodles, which are thicker but also transparent and delightfully slithery.

3½ oz (100g) bean-thread noodles
   (or sweet potato noodles)
3 tbsp cooking oil
3½ oz (100g) finely ground pork
½ tbsp Shaoxing wine
1 tsp light soy sauce
1½ tbsp Sichuan chile bean paste
1 tbsp finely chopped ginger
1 tbsp finely chopped garlic
1½ cups (350ml) everyday stock (see p. 463)
½ tsp dark soy sauce
4 tbsp finely chopped scallion greens
Salt

**Cover the bean-thread noodles** with hot water from the kettle and let soak for a few minutes to soften. (If using sweet potato noodles, soak them in cold water for at least 2 hours or overnight.)

Meanwhile, heat 2 tbsp oil in a seasoned wok over high heat. Add the pork and stir-fry, breaking it up into tiny pieces as you do—remember, it's supposed to look like ants. When the meat is cooked, splash in the Shaoxing wine, then stir in the light soy sauce and a pinch of salt.

When the pork is fragrant and a little brown, tilt the wok and push the pork up one side, to let the oil pool in the base. Add 1 tbsp oil, followed by the chile bean paste, and stir-fry until the oil is red and fragrant—turn the heat down a little to avoid burning, if necessary. Add the ginger and garlic and stir-fry until they too smell delicious. Tilt the wok back and stir the pork into the sauce, then add the stock, dark soy sauce and the well-drained noodles and mix thoroughly.

Turn the heat back up to high and stir until the liquid has been absorbed by the noodles, then add the scallion greens, mix well and serve.

### Variation

*Instead of ground pork, use ground beef, and replace the scallion greens with the same amount of finely chopped celery.*

# Sweetcorn Kernels with Green Peppers

## qingjiao yumi
## 青椒玉米

Sweetcorn has a poetic name in Chinese—"jade rice"—but is not considered a prestigious food. In Sichuan, it is generally associated with subsistence eating in the poor mountainous areas of the province. Cornmeal is made into some snacks and sweets, for example a type of coarse, conical steamed bun known as *wowotou* that is still a peasant staple but is also served in some fashionable restaurants as a pseudo-rustic novelty snack. Fresh sweetcorn kernels are often stir-fried, as in the following recipe.

This is the kind of everyday dish you won't often find in recipe books, but it crops up frequently on the menus of low-key Sichuanese restaurants and in home kitchens. You can use frozen or unsweetened, canned sweetcorn instead of fresh corn cut from the cob, if you wish. I recommend using thin-fleshed Turkish green peppers, but the regular kind is fine too. This definitely tastes best with plenty of salt—maybe a little more than you would put into other dishes.

1½ cups (250g) sweetcorn kernels
   (about 2 corn cobs' worth)
3 long green Turkish peppers
   or 1–2 green bell peppers (about 5¼ oz/150g)
2 tbsp cooking oil
Salt

**If using fresh sweetcorn,** strip the kernels from the cobs—you can do this by inserting the blade of a table knife into the gaps between the rows of kernels and gently levering them off. When you've cleared a few rows, use your thumb to lever off the rest (it doesn't take as long as you might think).

Chop the peppers into little chunks, about the same size as the sweetcorn kernels.

Heat the oil in a seasoned wok over high heat. Add both vegetables and stir-fry for 4–5 minutes, until piping hot and sizzly, adding salt to taste.

# Stir-fried Amaranth Leaves with Garlic

chao hancai
炒苋菜

This spring and summer vegetable, known as *hancai* in Sichuanese and *xiancai* in Mandarin, is the tender young leaves and stems of a species of amaranth (*Amaranthus tricolor*). The leaves have purple centers and green edges, and can have rounded or pointed ends, depending on the variety. The Sichuanese traditionally eat this vegetable on the fifth day of the fifth lunar month, during the Dragon Boat Festival, along with salted duck eggs and leaf-wrapped cones of glutinous rice (*zongzi*). It can be cooked in a number of ways, but is most commonly—and most deliciously—stir-fried with garlic. The cooking releases the purple pigments in the leaves, coloring the juices the most beautiful pink. Amaranth can be found in some Chinese and Vietnamese food shops. For convenience, you can cut the amaranth into longish, chopstickable lengths (the Chinese normally stir-fry without cutting).

*9 oz (250g) amaranth leaves*
   *(with any fibrous stalks discarded)*
*3 tbsp cooking oil*
*3 garlic cloves, peeled and sliced*
*Around 3 tbsp hot stock or water,*
   *if needed*
*Salt*

**Rinse the amaranth and shake dry.** Heat the oil in a seasoned wok over high heat. Add the garlic before the oil gets too hot, and stir-fry as it sizzles and releases its aromas.

Before the garlic colors, add the amaranth and stir-fry briskly until the leaves are wilted and the stems tender. If the wok seems too dry, add the stock or water: you want to end up with a small pool of pink juices from the leaves.

Season with salt to taste, then serve.

## Variations

*Many other leafy vegetables are delicious stir-fried with garlic, including spinach, water spinach, wild winter vetch and other wild vegetables. With coarser vegetables such as chard, it's best to add a little liquid after the initial stir-frying, then cover the wok and cook over medium heat until tender, stirring occasionally to make sure they don't stick.*

# Stir-fried Mixed Mushrooms

shanzhen hui
山珍烩

When I paid a late-summer visit to the Wolong Nature Reserve in western Sichuan, I discovered that one of the local cooks was, like me, a former student of the Sichuan Institute of Higher Cuisine in Chengdu. In China this "same-school" (*tongxue*) bond is an important one, and I was welcomed as one of the family. My *tongxue* Peng Rui and I pottered around in the kitchen while his mother smoked bacon over a smoldering fire in the shed at the back. The highlight of the visit, however, was a trip we made up the valley in search of wild food plants.

We chugged up the road on a borrowed moped, the immense, pine-clad mountains rising steeply on either side, their peaks shrouded in mist. In the valley a peacock-blue river tumbled over a mass of boulders. Small-scale farmers worked the steep lower slopes, carving out a patchwork of tiny plots: dark leaves shielded the hearts of cabbages and pinky-white radishes swelled out of the earth. Yellow corncobs and scarlet chiles dangled in huge bundles from the wooden eaves of scattered cottages. At one point we left the road and continued on foot through a craggy gorge, where cataracts spilled into a mountain stream. Here, I was told, the changing seasons brought walnuts and crabapples, tiny wild strawberries and an abundance of fungi.

The following recipe was created in homage to a dish of stir-fried wild mushrooms Peng Rui made that night. You can vary the mushrooms as you will—just try to bring together a few contrasting colors and textures.

14 oz (400g) mixed mushrooms, such as shiitake, oyster, Chinese golden needle or Japanese enoki, maitake (hen of the woods), king oyster, button, dried bamboo pith fungus
2 scallions
3 tbsp lard or cooking oil
1 tbsp chicken oil (see p. 462, optional)
3 garlic cloves, peeled and sliced
¾ cup plus 2 tbsp (200ml) chicken or vegetable stock
1 tsp potato starch, mixed with 1½ tbsp cold water
Salt and ground white pepper

**If using bamboo pith fungus,** soak it for a few seconds in cold water to soften, then blanch briefly in boiling water; rinse under cold water and cut into 1½-inch (4cm) lengths. If you are using enoki or maitake mushrooms, gently pull them apart so they're not in one clump. Cut or tear oyster mushrooms into bite-sized pieces. Cut the other mushrooms into ⅛-inch (3–4mm) slices.

Cut off the white parts of the scallions, then lightly smack them with the flat of a cleaver blade or a rolling pin to loosen them. Thinly slice the green parts.

Heat the lard or oil (with the chicken oil, if using) in a seasoned wok over high heat. Add the scallion whites and stir-fry until wonderfully fragrant, then add the garlic and continue to stir-fry until aromatic but not colored. Remove and discard the scallion whites. Add all the mushrooms and stir them into the garlicky oil. Add the stock, bring to a boil and season with salt and pepper to taste. At first, it will look as if there is not enough liquid, then suddenly, as the mushrooms relax, there will be plenty. Cook, stirring, until the mushrooms are tender.

Give the potato starch mixture a stir and gradually add to the wok, stirring as you go, and adding just enough to thicken the liquid to a luxurious sauce. Stir in the scallion greens and then serve.

# Stewed Baby Taro with Greens

## yu'er baicai
芋儿白菜

1 lb 5 oz (600g) taro
2 cups (500ml) chicken, vegetable
   or everyday stock (see p. 463)
7 oz (200g) green bok choy
*Salt and ground white pepper*

Taro is a vegetable that is often overlooked in the West, but its starchy white corms have a gorgeously silky texture, like a softer and more delicate cousin of the potato (one of the Chinese names for the potato, a much later arrival in China, is *yangyu*, "foreign taro"). I love to eat it in this soothing dish: a simple, soupy stew of taro and leafy greens. If you don't have bok choy, feel free to use chard, spinach or other greens of your choice, adjusting the cooking times accordingly. This dish is particularly satisfying when the taro is stewed in advance, so that it has time to relax into the stock, resulting in an almost creamy consistency.

Taro can be found (under various names) in Chinese, African and West Indian shops, and can be identified by its ridged, bristly brown corms; choose smaller corms, if possible. Note that it's best to wear rubber gloves for peeling the taro, as their skin contains an irritant that is neutralized by cooking but can make your hands itch when handled raw.

**Put on some rubber gloves,** then peel and rinse the taro. Cut into bite-sized chunks and place in a saucepan with the stock. Bring to a boil, season with salt and pepper and then simmer for about 20 minutes until the taro is completely tender. Switch off the heat and set aside until needed.

Shortly before you wish to serve, return the taro to a boil. Cut the bok choy into bite-sized pieces and add to the pan; cover and cook briefly until the leaves are wilted and the stems tender. Adjust the seasoning, if necessary, then serve.

# Tiger-skin Green Peppers

## fupi qingjiao
## 虎皮青椒

This dish is so called because the frying method makes the skins of the peppers slightly wrinkled and golden in places, so that they look streaky—"like a tiger's skin." After the frying, the peppers are seasoned with salt and then dressed on the serving dish with a little aromatic vinegar and soy sauce, a delicious contrast to their rich, buttery flesh. The Sichuanese use small, thin-skinned green chiles that are generally 2½–3½ inches (6–9cm) long; at home in London, I use longer, thin-skinned Turkish peppers with a pleasing kick of heat.

Ordering this dish in a Sichuan restaurant is always a gamble because you never know exactly what kind of chile will be used—sometimes they are as sweet and mild as green bell peppers, other times so hot they'll leave you gasping (with its element of Russian roulette, the dish is perhaps a Chinese equivalent of Spanish padrón peppers). The peppers can be eaten hot or cold.

10 oz (300g) long green Turkish peppers
1 tbsp Chinkiang vinegar
2 tsp light soy sauce
Cooking oil, for deep-frying
Salt

Lightly smack the peppers with the flat of a cleaver blade or a rolling pin to loosen them. Trim off and discard the stems and cut the peppers into 2½–2¾-inch (6–7cm) sections, shaking off any obvious seeds. Mix together the vinegar and soy sauce.

Heat the deep-frying oil to 390°F (200°C) (hot enough to sizzle vigorously around a test piece of pepper). Add the peppers and stir for a minute or two until the skins are white and blistered and the flesh is tender. Carefully strain off the deep-frying oil from the wok, then return to high heat and stir the peppers as you season them with salt to taste.

Pile the peppers onto a serving dish. Pour the vinegar mixture around the edges of the dish (so it doesn't spoil the color of the peppers) and dip the peppers into it as you pick them up with your chopsticks.

## Stir-fried Celery with Ground Pork

lanrou xiqin

烂肉西芹

This simple, scrumptious stir-fry is typical of Sichuanese "home-style" cooking. The recipe, which is similar to the celery and beef dish from my book *Every Grain of Rice* but with an extra kick of chile oil and Sichuan pepper, is based on one from Zhang Guobin and Li Qi, respectively chef and owner of one of my favorite backstreet restaurants in Chengdu. It's easy to make and, with plain white rice, can serve as a meal for two in itself. In Sichuan they use Chinese celery, which is thinner and more aromatic than the kind typically eaten in the West, but I find the dish more delicious when made with regular Western celery, which is juicier.

*10 oz (300g) celery (about 5–6 sticks)*

*3 tbsp cooking oil*

*3½ oz (100g) ground pork*

*1½ tbsp Sichuan chile bean paste*

*1½ tbsp finely chopped ginger*

*1 tsp light soy sauce*

*1 tsp Chinkiang vinegar*

*¼ tsp ground roasted
  Sichuan pepper, or to taste*

*1 tbsp chile oil*

**Remove any strings from the celery sticks,** cut them lengthwise into ½-inch (1cm) strips, and then finely chop the strips.

Heat the cooking oil in a seasoned wok over high heat. Add the pork and stir-fry until pale, breaking the meat into tiny morsels as it cooks. Add the chile bean paste and continue to stir-fry until the oil is red and fragrant, then tip in the ginger and stir-fry until it also smells wonderful. Add the celery and continue to stir-fry until it is piping hot, adding the soy sauce as you go. Add the vinegar and give it a lick of heat.

Finally, stir in the Sichuan pepper and chile oil, and serve.

# Soups

"Many Sichuanese soups are modestly seasoned because of their role as palate-cleansers: a spicy relish is sometimes served on the side, for dipping solid ingredients before the broth itself is drunk"

# Soups 汤羹类

Soup plays a vital role in most Chinese meals, and has a far greater importance in Chinese food culture than it typically has in the West. Soup might be the only liquid consumed with a meal, serving as both food and beverage. It is part of the comfort of eating, rinsing the palate, soothing the throat and offering a pleasing contrast to "dry" rice and dishes. Noodles and dumplings are often served in soup; when they are not, a separate bowlful of broth may be provided. Because of this function as liquid refreshment, most Chinese soups are light and brothy, unlike the thick and creamy soups normally favored in the West. In Chinese, light, broth-based soups are known as *tang*; a different word, *geng*, is more often used for substantial soups full of finely cut ingredients. Chinese people also seem to have a more refined appreciation of the subtle flavors of a broth than most outsiders, savoring the distilled essences of the meat or poultry that are intrinsic to a good stock.

In Guangdong and elsewhere in southern China, soup is usually eaten at the start of a meal, to "open the stomach" (*kaiwei*) and whet the appetite. In Sichuan, however, soup is typically served at the end, to refresh the palate after a run of intense and spicy flavors. For this reason, Sichuanese soups tend to be clear and lightly seasoned. Sometimes they appear slight and modest in comparison with more sensational dishes, but that's the point: they are part of an overall harmony in which stimulating flavors are balanced by those that are calming and refreshing. When I first started eating in China, I found some of the soups a little boring; now I like to eat a simple soup with almost every meal, because it leaves me feeling so relaxed and comfortable. (Incidentally, the presence of gentle, understated soups on a the menu of a Chinese restaurant is usually a sign that it's frequented by Chinese people and not just Westerners.)

Some everyday soups are absurdly simple. They may consist of no more than a vegetable boiled in water or the silky, starchy liquid left over from cooking rice or noodles. In the countryside, vegetables are often cooked up in this "rice broth" (*mitang*) to make a rudimentary soup: tender winter vetch leaves, maybe, or Chinese mallow, perhaps with a dash of home-made lard for richness. The vegetable ingredients can be stir-fried (often in lard) before stock or rice broth is added. A soup like this can be a good home for odds and ends of vegetables left in the fridge.

For another type of broth, a whole fowl or some pork ribs, for example, may be slow-simmered to give a flavorful yet almost colorless broth; richer soups can be made by boiling poultry and meat bones with collagenous ingredients such as pig's trotters or knuckles to yield a milky, emulsified stock.

Many Sichuanese soups are modestly seasoned because of their role as palate-cleansers: a spicy relish is sometimes served on the side, for dipping solid ingredients before the broth itself is drunk. The soup can be consumed with a spoon or sipped directly from the rice bowl, rinsing away any stray grains at the same time. The Chinese always speak of "drinking" soup, rather than "eating" it.

Some soups are more substantial, including those made with a mash of dried yellow peas that have been soaked and boiled (*pa wandou*). Most tofu stalls in local markets serve this yellow pea mash, which may be fried up in a little lard with some aromatics and then boiled in water to make a delicious thick soup. Other pulses, including unusual local varieties of beans, are also made into thick nourishing soups, especially in country cooking; chopped leafy greens may be added to the pot.

Elegant sweet soups might also be served, particularly at a wedding, where they symbolize the hoped-for sweetness of married life. (Recipes for such sweet soups can be found in the Sweet Dishes chapter.)

Some of Sichuan's most famous soups look straightforward but are made with luxurious ingredients or demand high-level kitchen skills.

A whole duck may be stuck with as many dried caterpillar fungi (an expensive tonic ingredient from the Tibetan plateau) as the host can afford, and then stewed for hours to make a broth for a banquet. One dish that is rarely seen these days is "cabbage in boiling water" (*kaishui baicai*), a culinary witticism in which the tenderest hearts of Chinese cabbage are served in a limpid stock of consummate flavor made from chicken, duck and pork. It may look like "cabbage in boiling water," but elevated cooking technique is required to make a stock that is so pure and clear, unsullied by a single drop of oil.

I do recommend serving a soup with Chinese meals, if you can. It doesn't have to be complicated, especially if you keep home-made stock in the freezer, or even decent chicken stock cubes, or if you find you enjoy a simple boiled broth such as the pumpkin version on p. 315. (At home, I have to admit that I quite often cheat by making miso soup, which is not Chinese but satisfies my desire for a savory broth.) The following chapter contains several quick, easy soups as well as a few that require a little more time or labor. My personal favorites are the chicken and tofu soups made with pickled mustard greens (bright and refreshing), the fried egg and tomato soup (absolutely delicious), or, if you want something more substantial, try the sour-and-hot "flower" tofu soup or the soup with meatballs and mixed vegetables.

Most of these soups can be made with a basic everyday stock, but feel free to use a chicken or vegetable stock if you'd rather.

Lotus pond near Li Zhuang,
Yibin, southern Sichuan

# Fried Egg and Tomato Soup

## fanqie jiandan tang
## 番茄煎蛋汤

Egg stalls in Sichuanese markets are often stunningly beautiful. There will be neat piles of hen eggs—blue, brown and white—alongside large white duck eggs. Preserved duck eggs will be piled up in their coating of lime-laced mud and grain husks, one of them scraped clean and broken open to reveal jellied albumen and green-yellow yolk. Salted duck eggs will be coated in soot-black paste, and displayed with one of their golden, waxy yolks exposed as a sample. Loveliest of all are the smudged, speckled quail eggs, sold in wooden trays divided by lines of red cotton thread into tiny individual compartments, like jewellers' display cases full of rings.

Hen eggs, of course, are the most everyday ingredient. They go particularly well with tomatoes, as in this gorgeous soup, which I used to order often in the restaurants around Sichuan University. It's simple to make, and is surprisingly rich and delicious.

2 large eggs
2 medium-sized ripe tomatoes
   (about 6¼–7oz/175–200g)
1 quart (1 liter) everyday stock
   (see p. 463) or chicken stock
2 tbsp lard or cooking oil
A handful of spinach leaves,
   pea shoots or other tender greens
Salt and ground white pepper

Beat the eggs together in a small bowl. Slice the tomatoes. Bring the stock to a boil in a saucepan.

Heat the oil in a seasoned wok over high heat until the oil is very hot and the edges of the wok are smoking. Pour in the eggs and swirl them around. Fry until puffy and golden underneath, then flip over and fry the other side until golden. The omelet does not have to remain intact; you will break it up anyway.

Pour in the hot stock and bring to a boil, then let it bubble away for a minute or so until the soup has become rich and opaque. Season with salt and pepper to taste. Add the tomatoes and boil until they are just cooked. Tip in the greens and cook until just wilted, then ladle everything into a deep bowl and serve.

*Tomato and egg flower soup (fanqie danhua tang 番茄蛋花汤)*
*This is based on a recipe from a 1980s book of Sichuanese home-style recipes. Beat 2 eggs together in a small bowl. Blanch 2 large tomatoes (about 10–14 oz/300–400g) briefly in boiling water. When they are cool enough to handle, slip off their skins, discard the seeds and cores, and then finely dice. Combine 2½ tbsp potato starch with 6 tbsp cold water in a small bowl. Heat 2 tbsp lard or cooking oil in a wok over high heat, then add 2 tsp finely chopped ginger and briefly stir-fry until fragrant. Add 1 quart (1 liter) of stock and bring to a boil, seasoning with salt to taste. Give the potato starch mixture a stir and gradually add it to the wok, stirring as the stock thickens and adding just enough to give the soup a lazy, creamy consistency. Add the tomatoes and heat them through. Now turn the heat down to low and drizzle in the egg in a thin stream, moving the bowl in a circular motion to distribute it evenly through the soup. When the egg has set into little flowery wisps, give the soup a stir and then ladle into a serving bowl.*

# Simple Tofu Soup

## doufu tang
豆腐汤

This is a typical example of an everyday soup that is intended to be understated and refreshing. Plain white tofu is simply simmered in a seasoned broth with sliced tomato and greens. Serve it to cleanse your palate after a meal of spicy dishes.

*1 large tomato*
*10 oz (300g) plain white tofu*
*1 quart (1 liter) everyday stock*
    *(see p. 463) or vegetable stock*
*A good handful of choy sum leaves,*
    *pea shoots or other greens*
*Salt and ground white pepper*

Cut the tomato in half and then into slices about ¼ inch (5mm) thick. Cut the tofu into squares of a similar thickness and refresh in a pot of very gently simmering, lightly salted water for a few minutes.

In another pot or a wok, bring the stock to a boil and season to taste with salt and pepper. Add the drained tofu and simmer for a few minutes to let it absorb the flavors of the stock, then add the tomato slices and boil for 10–20 seconds until they are just tender. Add the greens, stir once or twice and then ladle everything into a serving bowl.

# Thick Split Pea Soup

## pa wandou tang
## 炖豌豆汤

Most tofu stalls in Sichuanese markets also sell a thick mash of cooked yellow dried peas (*pa wandou*) that can be used as a base for making soups. The mash is made with whole peas, but the split yellow peas commonly found in the West are just as good. One of my favorite Chengdu snack shops serves a thin broth made from dried peas and pork stock as a refreshing side dish with its spicy buckwheat noodles, steamed cakes and dumplings. The following version is thicker and more substantial, especially with the addition of chopped leafy greens. Feel free to use any leafy greens you have on hand, and to jazz up the finished soup with additional garnishes of fried peanuts and Bombay mix or croutons (in Sichuan, people would use peanuts and fried noodle dough, *sanzi*).

In Chongqing, they use the same pea mash to make heartier dishes, such as a thick pea soup with chopped pork intestines, and blanched greens covered generously with a thick, lard-enriched pea sludge—which sounds and looks clumsy, but is marvelously delicious.

*1½ cups (300g) split (or whole) yellow dried peas*
*1¼-inch piece (25g) ginger, unpeeled*
*2 scallions, white parts only*
*7 oz (200g) green bok choy or choy sum*
*3 tbsp lard or cooking oil*
*1 tsp whole Sichuan pepper*
*5 cups (1.2 liters) everyday stock*
  *(see p. 463) or vegetable stock*
*2 tbsp thinly sliced scallion greens*
*Salt and ground white pepper*

**Soak the peas overnight** in plenty of cold water. The following day, rinse and place in a saucepan. Cover the peas with fresh water and boil for 10 minutes, then turn down the heat and simmer until they are completely tender and disintegrating—this will probably take about an hour. Top up with water as necessary, but don't add more than you need: you want to end up with a thickish paste of peas. (This step can be done in advance.)

Lightly smack the ginger and scallion whites with the flat of a cleaver blade or a rolling pin to loosen them. Slice the bok choy or choy sum, or tear into bite-sized pieces.

Heat the lard or oil in a seasoned wok over high heat. Add the ginger and scallion whites and stir-fry briefly, until they smell delicious. Add the Sichuan pepper and stir-fry for a few seconds more, until you can smell it too. Use a slotted spoon or fine-mesh strainer to scoop out and discard the aromatics, leaving only the fragrant oil. Add the peas to the wok and stir-fry in the fragrant oil for a minute or so, then add the stock and bring to a boil. Season with salt and white pepper to taste. Add the greens and boil until just cooked, then ladle the soup into a bowl, sprinkle with the scallion greens and serve.

*Split pea soup with dough wriggles and greens*
*(doutang shishu miangeda 豆汤时蔬面疙瘩)*
*For a more substantial soup, make a very loose, wet dough from 3¼ cups (400g) all-purpose or Chinese low-gluten flour and 1⅓ cups (325ml) water; place in a bowl, cover with a damp dish towel and let rest for 10 minutes. Before adding the greens, hold the bowl over the soup, tilting it so the dough reaches up one side, and use a spoon to cut narrow strips from the edge and drop them into the liquid. Keep rotating the bowl as you nibble away at the dough. Boil until the dough scraps are cooked through, about 3 minutes. Add the greens, boil until just cooked, then serve as in the main recipe.*

# Clear-simmered Oxtail Soup

## qingdun niuwei tang
## 清炖牛尾汤

This wonderful winter soup is a specialty of Chongqing. A whole oxtail is simmered gently for many hours, until it is beautifully tender, the fat melty and delicious. The tail is served in a bowl of clear broth, with a spicy relish on the side for dipping. It's perfect for a soothing, refreshing end to a Sichuanese meal.

The most acclaimed oxtail soup is made by the Old Sichuan restaurant in central Chongqing, which specializes in beef dishes. This soup is said to have been invented by the restaurant's former chef Chen Qingyun. (Incidentally, I once made a version in Sydney with kangaroo tail, which was equally delicious.)

The cooking method that gives the dish its name, "clear simmering" (*qingdun*), is a way of stewing meat and poultry without the addition of salt or other flavorings. The ginger, Sichuan pepper and Shaoxing wine don't really count as flavorings, but are employed to subdue the strong, rank taste of beef, which is disdained by Chinese gourmets. The chicken, similarly, is not meant to give the dish a chicken flavor, but to enhance the natural, essential taste of the beef with its umami savoriness. Salt is added at the end, just before the dish goes to the table.

This way of stewing is often used to make tonic soups and stews, which are always about extracting the essences of nourishing ingredients rather than the thrill of complex flavors.  →

*1 large oxtail (2 lb 2 oz–3⅓ lb/1–1.5kg)*
  *or 2½ lb (1.2kg) thick chunks of oxtail*
*1 lb 5 oz–1½ lb(600–700g) chicken legs or carcasses*
*1¾-inch piece (35g) ginger, unpeeled*
*2 tsp whole Sichuan pepper*
*5 tbsp (75ml) Shaoxing wine*
*2 tbsp goji berries, rinsed*
*Cilantro leaves, to garnish*
*Salt*

*For the relish*
*1½ tbsp cooking oil*
*4 tbsp Sichuan chile bean paste*
*½ tsp dark soy sauce*
*2 tsp sesame oil*

**Remove any remnants of skin** from the oxtail. If you have a whole oxtail, use a sharp knife to cut through to the center of the tail at each joint, all the way round, taking care not to actually sever the joints. You should end up with a series of rings of flesh that are still attached to the central line of bone. Soak the chunks of oxtail in cold water for 20 minutes to remove some of the bloody juices, then discard the soaking water and rinse the oxtail.

Bring 2½ quarts (2.5 liters) of water to a boil in a large saucepan. Add the oxtail and bring back to a boil over high heat. When the water is boiling, use a fine-mesh strainer to skim off the froth that rises to the surface. Add the chicken legs or carcasses, return to a boil and skim again. Lightly smack the ginger with the flat of a cleaver blade or a rolling pin to loosen it, and then add to the pan, along with the Sichuan pepper and Shaoxing wine. Turn the heat down low and let the soup simmer away gently for several hours. The tail should be stewed until the meat is very tender and easily comes away from the bone: 3 hours should do it, although one of my sources suggests 7½. (Alternatively, pressure cook at high pressure for 45 minutes, then allow the pressure to release naturally.)

Meanwhile, to make the relish, heat the cooking oil in a seasoned wok over medium heat. Add the chile bean paste and stir-fry gently until the oil is red and richly fragrant. Tip into a small bowl. When the paste has cooled, stir in the soy sauce and the sesame oil. →

One closely related dish is clear-simmered beef soup (*qingdun niurou tang*), outlined in the variation here. Another is called ox whip soup with goji berries (*gouqi niubian tang*). I devoured this with enormous pleasure on my first visit to the Old Sichuan restaurant; it was only later that I discovered "ox whip" was not, as I had assumed, a fancy name for oxtail, but rather a euphemism for ox penis. Another Old Sichuan specialty, the dish is thought, perhaps predictably, to enhance masculine vitality and boost the *yang* energy of the body.

At the end of the cooking time, remove the oxtail and chicken pieces from the pan. Discard the chicken (or set it aside for other uses), then strain the soup through a muslin-lined sieve or colander into a clean saucepan. Discard the ginger, Sichuan pepper and any impurities, then return the oxtail to the soup.

When you are ready to eat, gently reheat the soup and then transfer the oxtail to a large serving bowl. Add the goji berries to the soup and season lightly with salt to taste, then pour over the tail. Serve the soup garnished with cilantro, and with the relish on the side.

*Clear-simmered beef soup (qingdun niurou tang 清炖牛肉汤)*
*Follow the recipe above, but instead of oxtail use a good chunk of marbled beef leg, on the bone. Toward the end of the cooking time, remove the beef from the soup and cut it across the grain into finger-sized strips, discarding the bones. Strain the soup, discarding the chicken, then return the beef and continue to simmer. Peel a daikon or two and chop into chunky strips to match the beef. Simmer the radish strips in fresh water until tender, then add them to the soup. Finally, add a few goji berries. To serve, place the radish strips at the bottom of the serving bowl, add the beef and pour over the soup. Scatter with cilantro leaves, if desired, then serve with spicy relish, as in the main recipe. (This recipe also works beautifully with brisket.)*

# Boiled Pumpkin "Soup"

shuizhu nangua
水煮南瓜

"Soup" is really too grand a name for this simple broth (shown in the photograph on the next page). It simply consists of boiled pumpkin chunks in water, with neither oil nor seasoning, but it's heavenly. No other dish will allow you to appreciate in the same way the *benwei*, or "essential root taste" of pumpkin, with the gentle sweetness and faint silkiness it lends to the cooking water. It's a reminder that in traditional Chinese home cooking, soup is often the only beverage served with the meal, and also that plain dishes are just as important as exciting ones in Chinese gastronomy; they are the *yin* to the *yang*, the mirror-twin, a vital part of a whole food system in which balance and physical wellness are inseparable from pleasure.

Think of serving this at the end of a meal that has included sensational dishes such as tingly-hot mapo tofu and Gong Bao chicken, to calm the spirits and refresh the palate. The recipe is so simple that you don't really need measurements; I've included them only as a guide.

One lovely and interesting version of this soup I enjoyed in southern Sichuan incorporated a few cooked mung beans and was then served cold and faintly sweetened with sugar.

*2 lb 6 oz (1.1kg) pumpkin*

Peel and core the pumpkin, then cut the flesh into bite-sized chunks. Place in a saucepan, cover generously with water (about 5 cups/1.2 liters) and bring to a boil. Skim off any froth, half-cover the pan and simmer for about 20 minutes until tender.

Serve. Eat the pieces of pumpkin with your chopsticks, then drink the soup from your bowl.

# Simple Choy Sum "Soup"

xiaocai tang
小菜汤

This is a recipe from a backstreet restaurant in Luzhou, the southern Sichuanese city best known for its fierce, fragrant "Old Cellar" liquor, *luzhou laojiao*: around the old brewery, the boozy smell of fermentation is so intense you could almost get drunk passing by. The soup we ordered with our lunch that day consisted of nothing more than tender, leafy greens served in the water in which they had been boiled, with a spicy dip. And so we plucked the green stalks out of the water and dipped them into a small bowlful of chile oil and soy sauce before eating, and then we drank the liquid, which was faintly green and had a soft, delightful sweetness to it.

Vary the vegetable as you please— you might use spinach, Malabar spinach, broccoli or green beans. Do regard the dip as optional: many people would enjoy both soup and vegetable with no seasoning at all, as a contrast to other, more flavorful dishes.

7 oz (200g) baby choy sum,
 or another vegetable of your choice

*For the dip*
*2–3 tsp chile oil, with sediment*
*1½ tbsp light soy sauce*
*1 tbsp thinly sliced scallion greens*
 *(optional)*

**To make the dip,** combine the chile oil, soy sauce and scallion greens (if using) in a small bowl.

In a saucepan, bring to a boil enough water to cover the greens. Add the greens and boil until just cooked, then transfer them and their cooking water to a serving bowl. Serve with the accompanying dip, or just as it is.

# Chicken Balls
in Clear Soup

## qingtang jiyuan
清汤鸡圆

A bowl of clear soup, with pale chicken balls floating, and wisps of green leaves drifting—this is a traditional Sichuanese banquet soup.

The chicken balls are made from breast meat, with a little seasoning and some egg white and starch to help bind the mixture together. Sichuanese chefs traditionally pummel the chicken breast to a paste using only the spines of their cleaver blades. It's time-consuming, but helps to make the final chicken balls wonderfully smooth; if you use a blender, the recipe is much quicker and easier to make (but for those who'd like to try the old-fashioned method, I've given instructions opposite). Please note that the chicken balls can be cooked in advance, kept in cold water in the fridge for a day or so and then reheated when you wish to serve them.

The same chicken mixture, with a little more egg white to loosen it, is used to coat tender mallow tips for another classic banquet dish, *jimeng kuicai*.

1 skinless, boneless chicken
   breast (about 6¼ oz/175g)
5 cups (1.2 liters) clear superior stock (see p. 464)
   or chicken stock (see p. 463)
7 tbsp (100ml) egg white (from 3–4 large eggs)
1 tsp potato starch,
   mixed with 2 tsp cold water
A handful of small choy sum
   leaves or pea shoots
Salt and ground white pepper

**Pluck out and discard the large tendons** that run down the center of the chicken breasts and any visible wisps of fat or smaller tendons. Cut the meat into small cubes and place in a blender with 3 tbsp stock, ½ tsp salt and the egg white. Start the blender slowly, then gradually increase the speed and whizz the mixture to a soft, elastic paste with a consistency a little like cake batter. Give the potato starch mixture a stir and blend it in, then transfer the chicken mixture to a bowl, scraping every last bit from the blender.

Bring a pot of water to a boil, then turn down to a very gentle simmer (the chicken balls will toughen if boiled). Now use your hands to make the chicken balls: take a small handful of chicken paste in one hand and make a gentle fist, thumb side up. Gently squeeze the paste up through the hole between your thumb and index finger until you have a blob about the size of a cherry tomato. Use your other hand, palm up, to scoop the blob from the top of your fist and drop it very gently into the simmering water—it is best to hold your hands very close to the surface of the water so the chicken ball keeps its shape. Repeat until you have used up all the chicken paste. When all the chicken balls are in the pan, simmer for 3–4 minutes, until they are all just cooked through (cut one in half to make sure). Use a slotted spoon to transfer the chicken balls to a bowl of cold water, and chill if not using them immediately.

Shortly before you wish to serve the soup, briefly blanch the greens in boiling water. Tip into a colander or sieve and immediately refresh under cold water to preserve their color, then place in a serving bowl.

Bring the rest of the stock to a boil and season lightly with salt and pepper. Add the chicken balls and poach gently to reheat, then scoop everything into the serving bowl.

*If you wish to make the chicken paste by hand*
*Place the chicken breasts on a chopping board, and pummel them with the blunt spine of a cleaver or—for speed—two cleavers. Keep whacking them with an up-and-down motion until they have been reduced to a fine paste; keep turning the pile of paste to ensure an even pummeling, plucking out any visible wisps of stringy white tendon. When the paste is fairly smooth, hold the cleaver blade almost parallel to the chopping board and draw the blade across the pulp, smearing the paste onto the board so you can see and remove every last tendon. The reason for using this laborious method, rather than a food processor or the sharp side of the cleaver blade, is that you won't chop up the tendons, and so with a little patience you can remove them all whole, giving the final paste a superlatively smooth texture. When you have pulverized the chicken, transfer it to a mixing bowl with 3 tbsp stock and ½ tsp salt and mix well. Using your dominant hand, whip the paste, stirring in one direction, as you gradually add the egg white. The paste will become thick and sticky. Finally, whip in the starch mixture and then shape and cook the chicken balls as in the main recipe.*

## Chicken Soup with Pickled Mustard Greens

suancai jisi tang
酸菜鸡丝汤

This soup is extremely easy to make and most delicious. The pickled greens lend it a pale jade color and a refreshing sourness; the chicken slivers are cooked so briefly that they remain silky and tender. The Sichuanese would always serve this soup at the end of the meal, to cleanse and refresh the palate, but it makes a fine Western-style starter. In Sichuan, it's a dish for special occasions.

A more everyday version, which is one of the most common after-dinner soups in Sichuan, is pickled vegetable soup with bean-thread noodles (*suancai fensi tang*): to make this, soak a few dried bean-thread noodles in hot water for about 30 minutes before you begin, and add these to the soup instead of the chicken slivers. Pork may also be used instead of chicken, for a less elevated dish. The pickled mustard greens are readily available in Chinese supermarkets, usually in plastic packages.

10 oz (300g) skinless, boneless chicken breast meat
7 oz (200g) pickled mustard greens
6¼ cups (1.5 liters) chicken stock (see p. 463)
Salt and ground white pepper

_For the marinade_
2 tsp Shaoxing wine
¼ tsp salt
1 tbsp potato starch
1 tbsp egg white

Cut the chicken as evenly as possible into very thin slices, and then into very thin slivers. Place in a bowl, add the marinade ingredients and mix well, stirring in one direction. Drain the pickled mustard greens and cut them into fine slivers to match the chicken.

Bring the stock to a boil in a wok or saucepan. When it is boiling, add the pickled mustard greens and simmer gently for a minute or so, until they have lent their flavor to the soup. Season with salt and pepper to taste (if you are serving the soup at the end of the meal, you may wish to follow Sichuanese practice and keep it slightly undersalted).

Add the chicken slivers, using chopsticks to separate them. As soon as they are cooked through and the liquid has returned to a boil, pour the soup into a deep bowl and serve immediately.

_Tofu soup with pickled mustard greens_
_(suancai doufu tang 酸菜豆腐汤)_
_If you have tofu in the fridge and a package of pickled mustard greens in the larder, you can make this soup in little more than the time it takes your stock to come to a boil—and if you don't have home-made stock on hand, you can use good stock cubes, because the pickles themselves add such a gorgeous flavor. Cut 7 oz (200g) pickled mustard greens into slivers. Cut 10 oz (300g) plain white or silken tofu into bite-sized cubes. If you are using plain white tofu, soak it in lightly salted hot water for a few minutes to refresh it, then drain (silken tofu can be used directly). Bring 6¼ cups (1.5 liters) of stock to a boil. Add the pickled mustard greens and tofu and simmer for 1–2 minutes to let the pickles flavor the soup. Season with salt and white pepper to taste. Add a few lengths of scallion before serving._

# Meatball and Vegetable Soup

## jiachang wanzi tang
## 家常丸子汤

A hearty soup made with meatballs and whatever vegetables are on hand is typical of Sichuanese home cooking. It may be served with other dishes, or as a simple meal with steamed rice and perhaps a small dish of pickles. I've based this recipe on a particularly gorgeous version made by Zhang Guobin, the chef at one of my favorite Chengdu restaurants. He uses chunky, hand-cut pork and slow-cooks the meatballs so they're as meltingly tender as the famous lion's head meatballs of Yangzhou.

With a pressure cooker it takes only 20 minutes to cook the meatballs, but if you don't have one and would rather make supper quickly, you can use 14 oz (400g) ground pork—in which case, simply cook the meatballs through before adding the vegetables, which should take 5–10 minutes (test one to check).

I've suggested using Little Gem lettuce leaves and tomatoes, but feel free to use any vegetables you have, adjusting the cooking time accordingly. Bean sprouts would be lovely, as would Chinese cabbage, winter melon and/or bean-thread noodles (the last soaked in hot water for a few minutes to soften them). Another variation includes a very small handful of dried wood ears or a few dried day-lily flowers, soaked in hot water for about half an hour and briefly warmed through in the soup just before serving.

The first stage of the recipe (making the meatballs and cooking them in the stock) can be done in advance.

2 quarts (2 liters) everyday stock
  (see p. 463)
1 tbsp light soy sauce
1 medium-sized tomato, sliced
10 Little Gem lettuce leaves
3 tbsp thinly sliced scallion greens
Salt and ground white pepper

_For the meatballs_
14 oz (400g) skinless pork belly
1-inch piece (20g) ginger, unpeeled
4 dried shiitake mushrooms
1 egg, beaten
4 tsp potato starch

**First make the meatballs.** For ease of cutting, place the pork in the freezer for about 2 hours to firm up. Lightly smack the ginger with the flat of a cleaver blade or a rolling pin to loosen it, then place in a small bowl, add just enough cold water to cover and let infuse. Place the shiitakes in another bowl, cover with hot water from the kettle and soak for at least 30 minutes to soften. Cut the chilled pork into ¼-inch (5mm) slices, and then into tiny dice. Place in a large bowl. Thinly slice the soaked shiitake caps (discarding the stalks) and add to the pork, along with the egg, potato starch, ¾ tsp salt, a couple of pinches of white pepper and 3 tbsp of the strained ginger-infused water (the ginger can then be discarded). Mix everything together well, stirring in one direction and using your hand to slap the mixture against the side of the bowl to firm up the texture.

Bring the stock to a boil in a pot or wok, add the soy sauce and season lightly with salt and pepper, then turn down to a gentle simmer. Shape the pork mixture into meatballs the size of walnuts and drop them into the simmering stock. Return to a boil, then turn the heat down and simmer for 2 hours, until they are beautifully tender. (Alternatively, pressure cook at high pressure for 20 minutes, then let the pressure release naturally.)

About 30 minutes before you wish to serve, return the stock and meatballs to a boil, adding more salt and pepper to taste, if necessary. Add the tomato and lettuce leaves to the broth. As soon as the lettuce leaves have wilted, turn off the heat and serve the soup, garnished with the scallion greens.

# "Along with the Pot" Pork and Daikon Soup

## lianguotang
## 连锅汤

This classic country soup is served at the end of the meal, and so is usually very lightly seasoned. Use your chopsticks to fish out the slices of tender pork and slippery daikon and dip them into the spicy relish. Finally, drink the refreshing broth, either with a china spoon or directly from your rice bowl.

The name *lianguotang*, which literally means "soup served along with the pot," refers to the old-fashioned winter custom of bringing the soup to the table in its cooking pot, which would traditionally be perched on top of a small clay stove containing embers from the kitchen fire to keep the liquid hot. Until recently, you would often see people in the countryside gathered around this kind of hotpot, using the soup to keep themselves warm in their draughty timber-framed farmhouses; these days, they are more likely to use an electric burner or a stove fueled by alcohol gel.

If you wish, you can enrich the soup by using stock instead of water, and seasoning it with salt and white pepper before serving, but I've given the traditional recipe here, bearing in mind that in the past, such quiet flavors were appreciated because soup was often the only liquid refreshment served with a meal. You will need a piece of pork with skin and a good layer of fat for this soup. Chinese cooks vary the vegetable according to the season; Chinese cabbage or celtuce both work well.

*1-inch piece (20g) ginger, unpeeled*
*2 scallions, white parts only*
*14 oz (400g) daikon*
*9 oz (250g) boneless pork leg, in one piece*
*½ tsp whole Sichuan pepper*

*For the dip*
*2 tbsp cooking oil*
*4 tbsp Sichuan chile bean paste*
*2 tsp light soy sauce*
*1 tsp sesame oil*
*6 dried chiles, 1–2 tbsp extra cooking oil and*
   *¼ tsp ground roasted Sichuan pepper (optional)*

**First make the dip.** Heat the cooking oil in a seasoned wok over medium heat. Add the chile bean paste and stir-fry gently until it is wonderfully fragrant and the oil is red. Take off the heat, then stir in the soy sauce and sesame oil. If you want to step up the heat, fry the optional chiles—snipped into ¾-inch (2cm) sections and seeds shaken out as much as possible—in the extra cooking oil. When they have darkened, but are not burned, remove with a slotted spoon and let cool, then chop finely and add to the dip with the Sichuan pepper. Divide between small serving dishes—one per person—and set aside.

Lightly smack the ginger and scallion whites with the flat of a cleaver blade or a rolling pin to loosen them. Peel the daikon and cut into rectangular slices about ⅛ inch (3mm) thick.

Place the pork in a pot with 2 quarts (2 liters) of water (or stock, if you prefer) and bring to a boil. Skim any froth from the surface, then add the ginger, scallion whites and Sichuan pepper. Turn down the heat to medium, cover the pan and simmer for 10 minutes, until you can poke a pointed chopstick easily through the skin of the pork. Turn off the heat and remove the meat from the pot, reserving the cooking liquid. When the meat is cool enough to handle, slice it as thinly as possible, trying to ensure that each slice has a strip of skin and a layer of fat.

Add the daikon slices to the reserved cooking liquid in the pot, cover and return to a boil, then simmer until beautifully tender, about 7 minutes. Add the pork, simmer for another couple of minutes and then serve, in the pot if you want to be traditional, with the spicy dip on the side. (If you wish, remove and discard the ginger from the soup before serving.)

## Sour-and-hot "Flower" Tofu Soup

suanla douhua tang
酸辣豆花汤

In the early 2000s, master chef Lan Guijun ran a popular restaurant opposite the People's Park in Chengdu called the Village Cook (*xiang chuzi*). It was usually packed, often with chefs who adored his and his wife's hearty, down-to-earth cooking. This is my version of one of the dishes I enjoyed there: a gorgeous, lip-slipping tofu soup with a good kick of heat from pepper and chiles and a refreshing chord of vinegar. The recipe is based partly on my memories and partly on a recipe in a 1980s cookbook called *Sichuanese Home Cooking*. Vegetarians may omit the optional lard and use a vegetable stock.

In Sichuan, the soup would be topped with a mixture of deep-fried soy beans and *sanzi* (morsels of crunchy, deep-fried dough strands). At home, I always use Bombay mix because it's much handier and creates a very similar effect.

1 lb 5 oz (600g) silken tofu
5 cups (1.2 liters) everyday stock
   (see p. 463) or vegetable stock
1 tbsp lard
¼ tsp ground white pepper
7 tbsp potato starch,
   mixed with 10 tbsp (150ml) cold water
2 tbsp light soy sauce
5 tbsp Chinkiang vinegar
1 tsp sesame oil
3 tbsp finely chopped preserved
   mustard tuber (zhacai)
2–3 tbsp chile oil, with sediment, to taste
¼–½ tsp ground roasted Sichuan pepper
3 tbsp thinly sliced scallion greens
A good handful of Bombay mix
Salt

**Open the packages of tofu,** drain off any water, and then run a fork through the tofu to break it up into smallish pieces.

Bring the stock to a boil in a pot or wok, and skim if necessary. Stir in the lard, white pepper and ¾ tsp salt. Give the potato starch mixture a stir, then gradually stir it into the stock, adding just enough to thicken it to a lazy consistency (this will ensure that the tofu distributes itself evenly through the soup). Now add the tofu and warm it through.

Switch off the heat and gently stir in the soy sauce, vinegar, sesame oil and preserved mustard tuber. Pour everything into a deep serving bowl. Drizzle the soup with the chile oil and sprinkle with the Sichuan pepper. Garnish with the scallion greens and Bombay mix and then serve, giving the soup a good stir before ladling it into individual bowls.

# Chicken with Ginkgo Nuts

## baiguo dun ji
## 白果炖鸡

1¼-inch piece (25g) ginger, unpeeled
2 scallions, white parts only
5¼ oz (150g) shelled, peeled ginkgo nuts
1 small chicken or guinea fowl (about 2 lb 2 oz/1kg)
2 quarts (2 liters) chicken stock (see p. 463) or water
2 tbsp Shaoxing wine
Salt and ground white pepper

The scenery at Qingcheng Mountain, northwest of Chengdu, is as romantic as a Chinese ink-and-water painting, with its towering crags, plunging cliffs and whispering trees. On its higher slopes, Daoist monks say their prayers; in the valley below, day-trippers feast on local delicacies like fiddlehead ferns, dark smoked bacon and ginkgo nuts. This delicate soup-stew is a specialty of the area, traditionally made with a free-range bird and locally harvested ginkgo nuts.

These nuts, the kernels of the *Ginkgo biloba* tree, are commonly known as "white fruits" (*baiguo*) or "silver apricots" (*yinxing*), and archaically as "fairy eyes" or "Buddha's thumbnails." Shelled and cooked, they have a soft and slightly sticky texture, with a pleasing hint of bitterness to their flavor (although they are thought to be unhealthy when consumed to excess). For convenience, I buy the yellow nuts shelled, peeled and vacuum-packed in the refrigerated section of a Chinese supermarket; if you buy them in their pointy white shells, you will need to crack them open and peel off the papery inner skins.

The soup is usually made with a small farmhouse chicken; I've sometimes used a guinea fowl instead. You will need a cooking pot that fits snugly around your bird, such as a Chinese claypot or similar. To intensify the flavor, cook the chicken in chicken stock rather than water.

Lightly smack the ginger and scallion whites with the flat of a cleaver blade or a rolling pin to loosen them. Remove and discard the tiny embryonic sprout that runs down the center of each ginkgo nut and is very bitter (you may have to split them in half to do this, or you may get away with just making a slit in one end).

Bring a pot of water to a boil. Add the chicken or guinea fowl and return to a boil, then drain in a colander, discarding the water, and rinse under cold water. Scrub out the pan, then return the bird, pour in the stock or water and bring to a boil, skimming off any froth from the surface. Add the ginger, scallion whites and Shaoxing wine, turn down the heat to low, half-cover the pan and simmer gently for 2 hours. (Alternatively, pressure cook at high pressure for 30 minutes, then allow the pressure to release naturally.)

At this stage, add the ginkgo nuts and about ½ tsp salt to the soup, then simmer for another 30 minutes. (If you've used a pressure cooker, bring the soup back to a boil, add the ginkgo nuts and salt and simmer for another 30 minutes.)

Finally, season the soup lightly with salt and pepper, then serve. Eat the chicken and ginkgo nuts with your chopsticks before drinking the broth.

Variations

*The same basic method can be used for a plain chicken soup (with no ginkgo nuts), or a chicken soup with other tonic ingredients. You can add reconstituted dried wild mushrooms to the brew instead of ginkgo, cooking them with the chicken. If you can get your hands on some fabulous (and fabulously expensive) dried sliced matsutake mushrooms, add a handful of slices when the chicken soup is ready, and simmer for another 10 minutes as magical aromas fill your kitchen.*

# "Rice Broth" with Vegetables

mitang zhu qingcai
米汤煮青菜

In the Sichuanese countryside, rice is often parboiled in plenty of water and then transferred to a wooden rice steamer (*zengzi*), where the grains swell and soften in their bath of steam. The parboiling water, milky with rice starch, is known as "rice broth" (*mitang*) and may be drunk as refreshment during a meal or used as the base for a simple soup. In recent years, soups of vegetables simmered in rice broth have become common on menus inspired by rustic cooking. They embody comfort, nostalgia and the careful economy of the rural kitchen.

In Sichuan, I've enjoyed soups like this made with wild winter vetch, the slightly mucilaginous leaves of Chinese mallow and many other vegetables. You can use any vegetables you like, either individually or in combination, including spinach, choy sum or pumpkin, to give just a few examples.

To make rice broth, rinse your rice, then place it in a saucepan and cover with plenty of cold water. Bring to a boil over high heat and then boil for 7–8 minutes, until the grains are partially cooked but still opaque and hard in the center. Off the heat, use a fine-mesh strainer to remove the rice, leaving the broth in the pan, and transfer it to a traditional wooden steamer or a regular steamer lined with muslin. Steam the rice over high heat for about 10 minutes, until the grains are fully cooked.

Reheat the reserved rice broth, adding some stock or water if you require more liquid, then add vegetables of your choice, along with a tablespoon of lard if you like, and simmer until tender. (Some cooks like to briefly stir-fry the vegetables in lard before adding the rice broth.) Season to taste and serve.

If you wish, you can serve the soup with a spicy dip, such as those for tender boiled vegetables (see p. 277) or clear-simmered oxtail soup (see p. 313). Some cooks also add a dollop of chile oil sediment to the broth just before serving.

# Rice

"Terraced paddy fields dominate the Sichuanese rural landscape, and rice is at the heart of almost every meal"

# Rice 米饭类

In Sichuan, as in most of southern China, rice is the staple food, and wheat an afterthought. Most people maintain that wheat takes less kindly to the warm, humid southern climate. Terraced paddy fields dominate the Sichuanese rural landscape, and rice is at the heart of almost every meal. Wheaten noodles and dumplings may be eaten as snacks and for more casual repasts; otherwise, to eat a meal is, as the Chinese term suggests, to "eat rice" (*chifan*).

A typical local breakfast is based on *xifan*, a thin rice porridge that is less substantial than congee but silky and soothing to the throat. People slurp a bowlful as they pick at small dishes with their chopsticks or take a bite from a steamed bun served on the side. For main meals, plain steamed rice (*bai mifan*, "white cooked rice") is served, usually toward the end of the meal, to fill up after the enjoyment of other dishes. In the countryside, rice is traditionally cooked in a great wooden steamer (*zengzi*): the grains are parboiled before being transferred to the steamer, and the milky parboiling water bubbling away beneath can serve as a simple soup, either on its own or with some added vegetables. Otherwise, rice is traditionally made by the absorption method in a covered pot, simmered with a measured amount of water until the grains are swollen and a delicious, toasty golden layer (*guoba*) has formed at the bottom of the pot. These days, of course, most people use an electric rice cooker, as do I.

Although the rice grains themselves are usually unseasoned and unadorned, they are always served with something tasty to "send the rice down" (*xiafan*), typically a little dish of home-made pickles drizzled with chile oil. Most old-fashioned restaurants in the backstreets of Chengdu have their own jars of home-made pickles fermenting away, and will send out small servings with the rice at a customer's request.

Leftover rice, chilled overnight, can be stir-fried the following day, with perhaps just a little beaten egg and some sliced scallions, or with morsels of wind-dried sausage or cured pork. One pickle-maker and restaurateur I know in Shuangliu, just outside Chengdu, likes to fry up leftover rice in lard with slivers of blanched daikon. He calls the dish "beggars' rice," an ironic reference to the way wealthy residents of nearby "Silver" Pixian and "Golden" Wenjiang used to say scornfully that "beggars come from Shuangliu"—ironic, because it is usually served at the end of a stupendous feast of rabbit, pork, stewed turtle and other amazing dishes. In the Bamboo Sea of southern Sichuan, a nature reserve of glorious bamboo forests, one can eat "bamboo tube rice" (*zhutongfan*), rice mixed with mung beans, smoked bacon and water and steamed in sections of bamboo, lending it a subtle fragrance.

The Sichuanese tend to eat long-grain, non-glutinous rice for most meals. Glutinous rice, both short- and long-grain, is an occasional treat, used in stuffings and sweet dishes rather than as a staple grain served with savory foods. It can also be steamed, mixed with wine yeast and left to ferment to give *laozao*, fermented glutinous rice wine, which explains why the Sichuanese dialect name for glutinous rice is "wine rice" (*jiumi*).

Both glutinous and non-glutinous rices are used, either separately or in combination, to make sweet dumplings and cakes (see pp. 387 and 447). Traditionally, they are often soaked overnight and then ground with fresh water to make a batter. The batter can be drained in muslin to make the dough used for glutinous rice balls (*tangyuan*), or left to ferment, sweetened and then steamed into cakes, either in a muslin-lined steamer or in little boats made from corn husks or other fragrant leaves. Non-glutinous rice batter can be mixed with an alkaline solution that gives it a yellow tint, simmered and then poured into molds to set to make "rice jelly" (*mi liangfen*), which is served hot in a lavishly spicy sauce. These days, many people use dried rice flour to make dumpling wrappers and cakes, but their flavors are considered inferior to those made with traditional "damp" rice flour.

Particularly in southern Sichuan, people like to dry-roast rice in a wok with spices, before grinding it. The coarsely ground meal, known as "rice powder" (*mifen*) in Chengdu and *zhafen* further south, has various uses. (The *zha* in *zhafen* is an ancient word for pickled fish, and this rice powder is still used in some pickles, which might account for the curious name.) As a coating for marinated meat, fish and poultry, it appears in many steamed dishes, like spicy steamed beef (see p. 165). It may also be mixed with pickled chiles to make *zha* chiles, a pantry relish that can be eaten after a swift stir-frying in oil (see p. 430).

Another intriguing rice is the "shady rice" (*yin mi*) of southern Sichuan (*yin* is the quiet, shady feminine counterpart to the driving, bright masculine energy of *yang*; *yin* and *yang* being the indivisible, eternal, complementary and mutually replenishing forces that nourish the universe). Here, people soak and then steam short-grain glutinous rice, but instead of eating it they put it in bamboo trays until it's completely dry; the rice is dried in a shady place because hot sun would split the grains, hence the name. When totally dry, the rice can be stored almost indefinitely. It is eaten for breakfast as a sort of porridge: the dried grains are fried in a little oil or lard until white and puffy, and then simmered with water and sugar to soften and sweeten them. The finished porridge has a particularly delicious flavor and richness that sets it apart from regular congee. It's a traditional tonic for women who have just given birth, especially with the addition of an egg (which may be broken into the porridge as it cooks).

The following chapter is a short one, focusing on rice as a staple; you will find some of the more complex dishes described above in other chapters.

# Plain White Rice

bai mifan
白米饭

The easiest way to cook rice is with an electric rice cooker: you simply measure and then rinse the rice, add a measured quantity of water, push a button—and then, in due course, perfect rice appears and is kept warm until you wish to eat it. The simplest models just make plain white rice; more sophisticated versions can cook white rice, sushi rice, brown rice and congee.

If you don't have a rice cooker, it's most convenient to make it by the absorption method, as in the following recipe. When I'm cooking for friends, I find judging quantities extraordinarily difficult: sometimes all the rice is eaten and I have to cook some more; other times I'm left with plenty for fried rice the following day. In general, I prefer to err on the side of generosity and recommend the quantity here, which yields enough for 2–3 rice bowlfuls for 4 people, a decent compromise. You may find you have some leftovers: use them to make fried rice the following day. I recommend Thai jasmine rice, which is easily available and highly esteemed in China. Please be aware that you should always serve Chinese food with slightly sticky East Asian varieties of rice: with chopsticks, it's hard to eat looser grains like basmati.

If you want to be really Sichuanese, serve the rice with a small dish of home-made pickled vegetables (see p. 420) dressed with chile oil.

*3 cups (600g) Thai jasmine rice*

**Put the rice in a bowl,** cover with cold water and use your hand to swirl it around. Drain and repeat until the water is clear. Tip into a sieve and let drain completely.

Put the rice into a heavy-bottomed pan with 4⅔ cups (1.1 liters) of cold water and bring to a boil over high heat. Stir to dislodge any grains sticking to the base of the pan, and then boil for a few minutes until the surface of the rice is dry and covered in little round "breathing" holes. Cover the pan tightly, turn the heat down as low as possible, and continue to cook for 12–15 minutes, until tender.

*Traditional steamer rice (zengzi fan 甑子饭)*
*Bring your rice to a boil in plenty of water, and then simmer for 7–8 minutes, until nearly cooked but still a little hard and starchy in the center of each grain. Drain the rice (reserving the water to use as "rice broth" if desired—see p. 327), then turn it out into a steamer basket lined with muslin and steam over high heat for about 10 minutes, until fragrant and fully cooked.*

## Smothered Glutinous Rice with Peas and Cured Pork

wandou larou menfan

豌豆腊肉焖饭

In Sichuan, while plain steamed rice is served with most meals, there are exceptions, like this delicious pot-cooked rice with cured meat and peas. You can make it with home-made Sichuanese bacon (see p. 424) or cured pork (see p. 427); alternatively, use a piece of Cantonese cured pork belly or sausage from your nearest Chinatown.

This old-fashioned recipe is inspired by a version cooked by Chengdu master chef Lan Guijun at his restaurant, Yuzhilan, and based on his instructions (except that I've used ground Sichuan pepper instead of roughly chopped whole pepper). When I visited his restaurant one winter, he served me this rice, made using his own, home-cured meat and finished with a quick steaming in a lotus leaf. He served it accompanied by a little dish of mustardy greens (see p. 63), dressed with soy sauce, vinegar, chile oil and sugar: sublime. You can, of course, also fry up leftover non-glutinous rice with peas and morsels of cured pork, which is also delectable. Please note that the glutinous rice needs to be soaked for several hours before cooking. Served with other Chinese dishes, this makes enough for 4 people.

1⅔ cups (300g) long-grain glutinous rice
3½ oz (100g) Sichuanese (or Cantonese) cured pork or bacon, skinless, and with as much fat as possible
1 tbsp cooking oil
½ cup (75g) fresh or frozen peas
½ tsp salt
½ tsp ground roasted Sichuan pepper

**Rinse the rice,** then cover generously with cold water and let rest in a cool place to soak for 4 hours or overnight.

Give the pork a good scrub under cold water to remove any remaining cure, then cut into ½-inch (1cm) dice.

Rinse the soaked rice under cold water and drain well. Put the kettle on to boil.

Heat the oil in a seasoned wok over high heat. Add the pork or bacon and stir-fry until it is tinged with gold and has given up its fragrant fat. Add the peas and stir-fry until piping hot. Tip in the rice, along with the salt and Sichuan pepper, and mix everything together, then take off the heat.

Transfer the contents of the wok to a heavy-bottomed saucepan and stir in 1¼ cups (300ml) hot water from the kettle. Bring to a boil over high heat, then turn the heat down to very low, cover and cook for about 15 minutes, by which time the rice should be cooked, with a nice golden crust on the bottom. Serve.

# Thin Rice Porridge

xifan
稀饭

While the Cantonese adore eating thick, porridgy rice congee for breakfast, the Sichuanese prefer, as a rule, a thin, watery version known as *xifan*; this is often translated, accurately but somewhat unattractively, as "rice gruel." Part food, part drink, *xifan* (shown in the photograph on p. 339) is slurped from the bowl, while steamed buns, dumplings, boiled eggs, pickles and other small dishes are served on the side. In hotels, there might be a huge range of accompanying relishes, buns and dishes; at home, people often warm up the previous night's leftovers and serve them with *xifan* and some steamed buns, plain or stuffed. Some people also like to have *xifan* for supper on a sultry summer's night, with steamed buns and cold dishes. In general, the porridge is insufficiently filling to serve as a starchy staple on its own, which is why it's almost always served with bready snacks.

Sometimes, people soak a handful of mung beans in cold water overnight before adding them to the pan with the rice and water; this mung bean thin rice porridge is seen as "cooling" in traditional Chinese medicine, an aid to reducing inner heat or inflammation. In summertime, you may also come across *xifan* that has been boiled with lotus leaves; the leaves are not eaten, but lend the porridge a pale green tint, a delicate aroma and similarly "cooling" properties.

However it's made, *xifan* is a Sichuanese comfort food: soft, modest and reassuring. This recipe makes enough for 4–6 servings.

*½ cup (100g) Thai jasmine rice*

**Put the rice in a bowl,** cover with cold water and use your hand to swirl it around. Drain and repeat until the water is clear. Tip into a sieve and allow to drain completely.

Bring 2½ quarts (2.5 liters) of water to a boil in a heavy-bottomed pan. Add the rice and stir to dislodge any grains that may have stuck to the base of the pan. Return to a boil, then turn the heat down to a very gentle simmer and cook for at least 1 hour (or up to 1½ hours), until the liquid is silky and opaque and the rice grains have ruptured and spilled their flesh—the Chinese call this *kaihua*, "bursting into flower."

Stir the porridge occasionally to prevent sticking. You may also need to add a little extra hot water from the kettle: you want to end up with a gruel that has the consistency of a thick soup rather than a porridge, so it can be consumed in a manner that is somewhere between drinking and eating.

*Mung bean thin rice porridge (lüdou xifan 绿豆稀饭)*
*Cover a handful of mung beans with cold water and let soak overnight, before draining and cooking them with the rice and water.*

*Lotus-leaf thin rice porridge (heye xifan 荷叶稀饭)*
*Give a large piece of lotus leaf a dunk in hot water to soften it, and then simmer with the rice and water. Remove before serving the porridge.*

# Eight-treasure Black Rice Porridge

## babao heimi zhou
八宝黑米粥

Every morning a woman used to set up her portable stove in the courtyard outside my apartment in Chengdu. She would heat up a great potful of black rice porridge and sell it by the bowlful to local residents. It was a wonderful, nutritious breakfast: a warm mess of rice, tinted purple by grains of black glutinous rice, and scattered with tiny green mung beans, red Chinese dates, goji berries and peanuts. I would eat it with a little sugar or honey, or perhaps a sprinkling of chopped candied fruit.

The following recipe is based on one taught to me by my Chinese teacher Yu Weiqin, who used to feed me such comfort foods whenever she thought I was sad or homesick. All the ingredients, which can be found in most Asian supermarkets, are considered to have healing properties in traditional Chinese medicine, making the dish nutritious as well as colorful. For a more simple, everyday breakfast, you can use ordinary rice plus a handful of mung or azuki beans. Although I've given exact measurements for the "treasure" ingredients, quantities are not critical: just aim for a very small handful of each. (Other possible additions are 1 tbsp (10g) raw barley and 1 tbsp (10g) dried foxnuts, which can be found in some Chinese supermarkets.) This recipe makes 4–6 servings.

A few (15g) dried lotus seeds
About 1 tbsp (15g) day-lily bulb pieces (baihe), fresh or dried
1 tbsp (10g) mung beans
1 tbsp (10g) azuki beans
2 tbsp (15g) raw peanuts, in their pink skins
2 tbsp (15g) walnuts
A few (20g) dried Chinese dates
   (pits removed, if you wish)
¼ cup (50g) black glutinous rice
¼ cup (50g) white glutinous rice
¼ cup (50g) Thai jasmine rice
2 tbsp (10g) goji berries
Brown or white sugar, crushed rock sugar
   or honey, to serve (optional)

Soak the lotus seeds, dried day-lily bulb (if using), mung beans and azuki beans in cold water overnight.

Next day, drain and rinse the seeds, bulbs and beans, then tip into a large saucepan. Give all the remaining ingredients except the goji berries and sugar or honey a good rinse, then add them to the pan, together with 3 quarts (3 liters) of water.

Bring to a boil, skim if necessary and then simmer over a very gentle heat for 1½ hours, stirring occasionally to prevent sticking and adding more water if necessary. (If you are using fresh day-lily bulb, add it to the pan for the last few minutes of cooking.) You should end up with a loose, soupy porridge.

Shortly before the porridge will be ready, add the goji berries and let them steep in the hot liquid for a minute or so. Serve warm, with sugar or honey to taste, if you wish.

# Noodles

"All over Sichuan, small, inconspicuous snack shops serve the most ravishing noodles: spicy and plain, soupy and dry, meaty and vegetarian–something for every mood"

# Noodles 面条类

All over Sichuan, small, inconspicuous snack shops serve the most ravishing noodles. One of my favorite haunts, the long-lost Mr. Xie's, near Sichuan University, was a tiny place with white-tiled walls on the ground floor of an old wooden building, open to the street, yet his dandan noodles were beyond compare. Recently, in the southern town of Luzhou, my friend Luo Jun took me on an early-morning tour of some of her favorite noodle shops, hole-in-the-wall outfits where we sat alongside locals on their way to work and sampled heavenly soup noodles with, variously, stewed pig's trotters, pickled vegetables and wild mushrooms. And on my last trip to Chengdu, I breakfasted at an unassuming noodle shop opposite my hotel on a different noodle dish every morning—spicy and plain, soupy and dry, meaty and vegetarian—something for every mood.

In northern China, where wheat is widely grown, noodles are regarded as a staple, along with breads, dumplings and other wheaten foods. In rice-loving Sichuan, however, they are not generally eaten for main meals, but for casual eating, rustled up quickly at home without ceremony, or scoffed in a noodle shop, where they are ordered by the *liang* (around 2 oz/50g) from a menu of dry-tossed (*ganban*) or soupy noodles (*tangmian*). Dry-tossed noodles, which are drained then mixed, typically, with spicy and savory seasonings, are often served with a bowlful of palate-cleansing stock or noodle-cooking water (*miantang*) on the side; many places also offer home-made pickles. Noodle shops usually have several potfuls of different stews bubbling away, any of which can serve as the topping (*miansao*) for a bowlful of soupy noodles.

The most famous Sichuanese noodles, of course, are dandan noodles: spicy and numbing, with their savory ground meat topping, they are irresistible. But in recent years, spicy Chongqing noodles have become popular—either as simple "small noodles," or topped with cooked peas or a ground pork sauce—and the town of Yibin is famed for its nutty "kindling" noodles. Cold noodles seasoned with an arresting array of sweet, savory and hot seasonings are a favorite summer snack, often enjoyed on outings to scenic spots. And aside from the dramatically flavored noodles, there are more soothing brews, such as "sea flavor" noodles, and noodles with ground pork and pickled mustard greens.

Many noodle shops buy freshly made noodles in long, snaky skeins from specialty producers. Some are made with a dough spiked with alkaline lime water, which gives them a yellowish tinge and a slightly springy consistency: these are favored for cold noodle dishes. Other kinds of noodles are usually made in-house, such as sweet-water noodles, a Chengdu specialty of chunky noodles cut from a sheet of dough that are boiled and soused in sweet soy sauce, chile oil and garlic. For buckwheat noodles, a specialty of Chongzhou, a buckwheat-flour dough is forced through a wooden press into boiling water. Sweet potato noodles, transparent and slithery, are made from a looser dough that is shaken and smacked through a colander into the pot.

Miniature bowls of dainty noodles may be served as a starchy filler during or at the end of a banquet. Occasionally, you may be lucky enough to try "golden thread" noodles (*jinsimian*), made from a wheat flour and egg yolk dough, and so fine they can be passed through the eye of a needle; they are typically served in a clear broth that shows off their delicate craftsmanship. "Silver needle" noodles, as you might guess, are made with egg white instead of yolk.

Noodles are among the easiest and most addictively delicious Sichuanese specialties to make at home. Just keep some basic seasonings and dried noodles in your larder or fresh noodles in your freezer, and it's easy to magic up a quick lunch or midnight feast. Although fresh wheat-flour noodles are traditionally used for many dishes, you can apply the same flavorings and techniques to whatever kind of noodle you fancy, including rice noodles, Cantonese egg noodles and noodles made from buckwheat and other flours.

Chengdu city center at night

# Traditional Dandan Noodles

## dandan mian
## 担担面

Dandan noodles are the most famous Sichuanese street snack. They were first sold by men who wandered the alleys of Chengdu, carrying their stoves, noodles and secret-recipe sauces in baskets hanging from a bamboo shoulderpole (*dan* means "to carry on a shoulderpole"). Older people can remember the days when these vendors were a common sight and their calls of "*dandan mian! dandan mian!*" rang out in every quarter. The noodles were served in small portions, just enough to ease the hunger of scholars working late or mahjong players gambling into the night. They were cheap and nourishing, and enjoyed by everyone from odd-jobbers to the very wealthy, whose servants were sent to the gateways of the old courtyard houses to flag down passing noodle-vendors. The name didn't originally refer to a particular style of noodles, but it is now firmly associated with the following recipe, made with Yibin *yacai* and ground pork.

Some say that dandan noodles were first sold in the mid-nineteenth century by a pedlar named Chen Baobao in the salt-mining city of Zigong and were originally vegetarian; only later, when they became popular in Chengdu, did people start adding ground pork. The distinguishing characteristic of dandan noodles, apart from their spiciness, is that they are "dry-tossed" (*ganban*)—that is, made without stock. They look quite innocent when served, but when you mix the noodles into the sauce at the bottom of the bowl, they come alive with spice and tinginess. This recipe makes 2 servings.

2 tsp sesame paste
1 tbsp cooking oil
2 tbsp Yibin yacai or Tianjin preserved vegetable, rinsed and squeezed dry
2 tbsp light soy sauce
½ tsp dark soy sauce
4 tbsp chile oil, plus 1 tbsp sediment
1 tsp Chinkiang vinegar
2 tsp melted lard (optional)
¼–½ tsp ground roasted Sichuan pepper
2 tbsp thinly sliced scallion greens
10 oz (300g) fresh or 7 oz (200g) dried wheat-flour noodles
A handful of leafy greens

*For the topping*
3 tbsp cooking oil
1 tsp finely chopped ginger
3½ oz (100g) ground pork (fatty, if possible)
½ tbsp Shaoxing wine
1 tsp sweet flour sauce
1 tsp light soy sauce
¼ tsp dark soy sauce
Salt

**First make the topping.** Heat the cooking oil in a seasoned wok over high heat. Add the ginger and stir-fry briefly until you can smell it, then add the pork and stir-fry until it changes color. Splash in the Shaoxing wine. When the pork has lost its water content and smells delicious, tilt the wok and push the pork up one side so the oil pools in the base. Add the sweet flour sauce to the oil and stir-fry until you can smell it. Tilt the wok back and stir in the pork, followed by both soy sauces. Stir thoroughly, then season with salt to taste and set aside.

Dilute the sesame paste with about 2 tsp oil from the jar, so that it has a runny consistency. Heat the cooking oil in a seasoned wok over medium heat. Add the preserved vegetable and stir-fry briefly until hot and fragrant. Divide the sesame paste and preserved vegetable between two bowls, along with all the other ingredients except the noodles and leafy greens.

Boil the noodles to your liking, adding the leafy greens for the last few seconds to wilt them. Tip the noodles and greens into a colander and drain well, then divide between the bowls and top with the pork mixture. Mix everything together before eating.

# Chongqing "Small" Noodles

## chongqing xiaomian
## 重庆小面

Over the last few years, snack shops selling Chongqing "small" noodles have sprung up all over China. Usually they are tiny places with makeshift tables, brightly colored plastic stools and noodle-slurping customers spilling out across the pavement. Their eponymous noodle dish is simple, as its name might suggest: just boiled noodles and a few green leaves in a spicy broth, with a smattering of seasonings, fried peanuts and pickles. You can, however, customize your noodles with one of a number of toppings: red-braised beef, cooked yellow peas, ground pork or a spoonful each of ground pork and peas. Alternatively, you might choose to have your noodles "dry-tossed" (*ganban*), the spicy seasonings undiluted with stock: in this case, you'll normally be served a bowlful of the noodle-cooking water (*miantang*) as refreshment on the side.

These noodles aren't usually terribly chile-hot, but most Chongqingers like to add enough ground roasted Sichuan pepper to make their lips dance and tingle as if they've been zapped by an electric current. Use any leafy greens you have on hand: spinach, water spinach, choy sum or pea shoots all work well. The following recipe is based on a few versions I've enjoyed in Chongqing and Chengdu: add as much or as little chile oil and Sichuan pepper as you wish. This recipe makes 2 servings.

10 oz (300g) fresh or 7 oz (200g) dried wheat-flour noodles
A good handful of choy sum or other leafy greens
¾ cup plus 2 tbsp (200ml) stock (or noodle-cooking water)
4 tbsp thinly sliced scallion greens

*For the seasonings*
1½ tsp sesame paste
1 tbsp cooking oil
3 tbsp Yibin *yacai* or *Tianjin* preserved vegetable, rinsed and squeezed dry
¼–½ tsp ground roasted Sichuan pepper, to taste
2 tbsp light soy sauce
4–6 tbsp chile oil, with sediment, to taste
1 tsp sesame oil
3 tbsp roasted or deep-fried peanuts (see p. 458)
2 tsp crushed or finely chopped garlic (optional)

**For the seasonings,** dilute the sesame paste with about 1½ tsp oil from the jar, so that it has a runny consistency.

Heat the cooking oil in a seasoned wok over medium heat. Add the preserved vegetable and stir-fry briefly until hot and fragrant. Divide the sesame paste, preserved vegetable and all the remaining seasonings except a few of the peanuts between two deep bowls.

Boil the noodles to your liking, adding the choy sum for the last few seconds to wilt them. If using stock, rather than just noodle-cooking water, bring it to a boil.

Pour the hot stock (or noodle-cooking water) into the two bowls, dividing it evenly. Tip the noodles and choy sum into a colander and drain well, then divide between the bowls. Garnish with the scallion greens and reserved peanuts and serve. Mix everything together before eating.

*Chongqing "small" noodles with yellow peas*
*(wandou xiaomian 豌豆小面)*
*Add a big spoonful of tender cooked yellow peas to the noodles just before serving. Whole dried yellow peas are easily found in Sichuan markets (¼ cup/50g dried peas, pre-soaked and then simmered until tender, will give about 2 servings); Chongqing noodle-makers abroad tend to use cooked chickpeas, which are more readily available and give quite a similar effect.* →

← *Chongqing "small" noodles with ground pork topping*
(cuishao mian 脆馅小面)

Just before serving, add a good spoonful of ground pork topping to the noodles. To make the topping, heat 6 tbsp cooking oil in a seasoned wok over high heat. Add 2 tsp finely chopped ginger and stir-fry briefly until you can smell it, then add 7 oz (200g) ground pork (a bit fatty, if possible) and fry until it changes color. Splash in 1 tbsp Shaoxing wine. When the pork has lost its water content and smells delicious, tilt the wok and push the pork up one side so the oil pools in the base. Add 2 tsp sweet flour sauce to the pool of oil and stir-fry until you can smell it. Tilt the wok back and mix in the pork, then stir in 2 tsp light soy sauce, ¼ tsp dark soy sauce and season with salt to taste. This makes enough for 2 servings of noodles with ground pork, or 4 servings of noodles with ground pork and yellow peas (see below).

*Chongqing "small" noodles with ground pork and yellow peas*
(wanza mian 碗杂面)

*Just before serving, add a spoonful each of cooked yellow peas (see previous page) and ground pork topping (see above); this version is also shown in the photograph on p. 348.*

*Dry-tossed Chongqing noodles* (ganban xiaomian 干拌小面)

*Use the same seasonings, but do not add any stock or noodle-cooking water. Drain the noodles and greens well (if you wish, save some of the cooking water to serve alongside), then divide between the bowls, top with cooked yellow peas and/or ground pork topping (see above) and quickly mix everything together before serving. You may need to add a little more chile oil to help it all mix together slickly. Some people add toasted soy flour, peanuts and walnuts to the seasonings for extra deliciousness. If you want to follow local practice, serve with bowlfuls of noodle-cooking water on the side.*

# Mr. Xie's Dandan Noodles

## niurou dandan mian
## 牛肉担担面

The following recipe is my own re-creation of a legendary and unique version of dandan noodles served in a tiny restaurant near Sichuan University. It is the fruit of repeated visits to the restaurant over a number of years, during which I begged and cajoled the unsmiling proprietor, Mr. Xie, for his culinary secrets. On one occasion he told me the ingredients of the delicious meaty topping; other times he let me watch as his cooks prepared the seasonings in the noodle bowls. He may have withheld a detail or two, but the following recipe has met with the wholehearted approval of several of the restaurant's most devoted customers. For the full authentic flavor, I tend to add some hotter chile oil to the milder chile oil I normally use. These noodles are not for the faint-hearted—they are shamelessly spicy, but utterly delicious. This recipe makes 2 servings.

*2 tsp sesame paste*
*1 tsp sesame oil*
*2 tbsp light soy sauce*
*½ tsp dark soy sauce*
*4 tbsp chile oil, plus 1–2 tbsp sediment*
*¼–½ tsp ground roasted Sichuan pepper*
*10 oz (300g) fresh or 7 oz (200g) dried wheat-flour noodles*

*For the beef topping*
*3 dried chiles*
*3 tbsp cooking oil*
*½ tsp whole Sichuan pepper*
*3½ oz (100g) ground beef*
*Scant 1 oz (25g) Yibin yacai or Tianjin preserved vegetable,*
*    rinsed and squeezed dry*
*1 tsp light soy sauce*
*¼ tsp dark soy sauce*

**First make the topping.** Snip the chiles into ¾-inch (2cm) sections and shake out the seeds as much as possible. Heat the oil in a seasoned wok over medium heat. Add the chiles and stir until they are fragrant and just turning color, then add the Sichuan pepper and stir very briefly until you can smell it. Add the beef and continue to fry, breaking it into tiny morsels. When the meat has lost its moisture and smells delicious, add the preserved vegetable, stir-fry briefly and then stir in both soy sauces. Set aside.

Dilute the sesame paste with about 2 tsp oil from the jar, so that it has a runny consistency. Divide this and all the remaining ingredients except the noodles between two bowls and mix together well.

Boil the noodles to your liking, then drain well and divide between the two bowls. Spoon over the beef topping and serve. Mix everything together while the noodles are hot, and eat as soon as possible.

## Spicy Noodles
## with Silken Tofu

douhua mian
豆花面

In the mid-twentieth century, a man named Tan Yuxian ran a makeshift snack stall near the Temple of Peace and Happiness in Chengdu. He became famous for his tender "flower" tofu, drizzled with fragrant oils and scattered with crunchy morsels of nuts and pickles. The following dish was one of Mr. Tan's specialties, and is still served in a Chengdu snack shop that bears his name. With its generous topping of tofu, this makes a scrumptious and nourishing vegetarian lunch. The dish is typically made with the flat, tagliatelle-type noodles that are known in Chinese as "chive leaf" noodles (*jiucaiye miantiao*), but I use the fresh round wheat noodles I can buy in my local Chinese shop. In Chengdu, the noodles are topped with crisp strands of deep-fried noodle (*sanzi*) and deep-fried soy beans; for convenience, I suggest you use Bombay mix and roasted or fried peanuts instead, which make a fantastic substitute.

If you keep noodles on hand and a package of silken tofu in the fridge, this recipe is extremely quick to make. It will serve 2 as a hearty lunch or 4 as a snack.

*10 oz (300g) silken tofu*
*10 oz (300g) fresh or 7 oz (200g) dried wheat-flour noodles*

*For the seasonings*
*1 tbsp sesame paste*
*3–4 tbsp chile oil, with sediment*
*4 tsp light soy sauce*
*¼ tsp ground roasted Sichuan pepper*

*For the toppings*
*3 tbsp finely chopped preserved*
    *mustard tuber (zhacai)*
*4 tbsp thinly sliced scallion greens*
*2 tbsp roasted or deep-fried peanuts (see p. 458)*
*2 small handfuls of Bombay mix*

**Spoon the tofu in chunks** into a small pot of boiling water and let it warm up over very gentle heat.

For the seasonings, dilute the sesame paste with about 1 tbsp oil from the jar, so that it has a runny consistency. Divide this and the other seasonings between two or four bowls.

Boil the noodles to your liking, then drain and divide these between the bowls too. Use a slotted spoon to remove the tofu from the water and place some on top of each bowl. Divide the toppings between the bowls and serve.

Mix everything together with chopsticks before eating.

# Soup Noodles with Shredded Pork and Pickled Greens

## suancai rousi mian
## 酸菜肉丝面

This gentle, refreshing dish is inspired by some delicious breakfast noodles I enjoyed during an early-morning noodle crawl in the Yangtze town of Luzhou with my friend Luo Jun. Thin slivers of lean pork are stir-fried and then combined with pickled mustard greens in a light broth perked up with white pepper.

The noodle topping can be made in advance and reheated when you wish to eat. If you prefer, you could use chicken instead of pork. This recipe makes 2 generous servings.

6¼ oz (175g) lean pork loin or tenderloin
7 oz (200g) pickled mustard greens
½-inch piece (10g) ginger
4 tbsp cooking oil
1 quart (1 liter) everyday stock (see p. 463)
2 tbsp thinly sliced scallion greens
1 tsp sesame oil
10 oz (300g) fresh or 7 oz (200g) dried wheat-flour noodles
Salt and ground white pepper

### For the marinade
¼ tsp salt
2 pinches of ground white pepper
1 tsp Shaoxing wine
1 tbsp potato starch

Cut the pork into thin slivers and place in a bowl. Add the marinade ingredients, mix well and set aside while you prepare the other ingredients. Cut the pickled mustard greens into slivers to match the pork. Peel the ginger and cut into similar-sized slivers.

Heat 2 tbsp cooking oil in a seasoned wok over high heat. Add the pork and stir-fry until the slivers have separated and turned pale, then remove from the wok and set aside. Wipe out the wok if necessary. Return the wok to high heat with the remaining 2 tbsp cooking oil, add the ginger and stir-fry briefly until you can smell it. Tip in the mustard greens and stir-fry them until they are hot and fragrant, then pour in 1⅔ cups (400ml) stock and return the pork to the wok. Bring to a boil and season with salt and pepper to taste, then set aside until needed.

When you wish to eat, bring a large pot of water to a boil. Divide the scallion greens and sesame oil between two bowls, with salt and pepper to taste. Reheat the remaining stock and, separately, your pork and pickle mixture.

Cook the noodles in the boiling water. When they are nearly done, divide the hot stock between the bowls. Drain the noodles and divide between the bowls, then top each with a good ladleful of the pork topping and serve.

# Sichuan Soup Noodles with Ground Pork Topping

## qingtang zajiang mian
## 清汤杂酱面

For those who don't wish to start their day with a jolt of chile and Sichuan pepper, these mild noodles make a delectable brunch or breakfast. The recipe can also be used as a template for making all kinds of soupy noodles, because you can vary the topping as you please. A spoonful of red-braised beef (see p. 168) is delicious, perhaps with a garnish of chopped cilantro; or you might use the remains of a stir-fried dish from the previous night. You could also serve the noodles in the remains of the chicken and ginkgo stew on p. 326.

Of course, since we're talking Sichuan, noodle shops typically offer a spicy, tingly option too, which is known as "vegetarian pepper noodles with ground pork topping" (*sujiao zajiangmian*). One of my favorite versions comes from Glasses Noodles, a hole-in-the-wall restaurant named, in typically charming Chengdu fashion, after the distinguishing feature of its bespectacled owner, Mr. Zhang.

To make this dish, place in each serving bowl: 2½ tsp light soy sauce, 2 tsp crushed peanuts or sesame paste, ¼–½ tsp ground roasted Sichuan pepper, ½ tsp crushed garlic, 1½ tbsp Yibin *yacai* preserved vegetable (for best results, first rinse this and stir-fry briefly in a little oil until fragrant), 1½ tbsp thinly sliced scallion greens and 1½ tbsp chile oil with sediment. Add the freshly cooked noodles, spoon over the ground pork topping and then mix everything together before eating.

This recipe makes 2 servings.

3 tbsp Yibin yacai *preserved vegetable*
1 tbsp cooking oil
1 tbsp melted lard (or cooking oil)
4 tsp light soy sauce
1 tsp sesame oil
4 tbsp thinly sliced scallion greens
2 cups (500ml) everyday stock (see p. 463) or chicken stock
10 oz (300g) fresh or 7 oz (200g) dried wheat-flour noodles
A good handful of leafy greens, perhaps spinach or choy sum
Salt and ground white pepper

*For the topping*
6 tbsp cooking oil
1 tbsp finely chopped ginger
7 oz (200g) ground pork
1 tbsp Shaoxing wine
2 tsp sweet flour sauce
2 tsp light soy sauce
¼ tsp dark soy sauce
Salt

**First make the topping.** Heat the cooking oil in a seasoned wok over high heat. Add the ginger and stir-fry briefly until it smells wonderful, then add the pork and stir-fry until it changes color, breaking the meat into small morsels with a wok scoop or spatula. Splash in the Shaoxing wine. When the pork is lightly browned and smells delicious, tilt the wok and push the meat up one side so the oil pools in the base. Add the sweet flour sauce to the pool of oil and stir-fry until you can smell it. Tilt the wok back and mix in the pork, then stir in both soy sauces and season with salt to taste. Set aside until needed.

Rinse the preserved vegetable and squeeze dry. In a small pan, heat the cooking oil and briefly stir-fry the preserved vegetable until fragrant. Divide between two deep bowls, along with the lard, light soy sauce, sesame oil and scallion greens. Add a good pinch of pepper and salt to taste to each one.

Bring the stock to a boil and keep it warm. In another pan, boil the noodles to your liking. When they are nearly done, add the greens to a boiling water and let them wilt for a few seconds. Divide the hot stock between the bowls, then drain the noodles and greens in a colander and divide between the bowls too. Spoon over the pork topping and serve. Mix everything together before eating.

# Hand-made Sweet-water Noodles

## tianshui mian
## 甜水面

These gorgeous hand-cut noodles are bathed in a glossy and totally irresistible sauce of chile oil, sweet soy sauce, crushed nuts and garlic. A popular snack across Chengdu, they are also one of the specialties of Second Brother Zhang's bustling snack shop opposite the Wenshu Monastery. Here, in the back kitchen, one of several longtime cooks, Master Jiang, mixes and kneads his dough by hand, then rolls it out on a wooden counter. Using a long wooden rolling pin as a guide, he slices the sheet of dough into thick strands, snatches up several at a time, stretches them and whacks them onto the counter before tossing them into a great potful of boiling water. When the noodles are ready, they are brought to a team of ladies, who slather them in sauce, oil and nuts with incredible speed before shoving them through the hatch to the eagerly waiting customers.

According to local sources, this was first sold during the late Qing dynasty by street vendors in the old imperial city of Chengdu (which stood where the Mao statue is today), but only became famous in the 1940s as a specialty of the area around the White Cloud Temple.

The flour you need to make the noodles is the sort used for steamed buns, which you should be able to find in Chinese supermarkets. Some cooks like to add crushed sesame seeds or toasted soy flour to the cooked noodles, others chopped peanuts. Because of the desired chunky shape of the noodles, no perfectionism is needed here: this is a forgiving recipe. It makes 2 servings.

½ tbsp crushed garlic, mixed with
   a pinch of salt and ½ tbsp cold water
2 tbsp chile oil, plus 1 tbsp sediment
2 tbsp sweet aromatic soy sauce (see p. 459)
2 tbsp (15g) roasted or deep-fried peanuts (see p. 458)

*For the noodles*
2 cups (250g) Chinese low-gluten (bun) or all-purpose flour,
   plus more for dusting
1 tsp salt
1 tbsp cooking oil

**First make the noodles.** Pile the flour and salt on a surface and make a well in the center. Gradually add ½–⅔ cup (125–150ml) lukewarm water (at about 85°F/30°C), drawing the flour into the center and adding just enough water to make a soft but firm dough. Knead for at least 5 minutes until smooth and even, dusting with flour if you need to, then cover with a damp cloth and set aside to rest for 20 minutes.

Bring a large pot of water (a pasta pot is ideal) to a boil and keep at a simmer while you roll out the dough and cut the noodles. Dust a work surface with flour and roll the dough out evenly to about ¼ inch (5mm) thick, forming it into a shape as near as possible to a long rectangle (in practice, it will be oval). If the dough resists being rolled out thinly, let it rest for a couple of minutes before proceeding. Then, using a long knife or the edge of a ruler, cut the whole sheet of dough into ½-inch (1cm) strips; dust them with a little more flour so they don't stick together.

Return the water to a good rolling boil. Then, using both hands, pick up both ends of 5–6 strips of noodle and stretch them out, whacking them onto the work surface if you dare: you want to end up with noodles about as thick as chopsticks. Cut off and reserve the bunched-up ends, then toss the rest of the noodles into the water, giving them a quick stir with long cooking chopsticks or tongs so they don't stick together. Repeat with the rest of the noodles, then make a few extra noodles with the offcuts. Once all the noodles are in the pan, boil them for about 5 minutes, until cooked through (test one to make sure).

Tip the noodles into a colander and quickly rinse under cold water, then drizzle over the cooking oil and toss briskly so they don't stick together. Divide between two bowls and add all the remaining ingredients. Mix well before devouring.

<u>Sesame-flavored sweet-water noodles</u>
*Dress the noodles with the following, divided between the bowls: 2 tsp sesame paste diluted with about 2 tsp oil from the jar, 2 tbsp sweet aromatic soy sauce (see p. 459), 2 tbsp chile oil plus 1 tbsp sediment, ½ tsp sesame oil, 2 tsp crushed toasted sesame seeds and ½ tbsp crushed garlic mixed with a pinch of salt and ½ tbsp cold water.*

# Mr. Xie's "Sea Flavor" Noodles

## haiwei mian
## 海味面

Because Sichuan is an inland province, ringed by mountains and cut off from the plains and oceans to the east, fresh seafood has historically been absent from the local diet. Dried seafood, however, was brought to the region by traders from the coast, who exchanged it for local medicinal plants and other forest exotica. Expensive delicacies such as dried shark's fin and sea cucumber have long been part of Sichuanese *haute cuisine*. But while eating exotic dried seafood is still the privilege of the wealthy, other fruits of the sea, including dried shrimp, mussels, squid and cuttlefish, find their way into everyday dishes and are sold in most local markets.

The following noodle dish is called "sea flavor" noodles because it includes a small amount of dried seafood, usually shrimp and mussels, in addition to the more ordinary pork and mushrooms. It's a well-established Chengdu snack, but this recipe is based on the peculiarly delicious version served by Mr. Xie— of dandan noodles fame—in his noodle shop near Sichuan University. Since I'm unable to find dried mussels or cuttlefish in London, I've included only dried shrimp in the recipe, but you might like to add a small handful of pre-soaked dried mussels or cuttlefish too, if you have them.

This makes enough "sea flavor" stew for 4 servings of noodles. (If you're cooking for fewer people, the leftover stew will keep for a couple of days in the fridge, or much longer in the freezer.)

3 tbsp dried shrimp
3 dried shiitake mushrooms
¾ cup (100g) fresh or canned bamboo shoots
9 oz (250g) skinless, boneless pork belly
2 cups (100g) fresh mushrooms, such as button, chestnut or shiitake
¾-inch piece (15g) ginger
1 scallion, white part only
2 tbsp cooking oil
1 tbsp Shaoxing wine
About 7¼ cups (1.75 liters) everyday stock (see p. 463)
Salt and ground white pepper

*To serve, per person*
½ tbsp melted lard (optional)
5¼ oz (150g) fresh or 3½ oz (100g) dried wheat-flour noodles
1 tbsp thinly sliced scallion greens

**Cover the dried shrimp with hot water** from the kettle and set aside for at least 30 minutes to soften. Do the same with the dried mushrooms. Cut the bamboo shoots into thin slices and blanch briefly in lightly salted boiling water, then refresh under cold water. Let soak in a bowl of cold water until needed.

Drain the mushrooms and thinly slice the caps, discarding the stalks. Drain the shrimp. Cut the pork and the fresh mushrooms into ⅛–¼-inch (4–5mm) slices. Peel and thinly slice the ginger. Lightly smack the scallion white with the flat of a cleaver blade or a rolling pin to loosen it.

Heat the oil in a seasoned wok over high heat. Add the ginger and scallion white and stir-fry briefly until they smell wonderful, then add the pork and stir-fry until pale. Add the Shaoxing wine and stock and bring to a boil. Skim off any froth, then fish out and discard the scallion white. Add the drained shrimp, mushrooms and bamboo shoots, along with the fresh mushrooms, and return to a boil. Season with salt and pepper to taste, then turn the heat to low and simmer for 1 hour.

To serve, place some melted lard, if using, in each bowl, along with salt and pepper to taste. Boil the noodles to your liking. When they are nearly done, spoon a little stock from the wok into each bowl. Drain the noodles and divide between the bowls, then spoon over some of the stew and top up with more stock. Sprinkle with the scallion greens and serve.

# Copper Well Lane Vegetarian Noodles

## tongjing xiang sumian
## 铜井巷素面

In the early twentieth century, an itinerant noodle-seller opened a shop in Copper Well Lane in Chengdu that became known for its delicious vegetarian noodles. Although the shop has long since disappeared, "Copper Well Lane vegetarian noodles" still appear on restaurant menus and in some cookbooks. This recipe is based on one I tasted in a Chengdu snack shop, although there they made their topping with tea-tree mushrooms (*chashugu*) rather than shiitake; if you can find dried tea tree mushrooms, recognizable by their long stalks and small, soft-brown caps, feel free to use them instead. The dish is largely a vegetarian version of dandan noodles, and perhaps closer to the original dandan, which is said to have been vegetarian when first sold by street vendors in Zigong.

This recipe makes 2 servings.

2 tsp sesame paste
2 tbsp light soy sauce
1 tsp Chinkiang vinegar
4 tbsp chile oil, with sediment
1 tsp sesame oil
¼–½ tsp ground roasted Sichuan pepper
2 tbsp thinly sliced scallion greens
4 tsp finely chopped or crushed garlic
10 oz (300g) fresh or 7 oz (200g) dried wheat-flour noodles
A small handful of leafy greens, perhaps spinach or choy sum

*For the topping*
3 dried shiitake mushrooms
2 dried chiles
2 tbsp cooking oil
½ tsp whole Sichuan pepper
2 tbsp Yibin yacai or Tianjin preserved vegetable, rinsed and squeezed dry
2 tsp light soy sauce
¼ tsp dark soy sauce
Salt

**First make the topping.** Cover the dried mushrooms with hot water from the kettle and let soak for at least 30 minutes to soften. Drain the mushrooms, then discard the stalks and finely chop the caps. Snip the dried chiles in half or into ¾-inch (2cm) sections and shake out the seeds as much as possible. Heat the cooking oil in a seasoned wok over medium heat. Add the chiles and stir-fry until they are beginning to darken, then add the Sichuan pepper and sizzle for a few moments until it smells wonderful, taking care not to let it burn. Remove the spices with a slotted spoon or fine-mesh strainer and discard. Add the mushrooms to the infused oil and stir-fry until fragrant and crisp around the edges. Tip in the preserved vegetable and stir-fry briefly until fragrant. Season with both soy sauces, and salt to taste.

Dilute the sesame paste with about 2 tsp oil from the jar, so that it has a runny consistency. Divide this and all the remaining ingredients except the noodles and leafy greens between two bowls and mix.

Boil the noodles to your liking, adding the leafy greens for the last few seconds to wilt them. Tip the noodles and greens into a colander and drain well, then divide between the bowls. Top with the mushroom mixture and serve. Mix well before eating.

# Spicy Cold Noodles with Chicken Slivers

jisi liangmian
鸡丝凉面

Spicy cold noodles are a popular summer snack in Sichuan. They are often enjoyed, along with cool starch jellies and "flower" tofu, as a pick-me-up on day-trips to scenic attractions like Qingcheng Mountain. Usually tossed with blanched bean sprouts and sometimes topped with hand-torn slivers of chicken, the noodles are seasoned with a giddy "strange flavor" (guaiwei) mix of ingredients: sweet aromatic soy sauce, sugar, vinegar, chile oil, garlic and Sichuan pepper. (If you don't want to make the sweet aromatic soy sauce, just use 1 tsp light soy sauce, ½ tsp dark soy sauce and an extra 1 tsp superfine sugar instead.) The chile oil gives the noodles a ruby sheen and the Sichuan pepper will make your lips tingle. When alkaline noodles are used, the noodles themselves have a yellowish tint and a slightly springy consistency. Vegetarians can simply omit the chicken, as the noodles are also superbly delicious without it.

If you can find alkaline noodles (made with wheat flour, water and a solution of sodium carbonate, also known as soda ash), they're ideal; otherwise, plain wheat-flour noodles will be delicious too. Do make sure you oil the noodles as soon as they're cooked and spread them out to dry as quickly as possible: this will help to prevent sticking. You can either serve these noodles in a large bowl to share, or street-style on four small plates. Any leftover sauce will taste incredible with cold chicken or blanched leafy greens. This recipe makes 4 servings.

10 oz (300g) fresh or 7 oz (200g) dried wheat-flour noodles
A little cooking oil
¾ cup (75g) bean sprouts
1¾–3½ oz (50–100g) leftover cooked chicken breast meat
1 tsp sesame seeds
4 tbsp thinly sliced scallion greens (optional)

_For the sauce_
2 tbsp sesame paste
2 tbsp sweet aromatic soy sauce (see p. 459)
1½ tsp superfine sugar
1 tbsp Chinkiang vinegar
3 tbsp chile oil, with or without sediment
2 garlic cloves, crushed and mixed with 2 tsp cold water
¼–½ tsp ground roasted Sichuan pepper
  or ½–1 tsp Sichuan pepper oil
1 tsp sesame oil

**Boil the noodles in plenty of boiling water** until they are just done—take care not to overcook them. Tip the noodles into a colander and briefly rinse under cold water. Give them a shake in the colander, then quickly spread them out on a baking sheet to dry. Sprinkle with cooking oil and mix it in with long cooking chopsticks or tongs to prevent the noodles from sticking together.Shortly before serving, blanch the bean sprouts for a few seconds in boiling water, then refresh in cold water. Drain them well, then place them in the base of a large serving bowl or divide among four small plates. Lightly smack the chicken meat with the flat of a cleaver blade or a rolling pin to loosen the fibers, then tear or cut into thin slivers. Toast the sesame seeds gently in a dry frying pan until golden.

For the sauce, place the sesame paste in a small bowl, dilute it with a little oil from the jar and stir and mash until smooth: you should end up with a thick liquid the consistency of cream. Add the remaining ingredients and mix well.

Put the noodles in your serving bowl or on plates. Drizzle over the sauce, then top with slivers of chicken, sesame seeds and the scallion greens, if using. Mix together before eating.

_Spicy peanut butter noodles_
_Once, when trying to devise a recipe for a magazine feature about cooking with pantry ingredients, I made a version of this recipe using peanut butter instead of sesame paste, and it_

turned out to be among the most popular I've ever published. Here it is: instead of the above sauce, mix together 2 tbsp smooth peanut butter, 1 tbsp light soy sauce, ½ tsp dark soy sauce, 1½ tsp Chinkiang vinegar, 2–3 tbsp chile oil (with or without sediment), 1 tsp sesame oil, 2 tsp crushed garlic (mixed with 1 tsp cold water) and 2 tbsp stock or water. If you wish, add ¼–½ tsp ground roasted Sichuan pepper. Sprinkle with 2 tbsp sliced scallion greens and 1 tsp toasted sesame seeds.

# Yibin "Kindling" Noodles

## yibin ranmian
## 宜宾燃面

Yibin is sometimes dubbed "the first city on the 10,000-mile Yangtze" because it sits at the confluence of the Min and Jinsha rivers, where they join to become what is known in Chinese as the "Long River" (*changjiang*). This fragrant, nutty noodle dish is one of the city's most famous exports, along with *wuliangye* "five-grain" liquor and Yibin *yacai* (spiced preserved mustard greens). Its Chinese name is hard to translate, but *ran* literally means to ignite or kindle a flame, which is why I've translated it as "kindling" noodles. Some say the dish is so called because the noodles, in their dry, oil-based sauce, resemble the rush wicks used in old-fashioned oil lamps; others that it's because the noodles are sometimes finished with a drizzle of smoking-hot oil, which makes them crackle like a fire. A possible, though perhaps alarming, alternative translation might be "inflammable" noodles.

The secret ingredient is an oil infused with chiles, Sichuan pepper and sometimes many other spices: specialty Yibin noodle shops often have great potfuls of this oil, packed with spices and aromatics, simmering away for hours. The noodles should be well drained: local noodle-cooks shake them hard in a bamboo net before tossing them in the spiced oil and scattering over the crunchy nuts. Like most "dry" noodle dishes, these may be served with a bowlful of noodle-cooking water or, in summer, chilled mung bean soup (see p. 450). You can add lard to the oil for extra richness, but I usually omit it to give a fine vegetarian lunch. This recipe makes 2 servings.

⅓ cup (40g) walnuts
About ¾ cup plus 2 tbsp (200ml) cooking oil
⅓ cup (40g) roasted or deep-fried peanuts (see p. 458)
3 tbsp Yibin *yacai* or *Tianjin* preserved vegetable, rinsed and squeezed dry
2 tsp sesame seeds
10 oz (300g) fresh or 7 oz (200g) dried thin wheat-flour noodles
1 tbsp light soy sauce
3 tbsp thinly sliced scallion greens

*For the infused oil*
2 tbsp coarsely ground chiles
¾-inch piece (15g) ginger, unpeeled
7 tbsp (100ml) rapeseed oil
3 tbsp (20g) walnuts, roughly chopped
1½ tsp whole Sichuan pepper
2 tsp sesame oil
2 tbsp melted lard (optional)

**First make the infused oil.** This can be done in advance, and makes more than you will need (the leftovers keep well and can be used in this and other, improvised, noodle dishes). Place the ground chiles in a small heatproof bowl. Lightly smack the ginger with the flat of a cleaver blade or a rolling pin to loosen. Heat the rapeseed oil in a wok over high heat and add the ginger: the oil should be hot enough to sizzle vigorously around it. Add the 3 tbsp (20g) walnuts, reduce the heat and let them sizzle for a minute until fragrant. Switch off the heat, add the Sichuan pepper and leave for 30 seconds to infuse, then strain the hot oil over the chiles: it should sizzle and smell delicious, without burning the chiles. When the oil has cooled, add the sesame oil—and the lard, if using. (Pick out the toasty bits of walnut from the sieve as a nibble while you work!)

Next, place the ⅓ cup (40g) walnuts in a seasoned wok, add enough oil to almost cover, and then heat over medium heat, stirring often, until the oil begins to fizz around the nuts. Turn the heat down low and fry the nuts gently for 1–2 minutes, until crisp and golden, then remove from the oil and set aside to drain on paper towels. When cool, chop into small pieces "the size of rice grains." Chop the peanuts in a similar fashion.

Carefully pour off all but about 1½ tbsp oil from the wok and return to medium heat. Add the preserved vegetable and stir-fry briefly until fragrant, then set aside in a small bowl. Toast the sesame seeds gently in a dry frying pan until golden, then transfer to another small bowl.

Boil the noodles to your liking. Tip the noodles into a colander and drain well, then divide between two shallow dishes. Working quickly, add 2 tbsp infused oil (with its chile sediment) and ½ tbsp soy sauce to each dish and mix through the noodles. Top with small piles of walnuts, peanuts, preserved vegetable, sesame seeds and scallion greens and serve. Mix everything together before eating.

# Cold Buckwheat Noodles

## liang qiaomian
## 凉荞面

Both sweet and bitter (or tartary) varieties of buckwheat are grown in Aba Prefecture and other dry, mountainous parts of Sichuan. Bitter buckwheat, which is thought to help regulate blood sugar and is therefore recommended for diabetics, has become fashionable in recent years in the form of a herbal tea that has a satisfying, roasty taste. Buckwheat is also used to make noodles, which are a particular specialty of Chongzhou, just west of Chengdu. Buckwheat flour made from the ground seeds is worked with water and a little lime solution into a soft dough, which is squeezed through holes in a wooden press so the noodles fall directly into a wokful of boiling water. The boiled noodles, quickly rinsed in cold water, can be eaten hot with a spoonful of red-braised beef stew, or cold with sour and spicy seasonings, as in the following recipe, which is inspired by the one served at a specialty buckwheat noodle restaurant in Chengdu, Granny Wang's.

Dried buckwheat noodles can be fragile and prone to disintegration, while those made from a mixture of buckwheat and wheat tend to hold their shape better: use whichever you prefer. Do regard this recipe as a template for experimentation: try adding crushed garlic, sesame oil, deep-fried soy beans, roasted or fried peanuts, or chopped cilantro, for example. This dish makes a quick, fabulous vegetarian snack—the recipe makes 2 servings.

7 oz (200g) dried buckwheat or buckwheat-and-wheat noodles
2 small handfuls of finely chopped celery (1–2 celery sticks)
4 tbsp thinly sliced scallion greens
½ tsp toasted sesame seeds

*For the seasonings*
¼ tsp salt
4 tsp light soy sauce
2 tbsp Chinkiang vinegar
½ tsp superfine sugar
2 tbsp chile oil, plus 1 tbsp sediment
¼–½ tsp ground roasted Sichuan pepper (optional)

**Boil the noodles to your liking.** Divide all the seasonings between two bowls. When the noodles are ready, tip them into a colander and quickly rinse under cold water, then drain well. Divide the noodles between the bowls and mix well.

Scatter over the remaining ingredients and serve.

Variations

*In Sichuan, people also love to serve buckwheat noodles with soupy red-braised beef (see p. 168). To do this as they do at Granny Wang's, season the noodles with a little light soy sauce, vinegar and ground roasted Sichuan pepper, to taste, then top with a good ladleful of red-braised beef. Finish with chile oil and plenty of chopped garlic and sliced scallion greens. Mix well before eating.*

# Sour-and-hot Sweet Potato Noodles

## suanla fen
## 酸辣粉

With a slippery mouthfeel and a refreshing sour-and-hot flavor, this is a gorgeous snack—and it's particularly easy to make. Skeins of glassy, pale-brown, dried sweet potato noodles can be found in Chinese supermarkets worldwide, but in the backstreets of Chengdu you can still see them being made from scratch. The noodles, made with sweet potato starch, alum and water, are fashioned from a shape-shifting dough that can be kept in a ball in the hands with constant manipulation, but subsides into molten batter when left alone, even momentarily (like a paste made from cornstarch and water). A young man, usually, will hold a wide-eyed colander filled with sweet potato paste a couple of feet above a huge wokful of boiling water, and then use his hand to thump the paste so it streams through the holes into the steaming cauldron. When the strands of liquid paste enter the water, they instantly coalesce into transparent noodles, which are boiled briefly and then whipped out with chopsticks and plunged into cold water to arrest their cooking. The whole process is remarkable to watch. This recipe makes 2 servings.

14 oz (400g) dried sweet potato noodles
1 quart (1 liter) everyday stock (see p. 463)
 or chicken stock
2 handfuls of bean sprouts
2 tbsp thinly sliced scallion greens
2 tbsp finely chopped preserved mustard
 tuber (zhacai)
2 tbsp finely chopped celery
2 tbsp crisp deep-fried soy beans,
 or roasted or deep-fried peanuts (see p. 458)

### For the seasonings
2 tsp finely chopped garlic
½ tsp ground roasted Sichuan pepper
 or 1 tsp Sichuan pepper oil
¼ tsp salt
4 tsp Chinkiang vinegar
1 tbsp light soy sauce
¼ tsp dark soy sauce
3–4 tbsp chile oil, plus 1 tbsp sediment
2 tsp lard (optional)

**Cover the noodles with cold water** and soak overnight. (Or you can soak them in warm water for just a few minutes—but if you soak them in cold water, they are less likely to disintegrate.)

Bring the stock to a boil. Divide all the seasonings between two bowls.

Blanch the bean sprouts in the hot stock, then remove with a slotted spoon and divide between the bowls, adding about 7 tbsp (100ml) stock to each one. Drain the noodles, add to a boiling stock and dunk for a few seconds until slippery, tender and transparent. Remove the noodles with long cooking chopsticks or tongs and a slotted spoon and divide between the bowls. Sprinkle over the remaining ingredients and serve.

## Variation

*In one popular local version of this dish, sweet potato noodles are served with stewed pig intestines (feichang fen): the noodles and bean sprouts are blanched in the milky stock in which the intestines have been cooked, and the whole dish is topped with a spoonful of intestines. People often like to eat them with a crisp guokui (see p. 393) or another pastry snack.*

# Small Eats

"Chengdu boasts literally hundreds of specialty snacks: from spicy noodles to sweet dumplings and crunchy flatbreads, from steamed buns to silken tofu and aromatic cold meats"

# Small Eats 小吃类

If you sit down in one of the busy market streets of old Chengdu and close your eyes, you will gradually hear, amid all the hubbub, the sounds of the itinerant street traders. The shoe cleaner passes first, knocking his wooden shoe brush against a wooden stool, beating out a gentle but insistent rhythm. Then there's the toffee man, sounding his arrival with a metal clapper: *ding ding dang, ding ding dang.* Without even looking, you know that he'll be carrying a pair of woven baskets on a bamboo shoulderpole, each one filled with a pale, chewy malt-sugar toffee that is called, unsurprisingly, dingding toffee (*dingding tang*). Next, the sound of a man's voice calling *"Dou hua'er! Dou hua'er!"*—and it's the "flower" tofu vendor with his red-and-black wooden barrels filled with warm curd and seasonings. And if there's a teahouse nearby, spilling its chairs and tables onto the street, you might even hear the metallic click of the ear-cleaner's tongs as he does his rounds, touting for custom.

Chengdu has long been known for its bustling street life and the city is still alive with the flower sellers and toy makers, the knife grinders and bamboo flute vendors who gave it this vibrant reputation. Above all, however, the city is famed for its diverse and delicious "small eats" (*xiaochi*). Chengdu boasts literally hundreds of specialty snacks: from spicy noodles to sweet dumplings and crunchy flatbreads, from steamed buns to silken tofu and aromatic cold meats. Most of these tidbits were originally made by street vendors who plied their trade all over the city: a few are still sold this way.

Elderly residents of Chengdu remember the early twentieth century as a golden era for this kind of eating; they describe how the street vendors lived or died by the quality of their food, so they were driven to create snacks of unparalleled flavor. Some sigh as they recall from their childhoods the aroma of a favorite dumpling, drifting on the warm spring air.

Many of today's most popular snacks date from the late imperial and early republican periods.

Some of their creators have entered popular legend for the excellence of their craft, their names inextricably linked with the delicacies they invented. Many of the more successful vendors ended up opening restaurants, some of which have lasted generations. Fu Chongju's *Survey of Chengdu*, published in 1909, offers a fascinating snapshot of the street life of that period. The book lists "small eats" that remain popular today, such as buckwheat noodles, sweet-water noodles and glutinous rice balls, and features sketches of street traders with their shoulderpoles and the rest of their gear, including makers of *guokui* pastries and sellers of wontons and cool starch jellies.

Some notable snacks are named after their creators, for example Zhong boiled dumplings, the specialty of a man named Zhong Xiesen, and Mr. Lai's glutinous rice balls, made to perfection by one Lai Yuanxin. Others are named after their regions of origin, like North Sichuan cool starch jelly and Yibin "kindling" noodles. Still others take their names from the calls of their original vendors, such as dingding toffee, dandan noodles (*dan* means to carry on a shoulderpole), and the delicate steamed dumplings known as *zhengzheng gao* (literally "steamed steamed cakes").

Many of Sichuan's most famous snacks can be found in Chengdu, but there are countless local specialties outside the provincial capital. Chongqing, Sichuan's hilly second city, is known for its tiny glutinous rice balls ("mountain city little rice balls"—*shancheng xiao tangyuan*), the village of Juntun for its spicy, crunchy flatbreads layered with ground meat. Wherever you go in Sichuan you'll find unusual delicacies: at one recent lunch in Yibin I tasted several intriguing steamed rice dumplings wrapped in different fragrant leaves. When I spent the Lunar New Year in a village near Hejiang, everyone interrupted their games of cards and mahjong at midnight, not only to light firecrackers but also to scoff sticky rice dumplings stuffed with pork, wild scallions and Sichuan pepper—known in these parts as "piglet dumplings" (*zhu'er ba*) because of their resemblance to piglets snuggled inside their leaves. There are also seasonal specialties, like spring roll pancakes and *zongzi*, the cones of glutinous rice wrapped in giant bamboo leaves made for the Dragon Boat Festival on the fifth day of the fifth lunar month.

Although many Sichuanese "small eats" are dumplings, cakes and noodles, the term also encompasses meat dishes such as "man-and-wife" offal slices, sweet soups and soothing porridges.

Like most aspects of Chinese culture, Sichuanese street food was shaken by the turbulent political events of the twentieth century. During the Cultural Revolution, individual enterprise was branded as capitalist and individual traders were driven off the streets. Private restaurants were collectivized, and street snacks were recycled on set menus in a new generation of impersonal, state-owned establishments. The incentive for achieving excellence disappeared, and by all accounts Sichuanese street food went through a period of stagnation and decline. After China began its economic reforms, there was something of a renaissance, as laid-off workers took to snack-selling to make a little extra cash. When I was a student in Chengdu, in the mid-1990s, you might buy hot leaf-wrapped dumplings (*ye'er ba*) from a man with a bicycle cart, or run into an elderly retired worker in the market with a basketful of home-made dough twists (*mahua*).

These days, it is harder to find these lone traders in Chengdu. A few of them cluster around the Buddhist and Daoist temples, frying up glutinous rice balls glazed in toffee or filling little pancakes with crushed nuts and sugar. For the most part, however, street food has been moved into tourist zones, where the snack-makers work for absentee bosses and often lack the skills and dedication of their forebears. Fortunately, many of the old "small eats" are still made and sold in specialty restaurants, where you can order set menus of a dozen or more delicacies served in individual, snack-sized portions. A couple of Zhong dumplings, drizzled in a scrumptious spicy sauce; a dish of smoked duck;

two glutinous rice balls stuffed with black sesame seeds and sugar; some cold pea jelly in a hot bean sauce; a fragile rippled-silk fried dumpling. . . . By the time the waiters have finished dispensing their goodies, every inch of the table will be covered with a sumptuous array of snacks. This is where I go to feed my nostalgia for the old street food of Chengdu. (Please see the photographs on the next two pages for my re-creation of one of these meals.)

Aside from being eaten as snacks between meals or as part of a street-food feast, dainty versions of "small eats" are also served on the side at banquets. At more formal meals, rice is not usually offered, so a tiny bowlful of noodles may be served in its place, to fill the stomach toward the end of the repast; otherwise, elegant dumplings may appear at intervals throughout the feast. Banquet snacks are often elevated versions of those eaten on the streets, made with exquisite artistry and beautifully presented. At his banquets, the brilliant chef Yu Bo serves a selection of dazzling snacks that include tiny hedgehog-shaped steamed buns with sesame-seed eyes and more than a hundred spiky quills, each snipped into the dough by hand, with a pair of nail scissors.

Some of the most famous Sichuanese snacks require specialty equipment, unusual ingredients or technical skills that are hard to master. I have not attempted to give recipes for these, but have included brief descriptions of some of the most interesting at the end of this chapter. The following recipes can all, I hope, be reasonably made at home.

Several "small eats" have found their way into other chapters of the book: for example, "man-and-wife" offal slices (see p. 97) and North Sichuan cool starch jelly (see p. 110) are in Cold Dishes; sour-and-hot "flower" tofu (see p. 256) is in Tofu; and all the noodle snacks can be found in the Noodles chapter. You will also find a few sweet snacks that are generally included under the "small eats" umbrella, such as Mr. Lai's glutinous rice balls (see p. 440), in the Sweet Dishes chapter.

Chengdu "small eats" (clockwise spiral from lower left): rabbit with peanuts in hot bean sauce, pot-sticker dumpling, Dragon wontons, Zhong crescent dumplings, sour-and-hot "flower" tofu, "big bang," steamed bun with spicy beansprout stuffing, numbing-and-hot dried beef, leaf-wrapped glutinous rice dumpling, pearly rice ball

(clockwise from lower left): green soy beans in a simple stock sauce, silver ear fungus and rock sugar soup, steamed pork and pumpkin dumpling, dandan noodles, sour-and-hot wood ear salad, North Sichuan cool starch jelly, Mr. Lai's glutinous rice balls with sesame stuffing and sesame dip, stuffed eggy pancakes

374

# Zhong Crescent Dumplings

zhong shuijiao
钟水饺

We were trying to find an underground dumpling restaurant. The residential compound didn't look promising, with its lines of brightly colored laundry and gaggles of old ladies knitting at the gates, but rumor had it that a retired chef from a famous Chengdu restaurant was running a snack shop in one of the apartments. We snooped around until we spotted a handwritten menu on the wall of one of the blocks. Inside, two rooms were crammed with people guzzling spicy dumplings, while the chef worked away in the steamy kitchen and members of his family handed out food and barked orders. The dumplings in question were the famous Zhong pork dumplings, with their heavenly-delicious dressing of garlic, chile oil and sweet aromatic soy sauce. A dainty Sichuanese version of northern *jiaozi*, they are said to have been invented by a pedlar, Zhong Xiesen, who set up shop in Lychee Lane in 1893.

The Chinese have been eating crescent-shaped dumplings like these for more than a thousand years: archeologists found a wooden bowl filled with desiccated *jiaozi* in a Tang-dynasty tomb excavated in remote Turpan, which you can still see in the local museum.

The Sichuanese tend to use smaller dumpling skins than those typically sold in Chinese supermarkets, but you can of course buy wrappers and make larger dumplings to save time. If you use fresh pork, the dumplings can be frozen and simply boiled and dressed before serving. The recipe makes 25–35 dumplings, depending on size—enough for 4–6 people.

3 tbsp sweet aromatic soy sauce
   (see p. 459)
2 tbsp chile oil
4 tsp crushed garlic, mixed with
   about 1 tbsp cold water
A few toasted sesame seeds, to garnish

For the wrappers
2 cups plus 6 tbsp (300g) Chinese high-gluten (dumpling)
   or bread flour, plus more for dusting (or about
   40 store-bought round dumpling wrappers)

For the stuffing
1 tsp ground roasted Sichuan pepper
1½-inch piece (30g) ginger, unpeeled
7 oz (200g) lean ground pork
½ tsp sesame oil
2 tbsp beaten egg (about 1 egg)
Salt and ground white pepper

If you're making your own wrappers, place the flour in a bowl or on a work surface, and make a well in the center. Gradually add about 10 tbsp (150ml) cold water, mixing it in with your hands, until you can make a fairly firm dough. Knead the dough until smooth and elastic, then cover with a damp dish towel and set aside to rest for at least 30 minutes.

Meanwhile, make the stuffing. Place the Sichuan pepper in a small heatproof bowl and cover with a little hot water from the kettle. Smack the ginger with the flat of a cleaver blade or a rolling pin until it is falling apart, then place in a pitcher and cover with about 10 tbsp (150ml) cold water.

Place the pork in a bowl. Add ½ tsp salt, a couple of pinches of white pepper, the sesame oil and beaten egg and mix vigorously, stirring in one direction—it's easiest to use your hand for this. The mixture should become sticky and a little elastic. Add 1 tbsp of the strained Sichuan pepper water and mix it in, again stirring in one direction. Now gradually add about 7 tbsp (100ml) of the strained ginger water, making sure each addition has been absorbed before you add the next. You should end up with a soft, fragrant paste.

Working on a lightly floured surface, take about a third of the dough and roll it into a sausage ¾–1 inch (2–2.5cm) thick. →

← Use a knife to cut the dough into pieces the size of large cherries (about ⅓–½ oz/12–15g each). Use the palm of your hand to flatten them into fat discs, then roll out into circular skins around 2¾ inches (7cm) in diameter. (If you are not used to making dumplings, it may be easier to start by making them a little larger than this.)

Place a dumpling skin in the palm of your non-dominant hand. With your other hand, place some stuffing in the center and fold over to make a semi-circle. Press the edges together, making sure they are sealed. Set aside on a floured plate or board. Repeat with the rest of the dough and stuffing.

Bring a large pot of water to a boil. Drop in around 10–12 dumplings and stir gently to prevent sticking, then bring back to a boil and cook for 5–7 minutes. When the water starts boiling very vigorously, add a dash of cold water to calm it down—you will need to do this two or three times. When the dumplings are done and the pork is cooked through (cut one open to make sure), drain well and divide between bowls, serving about 6 per person. Repeat with the rest of the dumplings.

Drizzle each bowlful of dumplings with 2 tsp sweet aromatic soy sauce and ½ tbsp chile oil, then top with about 1 tsp crushed garlic and sprinkle over a few sesame seeds. Mix everything together before eating.

# Dragon Wontons

## long chaoshou
## 龙抄手

Wontons are probably China's most ancient type of dumpling. According to scholars, they have been around since the Western Han dynasty (206 BC–24 AD), which makes them even older than the northern-style *jiaozi*. By about the fifth century AD they were a common snack, and over the next couple of centuries they reached great levels of sophistication—one Tang-dynasty source mentions 24 styles of wonton with various forms and fillings.

These days wontons are eaten all over China, and are prized for their silky, slippery mouthfeel. Known by different names in different regions, their Sichuanese dialect name is *chaoshou*, which means "folded arms," a reference to the crossover folding of the dumplings.

This particular sort, stuffed with pork and ginger and served in a rich broth, is the eponymous specialty of the Dragon Wonton (*long chaoshou*) restaurant in Chengdu. The "dragon" in the restaurant's name was a pun on the name of the teahouse where the three founders met to discuss their business plans before opening the place in 1941.

Dragon wontons (shown in the photograph on p. 374) may look plain but they're delicious. If you're buying wonton wrappers, select the thinnest available. Wontons wrapped in thicker skins are still tasty, but lack the exquisite mouthfeel of finer versions, which ruffle up and cling to the stuffing, their edges fluttering free like goldfish tails. You can make your own wrappers (see next page), but getting them sufficiently thin and strong is an art and I don't recommend it for the home cook. →

Around 40 thin wonton wrappers
2 tbsp melted lard (optional)
Salt and ground white pepper

*For the stock*
2 pig's trotters
1 lb (450g) chicken wings or legs
1-inch piece (20g) ginger, unpeeled
2 scallions, white parts only

*For the stuffing*
3-inch piece (60g) ginger, unpeeled
7 oz (200g) finely ground lean pork
2 tbsp beaten egg (about 1 egg)
1½ tsp Shaoxing wine
1 tsp sesame oil
½ tsp salt
A good pinch of ground white pepper

**First make the stock.** Place the trotters and chicken wings or legs in a large stockpot, cover with cold water and bring to a boil. Let it boil for a minute or so to allow any impurities to rise to the surface. Drain the meat in a colander, discarding the water, and rinse well.

Scrub out the pan, then return all the meat to the pan, cover with 1⅓ gallons (5 liters) of water and bring to a boil. Skim off any froth. Lightly smack the ginger and scallion whites with the flat of a cleaver blade or a rolling pin to loosen them and then add to the pot. Boil the stock for 2 hours until rich and milky in appearance. (The stock needs to boil rather than simmer to become milky, but does not need to boil at maximum heat: just make sure the liquid bubbles energetically.) Turn the heat down low and simmer for another hour. You should end up with about 3⅓ cups (800ml) rich, milky-opaque stock.

Next make the stuffing. Smack the ginger with the flat of a cleaver blade or a rolling pin until it is falling apart, then put in a pitcher and cover with about 1 cup (250ml) cold water. Place the pork in a bowl, then add the beaten egg, Shaoxing wine, sesame oil, salt and pepper and mix briskly with your hand, stirring in one direction, until the meat has become sticky and elastic. Gradually mix in ¾ cup plus 2 tbsp (200ml) strained ginger water, making sure each addition has been absorbed before you add the next. You should end up with a loose but coherent paste. →

← Wontons can be frozen raw and boiled directly from the freezer. Please note that the stock for this dish takes some time to cook, and so is best made in advance. This makes about 32 wontons, enough for 4 as an appetizer or light meal.

← Use a flexible knife or a small spatula to place 1–2 tsp stuffing in the center of a wonton wrapper. Fold the wonton in half diagonally, wetting one edge so you can press the two edges together. (For more advanced folding, you can then curve the two opposite corners to meet and press them together, forming what the Chinese call a "water caltrop" shape, but this isn't necessary.) Place the wontons on a lightly floured surface.

Bring a large pot of water to a boil over high heat and reheat the stock in another pot. Place the following seasonings in each of four bowls: a pinch of ground white pepper, a good pinch of salt, and, if you like, ½ tbsp melted lard.

When the water is boiling, give it a stir, then drop in about half the wontons and stir once to prevent sticking. When the water has returned to a boil, add one coffee-cupful of cold water. Allow the water to return to a boil once more, by which time the wontons should be cooked through (cut one open to make sure). When the wontons are nearly ready, add about ¾ cup plus 2 tbsp (200ml) hot stock to two of the bowls. Remove the wontons from the water with a slotted spoon and divide between the bowls. Repeat with the rest of the wontons and the other two bowls.

*If you wish to make your own wonton wrappers*
*Pile 3⅔ cups (450g) all-purpose flour on a work surface and make a well in the center. Add 1 beaten egg and about ¾ cup plus 2 tbsp (200ml) cold water. Mix the egg and water with your fingertips, then draw in the flour and mix to a stiff dough (you can add a little more flour or water if necessary to get the right consistency). Knead vigorously for several minutes, then cover with a damp dish towel and set aside for 30 minutes. On a surface dusted with potato starch, roll out the dough thinly and evenly, before cutting into strips 2¾ inches (7cm) wide (about the width of your four fingers) and then into squares.*

# Chengdu Wontons with Dried Chile Sauce

## ganban chaoshou
干拌抄手

One spring evening, my friend Kun led me to the eastern outskirts of Chengdu for a wonton supper. I followed him into a compound where a makeshift staircase led to the window of a ground-floor apartment. Bending our necks so we didn't bang our heads on the window-frame, we stepped down a crazy step-ladder contraption into a small dining room filled with people scoffing spicy wontons. Mrs. Li's pop-up restaurant, Dried Chile Wontons, had acquired a cult following in the city. After our meal, I could see why. We ate plump, juicy wontons with slippery skins, doused in various sauces. There were dry-tossed wontons scattered with ground chiles, sesame seeds and crushed peanuts; cold-tossed wontons in a spicy sauce laced with the tingle of Sichuan pepper and a hint of sweet-and-sour flavor, and wontons in a sumptuous clear broth made from chicken and dried matsutake mushrooms. (There was even a choice of wonton filling: either plain ground pork, or ground pork combined with shrimp.)

The following recipe is my homage to Mrs. Li's dry-tossed wontons. Below it you will find a couple of her variations, as well as some of the more classic Sichuanese wonton serving styles. If you have a good pot of stock and a few seasonings on hand, it is easy to serve several of these at one meal, to the inevitable delight of your guests. The quantities here are for about 32 wontons. For maximum spice and fragrance, make your own ground chiles (see p. 454); for ease, feel free to use Korean coarsely ground chiles.

*2 tbsp light soy sauce*

*4 tbsp chile oil, plus 2–4 tsp sediment*

*4 good pinches of ground roasted Sichuan pepper*

*1 batch of wontons (see p. 377)*

*2–4 tsp ground chiles*

*2 tsp toasted sesame seeds*

*4 tbsp crushed roasted or deep-fried peanuts (see p. 458)*

*6–8 tbsp thinly sliced scallion greens*

**Divide the soy sauce,** chile oil and sediment and Sichuan pepper among four bowls.

Make and cook your wontons as described on pp. 377–378, then divide them among the bowls.

Scatter over all the other ingredients, dividing them evenly among the bowls too. Mix together before eating.

*Dry-chile wontons (ganhaijiao chaoshou 干海椒抄手)*
*Follow the recipe for dry-tossed wontons above, but before adding the wontons to the bowls, pour 5 tbsp (75ml) chicken or everyday stock (see p. 463) into each bowl (1¼ cups/300ml in total). Mix before eating.*

*Cold-tossed wontons (liangban chaoshou 凉拌抄手)*
*This is also based on one of Mrs. Li's delicious variations. Place the following seasonings in each bowl: ½ tsp superfine sugar, ½ tsp Chinkiang vinegar, 1½ tsp light soy sauce, 1 tbsp chile oil plus 1 tsp sediment, ½ tsp finely chopped garlic and a couple of good pinches of ground roasted Sichuan pepper, to taste. Top each bowl with 1 tsp crushed roasted or deep-fried peanuts, ½ tsp toasted sesame seeds and 2 tbsp thinly sliced scallion greens. Mix before eating.*

*Wontons in chile oil sauce (hongyou chaoshou 红油抄手)*
*Place the following seasonings in each bowl: 1 tbsp chile oil with or without sediment, 2 tsp sweet aromatic soy sauce (see p. 459; or substitute 1½ tsp light soy sauce and 1 tsp superfine sugar) and 1 tsp crushed garlic.* →

← *Wontons in sour-and-hot soup (suanla chaoshou 酸辣抄手)*
*Place the following seasonings in each bowl: ½ tsp light soy sauce, 2 tsp Chinkiang vinegar, ½ tsp melted lard, ½ tsp sesame oil, 1 tbsp thinly sliced scallion greens, 7 tbsp (100ml) piping-hot clear stock (see p. 464), a couple of good pinches of ground white pepper and salt to taste. This variation is considered to be a pleasant summer dish.*

*Wontons in clear stock (qingtang chaoshou 清汤抄手)*
*Place the following seasonings in each bowl: 2 tsp Yibin yacai or Tianjin preserved vegetable (rinsed and squeezed dry), 1 tbsp thinly sliced scallion greens, ½ tsp sesame oil, ½ tsp light soy sauce, 10 tbsp (150ml) piping-hot clear stock (see p. 464), a good pinch of ground white pepper, ½ tsp melted lard and salt to taste. The soup is light and refreshing, with an enticing flash of sourness from the preserved vegetable.*

*Wontons in "sea flavor" soup (haiwei chaoshou 海味抄手)*
*You will need to make the stew used for the "sea flavor" noodles on p. 358, and keep it warm while the wontons are cooking. Place the following seasonings in each bowl: 1 tbsp thinly sliced scallion greens, ½ tbsp melted lard (optional) and salt and ground white pepper to taste. Just before serving, add a little of the liquid from the "sea flavor" stew. Add the cooked wontons, top with a good ladleful of the other ingredients, and finally top up with more liquid from the stew.*

*Wontons with ground pork topping (saozi chaoshou 臊子抄手)*
*You will need to make the ground pork topping used for the noodles on p. 354. You can also add a handful of blanched leafy greens such as choy sum, if you wish. Place the following seasonings in each serving bowl 2 tbsp Yibin yacai or Tianjin preserved vegetable (rinsed and squeezed dry), 1 tbsp thinly sliced scallion greens, ½ tsp sesame oil, ½ tsp light soy sauce, 10 tbsp (150ml) piping-hot clear stock (see p. 464), a good pinch of ground white pepper, ½ tsp melted lard and salt to taste. Add the cooked wontons and finish with a spoonful of the ground pork topping and some leafy greens, if using.*

# Pot-sticker Dumplings with Chicken Stock

## jizhi guotie
鸡汁锅贴

These tempting dumplings are the Sichuanese version of the gyoza sold in Japanese restaurants in the West. They take their name, "pot-sticker" (*guotie*) from the way they are cooked: in a single layer in a covered frying pan by a method that part-steams, part-fries them, so they end up moist and tender with golden, toasty bottoms. These Sichuanese pot-stickers, stuffed with ground pork mixed juicily with chicken stock, were invented in the 1940s by the Second Sibling Qiu restaurant in Chongqing. They are typically served with a bowlful of simple chicken broth (*dunjitang*), but also taste delicious with a dip of refreshing vinegar. (A pot-sticker dumpling is shown in the photograph on p. 372.)

You will need a heavy-bottomed non-stick or cast-iron frying pan about 10 inches (26cm) in diameter, with a lid.

This recipe makes around 16 pot-sticker dumplings.

4 tbsp cooking oil or melted lard
Chicken stock (or Chinkiang vinegar),
  to serve

### For the wrappers
½ cup plus 2 tbsp (75g) Chinese low-gluten (bun)
  or all-purpose flour, plus more for dusting
½ cup plus 2 tbsp (75g) Chinese high-gluten (dumpling)
  or bread flour
½ tsp cooking oil

### For the stuffing
¾-inch piece (15g) ginger, unpeeled
1 scallion, white part only
5¼ oz (150g) ground pork
5 tbsp cold chicken stock
½ tbsp Shaoxing wine
¾ teaspoon salt
½ teaspoon superfine sugar
A couple of pinches of ground white pepper
½ tsp sesame oil

**First make the dough** for the wrappers. Place both flours and the cooking oil in a bowl and mix together. Sprinkle about 7 tbsp (100ml) hot water from the kettle over the flour mixture and stir rapidly with the handle end of a wooden spoon to incorporate. Let rest for a few moments to cool down, then mix in just enough cold water to bind the mixture and make a dough. Knead until smooth, then cover with a damp dish towel and set aside to rest for 30 minutes.

Meanwhile, make the stuffing. Smack the ginger and scallion white with the flat of a cleaver blade or a rolling pin until they are falling apart, then place in a bowl, just cover with cold water and set aside for 5–10 minutes. Place the pork in a bowl. Add 3 tbsp strained soaking water from the ginger and scallion white, and mix well until it has been absorbed, stirring in one direction. Gradually add the chicken stock, mixing well and making sure each addition has been absorbed before adding the next—you should end up with a loose, wet paste. Add all the other stuffing ingredients and mix well.

Working on a lightly floured surface, divide the dough in half, then roll each half into a sausage about ¾ inch (2cm) thick. Cut or break off ½-oz (15g) pieces and flatten them with the palm of your hand, then use a rolling pin to roll into circles 3¼–3½ inches (8–9cm) in diameter. (Unless you work very quickly, cover the remaining dough with a damp dish towel to prevent it from drying out.)

Place about 1 tbsp stuffing into the center of each wrapper, then fold gently in half and, starting at one end, pinch the two edges together into a classic *jiaozi* dumpling shape. Place the finished dumpling on your work surface, pushing it down slightly to give it a flat base. Repeat with the rest of the wrappers and stuffing.

To cook the dumplings, heat a non-stick or heavy, flat-bottomed frying-pan over medium heat. Add 2 tbsp cooking oil or lard to the pan and swirl it around. When the oil is hot, arrange all the dumplings in the pan in neat rows. Drizzle over 7 tbsp (100ml) hot water from the kettle, then cover the pan with a lid and steam the dumplings over medium heat for 4–5 minutes, until you hear a sizzling sound, which means the water has mostly evaporated. Remove the lid to allow the remaining steam to escape, drizzle over another 2 tbsp oil or lard and fry for about 3 minutes more, until the bottoms of the dumplings are toasty and golden brown: as they cook, move the pan around the heat source to brown them evenly.

Remove the dumplings with a spatula and place them upside down on a serving plate, revealing their golden bottoms. Serve immediately, with bowlfuls of hot chicken stock (or little dipping dishes of Chinkiang vinegar).

# Steamed Pork and Pumpkin Dumplings

nangua zhengjiao
南瓜蒸饺

These delectable dumplings look gorgeous when brought to the table in a bamboo steamer, fresh from the stove. Like many steamed dumplings, they have wrappers made with a "scalded" dough (*tangmian*): the hot water partially cooks the flour and gives the finished dumplings a soft and slightly glutinous texture. Typically, steamed dumplings are filled with a stuffing that is already cooked and simply requires heating through before serving, as in the following version, which is based on a classic Chengdu recipe. If you wish, you can replace the pumpkin with leafy greens, which should be blanched, refreshed under cold water, squeezed dry and then finely chopped before being stirred into the cooked and seasoned pork.

You can either oil your steamer or line it with perforated parchment paper. Some Chinese supermarkets sell pre-made liners for steamer baskets. Alternatively, follow the example of chef Guirong Wei and make your own: use scissors to cut a circle of parchment paper and fold it in half several times until you have a narrow triangle of layers of folded paper. Now make little snips along the edges, just as you would when making a paper snowflake. Unfold the circle and it will be scattered with little holes (just like the one lining the steamer basket in the photograph).

In Sichuan, the dumplings are served on their own, but they also taste wonderful with a dip of Chinkiang vinegar.

This recipe makes 20–25 dumplings.

*For the stuffing*
About 9¾ oz (275g) pumpkin
3 tbsp cooking oil
1 tbsp finely chopped ginger
7 oz (200g) ground pork
½ tbsp Shaoxing wine
1 tbsp light soy sauce
1 tsp dark soy sauce
3 tbsp thinly sliced scallions
1 tsp sesame oil
Salt and ground white pepper

*For the wrappers*
1½ tsp cooking oil
2 cups (250g) Chinese low-gluten (bun)
  or all-purpose flour

**First make the stuffing.** Peel the pumpkin and discard its pulp and seeds. Cut the flesh into ⅛-inch (3mm) slices, then into strips and finely into tiny dice (the size of mung beans, in Chinese kitchen jargon). Bring a pot of water to a boil, tip in the pumpkin and boil for about 1 minute, until just tender. Drain in a colander, rinse under cold water and then shake dry.

Heat the cooking oil in a seasoned wok over high heat. Add the ginger and stir-fry very briefly until it smells delicious. Tip in the pork and stir-fry until pale, then splash in the Shaoxing wine. When the pork is nearly cooked, add both soy sauces and salt and pepper to taste: the mixture should be on the salty side, as the dumpling wrappers will be unsalted. Tip in the pumpkin and stir-fry until piping hot, adjusting the seasoning as necessary. Off the heat, stir in the scallions and sesame oil. Set aside to cool and then chill until needed.

Next make the dough for the wrappers. Place the cooking oil in a small pan with 1 cup (225ml) water and bring to a boil. Switch off the heat, then immediately tip in all the flour and stir rapidly, scraping the bottom of the pan: you will end up with a rubble of half-made dough. When the mixture is cool enough to handle, knead for a minute or so to make a smooth dough. Cover with a damp dish towel until needed.

When you're ready to make the dumplings, divide the dough in half and roll each half into a sausage 1 inch (2–3cm) in diameter. →

← Break or cut the dough into pieces the size of small walnuts (about ¾ oz/20g). Take a piece at a time—keeping the rest of the dough covered with a damp dish towel, so it doesn't dry out—and flatten it with your palm into a fat disc. Use a rolling pin to roll it out into a thin disc about 3¼ inches (8cm) in diameter, then place about 1 tbsp stuffing in the center. Place the wrapper in your non-dominant hand. With your other hand, pinch the wrapper together at the end nearest to you, then pleat the far edge of the wrapper against the near edge, pressing the two edges together after each pleat (the easiest way to learn how to do this is to ask a Chinese friend to show you, or watch a video on the internet); make sure the dumplings are tightly sealed, or they may rupture during cooking.

Place the dumplings in a single layer in an oiled or lined bamboo steamer, then steam over high heat for about 7 minutes, until they are piping hot all the way through. Serve immediately.

Variation

*You can also stuff these dumplings with mashed or chopped-up leftovers of red-braised pork (see p. 143), or indeed any other collagenous meat stew: the key is that the stew must be allowed to cool and set before you try to wrap it into the dumplings. In London, I've even made an anglicized version of these dumplings with a pheasant and pork belly stew: delicious.*

# Leaf-wrapped Glutinous Rice Dumplings

## ye'er ba
叶儿粑

Sometimes you can still catch, fleetingly on a Chengdu street corner, a vendor of these glistening leaf-wrapped dumplings. He'll have a huge round steamer on a portable stove, all precariously balanced on the back of his tricycle. The steamer will be packed with smooth glutinous rice dumplings, each half-wrapped in a piece of fragrant leaf. Some are sweet, stuffed with roasted nuts, candied fruits or blossoms; others are filled with a salty mix of pork and preserved vegetable. They are eaten there and then, nibbled from the leaf, the moist filling oozing out from the succulent rice dough.

This typical Chengdu pork and preserved vegetable ye'er ba originated in Yibin, home of the famous yacai preserved vegetable. But these are just the best known of a multitude of steamed, leaf-wrapped dumplings that are eaten across southern Sichuan. The dumplings are traditionally shaped from a dough made with freshly milled, soaked glutinous rice; using flour is a modern convenience.

Ye'er ba may be wrapped in lesser galangal, hardy banana (Musa basjoo), pomelo or tangerine leaves, each of which has an enticing scent. You can buy frozen banana leaves in East Asian shops; I also salvage any leaves from among the tangerines in my local Turkish supermarket and store them in my freezer for making ye'er ba. The dumplings can be frozen before cooking and steamed directly from the freezer—this recipe makes 20–25 dainty dumplings (or fewer if you want to make them larger).

A few banana leaves or
  20–25 tangerine leaves
A little cooking oil
1⅔ cups (50g) spinach leaves
1¼ cups (200g) glutinous rice flour
⅓ cup (50g) rice flour
1½ tbsp melted lard

_For the stuffing_
5 tbsp lard
3½ oz (100g) fatty ground pork
½ tbsp Shaoxing wine
1 tsp light soy sauce
½ tsp dark soy sauce
4 tbsp Yibin yacai preserved vegetable,
  rinsed and squeezed dry
2 tbsp finely chopped scallion whites
1 tsp sesame oil

**First make the stuffing.** Heat the lard in a seasoned wok over high heat. Add the pork and stir-fry to separate, breaking it up as much as possible. As the pork becomes pale, splash in the Shaoxing wine. When the pork is cooked through, add both soy sauces, then stir in the preserved vegetable and stir-fry briefly until fragrant and piping hot. Add a little salt to taste: the filling should taste a bit too salty, because the rice-flour dough will be unsalted. Add the scallion whites and give them a lick of heat. Off the heat, stir in the sesame oil, then let cool completely and set (this will make stuffing the dumplings easier).

Meanwhile, blanch the banana or tangerine leaves in boiling water with a drop of cooking oil until slightly softened. Refresh in cold water, pat dry with paper towels, and then rub both sides with a little oil. If you are using banana leaves, use scissors to cut them into 2½–2¾ inch (6–7cm) squares.

When you are ready to make the dough, blitz the spinach with 7 tbsp (100ml) cold water in a food processor, then strain the juice through a fine tea strainer or a muslin-lined sieve. Combine both rice flours in a bowl, then stir in the lard and about 4 tbsp spinach juice, along with just enough cold water to make a soft, putty-like dough. Knead until smooth.

Brush the base of a steamer basket with a little cooking oil. →

←     Divide the dough in half and roll each half into a sausage about 1¼ inches (3–4cm) thick. Break or cut off 1¼-inch (3–4cm) pieces (about 1 oz/25–30g each), then roll each one into a ball and flatten with the palm of your hand. Take a piece of dough in your non-dominant hand. Use your other hand to press 1–1½ tsp stuffing into the center, then draw in the sides of the dough and pinch them together. Roll the dumpling into a little cylinder and place in the center of a piece of banana leaf (or a whole tangerine leaf), drawing the ends of the leaf up the sides. Place the dumpling, leaf side down, in the steamer. Repeat with the rest of the dough and stuffing, arranging the dumplings in rows. (If you have any leftover stuffing at the end, serve it as a relish with rice.)

Steam over high heat for 10–15 minutes until heated through and then serve hot, straight from the steamer.

*Sweet leaf-wrapped dumplings*
*In Chengdu snack restaurants, ye'er ba are often served in pairs, with each guest being offered one green dumpling with a savory filling and one white dumpling, decorated with a dot of pink food coloring, with a sweet filling. For sweet dumplings, instead of spinach juice, add a little more water to the dough, and then stuff with the following mixture.*

5 tbsp fried peanuts, toasted sesame seeds or candied fruits
1½ tbsp all-purpose flour
6 tbsp (75g) superfine sugar
3 tbsp melted lard
A few drops of cochineal or 1 tbsp Chinese red yeasted rice

*If you are using peanuts, peel and coarsely chop them; crush sesame seeds to a coarse powder with a mortar and pestle; finely chop candied fruit. Toast the flour in a dry frying pan until cooked and very slightly golden, then transfer to a bowl. Stir in the sugar and lard, followed by the nuts, seeds or candied fruits.*

*If you are using cochineal, dilute it with a few drops of cold water. If using Chinese red yeasted rice, place in a small cup, add 1–2 tbsp hot water from the kettle, mash together and let steep for a few minutes, then squeeze through a tea strainer to extract the pink juice.*

*After stuffing and steaming the dumplings as in the main recipe, use a chopstick to dot each one with a spot of pink coloring and then serve.*

# Steamed Buns with Spicy Beansprout Stuffing

## douya baozi
## 豆芽包子

Round steamed buns with moist, meaty stuffings—known as *bao* or *baozi*—are eaten all over China, but the Sichuanese have their own particular recipes. One famous *baozi*-maker was Liao Yongtong, who began his career on the streets of Chengdu in the 1930s and devised an acclaimed "dragon-eye" *baozi*, so called because its pork stuffing peeped up through a small round hole at the top of the bun, like a beady eye. In the 1990s, there was still a small restaurant in the city selling Mr. Liao's buns (the restaurant was named after his distinguishing facial characteristic—a large mole with a few long, sprouting hairs!). Another famous Sichuanese steamed bun is the Han *baozi*, devised by a Mr. Han in the 1920s; stuffed with ground pork, fresh shrimp and spices, they are still sold in Chengdu outlets that bear his name.

The Chinese have a striking (and probably spurious) legend about the origin of these buns, which were once known as *mantou*—a word that now more commonly refers to plain steamed buns. During the third-century Three Kingdoms period, so they say, the great statesman and strategist Zhuge Liang was fighting barbarians on the southern fringes of the country when he ran into difficulties while trying to cross a raging river. He was instructed to follow local custom and propitiate the river gods by making sacrifices of barbarian heads. Zhuge Liang, unwilling to sanction such slaughter, instructed his troops to dupe the gods by offering them stuffed steamed buns instead of human heads. →

2 cups (250g) Chinese low-gluten (bun) or all-purpose flour, plus more for dusting
1 tsp fast-acting dried yeast
½ tsp superfine sugar
½ tsp baking powder
1 tsp cooking oil or melted lard

*For the stuffing*
2 cups (200g) bean sprouts
3 tbsp cooking oil
7 oz (200g) fatty ground pork
1 tbsp Shaoxing wine
2½ tbsp Sichuan chile bean paste
2 tsp finely chopped ginger
2 tsp light soy sauce
¼ tsp dark soy sauce
1 tsp superfine sugar
3 tbsp thinly sliced scallion greens
2 pinches of ground white pepper
1 tsp sesame oil
Salt

**First make the stuffing.** Cut the bean sprouts into roughly ½-inch (1cm) lengths. Heat the cooking oil in a seasoned wok over high heat, then add the ground pork and stir-fry. As the meat separates and turns pale, splash in the Shaoxing wine. When the pork is fragrant and the oil is sizzling, add the chile bean paste and stir-fry until it smells wonderful and the oil has reddened. Add the ginger and stir until you can smell it. Stir in both soy sauces and the sugar, and season with salt to taste (the stuffing should be on the salty side as the dough is unsalted). Tip in the bean sprouts and stir-fry for a little longer, until they are piping hot. Off the heat, stir in the scallion greens, pepper and sesame oil. Set aside to cool, and then chill in the fridge until needed.

To make the dough, mix the flour, yeast and sugar together in a bowl or on a clean work surface. Make a well in the center and gradually pour in just enough lukewarm water (around 10 tbsp/150ml, and ideally at about 80°F/27°C), drawing in the flour to make a soft but not sticky dough. When the dough has nearly formed, add the baking powder and oil or lard and mix well. Knead briefly until evenly mixed, then cover with a damp dish towel and set aside in a warm place for 20 minutes. →

The ruse worked, and apparently this is how the buns acquired the curious name *mantou*, which in Chinese sounds the same as "barbarian heads."

The following *baozi* is one of the most distinctively Sichuanese. Nowhere else in China do you find a *baozi* flavored with chile bean paste. Sichuanese cooks make the stuffing with soy-bean sprouts, but the more readily available mung-bean sprouts are a fine substitute. For maximum lusciousness, select ground pork that is thirty percent fat. Below the main recipe you will find a delicious vegetarian stuffing (note that the pork and preserved vegetable stuffing on p. 397 is also fantastic in *baozi*).

You will need a bamboo steamer with a couple of tiers. The recipe should make around 12 buns, depending on their size.

← Punch back the dough and knead for 5–10 minutes until pale and smooth, then cover with a damp dish towel and set aside for another 15 minutes. Meanwhile, cut out about a dozen 2½-inch (6cm) squares of parchment paper. Knead the dough briefly again, then divide in half and shape each half into a sausage with a diameter of 1½ inches (4cm). Break or cut off 1 oz (30g) pieces (about the size of a walnut), stand them on their ends and flatten with your hand to make fat discs. Use a rolling pin to roll them into 3½-inch (9cm)-diameter circles that are thinner around the edges. Take a disc in your non-dominant hand, place about 1½ tbsp stuffing on it and press down into the center. Use your other hand to draw up and pleat the edges of the circle around the stuffing, turning it as you do so. Seal the bun tightly. Repeat with the rest of the dough and stuffing.

Set the buns on the parchment squares and place in the steamer tiers, spacing them out, as they will expand. Put the lid on the steamer and let rise in a warm place for 20 minutes. Fill your wok with water, bring it to a boil and add the steamer tiers, covered with the lid. Steam over high heat for about 8 minutes, until the stuffing is heated through and the dough is cooked but retains a little springiness. If the buns appear flattened and droopy after steaming, they're overcooked.

### Vegetarian stuffing

*This simple but satisfying stuffing comes from a breakfast stall in Chengdu. Cover 2 dried shiitake mushrooms with hot water from the kettle and let soak for 30 minutes. Finely shred 7 oz (200g) pointy "sweetheart" cabbage and place in a bowl, then add about ½ cup (60g) peeled and finely shredded carrot. Sprinkle over ½ tsp salt and scrunch it into the vegetables, then set aside for at least 20 minutes to soften. Finally, mix in 1 tsp sesame oil.*

### Lotus-leaf buns (heyebing 荷叶饼)

*These are a traditional accompaniment to fragrant and crispy duck (as shown in the photograph on p. 206) and other substantial dishes. Omit the stuffing. Roll out the dough into discs, but make them an even thickness throughout. Brush half of each disc with cooking oil and lay a chopstick across the middle to help you fold it into a semi-circle. Use the teeth of a clean comb to make "veins" on the top of the leaf, then push in the edge of the leaf at the end of each "vein" using the back of the comb. Let rise for 20 minutes, then steam over high heat for 8 minutes. If you are making these in advance, simply reheat in the steamer before serving; they freeze well too.*

# Juntun Guokui Pastries

## juntun guokui
## 军屯锅魁

When I was a student at Sichuan University, an elderly couple had a stall on the campus where they made Juntun *guokui* every morning, rolling out their hand-made dough into long tongues, slathering them with ground pork laced with scallion and Sichuan pepper, and then rolling them up into fat little spirals. These were then rolled thin and fried in rapeseed oil in a skillet, before being baked in the fiery furnace beneath it until they were crisp and toasty on the outside but still bready within. The aroma of these twirly flatbreads sizzling in the hot oil was irresistible, as was their taste: I think they may have been the first Sichuanese snack I fell in love with.

The Juntun *guokui*, a specialty of the town of Juntun, is just one of a whole range of *guokui* pastries. *Guokui* literally means "chief-of-the-pot" and there are numerous different versions, most of them to be found in northern China, where they presumably originate. Northern *guokui* are typically larger, plainer flatbreads, and northerners use a different Chinese character (*kui*) in their name, so the word means "pot helmets."

In Sichuan the term encompasses various flatbreads and pastries, sweet and savory, with textures ranging from soft and fluffy to crisp and fragrant. In central Chengdu, a famed artisanal baker named Second Brother Qiu still rises at five every morning to knead his dough: he makes plain, fluffy round flatbreads and others stuffed with molten brown sugar or interleaved with a shortening spiked with salt and Sichuan pepper. →

*2 tbsp black or white sesame seeds*
*Cooking oil, for oiling and shallow-frying*

*For the dough*
*3 cups plus 6 tbsp (425g) all-purpose flour*
*¼ tsp fast-acting dried yeast*
*5 tbsp (75ml) rapeseed oil*
*1 tsp salt*

*For the stuffing*
*10 oz (300g) fatty ground pork*
*3 tbsp finely chopped scallion whites*
*2 tbsp finely chopped ginger*
*½ tsp salt*
*1 tsp ground roasted Sichuan pepper*
*2 good pinches of ground white pepper*
*3 good pinches of five-spice powder*

**First make the leavened dough.** In a bowl, combine ½ cup plus 2 tbsp (75g) flour and the yeast. Make a well in the center. Gradually mix in enough tepid water (3–4 tbsp) to make a soft dough. Knead for 5 minutes until smooth and glossy. Place in a lightly oiled bowl and turn to coat all over. Cover the bowl with a damp dish towel and set aside to rise for about 3 hours, until doubled in size.

For the unleavened dough, place 2 cups plus 6 tbsp (300g) flour in a bowl or on a clean work surface and make a well in the center. Gradually mix in enough cold water (about ¾ cup/175–200ml) to make a very soft but not sticky dough. Knead the dough for a few minutes until smooth. Place in a lightly oiled bowl and turn to oil it all over. Cover the bowl with a damp dish towel and set aside for at least 30 minutes.

Now make the layering oil that will be used to brush the dough. Place the remaining 6 tbsp (50g) flour and the salt in a heatproof bowl and mix. Heat the rapeseed oil until smoking, then pour it over the flour, mixing it in swiftly as the mixture fizzes and becomes fragrant, then set aside until needed.

Combine the stuffing ingredients and refrigerate until needed.

Next make the pastries. Knead the two doughs together on an oiled worktop, then cover with a damp cloth and let rest for 10 minutes. →

← Meanwhile, in Huaxing Street, next to the Yuelai opera teahouse, you may line up at a hatch in the wall of the Pansunshi restaurant for slurpsome *guokui* stuffed with luscious slow-cooked pork, spicy beef offal or a tingly vegetable salad. Another fabulous type of *guokui* is a crisp pocket of dough stuffed with ribbons of cool pea-starch jelly in a spicy dressing: the textural contrast between the crisp crust of the freshly baked bread and the cool, spicy slitheriness of the jelly is sublime.

Making Juntun *guokui* is laborious (they are not normally made at home), but I hope you'll agree that they're extraordinarily delicious—and, unless you happen to be in Sichuan, there may be no other way to get your hands on them. The key to this recipe is to rest the dough for a few minutes at every stage, to allow it to relax and become willing to cooperate; otherwise, it will be too springy to form the pastries.

This recipe makes about 8 *guokui*.

← Break off balls of dough the size of a large plum (about 2¼ oz/60g) and roll into sausage shapes, then smear lightly with oil and let rest for 3 minutes.

Use an oiled rolling pin to roll each ball of dough away from you into a long, thin strip about 10–12 inches (25–30cm) long and 2½–2¾ inches (6–7cm) wide. If you find the dough is too springy to roll out thinly, rest for another 2–3 minutes to allow it to relax more, and then roll it out thinner. Give the layering oil mixture a stir and use a pastry brush to paint 1–2 tbsp over each strip of dough, then use your fingers to press a scattering of 2–3 tbsp stuffing along each strip, staying clear of the edges.

Pick up one end of a strip of dough and start to roll it up; after one turn, fold in the sides of the end of the strip to make a little nugget of stuffed dough, then roll the nugget up in the rest of the strip of dough, pulling gently as you go so that you stretch the dough and make it thinner with every roll (the thinner the layers, the better the mouthfeel of the finished pastry). When you have reached the end of the strip, tuck the end of the tongue of dough into the top of the spiral you have made, turn the spiral on its end and push your finger into the top. Let rest for a few minutes while you roll up the other strips.

Tip the sesame seeds out onto the work surface and place a little water in a small bowl. Dip your finger into the water and wet the top of each spiral, then press in a good pinch of sesame seeds (the water will help them stick). Turn each spiral upside-down and gently roll out into a disc about ½ inch (1cm) thick. Repeat with the rest. Again, if the dough resists being rolled, rest it for a couple of minutes before proceeding.

When you're ready to cook the pastries, preheat the oven to 425°F (225°C). Heat a heavy-bottomed frying pan over medium heat and pour in cooking oil to a depth of about ¼ inch (5mm). When the oil is hot, place the pastries in the pan and fry for 1–2 minutes on both sides until golden brown, then transfer to a baking sheet and bake for about 5 minutes until cooked through. Eat while they are still hot.

# Stuffed Eggy Pancakes

## dan hong gao
## 蛋烘糕

In the streets around the Wenshu Monastery in Chengdu, you can still find makers of these eggy pancakes, which seem to have been enjoying a renaissance in recent years. In the vendors' glass cabinets, perched on the back of bicycle carts, are arranged bucketfuls of frothy batter, tiny stoves and various fillings, including ground pork with preserved vegetable, strawberry jam, and mixtures of toasted nuts and sparkly sugar. The traders make the pancakes in tiny, bespoke copper pans with convex bases and matching lids. They pour a little batter into each pan and let it cook, then add a spoonful of stuffing, fold the pancake in half and cover it with the lid until it's golden on the outside and fluffy on the inside.

The snack is said to date back to the early twentieth century and appears to have been inspired by Western pancakes. One of my local sources suggests the pancakes acquired their present name after being popularized in the early 1940s by a street vendor who had a stall near the city's West China Hospital, which was founded by foreign missionaries.

This recipe makes about 18 small pancakes. You can fill them with sweet or savory stuffings: at the Dragon Wonton restaurant in Chengdu they often serve each guest one of each. Do feel free to cheat by stuffing the pancakes with chocolate hazelnut spread or strawberry jam, if you wish.

1⅔ cups (200g) all-purpose flour
½ tsp fast-acting dried yeast
5 tbsp (60g) white or brown sugar
2–3 large eggs (total 4.2 oz/120g without shells)
A little cooking oil

*For the stuffing*
5 tbsp cooking oil or lard
3½ oz (100g) fatty ground pork
½ tbsp Shaoxing wine
1 tsp light soy sauce
4 tbsp Yibin yacai *preserved vegetable,*
  *rinsed and squeezed dry*
1 tsp sesame oil

**Place the flour and yeast in a bowl** and mix well. In a heatproof pitcher, dissolve the sugar in 7 tbsp (100ml) hot water from the kettle, then allow to cool. Lightly beat the eggs and add them to the pitcher, along with 7 tbsp (100ml) cold water. Gradually whisk this liquid into the flour to make a smooth batter. Cover the bowl with a damp dish towel and set aside until frothy: this could take up to 2 hours, depending on the temperature.

Meanwhile, make the stuffing. Heat the oil or lard in a seasoned wok over high heat. Add the pork and stir-fry to separate, breaking it up as much as possible. As the pork becomes pale, splash in the Shaoxing wine. When the pork is cooked through, add the soy sauce and preserved vegetable, and stir-fry until fragrant and piping hot. Off the heat, stir in the sesame oil.

To cook the pancakes, heat a heavy-bottomed frying pan over very gentle heat. Lightly oil the pan, then drop little pools of batter (about 2 tbsp each) into the pan and cover with a lid. Cook very gently for 1 minute, by which time the pancakes should be nearly cooked, but just a little wet on top. Add a spoonful of stuffing to each one and use a spatula to fold in half, then cover and cook for another 10 seconds or so. Repeat with the rest of the batter and stuffing. Serve while still hot.

*Sweet stuffing*
*Peel and coarsely chop 5 tbsp fried or roasted peanuts to make a peanut rubble. Mix with 2 tsp toasted sesame seeds and 6 tbsp (75g) superfine sugar.*

# Spiced "Oil Tea" with Crunchy Toppings

## wuxiang youcha
五香油茶

Every morning, in the quiet streets of the ancient Sichuanese city of Langzhong, Mrs. Zhu dispenses "oil tea" from her wheeled cart, as her family has done for four generations. She fills a bowl with the steaming, smooth rice porridge, fragrant with Sichuan pepper, and spoons over chile oil, crushed nuts, chopped pickles and herbs, finishing off with a great handful of *sanzi* (strands of crunchy fried noodle dough).

Despite its name, "oil tea" contains no tea or oil, although it may be related to other versions traditionally eaten by Chinese minorities such as the Miao and Tujia, which are made by various methods involving tea leaves, oil, glutinous rice and other ingredients. "Oil tea" is eaten all over China, but in the north it is mostly made with a combination of toasted wheat flour and ground nuts and seeds, rather than rice, as in Sichuan. Sometimes the paste is enriched with rendered ox bone marrow.

Most recipes suggest using a mixture of non-glutinous and glutinous rices, which are washed and then ground with water to make a fine paste. To save time, I've suggested using only brown rice flour, which makes a delicious and nutritious breakfast. Sichuanese street vendors garnish the porridge with deep-fried soy beans and noodle dough (*sanzi*), but I like to use Bombay mix instead, which provides the perfect crunchy note. This recipe makes 4 servings.

⅔ cup (100g) brown rice flour
¾-inch piece (15g) ginger, unpeeled
1 scallion, white part only
¾ tsp dark soy sauce
A couple of pinches of five-spice powder
Salt

*To serve*
2 tbsp chile oil, plus 2–4 tsp sediment
¼–½ tsp ground roasted Sichuan pepper
   or Sichuan pepper oil, to taste
2 tsp finely chopped ginger
4 tbsp finely chopped preserved
   mustard tuber (zhacai)
2 tsp toasted sesame seeds, crushed
8 tbsp thinly sliced scallion greens
4 handfuls of Bombay mix

Place the rice flour in a bowl and gradually stir in 10 tbsp (150ml) cold water, mixing well to make a smooth batter.

Lightly smack the ginger and scallion white with the flat of a cleaver blade or a rolling pin to loosen them. Place in a saucepan with 3¾ cups (900ml) water and bring to a boil over high heat, then fish out and discard the ginger and scallion white from the infused water.

Give the batter a stir, then gradually add it to the pan of infused water, stirring constantly to avoid the formation of lumps. Bring to a boil, then stir in the soy sauce and five-spice powder. Turn the heat down low and simmer, stirring often, for about 10–15 minutes, until you have a thick, gravy-like porridge. Season lightly with salt to taste (do not oversalt, because some of the garnishes are salty).

Divide the mixture among four bowls, then divide all the other ingredients between the bowls, finishing with a handful of Bombay mix. Stir everything together before eating.

## Variation

*If you'd like to make the rice paste from scratch, use one part glutinous rice to four parts regular non-glutinous rice; rinse well and then blend to a fine paste with 10 tbsp (150ml) cold water.*

## Other specialty snacks

The following is a selection of fascinating Sichuanese "small eats" that are particularly worthy of mention, although difficult to make at home because they demand unusual ingredients or specialty equipment.

### Ice jelly
*bingfen* 冰粉

On midsummer days, when a blanket of suffocating heat and humidity settles over southern Sichuan, few snacks are more appetizing than a bowlful of ice-cold *bingfen*, a transparent, wobbly jelly made from the small, reddish seeds of the shoo-fly plant (*Nicandra physalodes*). To make the jelly, the seeds are wrapped in a piece of muslin and then kneaded and rubbed in cold water until nothing but skins are left in the cloth; the clear liquid, now carrying the seeds' magical substance, is doctored with a little lime solution and left to set.

In the past, *bingfen* was normally sold on the streets; recently, I tried it at Mr. Huang's King of Ice Jelly snack shop in Luzhou. Mr. Huang presided over a gleaming stainless-steel counter covered in pots of sauces and sprinkles, ministering to the sweltering customers who perched thirstily on stools. Your *bingfen* could be dressed with lemon, mint or osmanthus syrups, or with honey or fermented glutinous rice wine—and then scattered with dried fruits and nuts, or chopped water chestnut, pineapple or mango. My favorite, however, was the old-fashioned classic, with a simple libation of brown sugar syrup.

### Cool rice pudding
*lianggao* 凉糕

Another glorious summer's treat is this cold, wobbly rice pudding, like a Chinese crème caramel. Made from milk produced from a particular variety of rice, it is distinguished by its pale color and satiny smoothness on the tongue, but with an extra hint of tautness that gives it the most exquisite wobble. It has a slightly alkaline taste because of the lime used in its making. People in southern Sichuan like to eat it with a spoon on sultry days, with a gorgeous sheen of brown sugar syrup. This pudding is delicious in its own right,

but is a special delight for anyone on a dairy-free diet. Sichuanese friends remember how, before the advent of refrigeration, *lianggao* vendors would keep the puddings cool by suspending them inside a well.

### Dingding toffee
*dingding tang* 丁丁糖

The "ding ding dang" sound made by sellers of malt-sugar toffee, usually elderly men, is part of the soundscape of old Chengdu. Since ancient times, malt sugar has been made in China by inoculating steamed glutinous rice with sprouted wheat grains, waiting until the starch in the grains has been transformed into sugars and then heating the resulting liquid to make toffee.

One maker I chatted to recently, Liu Tinggao, sold three kinds of dingding toffee: the most common kind, a pale, opaque candy, deliciously flavored with sesame seeds and tangerine peel; a clear, amber-like toffee; and an incredible version called "hollow flower" toffee (*konghua tang*) that had somehow been manipulated to create long, pale, batons of rippled, paper-thin toffee with chambers running through it like a honeycomb. The batons, studded with sesame seeds, were crisp, crunchy and fragrant, and then chewy: I was astonished by their texture and form.

### Toffee-glazed glutinous rice dumplings
*tangyou guozi* 糖油果子

These are a favorite of Chengdu schoolchildren: sticky glutinous rice balls that are cooked slowly in a wokful of oil and caramel, giving them a gorgeous sheen. Speckled with a few sesame seeds, they are strung up on skewers to be sold. Inside their crisp, lacquered shells, they are soft, airy, chewy and utterly delicious. You can still find makers of these dumplings in the streets around the Wenshu Monastery.

### Spring pancakes and spring rolls
*chunbing* 春饼

Deep-fried spring rolls are one of the archetypal "Chinese restaurant" appetizers in the West, but in Sichuan people prefer the unfried version, made by wrapping pale "spring pancakes" around refreshing salads or simple stir-fried dishes. The pancakes are normally bought from specialty vendors in the markets, who are fascinating to watch. They grab a handful of a wet, almost-liquid dough, keeping their wrist in constant motion to prevent its escape, and dab it onto a hot griddle so that a thin, round film of dough adheres to the metal surface. When the pancake is cooked but still alabaster-white, the vendor plucks it from the griddle and adds it to the pile.

The fresh wrappers are sold with a colorful selection of vegetables, including slivered carrot, radish and kelp, stems of cilantro and bean sprouts, which can be mixed to order with a piquant dressing. Traditionally, the trade peters out as the weather becomes sultry and the fresh pancakes begin to stick together in the heat.

These fresh spring rolls are the modern incarnation of an ancient food custom. As long ago as the third century AD, Chinese people celebrated the first day of the lunar year with *chunpan*: "spring platters" of pungent vegetables like garlic and chives which were eaten to purge the qi energy of the vital organs. By the Tang dynasty, these sprightly vegetables were served with thin pancake wrappers called *chunbing*, "spring pancakes." During China's last dynasty, the Qing, the actual word "spring roll" (*chun juan*) finally appeared. (By Chinese standards, the deep-fried spring roll is a fairly recent invention, having appeared in written records only in the thirteenth or fourteenth century.)

The link between spring rolls and the Lunar New Year has long since been broken, but the pancakes remain a seasonal delicacy, and the Sichuanese way of eating them with slivered vegetables pepped up with chile oil or mustard is a throwback to the "spring platters" of the distant past. (They may also be served with stir-fries of pork or chicken slivers with yellow chives or garlic stems.)

### Zhengzheng cakes
*zhengzheng gao* 蒸蒸糕

These delicate concoctions of steamed rice powder, with sweet fillings made from lotus seeds or pine kernels, were traditionally sold by street vendors who used to call out the name of their wares (which is why their name, *zhengzheng gao*, has such a delightful ring in Chinese—it simply means "steamed steamed cake"); in Chongqing, they are known as *chongchong* cakes. Food scholars trace their origins back at least three centuries. Sadly, these street vendors have now disappeared, but the snack lives on in specialty restaurants like the Dragon Wonton in Chengdu.

To make *zhengzheng gao*, you need specially designed individual wooden dumpling molds which fit onto a gadget on a stove that channels steam directly through each hexagonal dumpling. The rice itself is a mixture of regular and glutinous rice, soaked and then ground to a coarse powder that is squeezed dry, gently toasted and then layered into the molds with a nugget of sweet paste at the center. The finished dumplings have a consistency somewhere between sponge cake and cooked rice—moist, crumbly and delicious. They are usually decorated with candied fruits, roasted peanuts or white sugar.

### Rippled-silk fried dumplings
*bosi yougao* 波丝油糕

Rippled-silk dumplings are made from a hot-water dough enriched with lard that blooms into great diaphanous waves when they are deep-fried. They have a most delectable texture: a crisp, delicate outer coating that melts in the mouth, and sweet, heavy centers. The dumplings were invented by one of the great Sichuanese cooks of the twentieth century, Kong Daosheng. His students included my pastry teacher in Chengdu, Li Daiquan, and the head chef of the Dragon Wonton restaurant, Fan Shixian. According to Mr. Fan, Master Kong told his students that the snack originated in a happy accident at a small Sichuanese restaurant. The restaurant's owner was fiddling about with a small blob of leftover pastry, and he repeatedly smeared his hands with oil to keep it from sticking. After a while he grew bored and flicked the blob into the deep-frying pan to get rid of it, where to his amazement it puffed up like a flower. Master Kong heard about the discovery, added a stuffing to the oily dough, and created *bosi yougao*. "Rippled silk" is the local dialect name for cobwebs, so the name could also be translated (perhaps less appealingly) as "cobweb dumplings."

### Leaf-wrapped glutinous rice with salt and Sichuan pepper

_jiaoyan zongzi_ 椒盐粽子

As the Dragon Boat Festival approaches, in the fifth lunar month, people across Sichuan start making _zongzi_, pointy parcels of glutinous rice wrapped in the dark-green Indocalamus or giant bamboo (_zong_) leaves from which they take their name. On the day of the festival itself, people eat _zongzi_ with salted duck eggs and stir-fried purple amaranth. (Some people still follow ancient tradition and accompany the meal with _xionghuangjiu_, a tonic liquor that contains traces of an arsenic compound.) _Zongzi_ are eaten all over China. Northerners often prefer sweet versions, while in Sichuan they usually mix the soaked rice with red beans, nuggets of soy-marinated pork and a tingle of Sichuan pepper.

The tradition of eating them for the festival can be traced back at least sixteen centuries, but its origins are uncertain. Some scholars suggest they were eaten as part of ceremonies held in honor of the gods or ancestors, but the folk explanation, which dates back to the sixth century, is that they were eaten to commemorate the death of Qu Yuan. A poet who lived in the third century BC, Qu Yuan is remembered as a loyal and sagacious adviser to the Duke of Chu. He committed suicide by throwing himself into the Miluo River after the duke's failure to heed his advice led to political disaster. Mourners are said to have thrown parcels of rice into the river in the hope that the fish would eat them and leave the poet's body untouched.

In the countryside, people still bind their rice parcels with strands of leaf fiber. They strip a large leaf so that all that remains is a cluster of veins, and use each vein to bind a single _zongzi_, so they end up with a bundle of parcels still attached to the stem of the leaf.

# Hotpot

"The Sichuanese love to spend whole days or evenings eating hotpot, sitting around the simmering wok for hours on end"

# Hotpot 火锅

If you wander around Chengdu on a summer's evening, you'll find the streets filled with diners, their tables scattered on the pavement in the shade of leafy trees. Many will be gathered around bubbling hotpots, in which multitudes of dried chiles and Sichuan pepper bob up and down in an oily red broth, and they'll happily while away the hours chatting, sipping beer and dipping morsels of food into the broth to cook. Hotpot—literally "fire-pot"—is one of Sichuan's most popular dishes, and a favorite excuse for a get-together with family or friends. Untold thousands of restaurants across the region are devoted to it, and in its hometown of Chongqing there is even a "Hotpot Street"; according to the local hotpot association, there are now some 40,000 hotpot restaurants in greater Chongqing alone. Fancy restaurants lavish with marble and chandeliers serve it up for the rich, while beneath the steel supports of city flyovers, jobbing laborers crouch to eat it, paying a few *jiao* a time for a skewer of food to plunge into the spicy broth.

The "hotpot" itself, a wok or saucepan filled with a rich, oily broth resplendent with chiles, sits on a simple stove, whether it's a charcoal brazier on the pavement, a gas burner in a specially cut-out restaurant table, or just an electric ring on the floor at home. Around it, "like stars around the moon," are arranged dozens of small plates, each piled high with a different ingredient. Esoteric cuts of offal, many varieties of mushroom, bamboo shoots, ribbons of celtuce, crisp green leaves and sweet potato noodles are usually favored, but high-class restaurants will also serve exotic seafood and whole little fish. Guests select pieces of food from this tempting array and plunge them into the soup to cook; some ingredients need only be briefly scalded, others are simmered for several minutes. When the tidbits are ready, they are fished out with chopsticks and dipped into sesame oil seasoned with garlic, salt and MSG, and sometimes also chopped scallions and cilantro.

The Sichuanese love to spend whole days or evenings eating hotpot, sitting around the simmering wok for hours on end. The end of the meal is comfortably undefined: you just cook and eat, and eat and cook, for as long as you fancy. The pace ebbs and flows, with bursts of enthusiastic guzzling followed by gentle lulls of inactivity. Even when the meal is naturally drawing to a close, there is usually someone still exploring the broth for a forgotten tidbit. If you watch a group of Sichuanese people eating hotpot, you'll notice that they tend to spurn the lean meat and shrimp balls favored by foreigners, pouncing instead on the slithery or rubbery offal delicacies: pimpled gray sheets of tripe; jagged strips of ox or pig aorta, curling duck intestines, rabbit kidneys and coils of pig intestine.

Hotpot makes a fiery winter dish, potent at expelling the creeping dampness of the Sichuan winter. But the Sichuanese are peculiar among the Chinese in eating their spicy hotpot all year round. Even at the height of summer, hotpot restaurants will be overflowing with customers fanning themselves in the sweltering heat even as they swallow another mouthful of chile-laden food. The casual informality and delirious heat of hotpot encourages raucous behavior; popular hotpot restaurants are themselves like cauldrons full of cacophony and laughter.

Eating Sichuan's numbing-and-hot hotpot produces the most delicious physical sensation, a warmth and relaxation that begins in the belly and radiates out to all the extremities of the body, soothing away tension and anxiety, calming the mind and spirits. In the past, opium was sometimes thrown into the broth to enhance this effect, and used by devious restaurant owners to make sure their customers came back for more. Today, the practice is illegal, but it still crops up occasionally, with newspaper reports of restaurateurs being fined large sums for slipping opium and other narcotics into their broth. Amazingly, however, the heads of opium poppies (used as a traditional medicine) can still sometimes be found in the markets of Sichuan, nestling innocently among the cassia bark and star anise as though they were any other spice. I encountered them once during a summer lunch party in a small town near Chengdu. Some friends set up a hotpot on their kitchen floor and we all sat around it on little stools to eat. There was a perceptible change of mood as the meal progressed. Conversation at the beginning was animated, with wit and laughter, but gradually an intoxicated stupor overcame us all and we just fell asleep, on armchairs, sofas, anywhere. Only later, after a long, blissful siesta had restored me to my senses, did I notice the poppy-heads bobbing around in the pot.

Chinese scholars trace the origins of this kind of eating back thousands of years. People in China were cooking food in a soup over a fire, an embryonic form of hotpot, even before the time of Confucius, who lived in the fifth century BC. The Song-dynasty cookbook author Lin Hong wrote an account of a meal in the country in which he and his friends used their chopsticks to scald slices of rabbit in a potful of soup bubbling away on a tabletop stove.

The practice is thought to have gained popularity during the Ming and Qing periods; the famous eighteenth-century gourmet Yuan Mei declared that "when entertaining guests on winter days, it is customary to serve hotpot." During the Qing dynasty, the hotpot was adopted by the imperial court and appeared on the emperor's winter menus: in 1796, the imperial kitchens offered 1550 hotpots for guests attending a banquet to honor the Jiaqing Emperor.

Sichuanese hotpot, with its characteristic spicy broth, has more humble origins. It was born on the banks of the river at Chongqing, where bamboo-pole-bearing pedlars sold their wares. Meat dealers would haul a load of water buffalo offal in from the countryside and wash, chop and parboil it. Then a potful of chiles, Sichuan pepper and broth would be set up on a stove by the river, and laborers would gather round to eat and warm up. This original beef-tripe hotpot (*maodu huoguo*) is the grandfather of today's more elaborate dish. In the old days in Chongqing, eating hotpot was a casual, communal affair, with strangers cooking their own ingredients in a common pot: metal frames (*jiugongge*), a legacy of this custom, are still sometimes slotted into a Chongqing hotpot, carving the space into nine separate chambers like a tic-tac-toe board so that different ingredients can be kept apart.

Only in the 1930s did a Chongqing restaurateur bring the Sichuan hotpot upmarket by embedding it in a restaurant table. Now, nearly a century later, the dish is enjoyed by rich and poor alike, wherever there are Sichuanese people, and has long since shed its reputation as a poor man's dish. Cynics point out that the proliferation of hotpot restaurants is related to the ease with which restaurateurs can make money: no high-level cooking skills are required, just a good master broth and staff who can slice up ingredients. But there's no denying that hotpot is delicious and fun, and that many people are totally addicted: Chongqingers often aver that while eating *too* much hotpot can encourage a fiery constitution, their health and happiness depends on consuming it at least twice a week.

While beef offal is still popular, the original riverside menu has expanded wildly since the early days, with the addition of ever more exotic meats, vegetables and seafood. Many restaurants give customers a form listing vast numbers of ingredients with boxes for ticking: beef tripe of various kinds, ox and pig aorta (*huanghou*), squid, crucian carp, eels, loach, poultry gizzards, pig's kidneys, smoked bacon, rabbit kidneys and stomachs, lean or fatty beef, goose and duck intestines, pork intestines, pig's brains, lunch meat, meatballs, shrimp balls, many kinds of mushroom, various seaweeds, celtuce, lotus root, winter melon, bamboo shoots, potatoes, konnyaku "tofu," sweet potato noodles, cauliflower, jellied duck's blood, tofu skin, Chinese cabbage, bean sprouts, water spinach, day-lily flowers, rice jelly, celery, various types of fish, duck tongues, frogs, chicken testicles. . . .

On the streets, a cheaper version of hotpot, known simply as "numbing-hot-and-scalding" (*malatang*), is still immensely popular. Here, customers help themselves to tiny morsels of food impaled on bamboo skewers, which they dip into a spicy soup. A single skewer (*chuan'er*) might hold a spinach leaf, a slice of tofu, a strip of eel or a rabbit kidney. Once cooked, the morsels may then be dipped into a mix of ground chiles, Sichuan pepper and salt. The final bill is calculated by counting the number of empty skewers each customer has acquired during the meal. There are many other types of hotpot, from the spicy fish-head hotpot served with dips of crushed nuts and cilantro, to the fabled "chrysanthemum flower pot," which includes a plate of white chrysanthemum blossoms with stems and stamens removed—a banquet dish of the highest order.

In Chengdu, many restaurants serve a related dish, *maocai*: selected ingredients cooked in a great potful of pork-bone broth. Customers select their own ingredients, which are placed in nets and dunked into the broth to cook, before being served up in a great bowlful of spicy seasonings. At one such restaurant, they prepared base seasonings in our bowl: mashed fermented black beans, plenty of chile oil with its ground chile sediment; sesame oil and a spice-infused mixture of lard and vegetable oil. They poured over some hot broth and mixed everything together. Then they piled in the (now cooked) vegetables we had chosen, followed by the meats, and garnished the lot with chopped garlic, scallions, cilantro and fresh red chiles.

There are also regional variations, like the famous "crossed-legs" beef hotpot (*qiaojiao niurou*) of Leshan, in southern Sichuan, home of the giant seated Buddha. In the 1930s, so they say, when sickness and poverty were rife in the area, a Chinese doctor with a charitable heart set up a potful of medicinal herbs on the riverside, using his brew to treat the ailments of poor passers-by. Later, he began to salvage the beef offal spurned by wealthy households and cook it in the broth. Word spread of his delicious tonic stew, and soon people were squeezing onto benches around the pot, crossing their legs to make more room—hence the name of the dish. I recently shared a crossed-legs beef lunch with Leshan friends; we sat around a claypot of beef broth and tonic herbs, and in it we cooked slices of lean beef, beef liver, tongue, tripe and vegetables, seasoning the scalded food in dips of mashed fermented tofu mixed with chopped chiles, scallions and cilantro, and a spoonful of broth from the pot. On the side were served puffy fried pastries stuffed with ground beef or brown sugar.

The original Chongqing hotpot is the fieriest of them all—a response to the oppressively humid climate of this "furnace" city. Chongqing people make their hotpot with small, pointed chiles that are much hotter than the popular Chengdu varieties, and they use them with reckless abandon. The last time I ate hotpot in Chongqing, the early summer heat was already so intense that the air was almost soupy, and people were walking around in slow motion, fanning themselves and mopping their brows. We sat, my friends and I, by the banks of the river where the laborers used to gather, fighting the steamy atmosphere with the searing heat of chiles. In Chengdu, however, eating hotpot doesn't have to be such an intense experience. Most restaurants offer hotpots with a central partition in a "yin-yang" design, so you can have one half filled with the traditional spicy broth, and one half filled with a mild broth made from fish and chicken.

# Numbing-and-hot Hotpot

## mala huoguo
## 麻辣火锅

Making a Sichuan hotpot is a wonderfully easy and delightful way to entertain. You can make the hotpot broth in advance; preparing the dipping ingredients doesn't take long. It's also a relaxed way of eating, and particularly enjoyable outdoors on a warm summer's evening. You do need a cooking ring that can sit in the center of your dining table, within reach of all your guests. The hotpot itself can be a wok or a wide saucepan deep enough to hold the broth. If you can find a special hotpot wok with a central partition, you can serve both a spicy and a mild broth at the same meal, and allow people to cook in them according to their tastes. You can also provide, if you wish, slotted spoons or little wire nets for catching elusive morsels of food.

The following is a recipe for a classic Chongqing numbing-and-hot hotpot broth (*hong tang lu*), which can be made in advance and stored in the fridge for a few days. (Although cheats might like to know that these days most Chinese supermarkets sell packages of pre-made hotpot soup base—*huoguo diliao*—which can simply be boiled up with stock or water.) The hotpot broth is not itself meant to be consumed. If you wish, you can strain off the liquid and freeze it for re-use another time; just replenish it with more stock or water, fried chiles and Sichuan pepper as required.

Obviously, the amount of heat and numbingness is a matter of personal taste and will also depend on the heat level of the chiles you use: please feel free to adjust quantities of dried chiles and Sichuan pepper as you wish.

2½ oz (75g) dried chiles, or to taste
¾ cup plus 2 tbsp (200ml) cooking oil
¼ cup (1 oz/30g) fermented black beans
4 tbsp Shaoxing wine
2-inch piece (40g) ginger, unpeeled
7 oz (200g) beef tallow
6 tbsp (100g) Sichuan chile bean paste
Around 2½ quarts (2.5 liters) beef stock,
    store-bought or home-made (see below)
½ oz (15g) rock sugar (or granulated sugar)
7 tbsp (100ml) strained fermented glutinous
    rice wine (see p. 460; optional)
1 tbsp salt
2 star anise
3 tbsp whole Sichuan pepper, or to taste

*For the stock (if you wish to make your own)*
3⅓ lb (1.5kg) beef bones
1 lb 2 oz (500g) pork ribs
2½-inch piece (50g) ginger, unpeeled
2 scallions, white parts only
2 tbsp Shaoxing wine

If you're making your own stock, place the bones and ribs in a large stockpot and cover with cold water. Bring to a boil and then let it bubble for a couple of minutes to allow any impurities to rise to the surface, then tip the bones into a colander and rinse under cold water. Scrub out the pan before returning the bones and ribs. Cover them with plenty of fresh water and bring back to a boil over high heat. Lightly smack the ginger and scallion whites with the flat of a cleaver blade or a rolling pin to loosen them.

Skim any froth from the surface, then add the ginger, scallion whites and Shaoxing wine. Turn the heat down low and simmer for at least 3 hours. Strain out the solid ingredients and let the stock cool.

Now make the hotpot soup base. Snip the dried chiles in half or into ¾-inch (2cm) sections and shake out the seeds as much as possible. Heat 3 tbsp oil in a wok over medium heat, add the chiles and stir-fry until they have turned a deeper red and are crisp—but are definitely not burned. Remove from the wok and set aside. When the chiles have cooled, place about half of them on a chopping board and chop finely; leave the rest unchopped. →

← Rinse and drain the black beans, then place in a mortar, along with 1 tbsp Shaoxing wine, and mash to a paste with a pestle. Thinly slice the ginger.

Heat the beef tallow and the remaining oil in the wok over gentle heat. When the tallow has melted, turn the heat up to medium and add the chile bean paste. Stir the paste for about 5 minutes until the oil is reddish and the paste is soft and fragrant. Take great care not to burn the paste: the oil should just sizzle gently around it. Add the black bean mash, ginger and chopped chiles and continue to stir-fry gently for another 5 minutes or so until they smell delicious.

Tip in 1 quart (1 liter) of the stock and bring to a boil. Add the rock sugar, the rest of the Shaoxing wine, the strained glutinous rice wine (if using), the salt, star anise, Sichuan pepper and the remaining chiles and simmer for about 20 minutes to allow the flavors to mingle. This is your soup base.

When you wish to serve the hotpot, transfer this soup base to a pot that will fit on your tabletop burner, topping up with more of the stock if necessary. Bring to a boil, then place on the tabletop burner.

Bring the rest of the stock to a boil and keep warm: use it to top up your hotpot as the liquid evaporates.

### Dipping ingredients

What you dip into your hotpot is very much a matter of personal taste. The greater the variety in flavors, colors and textures, the more enjoyable the hotpot will be. Preparing the dipping ingredients is also very easy, so assemble as many kinds as you can. Aim for at least 8–12 different ingredients for a party of 4–6 people. Buy enough of each ingredient to pile high on a small plate. In Sichuan it is customary to serve each dipping ingredient on a separate plate, but you can pile them up on one large platter if you wish. (If you live near a Japanese supermarket, it's worth knowing that they often serve ready-sliced meats for the Japanese equivalent of hotpot, shabu shabu, which are also perfect for cooking in a Sichuan hotpot.) Do remember to follow basic hygiene practices when eating hotpot, particularly making sure that any chopsticks which have been in contact with raw meats are held in the boiling broth for a few seconds before they touch food that will be eaten.

In Chongqing, the home of hotpot, the ingredients cooked in hotpot invariably include several different types of offal. The most esteemed include goose intestines, which have an intriguing slithery-crisp texture after cooking, and different kinds of beef tripe, which offer a bolder, more rubbery crunch. Many of these kinds of offal are simply unavailable in the West, and unless you have a real appreciation of texture as the Chinese do, you may not see the point of eating them anyway.

For these reasons, I have suggested some dipping ingredients that are both appealing to Western tastes and in keeping with Sichuanese tradition, but please feel free to improvise.

Here are a few ideas
– chicken breasts, very thinly sliced
– pork tenderloin, very thinly sliced
– lean beef or lamb, very thinly sliced
– Chinese wind-dried sausage, cut into short sections
– cooked meats of all kinds, sliced
– pig's kidneys, halved, cored and very thinly sliced
– smoked bacon, thickly sliced
– firm tofu, thickly sliced
– tofu skin, cut into bite-sized pieces
– hard-boiled quail eggs, shelled
– shiitake mushrooms, whole
– oyster mushrooms, whole
– button mushrooms, whole
– enoki mushrooms, whole
– large flat mushrooms, cut into chunky slices
– any other kind of fresh mushroom
– dried wood ear mushrooms, soaked in hot water
   for at least 30 minutes
– Chinese dried mushrooms, soaked in hot water
   for at least 30 minutes
– daikon, peeled and thickly sliced
– lotus root, peeled, sliced and left in lightly salted
   water until served
– potatoes, peeled, thickly sliced and left in lightly
   salted water until served
– thick sweet potato noodles (soaked for at least
   2 hours, until supple)
– water spinach, cut into lengths

– Chinese cabbage leaves
– bean sprouts
– cauliflower, cut into florets
– broccoli, cut into florets
– winter melon, seeded, peeled
   and cut into thick slices
– pea shoots
– fresh cilantro

Less traditional ingredients include
– squid, cut into bite-sized pieces
– shelled raw shrimp
– meatballs made from ground pork,
   beef or shrimp
– *jiaozi* dumplings

Seasoning dips

Every guest can make up their own dip, mixing the seasonings in a small rice bowl. Aim for a ratio of two parts sesame oil to three parts vegetable oil for the base of the dip. Add plenty of chopped garlic, salt to taste and, if you feel like it, some MSG (about the same amount as the salt). You can also stir in some thinly sliced scallion greens and/or chopped cilantro leaves.

Although I never use MSG in my own cooking, I always stir it into my hotpot dip, because it seems to lighten the oiliness and makes everything taste delicious.

The following are suggested quantities
for one person's dip
4 tsp sesame oil
2 tbsp vegetable oil
Salt, to taste
1–2 tbsp finely chopped garlic
About ½ tsp MSG, to taste (optional)
Thinly sliced scallion greens, to taste (optional)
Chopped cilantro, to taste (optional)

Place the oils and salt, together with a bowl of finely chopped garlic (and the MSG, scallion greens and cilantro, if using) on the table, so people can top up their dips as they need to. →

You can serve your hotpot broth in a wok or saucepan, as you please—if you use a round-bottomed wok, make sure it is stable. Place the pot on a cooking ring in the middle of the dining table. Arrange all the dipping ingredients on plates around the hotpot. Give each guest a small rice bowl and a pair of chopsticks, and let them mix their own seasoning dips.

Bring the hotpot to a boil and allow all the beef tallow to melt if you are heating it from cold. When it is bubbling away merrily, you can begin to cook, and eat. Just encourage everyone to slip pieces of the prepared food into the hotpot at their leisure, and let them cook. When the food is ready it can be fished out with chopsticks, dipped into the seasonings and eaten; the whole Sichuan pepper and chiles are not meant to be eaten. Some kinds of food, such as bean sprouts, will be ready very quickly; others, such as potatoes, will take several minutes. Do make sure raw meats are cooked through properly.

As the liquid in the hotpot evaporates, top it up with more stock, adding more salt if necessary. Allow the stock to return to a boil before you continue cooking.

If you have any food left over, the same hotpot broth can be chilled and then reheated the following day.

*Mild hotpot broth* (bai tang lu 白汤卤)
*If you would prefer to have a mild, non-spicy hotpot broth (bai tang lu) , simply fill your hotpot with clear superior stock (see p. 464), salted to taste, and add a couple of trimmed scallions and a few slices of beefsteak tomato before serving.*

# Preserved Foods

"A whole book could be written on
the Sichuanese art of fermentation,
with all its myriad local variations"

# Preserved Foods 泡菜腌腊制品类

Whenever we're cooking together in his Chengdu apartment, my friend Zeng Bo reaches into a great clay urn and plucks out handfuls of scarlet pickled chiles, pale young ginger stems and long green beans. Some of the chiles will be sliced and stir-fried with morsels of tender chicken; others will be chopped and fried in hot oil to coax out their flavor and intense red hue for a dish of fish-fragrant pork. The ginger may be stir-fried with duck, its fresh piquancy a pleasing contrast to the richness of the meat, and the green beans will be fast-fried with a scattering of ground pork, chiles and Sichuan pepper.

Pickled vegetables are fundamental to the spirit of Sichuanese cooking. Every household has its *paocai tanzi*—a rough earthenware pot with a rounded belly, a narrow neck, and a lip that functions as a water-seal. In the darkness within, crunchy vegetables steep in a pool of brine, with a splash of grain liquor and a selection of seasonings that probably include brown sugar, Sichuan pepper and ginger, perhaps with a little cassia bark and star anise.

The vegetables come and go, replenished every day or two with fresh supplies, but the pickling brine or "mother" liquor goes on, they say, forever. With each new batch of vegetables a little fresh brine and a splash of wine is added, and the spices and sugar will be renewed from time to time. But the rich, aromatic liquid base goes from strength to strength as the years, or even generations, pass. In some parts of Sichuan, a pickle jar was once part of a bride's dowry.

Some vegetables are pickled for a few hours only, like the "take a shower" tidbits served in modern Sichuanese restaurants. These, usually crunchy vegetables—such as radish, cabbage and celery—are steeped in fresh brine with just a splash of the rich mother liquor from an established pickle jar. They taste a little salty and aromatic, but lack the deep, fermented flavors of longer-pickled vegetables. Restaurants often display their "take a shower" vegetables in clear glass pickle jars on a countertop, while waist-high clay jars of more mature pickles will be lined up in a storeroom at the back.

Sichuanese pickles are eaten with thin rice porridge for breakfast and as a refreshing palate-cleanser, served with rice at the end of almost every meal. Most typical are pickled pink radish, the white flesh acquiring a rosy tint as the skin releases its coloring into the brine, and round white cabbage (*lianhuabai*); both are cut into bite-sized pieces and served in little dishes, often with a dressing of chile oil. This custom of serving pickles to "send the rice down" (*xiafan*) extends from the simplest home-cooked meals to extravagant restaurant dinners, and is something the Sichuanese often miss most when they are away from home.

Apart from their role as relishes to eat with rice, pickles are important ingredients in cooking. Ripe pickled mustard greens lend their delectable, refreshing sourness to soupy dishes, while pickled chiles bring heat and color to a whole range of different recipes. The most indispensable are *erjingtiao*, the long, scarlet chiles that are the key to traditional fish-fragrant dishes. Chopped to a fine paste or cut into pieces, they have a mild piquancy, a fruity flavor and a gorgeous color that beautifies any dish. The pairing of pickled red chiles with pickled ginger in myriad dishes is one of the culinary signatures of southern Sichuan. More discreet, but often surprisingly hot, are the small, pale green pickled chiles known as "wild mountain chiles," which play second fiddle to the *erjingtiao* and are particularly good in fish dishes. In the past, for extra savoriness, a couple of small, silvery crucian carp were sometimes added to a jarful of pickling chiles, which were then known as "fishy chiles" (*yu lajiao*): this practice is one (oft-disputed) explanation for the origin of the fish-fragrant flavor.

Dry-salting is another prevalent method of preserving vegetables. Vegetables are strung out in the sun to wilt before being rubbed with salt and spices and stashed in clay jars to ferment. When I recently visited Chengdu in early spring, the whole city seemed to be festooned with sun-drying mustard leaves, which were splayed on mats, hung up on lines and even spread all over motorbikes parked in the backstreets.

Sichuan has four famous vegetable preserves. Zhacai or "pressed vegetable" (sold outside China, often in tins, as "Sichuan preserved vegetable") is a salted mustard tuber with an assertively salty, sour flavor that is a specialty of Fuling, near Chongqing. The knobbly, chile-coated tubers are rinsed before being slivered or diced, and have a pleasingly supple-crisp texture. "Big-headed vegetable" (datoucai) is a type of turnip that is processed in a similar manner to zhacai, and is often eaten cold as a relish or sprinkled over noodles or tofu. It has been made commercially for more than 200 years, but is thought to have evolved from local turnip-preservation methods dating back to the sixth century. (In some parts of Sichuan, this variety of turnip is known as "Zhuge vegetable" because the great strategist of ancient times, Zhuge Liang, is said to have ordered his followers to grow it.) From Nanchong, in northern Sichuan, comes "winter vegetable" (dongcai), made from the leaves of a variety of mustard, which are semi-dried, mixed with salt and spices—including star anise, fennel seeds and tangerine peel—and then fermented in jars for two or three years; the finished pickle is particularly delicious stir-fried or steamed with pork.

Finally, the secret ingredient of dandan noodles, "kindling" noodles, dry-fried green beans and many other Sichuanese specialties is dark, crinkly yacai, a preserved vegetable made in the southern city of Yibin. Local people eat both salty and sweet versions of yacai, but the spiced and sugar-sweetened one is more widely known. To make savory or "white" yacai, tender stems of a local mustard variety (erpingzhuang) are sliced into long strands, sun-dried, rubbed with salt and then packed into earthenware jars and left to ferment for a couple of months. To transform this into the renowned sweet yacai, the salty pickle is mixed with a brown sugar syrup and spices such as Sichuan pepper and star anise, and then sealed once again into the jars for

a second fermentation that lasts around a year, by which time it has acquired its characteristic dark color and marvelous flavor. This unusual method is said to have been invented in Nanxi in the nineteenth century, and refined by pickle makers in nearby Yibin early in the following century. In old towns around Yibin, one still comes across people selling home-made yacai from tall clay jars brimming with its distinctive, sweet-spicy aroma.

Many Sichuanese people, even in the cities, still salt and smoke their own pork and make wind-dried sausages every winter. When I was a student in Chengdu in the mid-1990s, long loops of sausage and great tranches of cured pork hung under the eaves of the old wooden houses, wind-drying in the winter sun. While the Cantonese like to sweeten their wind-dried sausages, the Sichuanese, predictably, prefer to pep theirs up with ground chile and Sichuan pepper. Once they're cured, the chunky sausages are usually steamed and sliced before being arrayed on a serving plate, and they are fantastically delicious; leftovers may be cut into small pieces to add a jolt of umami intensity to fried rice or eight-treasure stuffings. In the mountains of Hanyuan county, where the finest Sichuan pepper is grown, people make clay-jar pork (tanzi rou) every winter, salt-curing great chunks of meat and then slow-cooking them in their own lard; the confit meat, covered in lard, is stored in great clay jars until it is eaten.

A whole book could be written on the Sichuanese art of fermentation, with all its myriad local variations; this chapter includes just a few key recipes that can easily be replicated at home.

At the end, I've provided descriptions of some notable preserves that are usually left to professionals or require hard-to-get ingredients, including the famous Pixian chile bean paste and the incredible "boozy eggs" (zaodan).

You will also find information about preserved duck eggs on p. 56, and about fermented tofu on p. 57.

# Sichuanese Pickled Vegetables

## sichuan paocai
## 四川泡菜

When rice is served toward the end of a typical Sichuanese meal, it will almost always be accompanied by a small dish of pickled vegetables to "send the rice down" (*xiafan*). The vegetables are normally pickled in a traditional clay jar with a swollen belly and a narrow mouth surrounded by a little channel filled with water; when the mouth is covered with an upturned bowl, the water functions as a seal, keeping the pickles snug but allowing their gassy emanations to bubble out. If you don't have one of these jars, you can make the pickles in a standard preserving jar with a rubber seal, but do make sure you open the lid from time to time in the early days to let the gases escape.

The base pickling liquid consists of brine with a few added spices and a dash of strong liquor to help keep it clean. You can vary the vegetables as you please. Young ginger, cauliflower, carrot and other crisp, crunchy vegetables work very well, as do the classic cabbage and pink-skinned radish. More watery vegetables like cucumber and peppers can be pickled, but are best left in the brine just for several hours or perhaps overnight. The pickled vegetables can be given a lick of chile oil (and perhaps a sprinkling of MSG) to be served with rice, or used in cooking, as with the pickled yard-long beans on p. 273. In general, the best way to treat home-made Sichuanese pickled vegetables is to pickle and eat them regularly, eating a small dish of pickles with every meal and replenishing the jar with fresh vegetables often. →

¼ cup plus 1 tsp (80g) rock salt or sea salt
2 tbsp strong Chinese *baijiu* grain liquor
   (50% alcohol or higher)
1½ tbsp dark brown sugar or rock sugar
3¾-inch piece (75g) plump, fresh ginger
2 long red chiles
1 tsp whole Sichuan pepper
*Vegetables of your choice—*
   *I used 4 small or 2 large (200g) carrots,*
   *1 stick (60g) celery and 9¾ oz (275g) daikon*

**Add the salt to 1 quart (1 liter) of water** in a saucepan and bring to a boil, stirring to dissolve the salt. Cover the pan and let the brine cool completely.

Next rinse your vegetables. Let dry completely, then prepare as follows.
*Carrots:* peel and cut into bite-sized batons.
*Cauliflower:* break into florets.
*Celery:* remove any strings and cut into batons.
*Celtuce:* peel the stems and cut into bite-sized batons.
   *Ginger:* select young ginger with thin, smooth skin if you can find it; otherwise, use the older kind with thicker skin, but make sure it's plump, juicy and not too fibrous. If you are planning to use the pickled ginger in cooking, peel it but otherwise leave it whole; if it's just to flavor the brine, slice it with the peel left on.
*Kohlrabi:* peel and cut into batons.
*Long red chiles:* keep whole, with stalks intact.
*Round cabbage:* cut lengthwise into quarters or eighths.
*White or pink-skinned long radishes:* cut into bite-sized batons.
*Yard-long beans:* top and tail, and either keep as one skein of beans, or cut into shorter lengths.

Make sure your preserving jar is completely clean and dry. Pour in the cooled brine and add all the other ingredients, leaving an inch or two of empty space at the top of the jar. If possible, set a clean stone or small dish on top of the vegetables to keep them submerged; alternatively, fill a small freezer bag with water, seal the bag and use that instead. Close the jar and place in a cool, shady place to ferment. For the first week or two, open the jar for a few seconds every day to allow gases to escape. After this, if you are replenishing the jar with fresh vegetables, keep opening it regularly; otherwise, you can leave it for much longer intervals, simply opening it to take out the pickles for eating. →

You can keep a pickle jar going indefinitely, simply topping up with brine, liquor and spices as needed; the flavor of the pickles it produces will improve over time. And you can add some pickle liquid from an existing jar to a new one, to kick-start the fermentation. Season the brine as you wish: some people add a few spices, such as star anise and cassia bark, or peeled garlic cloves—but don't overdo it. The main experience should be of crisp vegetables with a refreshingly salty, sour flavor. Sichuanese food aficionados insist that you need genuine Zigong well salt to achieve the true flavor of *paocai*; others simply advise that non-iodized salt is best. At home, in London, I use rock salt for making pickles. You will also need a two-quart (two-liter) preserving jar, or a traditional Sichuanese pickle jar; please see the note to the right for advice on using a traditional jar.

The first batch of pickles will take a couple of weeks to get going: you can tell when the fermentation is under way from the sour, fragrant aroma and the pressure release when you open the jar. Once the pickle jar is established, fresh vegetables will take 1–3 days to pickle in warmer weather and about a week in winter: just sample them to see when they are pickled to your liking. For "take a shower" vegetables, cut them thinly and steep in the brine for one night only before eating. You can leave your pickles steeping in the brine for much longer if you wish. In Sichuan, people eat these pickles on a daily basis, topping up the jar with fresh vegetables, brine, liquor and seasonings as they go along, in a very relaxed manner.

Notes

*Only pickle vegetables that are fresh and in good condition.*

*Always maintain good hygiene when pickling: make sure your hands, chopping boards, preserving jars and other implements are clean. Use scrupulously clean, grease-free chopsticks or tongs to remove pickles from the jar.*

*If you are using a traditional pickle jar, you should make sure the water in the channel around the top does not dry out. This water should be replenished regularly (you can soak up the old water with a cloth or sponge before adding fresh water). Do not let any of the water in the seal channel fall into the pickle jar.*

# A "Small Dish" of Radish Slivers

xiaocai

小菜

The Sichuanese always accompany a breakfast of rice porridge and buns with little dishes of pickles, preserves, fermented tofu or some other strongly flavored relishes. Many snack shops will scoop pink radishes from their pickle jar and simply chop them into little cubes. Others will whip up a quick relish of salted vegetables and spicy seasonings.

The following "small dish" is inspired by the version served with rice at one of my favorite Chengdu restaurants. It's easy to make and stupendously delicious: the perfect solution if you want to eat rice the Sichuanese way but don't have a pickle jar at the ready. Serve it in small dishes with your breakfast porridge or the plain steamed rice eaten at the end of a meal. The radish can also be served as an appetizer alongside other dishes.

1 lb 5 oz (600g) Asian long pink or daikon radish
2 tsp salt
2 tbsp superfine sugar
2 tsp light soy sauce
2 tsp Chinkiang vinegar
4 tbsp chile oil, plus 1 tbsp sediment
4 tbsp thinly sliced scallion greens
½ tsp ground roasted Sichuan pepper (optional)

Peel the radish or give it a thorough scrub. Cut into 3¼–4-inch (8–10 cm) sections, then cut these lengthwise into ⅛-inch (3–4mm) slices. Cut the radish slices into fine slivers and place in a bowl. Add the salt, scrunching it in, then set aside for about an hour.

Tip the radish slivers into a colander or sieve and squeeze out as much water as you possibly can, then transfer to a bowl. Add the sugar and stir until dissolved. Add all the other ingredients and mix thoroughly.

Serve as an appetizer, or as a relish with a bowlful of congee or plain steamed rice.

# Home-made Bacon with Sichuanese Flavorings

larou
腊肉

In the Sichuanese countryside, many people still cure and smoke their own bacon, hanging the finished meat under the eaves to wind-dry. Traditionally, it is made during the last lunar month (*layue*, "the month of winter sacrifices"). Sichuanese bacon has an intensity of flavor that is rarely found in the supermarkets of the West: just a few slivers will pep up a simple stir-fry of garlic stems or green peppers.

In Chengdu, the meat is cold-smoked until the fat is a dark, treacly yellow and the flesh a deep wine-red. In the mountains to the northwest, most famously Qingcheng Mountain, with its Daoist temples and romantic scenery, the bacon is smoked until it is actually black, which makes it easy to identify in market stalls. And in the Bamboo Sea nature reserve in southern Sichuan, I've eaten bamboo-leaf-smoked bacon so exquisite it left me speechless with pleasure. The most celebrated bacon is always what Westerners would call "organic" and Chinese people call *tu* ("rustic" or "earthy"), made with pork from free-range pigs reared on household scraps.

To make the bacon, strips of pork rump with plenty of fat are first cured for a week in salt, sugar, wine and spices. They are then hung up to dry, before being smoked over smoldering wood shavings, peanut husks, rice straw and leaves. Farmers often smoke their meat slowly over their kitchen fire; city dwellers make smokers out of metal drums; and specialty vendors keep a fire smoldering in a dedicated smokehouse. →

*3⅓ lb (1.5kg) pork rump, with skin and*
*a generous layer of fat*
*2 tbsp strong Chinese baijiu grain liquor*
*(50% alcohol or higher)*
*¾ tsp five-spice powder*
*1½ tbsp dark brown sugar*
*1½ tbsp whole Sichuan pepper*
*2½ oz (75g) curing salt*
*(use 5% of the weight of the pork)*

*For the smoking*
*7 oz (200g) nut shells (I used almond shells)*
*5¼ oz (150g) peanut shells or sunflower seed husks*
*1½ oz (40g) cypress clippings (a good handful)*
*Peel of 1 tangerine*

**Cut the pork lengthwise** into three or four long strips about 2 inches (5cm) wide; each strip should have skin, fat and lean meat. Prick the meat and fat all over with a skewer. Add the liquor, five-spice powder, sugar, Sichuan pepper and curing salt, and massage into the meat as evenly as possible. Place in a ceramic, glass or stainless-steel container, cover and let cure in the fridge for a week, turning the meat after 3–4 days.

Remove the meat from the cure, pierce each strip with a sharp skewer and then use a meat hook or twine to hang the meat in a cold, shady, well-ventilated place to dry for a day or two before smoking.

Line a dry wok with two layers of foil, pressing them closely against the metal. Mix together all the smoking materials, then scatter half into the wok. Place a metal trivet on top and set a round steaming rack on the trivet. Pick out and discard the Sichuan pepper from the pork, then place the strips of meat, lean side down, on the rack.

Turn the heat under the wok to high (and your exhaust fan up to maximum power) until the materials in the wok are smoking, then cover the wok and turn the heat down to medium. Smoke the meat for 45–60 minutes, until the smoking materials are exhausted and blackened. Do make sure that there is enough heat to keep the smoke coming.

Switch off the heat, carefully lift out the rack, trivet and meat, and remove and discard the exhausted smoking materials. →

← If you don't have a smokehouse on hand, the hot-smoking method here, based on one shown by a Sichuanese internet chef who calls himself "Brother Fire" (*huoge*), can be done in a wok and gives insanely delicious results. Even with a good exhaust fan, it will make your kitchen smell like a bonfire for some time. To preserve the meat and give it a good color, you will need a curing salt that contains nitrates and nitrites (I use Weschenfelder Supacure dry-cured bacon curing salts, which is 0.6% nitrates and nitrites). You will also need a sharp skewer and some meat hooks (they can be found in Chinese supermarkets), as well as a large wok with a lid, foil for lining the wok, a metal trivet and a round steaming rack (these can be found in larger Chinese supermarkets). The bacon should be made in the winter, when the air temperature is 50–60°F (10–15°C).

← Replace with the rest of the smoking materials and reassemble the trivet, rack and meat. Turn the meat over, cover and repeat the smoking for another 45–60 minutes, by which time the meat should be a dark, caramelized pink and the fat a gorgeous amber color.

Hook up the meat again and hang in a cold, shady, well-ventilated place for another 4–5 days before eating. Rinse the bacon thoroughly in warm water before cooking it.

If you do not wish to use it immediately, wrap and then store in the fridge or freezer, as you would with store-bought bacon.

**Some serving suggestions**

*Sliced bacon with spicy dips*
*The simplest way to eat the bacon is to steam it for about 20–30 minutes, then slice it and serve fanned out on a serving dish with dips of ground chiles and ground roasted Sichuan pepper. (You can also steam and slice the bacon in advance, and then briefly steam the plated slices before serving.)*

*Stir-fried bacon*
*Steam the bacon for 20–30 minutes. Allow to cool, slice and then stir-fry with vegetables (see p. 152 for an example of this, using green peppers).*

*Soups and stews*
*Chunks of bacon are delicious in soups and stews—they go especially well with pulses, and with vegetables such as bamboo shoots, daikon or yard-long beans.*

*Fried rice*
*Steam a piece of bacon and cut it into small dice; use to jazz up any fried or steamed rice recipe.*

# Cured Pork with Sweet Flour Sauce

## jiangrou
## 酱肉

3⅓ lb (1.5kg) pork rump or belly,
  with skin and a thick layer of fat
2 tbsp strong Chinese *baijiu* grain liquor
  (50% alcohol or higher)
1 tbsp whole Sichuan pepper
2½ oz (75g) curing salt (use 5% of the
  weight of the pork)

*For the sauce*
About ½ cup (5⅓ oz/150g) sweet flour sauce
3 tbsp brown sugar
½ tsp five-spice powder
1 tsp whole Sichuan pepper
3 tbsp Shaoxing wine

Many Sichuanese families, especially in the countryside, still make this most delectable of preserved meats at the end of the lunar year and serve it during their New Year festivities. It's the easiest cured meat to make at home, and as intensely delicious as bacon. Strips of pork hind leg or belly are cured in salt and then rubbed with a selection of quintessentially Sichuanese flavorings: Sichuan pepper, sweet flour sauce and fermented glutinous rice wine. They are then hung out to dry. The meat is eventually steamed, sliced and eaten cold as a first course or as a snack with alcoholic drinks; small morsels may also be added to fried rice or other dishes (see p. 336 for an example).

The meat should be prepared when the weather is cold but not freezing, and hung in a well-ventilated place at 50–60°F (10–16°C). You will need a sharp skewer and 3 or 4 meat hooks (they can be found in Chinese supermarkets) or some twine. And to help preserve the meat and give it a good color, you'll need a curing salt that contains nitrates and nitrites (I use Weschenfelder Supacure dry-cured bacon curing salts, which is 0.6% nitrates and nitrites).

Cut the pork lengthwise into three or four long strips about 2 inches (5cm) wide; each strip should have skin, fat and lean meat. Prick the meat and fat all over with a skewer. Add the liquor, Sichuan pepper and curing salts, and massage into the meat as thoroughly and evenly as possible. Place in a ceramic, glass or stainless-steel container, cover and let cure in the fridge for a week, turning the meat after 3–4 days.

Remove the meat from the cure, picking out and discarding the Sichuan pepper. Pierce each strip with a sharp skewer, and then use a meat hook to hang the meat in a cold, shady, well-ventilated place for a couple of hours, until dry to the touch.

Mix the sauce ingredients together in a bowl, then use a pastry brush to coat the entire surface of each piece of pork generously with the sauce. Place the pork in a dish, cover and refrigerate for a few hours or overnight.

Hang the meat up to dry again. When the meat is dry to the touch, use a pastry brush to add another layer of sauce; continue with this until the sauce is finished. Hang the meat in a cold, shady, well-ventilated place for 2 weeks, and then store in the fridge or freezer if not using immediately.

When you wish to use the meat, wash it thoroughly in warm water to remove the coating of paste, then place in a steamer basket and steam over high heat for 20–30 minutes, until cooked through. When it has cooled, slice thinly and serve with a dip of ground chiles. (The meat can also be treated like Sichuanese bacon: see opposite for some ideas.)

# Salted Duck Eggs

xian dan
咸蛋

*9 duck eggs*
*⅔ cup (200g) salt*
*1 tsp whole Sichuan pepper*

Many Chengdu restaurants display a jar of bluish duck eggs that have been salt-preserved. The eggs have a strong salty taste, their yolks an intriguing, slightly granular texture. They are often enjoyed with rice porridge for breakfast: the eggs are usually hard-boiled, and then halved or quartered still in their shells, so the flesh can be picked out with chopsticks. They can also be used in cooking: the yolk, in particular, has a delicious umami flavor. Traditionally, the eggs are cured by caking them in a paste made from salt, mud, ashes and a dash of strong liquor (sooty, ash-caked eggs are a common sight in Chinese markets), but at home the easiest method is to use a strong salt-water solution. The eggs are at their best after about 3 weeks—if you leave them in the brine for longer than this they can become unpleasantly salty. If you break one open raw, you will see that the yolk has hardened into a golden, waxy globe. You will need a two-quart (two-liter) preserving jar with a wide mouth and a tight-fitting lid.

Give the duck eggs a good rinse in cold water (with farmhouse eggs, you may need to scrub them with a vegetable brush to remove any dirt). Discard any cracked eggs.

Bring 3⅓ cups (800ml) water to a boil in a saucepan. Add the salt and stir to dissolve, then cover the pan and let this salt solution cool completely.

Carefully place the eggs in your preserving jar, then pour over the cooled salt solution. Set a small ceramic or glass dish at the top of the jar to keep the eggs submerged. Close the lid tightly and leave in a cool, dark place for 3 weeks.

When the eggs are ready, remove them from the brine and store in the fridge until needed.

# Some other important preserves

## Pixian chile bean paste
### pixian douban 郫县豆瓣

In the yard of the Shaofenghe factory in Pixian, waist-high clay jars stand in rows like a terracotta army, their broad mouths open to the misty air. They contain one of the core ingredients of Sichuanese cuisine: fermented chile and fava bean paste (doubanjiang or pixian douban). A specialty of Pixian county, near the Sichuanese capital of Chengdu, the rich, savory paste is made by mixing split fava beans with wheat flour and allowing them to grow moldy before fermenting them in brine; the beans are then mixed with salt-pickled chiles and left to ferment further, usually for a couple of years.

People often ask me for a recipe for the paste, but it's not usually made at home and I haven't tried myself because it's a long process that demands local chiles and specific climatic conditions. However, for anyone who does want to experiment, the following is a summary of what I have learned during my visits to Pixian (with particular thanks to the staff of the Pixian Douban Company and Shaofenghe).

The ingredients of traditional Pixian chile bean paste are local *erjingtiao* chiles (not excessively hot), dried fava beans, wheat flour and salt. At Shaofenghe, which is run by descendants of the original inventor of the paste, they use seven parts chiles to three parts beans, with wheat flour to encourage the development of the moldy ferment, and salt for preservation.

The dried beans are soaked in hot water, peeled and split, then briefly boiled, drained and then mixed with wheat flour and left in warm, shady conditions for about ten days until they have grown a coat of yellow mold, which is the ferment or *qu*; traditionally, a layer of rice straw keeps the beans snug as they mold. They are then submerged in brine and left to ferment in clay jars open to the elements for about six months, until they are a dark, yellowish brown (the jars are covered when it rains). Separately, fresh *erjingtiao* chiles are trimmed, coarsely chopped and mixed with salt, and then left to ferment for two to three months.

When both fava beans and chiles have reached a suitable stage of fermentation, they are mixed together, transferred to large clay jars and again left in the open air to mature. The paste is turned every day with special wooden paddles, and the jars are only covered when it rains (the conical lids were traditionally made of natural plant fiber; now plastic is generally used).

Over time, the scarlet paste dries out, becomes glossy and darkens to a deep red, then a chestnut brown and finally, after seven or eight years, a dark purplish color. It can be used after a year, but is generally held to be best after two or three years, which is the age of most Pixian paste on the market. Locals sum up the maturation process as *"fan, shai, lu"* (turn, sun-dry, bask in dew).

Legend has it that the origins of this delicious flavoring lie in a happy accident. In the late seventeenth century, during the great resettlement of the Sichuan basin, after the fall of the Ming dynasty, a Fujianese immigrant named Chen Yixian was on his way to Sichuan with a bagful of fava beans to eat on the road. When a spate of wet weather made his beans go moldy, he couldn't bear to waste them, so he let them dry and then ate them with a few fresh chiles. The beans were unexpectedly tasty, so when he settled down he continued to ferment his beans and eat them in a similar way. In Pixian, he set up a pickle factory that became renowned for its vinegars and fermented sauces.

According to Chen Yixian's descendants, he invented the paste in 1666, which makes the story problematic. Chiles were certainly being eaten in coastal Zhejiang province around that time, and soon afterward being grown in Hunan: it's possible that Mr. Chen, arriving amid the great wave of migrants of that period, brought some with him from the east. However, there are no records of chiles being grown in Sichuan until more than a century later, around the late eighteenth or early nineteenth century. (One hunch of mine is that perhaps the paste was originally made with fermented beans alone, and chiles were added later, when they became locally available.)

In any case, Mr. Chen's descendants continued the family tradition, founding two factories, Shaofenghe and Yifenghe, that became renowned for their chile bean paste. The companies were nationalized in the 1950s, under the umbrella of the Pixian Chile Bean Paste Factory, but the Shaofenghe brand was revived in the 1980s by a member of the Chen family, and is once again producing artisanal chile bean paste under the guiding hand of Chen Shucheng, who is the sixth-generation descendant of Chen Yixian, and his son Chen Wei.

There's a recipe that closely resembles today's method for making Pixian chile bean paste in a remarkable little cookbook written by a Sichuanese woman, Zeng Yi, around the late nineteenth century (the exact date is uncertain). This is my translation of the recipe in the book, which is titled Zhong Kui Lu:

*Soak some large fava beans in water and then scoop them out of the water; peel the beans and split them into halves; blanch them in boiling water and then place them in a bamboo basket. Mix them with a thin, even layer of flour; briefly air-dry them and then put them into a dark, shady room and cover with a layer of rice straw or a mat of reeds. Wait for six to seven days until they are covered in yellow mold, and then let them sun-dry during the day and absorb the dew by night. Wait until the end of the seventh lunar month and then put them into a clay vat filled with brine, and let them bake in the sun until the red chiles have ripened. Toward daybreak, mix them with finely chopped red chiles; leave for another two to three days to bake in the sun during the day and absorb the dew by night, then store in a pickle jar. Add a little sweet wine, and it will keep for years.*

Zeng Yi was a woman from a scholarly family from Huayang, just outside Chengdu. Both her father and her husband were government officials who served in postings across China; with them she traveled to many places in the Jiangnan or Lower Yangtze region. Her cookbook contains a variety of recipes, including those for Yunnan ham and Jiangnan-style drunken crabs, but the chile bean paste recipe is perhaps a sign that a part of her never left her native Sichuan.

## "Shady" chile bean paste
### yin douban 阴豆瓣

"Shady" chile bean paste is so named because it is not sun-baked like the classic Pixian paste. It has a brighter, redder color and a fresher taste than classic Pixian paste, and is often used in fish cooking and, uncooked, in cold dishes and dips. It is made by fermenting chiles with salt, sometimes with a little added Sichuan pepper and strong grain liquor. Some people add molded fava beans, which are usually bought from specialty suppliers, but many don't—although they still call the paste yin douban, which includes the characters for split beans. It might be exposed to the sun for a few days, but it is otherwise fermented and stored in its jar. The paste is topped with a layer of rapeseed oil that functions as a seal as it ferments. "Shady" paste is still more of a home-made pickle than a commercial product.

## *Zha* pickled chiles with ricemeal
### zha lajiao 鮓辣椒

For this preserve, roughly chopped erjingtiao chiles are mixed with salt, a dash of strong liquor and plenty of toasted, coarsely ground rice, before being packed tightly into clay jars to ferment. The pickle is ready to eat after a couple of weeks, but keeps for much longer. For eating, it is typically stir-fried in oil until the rice is cooked, perhaps with a handful of chopped green garlic. The resulting rubble of fragrant rice and chile is eaten as a relish with rice, to "send the rice down."

The preserve is a fascinating throwback to a method for preserving salted fish with rice that dates back some 2,000 years: the first character in its name, zha, includes the signs for both "fish" and an ancient antecedent of vinegar.

## Salty fermented vegetables xiancai 咸菜
The word xiancai, "salted vegetables," encompasses a vast range of dry-salted pickles. On sunny days, the Sichuanese lay out sliced or shredded vegetables on bamboo trays and spread cabbage leaves over every available surface to catch the rays. When the vegetables are semi-dried, they are rubbed with salt and spices and packed into clay jars (tanzi) to mature. Roughly speaking, the drier the vegetables and the

more added salt, the longer the pickle will keep. Sometimes, the jars are stored upside-down to allow any excess liquid to drain out as they ferment. The finished pickles may be eaten straight as an appetizer, as a relish with rice, or used in cooking: a favorite local dish is twice-cooked pork with salted greens.

## Fermented soy bean and sweet potato balls
### tuotuo douchi 坨坨豆豉

This delicious flavoring is made from fermented soy beans, which are mixed with cooked, mashed sweet potato, chopped ginger, ground chiles and Sichuan pepper, and then formed into little balls about the size of golf balls and sun-dried. The dried balls are typically roughly chopped and then used to bring a delicious umami savoriness to stir-fried dishes, particularly twice-cooked pork. Another farmhouse trick is to tuck one or two of these beany balls, each with a small nugget of lard, into a potful of rice that is approaching the end of its cooking time, and just allow them to heat through.

## Boozy preserved eggs
### zaodan 糟蛋

These extraordinary preserved eggs, pickled in booze and spices, are one of my favorite Sichuanese culinary curiosities. Once popular with literary types, they have almost entirely disappeared from the modern food scene. *Zaodan* are made by tapping duck eggs all over to crack their shells, while leaving their inner membranes intact. These fragile things are then steeped in a wonderfully aromatic liquid, dark as long-steeped tea, fragrant with fermented glutinous rice wine, strong *baijiu* grain liquor, brown sugar and spices, for up to three years. I'll never forget the first time I tracked one down, after a long, hard chase in Yibin with a few friends from Chengdu. I was presented with a shell-less, tea-colored egg that had a marvelous boozy fragrance. Following instructions, I gently removed the membrane and then pierced the egg; its outer layer was pale brown and split open to reveal golden clumps of yolk that resembled crab roe. With a small wooden spoon, I mixed in a dash of strong five-grain liquor (*wuliangye*), a sprinkle of sesame oil and a spoonful of sugar. It was an extraordinary, delicious taste: profoundly aromatic, with a gentle waft of sweetness, and perked up with a kick of strong alcohol. I could see why scholars were said to have eaten these eggs with a cupful of *baijiu* as a restorative for flagging spirits.

According to one local source, this unusual method of egg preservation was devised during the Tongzhi reign (1856–75) by a scholar from a wealthy local family named Zhang. He loved cooking, and the boozy egg was the result of one of his experiments; later, several local producers picked up the recipe. In recent years, the famous Yibin boozy egg had all but disappeared, but happily one company has now revived the method and is trying to develop a new market for the eggs.

# Sweet Dishes

"A sweet dish on the menu of
a Sichuanese wedding banquet is
seen as a symbol of the sweetness
of married life"

# Sweet Dishes 甜食类

Unusually among the world's great culinary nations, traditionally the Chinese have had relatively little taste for sweetness. Although sweets and candied fruits may be enjoyed as nibbles, especially around the Lunar New Year, and some specific regions have infamously sweet teeth, most meals are entirely savory, with sugar used only in small quantities as a seasoning. A sweet dish might feature on the menu of a formal Sichuanese banquet, especially for a wedding, where it is seen as a symbol of the sweetness of married life. One friend of mine whose parents both graduated in Western medicine at the renowned West China University in Chengdu says they remembered the pre-war days, when the finest restaurants either had just a handful of private rooms or would send chefs to prepare banquets in private homes: in that era, a formal meal always included eight dishes, with a sweet dish—often a sweet soup (gengtang)—served toward the end, before the main soup. With a typical Sichuanese meal, however, there is no dessert course. Instead, fruit may be served: at home, simply fruit with a knife for peeling, or, in a glamorous restaurant, a beautiful platter of cut fruit, served with little forks or cocktail sticks.

Many Chinese sweet dishes use ingredients that are not generally thought of as dessert ingredients in Western cuisines, such as root vegetables, pulses and even mushrooms. My favorite dish in this chapter is the "sweet cooked white," a rice pudding embraced by slices of fat pork: surprising to outsiders, perhaps, but extraordinarily delicious. The Chinese also enjoy drinking sweet soups, such as the silver ear fungus and mung bean soups in this chapter. Aside from regular white cane sugar, the Sichuanese use rock sugar to sweeten some dishes, especially tonic soups, and make syrups from aromatic dark brown sugars.

In the past, someone who did need to be fed sweet things was the Kitchen God (zaojun). Traditionally, he sat in the form of a statue on a plinth above the kitchen stove, keeping his eye on the family, or was represented by a wooden tablet inscribed with Chinese characters. Once a year, on the twenty-third day of the last lunar month, the Kitchen God rose up to Heaven and reported on the family's behavior to the Jade Emperor, which is why on that day people made their offerings to him, burning paper money, lighting incense and giving him sticky confections intended to seal his lips or sweeten his words. The tradition of paying homage to the Kitchen God is thought to have its roots in ancient fire-worship; by the time of the Han dynasty, some two millennia ago, he had been established as one of the most common household gods.

In some parts of rural China, people still pay their respects to the Kitchen God, but in Chengdu all such rituals have long since disappeared. One day, however, when I was walking around the streets near the Wenshu Monastery, I noticed for the first time that a familiar street was called "Kitchen God Temple Street" (zaojunmiao jie), and it jogged a memory of an old chef mentioning that there had been a shrine to the Kitchen God in that part of town. But although I scoured the street and asked the nuns in a nearby Buddhist convent for information, there was not a trace of it to be seen. Later, I discovered that a temple devoted to the Kitchen God had been built there in 1853, but had long since vanished.

Sichuan's wealth of street snacks also includes many sweet treats that are normally eaten between meals, such as Mr. Lai's glutinous rice balls and "three big bangs": I've chosen to include recipes like these in this chapter because they might appeal if you wish to serve a dessert course after a Sichuanese meal. Please note also that two of the recipes in the Small Eats chapter—leaf-wrapped dumplings (see p. 387) and eggy pancakes (see p. 397)—have both sweet and savory versions, and you might like to serve the sweet variety after dinner. But, equally, there's nothing wrong with just serving good Chinese tea, fruit and chocolates, and maybe some pre-made halva or baklava, after the meal.

# "Sweet Cooked White" Rice Pudding with Pork Fat

tian shaobai

甜烧白

You may not think that pork fat sounds like the perfect ingredient for a dessert, but I hope you'll change your mind after eating this gloriously huggy steamed pudding, a stalwart of Sichuan country feasts. *Tian shaobai* is a glistening, amber-colored dome of sticky rice enriched with lard and pork fat, sweetened with sugar and red bean paste. (Famous Chengdu chef Yu Bo uses black sesame paste instead of red bean paste for this dish, which is also fabulously delicious.)

The name of the dish literally means "sweet cooked white," "white" being a nickname for cooked fatty pork, and it's a sister dish to the "salty cooked white" bowl-steamed pork on p. 137. In the past, it was often one of the "nine great bowls" (*jiu dawan*) served at weddings and New Year's Eve dinners, and seems these days to be enjoying a revival as a nostalgic, rustic dish. The pork is cut into linked slices that allow for the insertion of a layer of sweet paste (*liandaopian*, which I always think of as "sandwich slices"). If you find the cutting too much hassle, you could just cut simple slices, layer them in the bowl, add some red bean paste, and then fill the bowl with the rice.

Starting with a 14 oz (400g) piece of pork belly should allow you to produce about 10 oz (300g) of neat slices (with some raggedy offcuts that can be used in another dish, such as the twice-cooked pork on p. 132). Do use the fattiest pork belly you can find: this dish is all about the fat; the lean flesh is largely irrelevant.

1¼ cups (250g) short-grain glutinous rice
14 oz (400g) fatty pork belly, with skin, in one piece
¼ tsp dark soy sauce
2 tbsp cooking oil
6 tbsp (100g) red bean paste or black sesame paste (see p. 440)
5 tbsp (60g) dark brown sugar
3 tbsp (40g) superfine sugar
1½ oz (40g) lard
1 tbsp granulated (or superfine) sugar

**Rinse the rice in several changes of water** until the water runs clear, then cover with cold water and soak for at least 2 hours.

Place the pork in a saucepan, cover with cold water and bring to a boil, then simmer until just cooked through. Remove from the pan, reserving the cooking liquid, and pat dry. Smear the dark soy sauce over the skin of the pork and set aside to dry off. (If the pork is wet, it will spit like crazy when you fry it.)

Heat the cooking oil in a seasoned wok over high heat. Add the pork, skin side down, and fry until deep brown and slightly puckered, taking care not to burn the skin; tilt the wok or turn the pork with tongs to ensure even coloring. Remove from the wok and return to the reserved cooking liquid for 5–10 minutes to soften the browned skin. Drain the pork and allow to cool, then chill in the fridge.

When the pork is cold, cut it into "sandwich slices." Trim the meat into a neat block and place it, skin side down, on a board. Make a thin slice into the meat, but don't cut all the way through; with the next slice, cut all the way through, so you end up with a pair of slices linked by the skin—ideally each pair will be ¼ inch (5–6mm) thick in total. Repeat until you have around eight sandwich slices. Now insert a layer of red bean or sesame paste into the slit in each slice. Arrange the slices, skin side underneath, in an overlapping layer across the base of your bowl, so that each strip of skin is in contact with the bowl.

Line a steamer with parchment paper, then use a fork or a skewer to make lots of holes in the parchment. Drain the rice, spread it over the parchment in a thin layer and steam over high heat for 20 minutes, until cooked through.

Meanwhile, dissolve the brown sugar and superfine sugar in 4 tbsp water. When the rice is ready, turn it out into a bowl

You'll need a heatproof bowl just deep enough to hold the ingredients, about 3-cup (750ml) capacity, that will fit in your steamer or pressure cooker. This recipe makes enough for 4–8 servings.

and, while it's still warm, mix in the lard, then the sugar mixture. Tip into the pork-lined bowl, flatten the top and cover with foil or a small plate. To make it easier to remove from the steamer when it's hot, tie it up like a parcel with a piece of twine.

Steam for 2 hours over boiling water (or for 45 minutes in a pressure cooker at high pressure, then allow the pressure to release naturally). To serve, invert the bowl over a serving dish and carefully remove to reveal a pork-topped dome of rice. Sprinkle with the granulated sugar and eat while warm.

# Mr. Lai's Glutinous Rice Balls with Sesame Stuffing

## lai tangyuan
赖汤圆

*1¼ cups (200g) glutinous rice flour,*
   *plus more for dusting*
*1 tsp cooking oil*
*3 tbsp sesame paste*
*4 tsp superfine sugar*

*For the black sesame stuffing*
*3 tbsp (25g) black sesame seeds*
*1½ tbsp all-purpose flour*
*2 tbsp (25g) superfine sugar*
*2 tbsp (25g) lard or coconut oil*
*A little glutinous rice flour, for dusting*

In 1894, a young man named Lai Yuanxin traveled from his native county town to Chengdu, where he took up a post as an apprentice in a restaurant. Sadly, it wasn't long before he fell out with his boss and lost his job. Stuck with no means to support himself, he borrowed money from a cousin, bought a bamboo shoulderpole and a few cooking utensils, and started selling glutinous rice balls on the streets. After making a living this way for many years, he was able to open a dumpling shop on Zongfu Street in the center of Chengdu. Mr. Lai's unusually good *tangyuan* are now famed all over Sichuan. The descendant of his original shop, which now serves a selection of Sichuanese snacks, has so far survived nationalization under the Communists and ruthless competition from a new generation of restaurants.

*Tangyuan* are a traditional snack all over China, and are eaten in great quantities as part of the Lunar New Year festivities. Like many festive foods, their name is treated as a luck-giving pun, in this case because it sounds like *tuanyuan*, which means "reunion"— a fitting symbol for the annual family get-together. In rural Sichuan, many households still make these rice balls (shown in the photograph on p. 443) according to the time-honored method, which involves soaking glutinous rice, then stone-grinding it to a paste that is squeezed in a muslin cloth to make the dough. This "damp flour" is regarded as far superior to the dried flour used as a convenience in modern cities.

**First make the black sesame paste** for the stuffing—this should be done at least a few hours in advance. Toast the sesame seeds in a dry wok or frying pan over gentle heat for 5–10 minutes, stirring constantly, until they smell and taste delicious. Because they are black, you won't notice a change in color, so take care not to burn them. Trust your nose and tongue to tell you when they're ready—the roasted taste is unmistakable. (You can also add a few white sesame seeds to the mix as an indicator: when they are turning faintly golden, all the seeds should be ready.) Pound the toasted seeds to a coarse paste using a mortar and pestle; this can be done in a food processor, but take care not to reduce the seeds to a powder—they are better with a little crunch.

Transfer the paste to a bowl. Gently toast the flour in a dry wok or frying pan until it smells cooked and toasty, then add it to the crushed seeds, along with the sugar, and mix well. Heat the lard or coconut oil over gentle heat until melted, and then stir into the seed mixture. Cool and then chill for a couple of hours or until set. When the stuffing has set, use a teaspoon or a small knife to gouge out small lumps and roll them into balls the size of small cherries. Dust lightly with glutinous rice flour and set aside until needed.

Next make the dough. Place the glutinous rice flour in a bowl with the cooking oil and gradually mix in just enough hot water (about 10 tbsp/150ml) to make a soft, putty-like dough. Knead until smooth. Cover with a damp dish towel.

Now make the rice balls. Break off a ball of dough about the size of a walnut (½–¾ oz/15–20g), keeping the rest of the dough covered with the damp dish towel, so it doesn't dry

Please note that the stuffing is much easier to handle if it is made several hours in advance (in Sichuan it is generally made in large batches and used as needed—it will keep in a refrigerator for months). You should be able to find black sesame seeds in Chinese supermarkets and natural food stores.

This recipe makes about 20 balls, enough for 4–5 servings.

out. Slightly flatten the ball of dough, then use your thumb to make an indentation in its center. Place a ball of stuffing in this indentation, then draw the edges of the dough up around it to enclose it completely and gently roll between your palms to make a ball (make sure there is no stuffing peeking out, or the rice ball will disintegrate when you cook it). Place the finished rice balls on a baking sheet or plate dusted with rice flour until you are ready to cook them (they can be made in advance and refrigerated overnight or stored for longer in the freezer).

Dilute the sesame paste with about 1 tbsp oil from the jar, so that it has a runny consistency. Divide between four little dipping dishes and stir 1 tsp sugar into each one.

Fill a large saucepan with water and bring it to a boil. Drop all the rice balls into the water, return to a boil and then simmer for 5–10 minutes until they are cooked through. Do not allow the water to bubble vigorously or the rice balls may rupture: if necessary, add a splash of cold water to calm the water down. They are ready when they have increased in size and are soft and squeezable when you pick them up with chopsticks (if you break one open, the stuffing should be molten and glossy).

Meanwhile, put the kettle on to boil. When the rice balls are cooked, pour hot water into four serving bowls and divide the rice balls between them. The water is not for drinking, just to keep the rice balls hot and silken. Serve with the sesame paste dips.

Variations

*Several fillings are used in Sichuan, most based on a simple mixture of white sugar and lard, with a little toasted flour to add body. For rose-flavored stuffing, add a small amount of candied rose petals to the sugar and lard base; for tangerine stuffing, add finely chopped candied tangerine peel and crushed rock sugar; for cherry stuffing, use glacé cherries; and for three-nut stuffing, add toasted, roughly chopped walnuts, melon seeds and peanuts. I've also had delicious* tangyuan *stuffed with crushed roasted peanuts and brown sugar.*

*Mr. Lai used to make stuffings out of sweet-scented osmanthus blossoms and jujube paste, serving four different types of* tangyuan *in the same bowl: this was known as* siwei tangyuan, *four-flavor* tangyuan. *It can be given an extra flourish by molding each type into a slightly different shape, so there are egg-shaped and pointed* tangyuan *as well as round ones.*

# "Three Big Bangs"

## san dapao
## 三大炮

1 cup plus 1 tbsp (200g) long-grain glutinous rice
½ cup (40g) soy flour, raw or toasted
   (the toasted sort can be found in Japanese
   shops, where it is sold as kinako)
5 tbsp dark brown sugar

One cool spring morning I went with some friends to the hills of Longchuanyi, just east of Chengdu, to celebrate the blossoming of the peach trees. This annual festival attracts crowds, and the whole area had been mobilized to cater for them. Makeshift teahouses and snack shops had been erected on the edges of the hilly orchards, artisans milled around selling children's toys made from paper and bamboo. Down below in the town, a temporary food market sold Sichuanese snacks and local produce. In the end there wasn't a single peach blossom to be seen, anywhere, because of a recent run of cold weather. We did, however, have a splendid day sampling various unusual snacks and dumplings, which I suppose was really the point in the first place. Many Chinese excursions appear, in the end, to be clever excuses for eating in unusual places and situations.

It was at Longchuanyi that I first encountered "three big bangs," warm nuggets of glutinous rice tossed in golden soy flour and draped in a dark sugar syrup. These are traditionally made in flamboyant style by pounding the hot, sticky mass of rice to a paste in a huge stone mortar with a long-handled wooden pestle before shaping it into balls. These are tossed with some force onto a wooden board that has little stacks of copper saucers at either side, from where they bounce into a panful of toasted soy flour. As you might guess, they get their name from the thudding sound and the metallic rattle of saucers when they hit the board. This recipe makes about 12–15 rice balls.

**Soak the rice overnight** in plenty of cold water.

If using raw flour, begin by briefly toasting it in a dry, heavy-bottomed pan over very gentle heat, stirring constantly, until it is evenly cooked and a light golden brown. Set aside.

Rinse and drain the rice. Line a steamer with perforated parchment paper (see p. 445) or muslin. Spread the rice out in the lined steamer and steam over high heat for about 40 minutes, until fully cooked.

Meanwhile, place the sugar in a small saucepan with 5 tbsp water and dissolve over gentle heat, then turn up the heat and boil for a few minutes until syrupy. Keep warm.

When the rice is cooked, put it in a deep bowl or pan and pound it with the end of a rolling pin or a large pestle to make a squidgy paste; it isn't necessary to break up all the rice grains completely. (If you're not making the rice balls immediately, keep the paste warm in the steamer, set over very gently simmering water.)

When the paste is just cool enough to handle, break off walnut-sized pieces and roll them in the soy flour. (You can shape the paste with clean hands or thin plastic gloves; alternatively you can squeeze it through a piping bag and snip off bite-sized lengths with a pair of scissors.) Place on a serving dish and serve, still warm, with a drizzle of syrup.

## Variation

*In the southern Sichuanese town of Hejiang, a couple named Zhou Hongxing and Yao Ruixin showed me how they make a local version of this snack known as* ciba, *and traditionally eaten during the rice harvest and the mid-autumn festival. Working in unison, they used two long-handled cudgels to pound the steaming rice, before tossing small pieces into a delicious mixture of white sugar, toasted soy flour and a scattering of crushed, toasted peanuts, sunflower seeds and sesame seeds.*

# Pearly Rice Balls

## zhenzhu yuanzi
## 珍珠圆子

These gorgeous steamed rice balls take their name from their outer layer of whole, plump, shiny glutinous rice grains, which gives them a pearly appearance. They can be sweet or savory, but are most commonly stuffed with pastes made from fruit or nuts and sugar. Several of these pastes, such as red bean paste and lotus seed paste, can be bought pre-made in Chinese supermarkets. According to some accounts, they were perfected by a chef named Zhang Herong in the early twentieth century, but may have developed out of an earlier type of "pearly cake" (*zhenzhuba*) made for festivals in western Sichuan. Some modern versions use tapioca pearls rather than rice grains. This recipe makes about 20 rice balls, enough for up to 10 servings.

½ cup plus 2 tbsp (110g) short-grain glutinous rice

About ⅔ cup (175g) red bean paste or lotus seed paste

1¼ cups (200g) glutinous rice flour,
   plus more for dusting

⅓ cup (50g) white rice flour

Potato starch or cornstarch, for dusting

A little cooking oil, if needed

About 10 glacé or maraschino cherries

**Soak the rice in plenty of cold water** for at least 4 hours or overnight.

Cut or break the red bean or lotus seed paste into small, cherry-sized pieces of about ¼ oz (7g) (pre-made, canned stuffings can be cut into ½-inch/1cm slices and then into cubes). Dust the pieces with glutinous rice flour so they don't stick together, then set aside (this step can be done in advance).

Mix the two rice flours together in a bowl, then add just enough hot water from the kettle (about 1 cup/250ml) to bring together into a putty-like dough.

Divide the dough in half, then roll each half into a sausage about 1 inch (2.5cm) in diameter. Break or cut off plum-sized pieces of dough (about ¾ oz/20g each), keeping the rest of the dough covered with a damp dish towel, so it doesn't dry out.

Slightly flatten the ball of dough, then use your thumb to make an indentation in its center. Place a piece of the paste in this indentation, then draw the edges of the dough up around it to enclose it completely and gently roll between your palms to make a ball. Place the finished rice balls on a baking sheet or plate dusted with glutinous rice flour.

Either lightly oil your steamer, or line it with a perforated circle of parchment paper. Some Chinese supermarkets sell liners specifically made for steamers. Alternatively, make your own: use scissors to cut a suitably sized circle of parchment paper, then fold it in half several times until you have a narrow triangle of layers of folded paper. Now make little snips along the edges, as you would if you were making a paper snowflake. Unfold the circle and it will be scattered with holes (just like the one in the photograph). →

← Drain the rice and scatter it on a plate. Roll the stuffed rice balls in the rice to give them a "pearly" coating, and then arrange in your oiled or lined steamer, spacing them out as they will expand slightly during the cooking.

Halve the cherries and place in a tiny dish that will fit into your steamer alongside the rice balls. (The cherries are steamed separately so they don't color the snowy-white rice balls.)

Cover and steam over high heat for 20 minutes, then use chopsticks to place a cherry half on top of each rice ball. Serve immediately.

### Other sweet stuffings

*In Sichuan, these dumplings may be stuffed with a mixture of sugar, glutinous rice flour, candied rose petals, lard and a little water; or ground toasted sesame seeds, also mixed with sugar, glutinous rice flour, lard and a little water.*

### Savory pork stuffing

*Stir-fry some finely chopped pork until golden, allow to cool and then add finely chopped scallion whites and salt or light soy sauce to taste.*

# Sweet Potato Cakes

## hongshao bing
## 红苕饼

These delicious potato cakes are crunchy and golden outside, buttery and smooth within. You can eat them just as they come, or with a dip of white sugar or honey—they are often served as a nibble toward the end of a hotpot feast. Some people fill them or dress them up with a rose-petal sauce, as a way to distract from what is seen as the natural muddiness of the sweet potatoes. The sauce recipe is my own adaptation: I've used honey and rosewater instead of the sugar syrup and candied rose petals that most recipe books suggest. Sometimes these cakes are filled with lotus seed or red bean paste, flattened slightly and then dipped in beaten egg and breadcrumbs before frying.

This recipe makes about 20 sweet potato cakes, enough for 6–8 servings.

1½ lb (700g) orange-fleshed sweet potatoes (2 large)
⅔ cup (100g) glutinous rice flour
Superfine sugar, to taste (optional)
A little potato starch, for dusting
Cooking oil, for deep-frying

*For the rose-flavored sauce (optional)*
4 tbsp honey
1 tsp rosewater

Peel the sweet potatoes and cut them into chunks. Steam over high heat for about 30 minutes, until they are completely tender. Let cool, then mash and mix with the glutinous rice flour. You can add a little sugar at this stage, if you wish.

Break off plum-sized pieces of the sweet potato mash (about 1 oz/30g each) and roll them into croquette shapes, then dust lightly with potato starch.

Heat the deep-frying oil to about 300°F (150°C). Add the sweet potato cakes and fry, stirring gently, until golden brown—this will take about 8 minutes. Keep an eye on the oil temperature, which shouldn't shoot up too much above 300°F (150°C): the oil should just bubble gently around the potato cakes.

If you want to make the rose-flavored sauce, gently heat the honey in a saucepan, then stir in the rosewater.

When the sweet potato cakes are ready, drain and serve immediately, drizzled with the rosewater and honey sauce, if using.

# Silver Ear Fungus and Rock Sugar Soup

## yin'er geng
## 银耳羹

Silver ear fungus (*Tremella fuciformis*) is normally sold dried, each head yellow, papery and somewhat resembling a dried chrysanthemum. Recently, for the first time, I saw the fresh fungus in a Chengdu market, and it was utterly beautiful, shy as a flower with its translucent, ivory-white petals.

This dish shows off the ethereal qualities of this delicacy, as it lolls in its sugared soup in diaphanous waves. The liquid, made satiny by the fungus, slips down the throat like a dream; it should be gently sweetened but not cloying.

Sweet soups may strike Westerners as a curious idea, but they make a gorgeously soothing nightcap or a quiet conclusion to a rousing meal. This one is sometimes offered as a final digestif after a banquet of Sichuanese snacks, served to each guest in a separate, tiny bowl. I have also enjoyed it at the end of a more standard Chinese dinner, served at the table from one large bowl.

According to traditional Chinese medicine, silver ear fungus moistens the lungs and replenishes the yin energies of the body. This soup is seen as particularly nutritious for the elderly. Some restaurants add a few peeled tangerine segments or pineapple chunks, but I prefer the simplicity of this recipe; it makes enough for 6–8 servings.

*1 large or 2 small heads of dried silver ear fungus (about ¾ oz/20g)*
*1 tbsp goji berries, rinsed*
*4¼ oz (125g) rock sugar, or more to taste*

Cover the fungus with cold water and let soften: this will only take about 15 minutes. Pluck or cut out and discard any knobbly or discolored bits, then rinse the frilly fungus well and gently break into smaller pieces. Cover the goji berries with cold water and set aside until needed.

In a saucepan, dissolve the sugar in 2 quarts (2 liters) of water over gentle heat. Bring to a boil, add the fungus and then simmer for about 1½ hours, until it is utterly silken and voluptuous. Skim off and discard any foam that has risen to the surface, then add more sugar to taste, if you like.

Drain the goji berries and scatter in a bowl. Pour over the hot soup and serve.

# Iced Mung Bean Soup

## lüdou sha
## 绿豆沙

Traditional Chinese medicine holds that many diseases are caused by a surfeit of inner heat, or, as they say, "rising fire" (*shanghuo*). Chinese people keep an eye out for symptoms of rising fire, like pimples or a dry cough, and then treat them by avoiding "heating" foods and drinks and choosing instead those that calm and cool. Mung beans, known as "green beans" (*lüdou*) in Chinese, are a classic cooling food, and are often added to congee or drinks. This particular soup-drink is commonly served in hot weather in Yibin, in southern Sichuan, often alongside a bowlful of spicy noodles. The recipe is inspired by a version I enjoyed with a bowlful of "kindling" noodles (see p. 362) at the Qian Mai Xiang restaurant in Yibin. It was lightly sweetened with sugar and served with a few ice cubes to keep it chilled. This recipe makes enough for 4 servings.

¾ cup (150g) dried mung beans
*Rock or white sugar, to taste*
*Ice cubes, to serve*

**Cover the mung beans with plenty of cold water** and let soak overnight.

Drain and rinse the beans. Place in a saucepan with 3 quarts (3 liters) fresh water and bring to a boil. Boil for 10 minutes, then turn the heat down and simmer for at least 30 minutes, until the beans are completely tender and disintegrating. Add a little sugar to taste.

Allow the beany soup to cool. Serve on a hot day, with added ice cubes.

# Eight-treasure Wok Pudding

## babao guozheng
## 八宝锅蒸

This sweet dish, traditionally served at Sichuanese banquets, has a moist cake-like texture and is studded with delicious pieces of candied fruits and walnuts.

The following recipe is based on the one I learned at cooking school in Sichuan and is made by gently frying wheat flour in lard before adding sugar, candied fruit and nuts. In an older Sichuanese cookbook, published in 1977, just after the end of the Cultural Revolution (and still featuring a quotation from Chairman Mao), I found another version made with rice flour and vegetable oil rather than lard, which is described as a halal dish made by Hui Muslims.

The methods for both recipes are strikingly similar to those of the halvas made for many centuries in Turkey, Persia and across the Middle East. There are well-known links between the culinary traditions of Central Asia and northern China, the fruit of at least 2,000 years of trade along the old Silk Road, and many echoes in northern Chinese cuisine of the confections, breads and dumplings found in communities that span the Eurasian continent. In the case of this pudding, the Muslim link suggests that it may be one of the dishes brought to Chengdu by Hui people who migrated to the city in the early Qing dynasty (see p. 21), with much older roots in Persian cooking.

The recipe is traditionally made with lard, but coconut oil makes a fantastic vegetarian (or halal) alternative. It makes enough for 6–8 servings.

3 tbsp (25g) walnuts
Cooking oil, for deep-frying
½ cup (50g) assorted dried or candied fruits
   (in Sichuan these might include candied
   cherries, jujubes, winter melon and tangerine peel)
¾ cup plus 3 tbsp (200g) lard or coconut oil
1⅔ cups (200g) all-purpose flour
¾ cup (150g) superfine sugar

**Place the walnuts in a wok** with just enough cooking oil to cover them and heat over medium heat until they are golden and fragrant. Remove, drain well and coarsely chop. Finely chop all the dried and candied fruits (local cookbooks recommend cutting them into morsels the size of mung beans).

Heat half the lard or coconut oil in a seasoned wok over medium heat. Add the flour and stir constantly for 5–10 minutes until it is fragrant and slightly golden (the flour should taste toasty and cooked by the time it's ready); turn the heat down, if necessary, to prevent sticking.

Put the kettle on to boil. When the flour is cooked, stir in 1¼ cups (300ml) hot water from the kettle, standing back to avoid the steam, then mix in the rest of the lard or coconut oil. Tip in the sugar and stir until it has dissolved. Finally, stir in the nuts and fruits and mix well. Serve immediately.

# Seasonings & Stocks

"Home-made seasonings such as
chile oil and ground roasted Sichuan pepper
find their way into numerous dishes,
while a home-made stock brings depth
of flavor to soups and stews"

## Ground Chiles

### haijiao mian
### 海椒面

In my favorite Chengdu market, there's a spice stall on a corner whose owner can often be seen pounding dried chiles in a great stone mortar with a pestle as tall as he is. The chiles are first trimmed and snipped into sections, then toasted in a wok until they are crisp and aromatic. Only then are they pulverized, with their seeds, to a coarse, rust-red powder. He sells ground *erjingtiao* chiles for their gorgeous color and fragrance, and "little rice chiles" (*xiaomila*) for added heat: customers can choose one or the other, or tailor their mix. (If the ground chiles will be used to make chile oil, he'll also add a spoonful of sesame seeds.)

*1¾ oz (50g) dried chiles*
*1 tbsp cooking oil*

**Snip off and discard the tops** of the chiles, with any attached stems, and then snip them into 1-inch (2–3cm) sections. There is no need to discard the seeds.

Place the oil in a wok and swirl it around the base. Add the chiles and heat over medium-low heat for 2–3 minutes, stirring constantly, until the chiles smell wonderfully aromatic and are just beginning to deepen in color ("cockroach color," as a Sichuanese chef friend says!). Then transfer them to a heavy stone mortar and allow to cool.

When the chiles have cooled, pound them with your pestle to a coarse powder. Use to make chile oil or store in an airtight jar until needed.

## Ricemeal

### mifen, zhengroufen
### 米粉，蒸肉粉

This coarsely pounded rice can be found in Chinese supermarkets, but it's easy enough to make your own.

*¾ cup (150g) Thai jasmine rice*
*1 star anise*
*A couple of pieces of cassia bark*

**Place the rice, star anise** and cassia bark in a dry wok. Heat over medium heat for about 15 minutes, stirring often, until the rice grains are brittle, yellowish and aromatic. Remove from the wok and allow to cool. Pluck out the whole spices and discard (or save to use in other dishes). Using a food processor or a mortar and pestle, grind the rice coarsely, until it has the consistency of fine couscous. Store the ricemeal in an airtight jar until needed.

# Chile Oil

## hongyou
## 红油

Chile oil is an indispensable ingredient in many Sichuanese sauces and dressings. Its common Sichuanese name is *hongyou*, "red oil," because at its best it is an astonishing ruby red. It is made by pouring hot oil onto coarsely ground chiles, which fizz dramatically before they settle into a layer of sediment. Usually, the red oil is used together with the chile sediment at the base of the jar, although upmarket restaurants often strain off the oil for a smoother appearance and mouthfeel. Any leftover sediment (known as "oily chiles," *youlazi*), can be added to dips or used as a table condiment to pep up a bowl of noodles or dumplings.

You can make chile oil with any kind of chile, but the Sichuanese favor the local *erjingtiao* variety for its delicious fragrance and gently building heat. In London, for convenience, I often use coarsely ground Korean chiles, but while they are reasonable as a substitute and give a wonderful rich red color to chile oil, they lack the mellow heat and gorgeous flavor of the Sichuanese chiles. I hope one day that *erjingtiao* chiles will be available outside Sichuan, but in the meantime, feel free to use your own choice of chiles in this recipe. The proportions of chiles and oil in the following recipe are classically Sichuanese, but can be varied according to taste. Many cooks add a few sesame seeds to the chiles for added fragrance.

*2 cups (500ml) cooking oil*
*1 cup (100g) coarsely ground chiles, with seeds*
*1 tsp sesame seeds*

**Heat the oil in a wok** or heavy-bottomed pan to about 390°F (200°C), then set aside for 10 minutes to cool to around 285°F (140°C).

Place the ground chiles and sesame seeds in a heatproof bowl. Have a little cool oil or a cupful of water on hand. When the oil has cooled to the right temperature, pour a little onto the chiles: they should fizz gently but energetically and release a rich, roasty aroma. Pour over the rest of the oil and stir. If you think the oil is too hot and the chiles may burn, simply add a little cool oil or water to release excess heat (standing well back if you add water). Do make sure the oil is hot enough to produce the right roasty aroma. If, having poured over all the oil, you realize the chiles are not sufficiently fragrant, you can decant the whole lot into a saucepan and heat gently, stirring constantly, until it smells fabulous and the color is a deep ruby red—taking great care not to burn the chiles.

When the oil has cooled completely, decant it and the chile sediment into glass jars and store in a cool, dark place until needed; it is best to leave the oil to settle for a day before using.

## Variation

*The above recipe gives the classic traditional method for making Sichuanese chile oil. Chengdu master chef Lan Guijun has devised his own method, which he has encouraged me to share with my readers. He heats 2 cups (500ml) rapeseed oil with a scallion white until the scallion white has turned the color of milky coffee (a sign that the oil has reached 355°F/180°C). He then switches off the heat, adds 5 cups plus 3 tbsp (500g) ground chiles and stirs furiously until the oil is red and aromatic and the chiles have achieved the right "scorched chile flavor" (hula wei). Then he immediately tips in 1 quart (1 liter) of cool oil to arrest the heating before the chiles burn. He favors this method because it enables him to control the exact level of flavor extracted from the chiles, and because he believes the higher proportion of unheated oil makes the finished chile oil more healthy.*

# Ground Roasted Sichuan Pepper

## huajiao mian
## 花椒面

An essential Sichuanese condiment, this aromatic powder is scattered on many hot dishes, used as a dip (often with salt) and mixed into dressings. It smells heavenly and will make your lips tingle as you eat. It's not worth making in large quantities as the fragrance dulls fairly quickly. In many Sichuanese households the pepper is freshly roasted and ground almost every day; I try not to keep it for longer than a week or two. Remember that you must use excellent, zingy Sichuan pepper to appreciate this flavoring. The amount here should give you 1–1½ tbsp ground roasted pepper, which goes quite a long way.

*2 tbsp whole Sichuan pepper*

**Heat a dry wok or frying pan** over very low heat. Add the Sichuan pepper and stir for a few minutes, until the pepper husks are toasty and richly fragrant—they will smoke very slightly as you cook them. Take care not to burn them or they'll taste bitter. Remove from the wok and allow to cool completely.

Grind the pepper to a fine powder in a spice grinder or with a mortar and pestle—Sichuanese cooks use weighty pestles and mortars made of iron (I use an electric coffee grinder that I keep for this purpose only). The fibrous inner husks of the pepper are harder to pound finely than the fragrant outer part; if you find you have visible pieces of husk in the pounded pepper, it's best to sift the powder through a fine-mesh tea strainer to remove them. Use the ground pepper soon or store in an airtight jar.

# Salt and Sichuan Pepper Dip

## jiaoyan
## 椒盐

When Chinese people talk about a "salt-and-pepper" flavor or a "salt-and-pepper" dip, they refer to the classic combination of roasted salt and Sichuan pepper: after all, Sichuan pepper was the original Chinese pepper (*jiao*); regular pepper is still known as "barbarian pepper" (*hujiao*) because of its foreign origins. This is often used in dips for roasted and deep-fried foods, and also in breads and pastries, including sweet ones: think of it as a Chinese answer to the salted caramel flavor popular in the West. Apart from its uses in Chinese cooking, *jiaoyan* makes a delicious sprinkle for roast potatoes and fries.

*1 tbsp whole Sichuan pepper*
*1½ tbsp fine-grain salt*

**Place the salt and Sichuan pepper** in a dry wok or frying pan and stir over gentle heat until the pepper is wonderfully aromatic and the salt has darkened slightly. Tip into a mortar and pound to a fine powder with a pestle.

Store in an airtight jar if not using soon.

# Toasted Sesame Seeds

## shu zhima
## 熟芝麻

Sesame seeds are widely used in Sichuan, especially as a crunchy garnish for noodles and cold dishes. They are always toasted before use.

Simply toast white sesame seeds in a wok or frying pan over very gentle heat until fragrant and pale golden. Black sesame seeds won't visibly change color, so you'll need to taste to make sure they are toasty but not burned, or include a few white sesame seeds which you can use to gauge their doneness. Set aside to cool, then store in an airtight jar until needed.

# Sesame Paste

## zhima jiang
## 芝麻酱

Chinese sesame paste is made by grinding lightly toasted sesame seeds to a fine powder and adding some oil to make the paste runny. It can be found in most Chinese supermarkets, but if you'd like to make your own, here is a recipe based on the instructions of Chengdu master chef Lan Guijun. The paste will separate if you don't use it immediately: simply mix the layers of oil and toasted seed residue together again before use. Do take care not to over-toast the sesame seeds, or the paste will be bitter.

*⅔ cup (100g) white sesame seeds*
*5 tbsp rapeseed oil*

Toast the sesame seeds in a dry wok or frying pan over very gentle heat for around 5 minutes, stirring constantly, until they are a pale golden color and can be broken with the pressure of a fingernail. Tip the toasted seeds into a bowl to cool.

Grind the seeds to a fine powder: you can either use a mortar and pestle or, as I do, a clean coffee grinder.

Heat the rapeseed oil in a wok to around 355°F (180°C): by this stage the sides of the wok will be emitting pale smoky fumes, and you will feel the heat when you hold your hand flat (at a safe distance) above the surface of the oil. Pour the oil over the ground sesame seeds and mix well. Let cool and then store in an airtight jar until needed.

# Deep-fried Peanuts

## yousu huaren
## 油酥花仁

Deep-fried peanuts are used in many dishes and snacks. Sprinkled with salt and ground roasted Sichuan pepper, they also make a delightful snack, served alone or alongside other cold dishes. Do resist the temptation to be impatient and deep-fry at too high a temperature— the nuts can easily burn and develop a bitter taste.

**Tip raw peanuts into a wok** and cover them with cooking oil. Heat slowly to 250–265°F (120–130°C), at which point the oil should be sizzling gently around the peanuts. Fry them at this temperature for about 20 minutes, taking care not to let the oil overheat. When they're done, the nuts should be crisp and fragrant, with a faintly golden color and toasty flavor. Remove the nuts from the oil with a slotted spoon, drain well, and spread out on paper towels to cool completely.

For crushed peanuts, place the fried peanuts (cooled) on a chopping board and crush them with the flat of a cleaver blade or a rolling pin. Pick out and discard the skins as much as possible. You want to end up with coarse choppings that can be used as a crunchy garnish.

# Caramel Coloring

## tangse
## 糖色

Where a rich, dark color is required to make a dish look more appetizing, Chinese chefs traditionally use a liquid made from caramelized sugar: the local equivalent of browning sauce. Dark soy sauce can be used instead, but its color is inkier and less lustrous than caramel, which is why most chefs prefer the latter, particularly for making *lucai*, the vast range of foods cooked in spiced broth and often served cold as appetizers. With caramel coloring, timing is crucial: if you arrest the browning of the sugar too early, the color won't be sufficiently dark; too late, and it will be bitter. At cooking school in Chengdu, we made caramel coloring with white sugar, but one *lucai* specialist I met told me she thought a mixture of rock sugar and white sugar worked best: I have followed her advice with this recipe. You may use ½ cup (100g) white sugar instead of the mix I've suggested if you prefer.

*1¾ oz (50g) rock sugar*
*2 tbsp cooking oil*
*¼ cup (50g) superfine sugar*

**Have 7 tbsp (100ml) hot water on hand** in a pitcher.

Place the rock sugar and oil in a wok with 2 tbsp cold water and stir constantly over very low heat until the sugar has completely dissolved (add a little more water if you need it). Add the superfine sugar and continue stirring until it has also melted. The sugar will become chunkier again before it melts completely: this is normal.

When the sugars are both molten, turn the heat up to high and stir constantly as the mixture darkens, and then becomes pale and frothy. Watch the caramel carefully until the froth has lost its paleness, and the bubbles are large and clear (the caramelized smell will be striking at this point). Quickly pour in the hot water from the pitcher, standing back to avoid the puff of steam that will be released, and stir it in.

Turn off the heat and allow to cool, then store the caramel coloring in a jar until needed.

# Sweet Aromatic Soy Sauce

## fuzhi jiangyou
## 复制酱油

"Re-made" soy sauce (*fuzhi jiangyou*), also known as "red" soy sauce (*hong jiangyou*) is one of the magical elixirs of the Sichuanese kitchen, used most famously in the sauces for street snacks like Zhong crescent dumplings and sweet-water noodles but also in dressings for cold meats and vegetables. To make it, just simmer light soy sauce with spices and sugar until it is sweet, fragrant and syrupy. There is no one formula for making it: every cook has their own combination of spices and sugars (some chefs add dried shiitake mushroom stalks to the brew for extra savoriness). I suggest you regard star anise, cassia bark or cinnamon, fennel seeds and Sichuan pepper as your core spices, and then improvise as you please. You can add the spices directly to the soy sauce and strain them out later, but it's easiest to tie them up in a piece of muslin. The simmering sauce will fill your kitchen with bewitching aromas. This makes about 1½ cups (375ml) sauce, and it keeps indefinitely.

1 small Chinese black cardamom pod
   or 3 green cardamom pods
1 star anise
1 slice licorice root
1 piece of cassia bark or
   ½ cinnamon stick
1 slice sand ginger
1 bay leaf
1 tsp fennel seeds
½ tsp whole Sichuan pepper
2 cups (500ml) light soy sauce
¾ cup plus 2 tbsp (175g) superfine sugar
½ cup (100g) dark brown sugar

**Lightly smack the cardamom** with the flat of a cleaver blade or a rolling pin to crack it open. For best results, tie up all the spices in a small piece of muslin.

Place the spices and soy sauce in a small saucepan and bring to a boil. Then turn the heat down very low and simmer gently for 30 minutes to let the spices infuse the liquid.

Remove and discard the spice bag (or strain out the spices using a fine-mesh sieve, if they were added loose). Add both sugars and stir to dissolve. Finally, return to a boil, and then allow to cool. Transfer to a jar or bottle and store in a cool place.

# Fermented Glutinous Rice Wine

laozao
醪糟

*2½ cups (500g) long-grain glutinous rice*
*1 wine yeast ball (⅓ oz/10g)*

This sweet, boozy liquid is used in marinades, "drunken" dishes and some sweet soups. It is made by mixing cooked glutinous rice with a powdered starter (*jiuqu*) and leaving it in a warm place for a few days until it ferments. The molds, yeasts and bacteria in the starter break down the rice starch into delicious sugars, alcohol and lactic acids, so you end up with pulpy, half-dissolved rice grains in a clear liquid. The juices can be used with or without the rice sediment. In Sichuan, *laozao* is often made by small-scale artisans who take it to market in the large clay pots used for fermentation. It can be found in many Chinese supermarkets, but is extremely easy to make at home. The wine yeast balls required can be bought in Chinese and Vietnamese shops. When the rice has fermented, the mixture can be stored in a jar in the refrigerator, where it will keep for months.

Occasionally, the yeasted rice will become sour or moldy, in which case it should be thrown away. To avoid this, use a scrupulously clean pot for the fermentation and make sure any implements you use are clean and grease-free. Also, crucially, the fermenting rice must be kept warm, like fermenting yogurt.

**Soak the rice in cold water** for 4 hours or overnight, then drain.

Cut a piece of parchment paper to fit the base of your steamer and come up the sides by ¾ inch (a couple of centimeters). Place in the steamer and use a skewer to perforate it with small holes, then tip in the rice in a loose, even layer. Steam over high heat for 40 minutes until tender.

Meanwhile, crush the wine yeast ball to a coarse powder with a mortar and pestle.

When the rice is cooked, turn it out into a colander and rinse under cold water to quickly reduce the temperature to lukewarm. Shake the rice dry and place in a bowl. Sprinkle in most of the crushed yeast, reserving a teaspoonful or two, and mix it in. (Make sure the temperature is only lukewarm when you add the yeast.)

Tip the rice mixture into a clean ceramic pot or bowl and make a well in the center. Sprinkle the remaining yeast over the rice. Cover the pot or bowl with a clean cloth or a loose-fitting lid.

Let the rice ferment in a warm place until it smells sweet and boozy: this will take a few days, depending on the temperature (the ideal temperature is around 85°F/30°C). A mildly alcoholic liquid will have pooled in the base of the pot or bowl and the rice grains will have become soft and sappy without completely losing their shape.

At this point, bring 10 tbsp (150ml) water to a boil in a small saucepan and then leave, covered, to cool completely. Transfer the fermented rice wine to a 1-quart (1-liter) jar, top up with the cooled boiled water and store in the fridge until needed.

# Red Spicy Infused Oil

## fuzhi tiaohe laoyou
## 复制调和老油 1

The secret mystery to many of the dramatically oily dishes of Chongqing, such as spicy blood stew (see p. 170), is a cooking oil that has previously been infused with aromatics and spices. If you don't use this kind of "remade old oil," as it's known in Chinese, such dishes will seem flat and simply oily; with the oil, they have that addictive deliciousness for which they are famed.

The following recipe, for a flavored oil colored red by chile bean paste, is a slightly simplified version of one in a book called *Chongqing-style Sichuan Dishes.* You should make it at least a couple of days before you wish to use it, to allow the flavors to infuse.

If you're keen on spicy Chongqing dishes, you may wish to make this oil in larger quantities, storing it in a jar or bottle and keeping it on hand.

1-inch piece (20g) ginger, unpeeled
2 scallions, white parts only
1 small shallot
1⅔ cups (400ml) rapeseed oil
2 "petals" of star anise
A thumbnail-sized piece of cassia bark
2 green cardamom pods, cracked
1 bay leaf
A good pinch of fennel seeds
5 tbsp Sichuan chile bean paste
2 tbsp ground chiles

**Lightly smack the ginger** and scallion whites with the flat of a cleaver blade or a rolling pin to loosen them. Peel and thinly slice the shallot. Pour the oil into a wok and heat to 355–390°F (180–200°C). Add the ginger, scallion whites and shallot and stir them until they smell delicious and are lightly browned. Add the star anise, cassia, cardamom, bay leaf and fennel seeds and stir briefly until you can smell them. Switch off the heat and let the oil cool to 250–265°F (120–130°C), then add the chile bean paste: the oil should sizzle gently around it. Return the wok to medium heat and stir-fry the chile bean paste until the oil is red and fragrant. Switch off the heat again, stir in the ground chiles, then pour into a heatproof container. Set aside in a cool place to infuse for 24–48 hours before straining off the oil, discarding the solids.

# Clear Spicy Infused Oil

## fuzhi tiaohe laoyou
## 复制调和老油 2

This colorless but wonderfully fragrant oil is used to make the famous boiled fish in a seething sea of chiles (see p. 223) and the similar fish with fresh chile and green Sichuan pepper (see p. 236). Make it at least a day before you wish to use it, to allow the flavors to develop. Store the oil in a jar or bottle until needed.

6 scallions
3¾-inch piece (75g) ginger, unpeeled
1 small onion (about 5¼ oz/150g)
2 cups (500ml) cooking oil
2 star anise
A good handful of cilantro stalks

**Lightly smack the scallions** with the flat of a cleaver blade or a rolling pin to loosen them, then cut into lengths. Slice the ginger, and peel and slice the onion. Pour the oil into a wok and heat to 355–390°F (180–200°C). Add the scallions, ginger and onion and stir for 5 minutes, until they smell wonderful and are lightly browned. Add the star anise and cilantro stalks, turn the heat down low and fry for 30 minutes, stirring occasionally. Ladle into a heatproof container and set aside in a cool place to infuse for 24–48 hours before straining off the oil, discarding the solids.

# Lard

zhuyou

猪油

Lard and rapeseed oil are the two main traditional Sichuanese cooking fats; lard is especially used in country cooking and is prized for its lusciousness and umami flavor. Many chefs these days like to cook with blended oil (hunheyou), a mixture of lard and rapeseed oil. You can buy lard in a supermarket, but I find the flavor purer when I either make it myself or buy it from an artisanal butcher.

The best ingredient for making lard is leaf fat ("stiff sheet fat," banyou, in Chinese), the fat that surrounds the viscera of the pig, but back fat or belly fat can also be used; a good butcher should be able to supply it if you place an order in advance. If the lard is clean and meat-free, it will keep excellently in the fridge, or even at room temperature.

*4½ lb (2kg) leaf lard, or pork back or belly fat, ground if possible*

Preheat the oven to 250°F (120°C).

If the fat is not ground, cut it into ¾-inch (2cm) strips and then into ¾-inch (2cm) chunks. Place in a wide roasting pan and add 3 tbsp (50ml) water. Put the fat, uncovered, in the oven and let it cook slowly for about 4 hours, stirring every 30 minutes or so. At first it will make soft, wet, blubbery sounds; later it will gently fizz and seethe as the fat yields up its pale golden liquor. By the end, the fat will be crisp and honey-colored (see note below for advice on what to do with these delicious cracklings).

Strain the molten lard through a sieve lined with clean muslin, then pour into sterilized jars and store in the fridge, or allow to cool and scoop into freezer bags for freezing.

Note

*The golden, crunchy bits left after making lard can be added to noodle soups or used in stir-fries, to delicious effect—try them in the cabbage recipe on p. 282. One restaurateur I know, Liu Shaokun, makes a fabulous version of twice-cooked pork with green garlic in which pork cracklings are used instead of sliced pork: the nostalgic taste, he told me, of his Sichuanese childhood. The deep green garlic cuts the richness of the fat, and the fermented beany seasonings give it a ravishing flavor.*

# Chicken Oil

jiyou

鸡油

Chicken oil is used to imbue a dish with a glossy richness and luxurious flavor. It is often added in small amounts to a wokful of stir-frying tender green vegetables toward the end of cooking time, or to a bowlful of noodles or a finished dish.

To make chicken oil, simply reserve the layer of yellow fat that solidifies on a cooled chicken stock.

If you want to keep it for longer than a few days, heat it in a wok to allow any water to evaporate, then cool and allow to set. Store in a cool place, or in the fridge.

# Everyday Stock

## iantang

羊汤

classic everyday Sichuanese stock
s made from a mixture of chicken and
ork bones: for the former, a mature
nd flavorful hen (known as "old
nother chicken," *laomuji*, in Chinese)
s preferred. The bones and meat are
lanched in boiling water to remove
mpurities, enhanced by the addition of
little crushed scallion and ginger, and
hen simmered for at least a couple of
ours to extract maximum flavor. The
ame method can be used to make a pure
hicken stock.

At home, I tend to buy chicken
arcasses and pork ribs from an excellent
utcher, with some additional chicken
vings if I want a richer stock. Quantities
re not critical, but obviously you will end
p with a richer stock if you use a good
roportion of meat to water. If you have a
ressure cooker, you can make this stock
n 30 minutes. I tend to make it in large
quantities and freeze it in batches.

*Chicken carcasses and wings*
*Pork ribs or other bones*
*1-inch piece (20g) ginger, unpeeled*
*2 scallions, white parts only*

Place the chicken and pork bits in a stockpot or large
saucepan, cover with cold water and bring to a boil over
high heat. For best results, tip the meat and bones into a
colander and rinse under cold water, then scrub out the pan
before returning them, covering with fresh water and bringing
back to a boil—but, to save time, you can simply skim off as
much as possible of the froth that rises to the surface.

Lightly smack the ginger and scallion whites with the flat of
a cleaver blade or a rolling pin to loosen them. Add to the
pan, then turn the heat down low and simmer for 2–3 hours.
(Alternatively, pressure cook at high pressure for 30 minutes,
then allow the pressure to release naturally.)

Strain the stock (discarding the meat, bones and aromatics)
and, if not using immediately, let it cool completely before
storing. It will keep in the fridge for a few days or in the freezer
for several months.

### Chicken stock
*Follow the recipe above, but just use chicken carcasses and
wings or, for a superior chicken stock, a whole chicken (a
mature hen if you can get your hands on one).*

### Vegetable stock
*Chinese vegetable stocks are typically made by simmering
dried and fresh mushrooms (and/or their stalks), bamboo
shoots and sprouted soy beans (or sometimes fava beans) in
water. While sprouted soy beans are widely sold in China, they
are hard to find in the West, so you will need to sprout your own.
A quick vegetarian stock for soupy noodle dishes can also be
made by seasoning hot water with light soy sauce and a little
sesame oil. You can also use non-Chinese vegetarian stock
cubes or stock powders to make stocks for Chinese dishes;
however, they are often very salty, so you may need to adjust
the quantities of any other salty seasonings used.*

# Clear Superior Stock

## gaotang
## 高汤

*½ free-range chicken (about 1 lb 10 oz/750g)*
*2 duck legs (about 1 lb/450g)*
*¾ lb (350g) pork ribs*
*2½ oz (75g) lean dry-cured Spanish or Chinese ham,*
  *in one piece*
*1-inch piece (20g) ginger, unpeeled*
*2 scallions*

The classic Sichuan banquet dish "cabbage in boiling water" (*kaishui baicai*) is a culinary witticism. It looks like a whole Chinese cabbage in a tureen of boiling water, but is actually a luxurious dish, in which a perfect cabbage heart is served in an extravagant and perfectly clear stock made from chicken, duck and ham. The Sichuanese call such a stock a "high stock" (*gaotang*) or a "clear stock" (*qingtang*); for the Cantonese, it's a "superior stock" (*shangtang*).

A classic Sichuanese superior stock is made from mature hens and ducks, pork ribs and a piece of fine ham, with a little ginger, scallion and sometimes Shaoxing wine to subdue "off-tastes" and refine its flavor. A huge potful will be left to simmer for many hours to extract the essences of the ingredients. Finally, it will be clarified by the addition of loose pastes of puréed meat that collect impurities as they rise to the surface: first a "red paste" (*hongrong*) made from lean pork, and then a "white paste" (*bairong*) made from chicken breast. Every chef has his own signature stock: in Chinese they say a chef's stock is like the voice of an opera singer, the means by which he expresses his art (*chushi de tang, changxi de qiang*).

An everyday stock (see previous page) is delicious enough for most purposes, but for a special occasion, this stock will give you extra depth of flavor. You will need a large stockpot for this recipe, which makes between 2½ and 3 quarts (2.5 and 3 liters) of stock, depending on the simmering time.

**Bring a large pot of water** to a boil. Separately, add the chicken duck legs, pork ribs and ham and blanch them, bringing the water back to a boil each time to allow any impurities to rise to the surface. Transfer each ingredient to a colander and rinse under cold water.

Place all the blanched ingredients in a stockpot and cover with 1 gallon (4.5 liters) of cold water. Bring to a boil over high heat, skimming off any froth. Lightly smack the ginger and scallions with the flat of a cleaver blade or a rolling pin to loosen them, then add to the pot. Turn the heat down low and simmer, uncovered, for at least 3 hours (or as many as 5, or even more—one chef I know leaves this stock to simmer for 10 hours). The surface of the water should murmur gently: don't let the water get too agitated or the stock will not be clear.

Strain the stock and chill overnight (you can use the leftover stock ingredients to make a quick milky stock, see opposite), then remove the oil that solidifies on the surface.

The stock will keep for a few days in the fridge or several months in the freezer.

# Milky Stock

naitang

奶汤

½ free-range chicken (about 1 lb 10 oz/750g)
2 duck legs (about 1 lb/450g)
1 lb 5 oz (600g) pork knuckle or trotter
1-inch piece (20g) ginger, unpeeled
2 scallions

A milky stock is so named because the proteins in the ingredients are sublimated into the liquid over its long boiling, giving it a pale, opaque, "milky" appearance. The stock is silky on the tongue because of all the melted collagen, and is wonderfully comforting. In banquet cooking, it can be used to lend richness to vegetable ingredients, as well as illustrious but tasteless ingredients such as fish maw. At home, you can make fabulous soups by simmering sliced or slivered ingredients—tofu and Chinese cabbage is a particularly lovely combination—in a milky stock, then simply seasoning with salt and white pepper, and garnishing with thinly sliced scallion greens for a splash of color.

Milky stocks are made with chicken and duck, but with added body from ingredients such as pork knuckle, marrow bones and pig stomach. The key to making a milky stock is the control of heat: while clear stocks are simmered over very gentle heat, milky stocks are left to cook at a rolling boil (fish stock is normally a milky stock, made by fast-boiling rather than slow-simmering). Most cooks advise that you should add the entire quantity of water at the start and let it reduce and intensify naturally.

(For a quicker and more economical but less rich milky stock, simply boil up the ingredients left over after making a clear stock—either the clear superior stock opposite or the everyday stock on p. 463—see to the right.)

You will need a large stockpot for this recipe, which makes around 3 quarts (3 liters) of stock.

Bring a large pot of water to a boil. Separately, add the chicken, duck legs and knuckle or trotter and blanch them, bringing the water back to a boil each time to allow any impurities to rise to the surface. Transfer each ingredient to a colander and rinse under cold water.

Place all the blanched ingredients in a stockpot and cover with 1½ gallons (6 liters) of cold water. Bring to a boil over high heat, skimming off any froth. Lightly smack the ginger and scallions with the flat of a cleaver blade or a rolling pin to loosen them, then add to the pot.

Cover the pot and boil for 3 hours, until the stock is milky. The water should bubble away merrily, but you don't necessarily need to use maximum heat; I find medium heat sufficient.

Strain the stock, which can be kept for a few days in the fridge or several months in the freezer.

*Quick milky stock*
*This is a tip from veteran Beijing chef Du Guangbei. Put the ingredients left over from making clear superior stock or everyday stock, such as chicken carcasses, pork ribs and bones, into a large pot. Cover with cold water, bring to a boil over high heat, then boil fast for 20 minutes until the broth is milky-looking. Strain the stock and store for a few days in the fridge or several months in the freezer.*

## Sauces and dips

The following is a concise selection of Sichuanese sauces and dips, gathered here for ease of reference, together with some of the ways they might be used.

### "Red-oil" sauce

Combine 4 tsp superfine sugar, 3 tbsp light soy sauce and 4 tbsp cold chicken stock in a bowl and stir to dissolve the sugar. Add 1 tsp sesame oil and 4 tbsp chile oil, with or without chile sediment.
*Typical uses:* cold meats and offal.

### Numbing-and-hot sauce

Place 3 tbsp light soy sauce, 1 tbsp superfine sugar and 4 tbsp cold chicken stock in a bowl and stir to dissolve the sugar. Add to this ¼–½ tsp ground roasted Sichuan pepper (or 1–1½ tsp Sichuan pepper oil), 1 tsp sesame oil and 3 tbsp chile oil, with or without sediment.
*Typical uses:* cold meats and offal.

### Chile oil dip

Mix together in a small bowl 1 tbsp chile oil plus 2 tbsp sediment, 3 tbsp light soy sauce, ½ tsp finely chopped ginger, 1 tbsp finely chopped garlic, about ¼ tsp ground roasted Sichuan pepper to taste and 1 tbsp thinly sliced scallion greens.
*Typical uses:* cold meats and offal.

### Garlicky sauce

In a small bowl, combine 3 tbsp sweet aromatic soy sauce (see p. 459), 1 tbsp cold water, 2–3 tbsp crushed garlic, 1 tsp sesame oil and 2 tbsp chile oil, with or without sediment.
*Typical uses:* cold meats, vegetables—including cucumber, fresh fava beans and fish mint or heartleaf (*zhe'er gen*).

### Quick "garlic paste" sauce

Combine in a bowl: 3 tbsp light soy sauce, 1 tbsp superfine sugar, 2 tbsp crushed garlic, 1 tsp sesame oil and 2 tbsp chile oil, with or without sediment.
*Typical uses:* cold meats, vegetables—including cucumber, fresh fava beans and fish mint or heartleaf (*zhe'er gen*).

### Pounded *ciba* chile dip

Snip off the tops of 10 dried chiles and shake out their seeds as much as possible. Snip into ¾-inch (2cm) sections and place in a small heatproof bowl, then cover with hot water from the kettle and let soak for 5 minutes. Drain the chiles and place in a mortar, together with 6 peeled garlic cloves. Pound to a paste, then stir in 3 tbsp sweet aromatic soy sauce (see p. 459) and 1 tbsp cold water. Add a little ground roasted Sichuan pepper, if you wish.
*Typical uses:* cold meats and offal.

### *Ciba* chile dip with hot oil

Snip 10 dried chiles in half or into ¾-inch (2cm) sections and place in a small heatproof bowl, along with 1½ tsp green or red whole Sichuan pepper. Cover with hot water from the kettle and let soak for 5 minutes. Drain the spices and place in a mortar with ¼ tsp salt, then pound to a paste (*ciba* chiles is the name for dried chiles that are soaked and pounded like this). Heat 3 tbsp cooking oil until hot enough to sizzle vigorously when dripped onto the chile paste; pour the hot oil over the paste and stir. Finally, stir in 3 tbsp light soy sauce and 3 tbsp finely chopped spearmint (or thinly sliced scallion greens, if you can't get it).
*Typical uses:* freshly made "flower" tofu.

### Chile bean paste and black bean sauce

Rinse 3 tbsp fermented black beans and drain well, then pound to a coarse paste with a mortar and pestle. Heat 4 tbsp cooking oil in a seasoned wok over medium heat. Add 3 tbsp Sichuan chile bean paste and stir-fry gently until the oil is red and fragrant. Add the black bean paste and stir until the beans are also fragrant. Off the heat, stir in ¼–½ tsp ground roasted Sichuan pepper and 2 tbsp chile oil.
*Typical uses:* cool starch jelly; also delicious as a relish with rice or noodles.

### Chile bean paste dip

Heat 1½ tbsp cooking oil in a seasoned wok over medium heat. Add 4 tbsp chile bean paste and stir-fry gently until the oil is red and richly fragrant. Tip into a small bowl. When the paste has cooled, stir in ½ tsp dark soy sauce and 2 tsp sesame oil.
*Typical uses:* oxtail soup.

## Chile oil dip

In a small bowl, mix together 3 tbsp chile oil or cold-pressed rapeseed oil and 3 tbsp chile oil sediment. Stir in 3 tbsp light soy sauce or salt to taste, followed by 3 tbsp thinly sliced scallion greens. If you can get it, add a few drops of lemony litsea oil (a special local ingredient in Guizhou province and the part of Sichuan that borders Guizhou).

## Ground chile dip

Mix together 2 tbsp ground chiles, ½ tsp ground roasted Sichuan pepper, 2 tbsp thinly sliced scallion greens, 3 tbsp light soy sauce and 1–2 tbsp cold-pressed rapeseed oil.

## "Strange flavor" sauce

In a small bowl, dilute 2 tbsp sesame paste with a little oil from the jar and about 2 tbsp cold water until it has the consistency of cream. In another bowl, combine ½ tsp salt, 1½ tsp superfine sugar, 2 tbsp light soy sauce and 1½ tsp Chinkiang vinegar and stir to dissolve the salt and sugar. Add the diluted sesame paste, ¼–½ tsp ground roasted Sichuan pepper (or 1–2 tsp Sichuan pepper oil), 2 tsp sesame oil and 4 tbsp chile oil plus 1–2 tbsp sediment.
*Typical uses:* cold chicken, cold noodles.

## Fish-fragrant sauce for cold dishes

Place 2 tsp superfine sugar, 2 tsp Chinkiang vinegar, 1 tbsp light soy sauce and 2 tbsp cold stock or water in a bowl and mix to dissolve the sugar. Heat 4 tbsp cooking oil in a seasoned wok over low heat. Add 4 tbsp sambal oelek (or seeded, finely chopped Sichuan pickled chiles) and stir-fry gently until the oil is red and wonderfully fragrant, then add this to the bowl. Stir it into the sauce, then add 1 tbsp very finely chopped ginger, 1½ tbsp very finely chopped garlic, 3 tbsp thinly sliced scallion greens and 1 tsp sesame oil and mix well.
*Typical uses:* cold meats or deep-fried green peas.

## Sichuan pepper and scallion sauce

Cover ½ tsp whole Sichuan pepper with a little lukewarm water and let soak for 20 minutes. Thinly slice 1¾ oz (50g) scallion greens (from about 1 bunch), then place on a board with the drained Sichuan pepper and a pinch of salt and chop extremely finely. Transfer the mixture to a small bowl, then stir in 6 tbsp cold chicken stock, 2 tbsp light soy sauce and 2 tsp sesame oil.
*Typical uses:* cold meats and offal, fresh walnuts.

## Chongqing sauce with bird's eye chiles and green Sichuan pepper oil

In a bowl, combine 7 tbsp (100ml) chicken stock (hot or cold) with 2 tbsp light soy sauce, ½ tsp salt, 2 thinly sliced bird's eye chiles (red and green), 1–1½ tsp green Sichuan pepper oil, 1½ tbsp cold-pressed rapeseed oil and 1 tsp sesame oil.
*Typical use:* cold chicken.

## Fresh chile dip

In a small bowl, mix together 3 tbsp light soy sauce, 1–2 tbsp thinly sliced red bird's eye chile, 1 tbsp finely chopped garlic, ½ tsp finely chopped ginger, 2 tbsp cold-pressed rapeseed oil and about ¼ tsp ground roasted Sichuan pepper, to taste.
*Typical uses:* cold meats and offal.

## Scorched green pepper sauce

Grill 7 oz (200g) long green Turkish peppers over charcoal until soft, puckered and browned but not burned; or roast them in a 400°F (200°C) oven for 20 minutes until browned and tender. Trim off the stem ends of the peppers, then peel away any blackened skin as much as possible. Finely chop the peppers to a mush, or pound them with a mortar and pestle, then transfer to a bowl. Crush 2–3 garlic cloves and add them to the bowl, along with 4 tbsp cold-pressed rapeseed oil and about ½ tsp salt, to taste. If you wish, you can also add 1 preserved duck egg (peeled, rinsed and finely chopped).
*Typical uses:* steamed eggplants, freshly made "flower" tofu.

## Ginger sauce

In a small bowl, combine 1½ tbsp very finely chopped ginger with 1 tbsp Chinkiang vinegar, ¾ tsp salt, 1½ tbsp cold stock or water and 1½ tsp sesame oil.
*Typical uses:* cold vegetables and meats.

# The 23 Flavors of Sichuan

Here follows a brief explanation of the 23 "official" complex flavors (*fuhewei*) at the heart of the Sichuanese culinary canon. The first four are the most famously associated with Sichuanese cuisine, while the following seven are also typically local. The remainder overlap more significantly with the tastes of China's other cooking regions. It's worth noting that only ten of the total use chile or Sichuan pepper: a reminder that true Sichuanese cuisine is not simply hot or numbing, but about a scintillating variety of flavors.

Do remember that this is just a set of guidelines, and that local chefs mix up and overlap their flavors in a spirited and undogmatic way. Many classic dishes combine more than one flavor: Gong Bao chicken, for example, blends "scorched chile" and "lychee" flavor; mapo tofu is a mix of "home-style" and "numbing-and-hot."

At the end of this section, I've also added a note on some of the other complex flavors that have been adopted by Sichuanese chefs over the past couple of decades.

## 1. home-style flavor (jiachang wei 家常味)

This uniquely Sichuanese flavor is based on the hearty tastes of home cooking: salty, umami-savory and a little bit hot (*xianxian weila*). The seasonings used are typically Sichuan chile bean paste, fermented black beans, salt and soy sauce. Pickled red chiles and sweet flour sauce may also play a role; sometimes cooks add a hint of sugar-sweetness or a touch of vinegar.

*Examples*: twice-cooked pork (p. 132), home-style tofu (p. 250), Taibai chicken (p. 185), stir-fried celery with ground pork (p. 300).

## 2. fish-fragrant flavor (yuxiang wei 鱼香味)

Another celebrated Sichuanese invention, based on the seasonings used in traditional fish dishes and sometimes thought to evoke the actual taste of fish, this flavor combines salty, sweet, sour and spicy notes, with the heavy fragrance of garlic, ginger and scallions. The core seasoning is pickled red chiles, either on their own or in the form of Sichuan chile bean paste, which give fish-fragrant dishes their distinctive orange-red hue. When this flavor scheme is used in actual fish dishes, the name "fish-fragrant" is not normally used.

*Examples*: fish-fragrant cold chicken (p. 72), fish-fragrant pork slivers (p. 145), fish-fragrant eggplants (p. 266).

## 3. strange flavor (guaiwei 怪味)

Also uniquely Sichuanese, this flavor is based on the harmonious mixing of salty, sweet, numbing, spicy-hot, sour, umami-savory and fragrant notes. No individual flavor should clamor for the attention at the expense of any other; each should be equally stressed. Ingredients typically include salt, soy sauce, chile oil, Sichuan pepper, sesame paste, sugar, vinegar, sesame seeds and sesame oil, and sometimes ginger, garlic and/or scallions.

*Examples*: "strange flavor" bang bang chicken (p. 70), "strange flavor" peanuts (p. 123).

## 4. numbing-and-hot flavor (mala wei 麻辣味)

This is the flavor most strongly associated with Sichuanese food, and particularly with the hearty riverside dishes of Chongqing. It is based on a delicious double whammy of chiles and Sichuan pepper, underpinned by salt and other seasonings such as sugar, sesame oil and occasionally five-spice powder. The level of fieriness varies widely from place to place: the people of Chongqing have a fabled appetite for extremely *mala* dishes, a consequence, they say, of the city's oppressively warm and humid climate.

*Examples*: numbing-and-hot dried beef (p. 120), mapo tofu (p. 245), boiled beef slices in a fiery sauce (p. 161), numbing-and-hot hotpot (p. 407).

### 5. red-oil flavor (hongyou wei 红油味)

This describes a delicious mixture of ruby-red chile oil, soy sauce and sugar, perhaps with a little sesame oil. The flavor combines salty, umami-savory, spicy-hot and fragrant tastes with a hint of sweetness in the aftertaste, and is used in cold dishes.

*Examples*: cold-dressed chicken (p. 68), slivered pig's ear in chile oil sauce (p. 114).

### 6. garlic paste flavor (suanni wei 蒜泥味)

A scrumptious combination of mashed garlic, chile oil and sesame oil with a special soy sauce that has been simmered with spices and brown sugar until it is dense and fragrant. This gently spicy sauce is used for cold meat and vegetable dishes, noodles and dumplings. The garlic should be added shortly before serving.

*Examples*: "white" pork in garlicky sauce (p. 85), smacked cucumber in garlicky sauce (p. 106), hand-made sweet-water noodles (p. 356), Zhong crescent dumplings (p. 375).

### 7. scorched chile flavor (hula wei 煳辣味)

As its name suggests, this flavor is derived from frying dried chiles in oil until they're crisp, aromatic and beginning to darken; the main ingredients are then added and tossed in the chile-flavored oil. The chiles are often fried with Sichuan pepper; for optimum results, add the pepper to the hot oil a few seconds after the chiles, because it takes marginally less time for them to become fragrant. Soy sauce, vinegar, sugar, ginger, scallions and garlic may be added. The crucial skill for making scorched chile dishes is *huohou*, the control of heat: the cooking oil must be hot enough to "scorch" the chiles but must not burn them. The best way to achieve this is to throw the chiles into the wok before the oil gets smoking-hot—you can then continue heating the oil until they sizzle, without running the risk of burning them immediately.

*Examples*: stir-fried water spinach with chiles and Sichuan pepper (p. 271), stir-fried lotus root with chiles and Sichuan pepper (p. 276), spiced cucumber salad (p. 108).

### 8. tangerine peel flavor (chenpi wei 陈皮味)

Dried tangerine peel gives this formula its distinctive taste, but always against a background of numbing-and-hot chiles and Sichuan pepper; there may also be a subtly sweet aftertaste. All Sichuanese cooks warn against using too much peel, lest the dish taste bitter. This flavor is typically used in cold meat and poultry dishes, such as spicy beef slices with tangerine peel.

### 9. Sichuan pepper flavor (jiaoma wei 椒麻味)

This distinctive flavor derives, unusually, from raw Sichuan pepper, which is finely chopped with scallion greens and salt, then mixed with a little soy sauce and sesame oil. The Sichuan pepper should give the sauce an amazing tingly quality—it's not worth making if your Sichuan pepper isn't fresh and bursting with fragrance. Used mainly in cold meat, poultry and offal dishes and also, in season, with fresh walnuts.

*Example*: chicken in Sichuan pepper and scallion sauce (p. 71).

### 10. Sichuan pepper and salt flavor (jiaoyan wei 椒盐味)

A simple combination of ground roasted Sichuan pepper and salt, which is used as a dip for deep-fried or roasted foods and to flavor breads and pastries, both sweet and savory. The Sichuan pepper is best roasted near the time you wish to use it, as it loses its fragrance if kept for too long.

*Examples*: stuffed eggplant fritters with Sichuan pepper dip (p. 269).

### 11. sour-and-hot flavor (suanla wei 酸辣味)

This flavor, more commonly known in English as hot-and-sour, has several variants. The classic sour-and-hot style, also found in northern China, combines the mellow taste of Chinese vinegar with a kick of white pepper against a salty background. In Sichuan, the pepper is often replaced or supplemented with chiles or chile oil and the vinegar with pickled vegetables. Most food experts stress that sourness is the crux of this flavor, with the spicy seasonings playing an "assisting" role.

*Examples*: sour-and-hot "flower" tofu soup (p. 324),

spinach in sour-and-hot dressing (p. 79), sour-and-hot sweet potato noodles (p. 366).

## 12. fragrant fermented sauce flavor (jiangxiang wei 酱香味)

This flavor is based on the heady fermented taste of sweet flour sauce, with additional notes of salt and sweetness.

*Examples*: stir-fried pork slivers with sweet flour sauce (p. 142), tofu with ground meat in fermented sauce (p. 252).

## 13. five-spice flavor (wuxiang wei 五香味)

As its name suggests, five-spice flavor involves several spices (though not necessarily five), either whole or ground to make five-spice powder. Five-spiced foods, including meat, offal, poultry, eggs and tofu, may be simmered in a rich, spiced broth (*lushui*, p. 100) and then served cold, usually with a dip of ground chiles or Sichuan pepper (for example, spiced chicken hearts, p. 100). They may also be braised in a spiced liquid that is ultimately reduced to a delicious sticky sauce, or steamed with a spicy marinade (as for fragrant and crispy duck, p. 205). The spices can vary, but normally include star anise, cassia bark and Sichuan pepper.

## 14. sweet-fragrant flavor (tianxiang wei 甜香味)

This flavor is found in hot, sweet dishes made by a variety of cooking methods. It derives its sweetness from white or rock sugar, sometimes with the addition of fruit juices or candied fruits.

*Examples*: eight-treasure black rice porridge (p. 338), silver ear fungus and rock sugar soup (p. 449).

## 15. fragrant-boozy flavor (xiangzao wei 香糟味)

Made with *laozao* or fermented glutinous rice wine (p. 460), which has a delicious, gently alcoholic aroma and taste—with perhaps a little extra salt, sugar, sesame oil and spices—this flavor is typically used for meat, poultry and other ingredients, such as ginkgo seeds and bamboo shoots.

*Example*: cold chicken with fragrant rice wine (p. 75).

## 16. smoked flavor (yanxiang wei 烟香味)

As you might imagine, this flavor arises through smoking salt-cured meat or poultry over smoldering wood shavings and fragrant leaves. The Sichuanese famously use tea and camphor leaves to smoke their ducks; other meats may be smoked over bamboo leaves, pine needles, rice straw, peanut husks or sawdust. In southern Sichuan, bamboo shoots are also smoked and dried: they are particularly delicious stewed with beef.

*Examples*: tea-smoked duck (p. 118), home-made bacon with Sichuanese flavorings (p. 424).

## 17. salt-savory flavor (xianxian wei 咸鲜味)

A very simple flavor that is designed to highlight the natural, fresh, umami taste (*xianwei*) of raw ingredients. Salt is the base flavoring, with stock (or MSG) often added to give a rounded umami taste; other seasonings such as sugar, soy sauce and sesame oil may be added judiciously, but should not overwhelm the flavor of the main ingredient. This flavor is used in hot and cold dishes.

*Examples*: stir-fried pig's liver (p. 155), green soy beans in a simple stock sauce (p. 77), chicken "tofu" (p. 203).

## 18. lychee flavor (lizhi wei 荔枝味)

This flavor does not involve any actual lychees, but is a variety of sweet-and-sour in which the sour notes stand out a little more than the sweet, recalling the fruit. The sour-sweet tastes are always played out against a background of gentle saltiness. Some experts distinguish between the lighter "small lychee flavor" of Gong Bao chicken and the heavier "big lychee flavor" of pork in "lychee sauce" with crispy rice.

*Examples*: pork in "lychee" sauce with crispy rice (p. 139), Gong Bao chicken with peanuts (p. 182).

## 19. sweet-and-sour flavor (tangcu wei 糖醋味)

The Sichuanese have their own version of this famous Chinese flavor combination. It usually relies heavily on sugar and vinegar, with a backbone of salt, and, when used for hot dishes, it is also flavored with ginger, garlic and scallions.

*Examples*: coral-like snow lotus (p. 81), three-sliver salad (p. 92), sweet-and-sour pork (p. 146), sweet-and-sour crispy fish (p. 231).

20. ginger juice flavor (jiangzhi wei 姜汁味)
Fresh ginger, salt and vinegar give this flavor its
distinctive taste and fragrance; soy sauce and
sesame oil are also added. Ginger juice sauces are
used with some cold meats and green vegetables,
and occasionally for hot dishes.
*Example*: fine green beans in ginger sauce (p. 82).

21. sesame paste flavor (majiang wei 麻酱味)
Another flavor used for cold dishes, this one relies
on toasted sesame paste, sesame oil, salt and stock
or water, sometimes with the addition of soy sauce
and/or sugar. Some chefs add a touch of chile oil.
It is used for offal and some vegetables.
*Example*: "phoenix tails" in sesame sauce (p. 102).

22. mustard flavor (jiemo wei 芥末味)
This flavor is used for cold dishes. It is based on
the salt-savory flavor, but with a hint of vinegar
sourness and a burst of hot mustard.
*Example*: three-sliver salad with a mustardy
dressing (p. 92).

23. salt-sweet flavor (xiantian wei 咸甜味)
A combination of umami-savoriness and sugar-
sweetness, used in varying proportions in some hot
meat and poultry dishes. Shaoxing wine and pepper
are usually added, perhaps with other spices.
*Example*: braised chicken with chestnuts (p. 188).

Other flavor combinations that were not in the
canon taught in the mid-1990s but have since
become fashionable include "fruit juice flavor"
(*guozhi wei* 果汁味); "tomato sauce flavor" (*qiezhi
wei* 茄汁味); "fragrant-and-hot flavor" (*xiangla wei*
香辣味); "pickled chile flavor" (*paojiao wei* 泡椒味);
and "chopped salted chile flavor" (*duojiao wei* 剁椒
味), a Hunan-style flavor with Hunanese chopped
salted chiles.

# The 56 Cooking Methods of Sichuan

The following are the 56 "official" cooking methods, as listed in the 1998 Sichuan culinary encyclopedia.

1. chao (炒)
A general term for stir-frying food in a wok, usually with oil as the heating medium (*youchao* 油炒), but occasionally using salt (*yanchao* 盐炒) or even sand (*shachao* 沙炒).

2. shengchao ("raw-frying" 生炒)
Stir-frying as above, where the main ingredient is raw when it enters the wok.
*Example*: salt-fried pork (p. 154).

3. shuchao ("cooked-frying" 熟炒)
Stir-frying where the main ingredient is cooked when it enters the wok.
*Example*: twice-cooked pork (p. 132).

4. xiaochao ("small-frying" 小炒)
Simple, quick stir-frying, where ingredients and seasonings are added to the wok in a single sequence, with no pre-frying of any ingredient. This method is typical of home cooking and is a particular favorite in southern Sichuan. A variant of this cooking method, typical of the Zigong area, is *xiaojian* (which also translates as "small-frying").
*Examples*: Gong Bao chicken with peanuts (p. 182), stir-fried chicken hodgepodge (p. 199), Zigong "small-fried" chicken (p. 184).

5. ruanchao ("soft-frying" 软炒)
Ingredients such as fava beans or chicken breast are mashed to a pulp, mixed with water, egg and starch and then stir-fried over high heat.

6. bao ("explode"-frying 爆)
Fast stir-frying in hot oil at a very high temperature. Used particularly for offal that needs swift cooking to preserve its slippery-crisp texture.
*Example*: fire-exploded kidney "flowers" (p. 157).

7. liu (熘)
A type of frying where small pieces of food are pre-cooked in oil (or steamed) and then married with a wok-cooked sauce. The pre-cooked pieces of food may be tossed into the sauce in the wok, or the sauce may be poured over food on the serving dish.

8. xianliu ("fresh liu" 鲜熘)
A variant of *liu* where soft pieces of fish or poultry are draped in a light egg-white batter and pre-fried in plenty of gently heated oil. Excess oil is then drained off and seasonings and other ingredients are added to the wok. This method keeps the main ingredients beautifully tender. It is also known as "slippery liu" (*hualiu* 滑熘) because of the final mouthfeel of the food.
*Examples*: chicken in a delicate vinegar sauce (p. 189), Gong Bao shrimp with cashews (p. 234).

9. zhaliu ("deep-fry liu" 炸熘)
A variant of *liu* where the food is first deep-fried at a high temperature and then added to a wokful of sauce, or turned out onto a serving dish to receive the sauce.
*Examples*: fish-fragrant eggplants (p. 266), fish-fragrant fried chicken (p. 200).

10. ganbian ("dry-frying" 干煸)
The main ingredient, cut into pieces, is stir-fried in no oil or scanty oil until part-cooked and fragrant; oil and seasonings are then added. In practice, many cooks replace dry-frying with deep-frying because the latter is faster.
*Examples*: dry-fried green beans (p. 274), dry-fried eggplants (p. 268), dry-fried beef slivers (p. 166).

11. jian (煎)
Pan-frying or shallow-frying over medium heat against the surface of a wok or pan, until the food is golden on both sides.

*Examples*: frying the egg for fried egg and tomato soup (p. 308), Juntun *guokui* pastries (p. 393).

### 12. guotie ("pot-sticking" 锅贴)

A combination of steaming and shallow-frying over gentle heat in a flat-bottomed pan. The food is not moved, so it develops a golden toasty crust beneath but remains succulent on top.

*Example*: pot-sticker dumplings with chicken stock (p. 382).

### 13. zha (炸)

Deep-frying food in plenty of oil, usually over high heat, until it is crisp.

### 14. qingzha ("clear deep-frying" 清炸)

Deep-frying once only in hot oil over high heat until the outside of the food is crisp and fragrant. The food is not coated in any starch or batter.

*Example*: lamp-shadow sweet potato chips (p. 112).

### 15. ruanzha ("soft deep-frying" 软炸)

The deep-frying of small pieces of food coated in an egg-white batter, first at a lower temperature and then at a higher, so the outside of the food is crunchy but the inside tender.

*Example*: frying the chicken for fish-fragrant fried chicken (p. 200).

### 16. suzha ("crisp deep-frying" 酥炸)

The food is coated in flour or batter or rolled up in some kind of skin, deep-fried briefly in hot oil to hold its shape, and then fried in even hotter oil until it is crisp and golden.

*Example*: frying the fish for sweet-and-sour crispy fish (p. 231).

### 17. jinzha ("soak deep-frying" 浸炸)

The food is placed in a wok of cool or warm oil and allowed to heat up very slowly until it is cooked.

*Example*: fragrant deep-fried peanuts (p. 122).

### 18. youlin ("oil-drenching" 油淋)

The food, often whole, pre-cooked poultry, is held over a wokful of hot oil and ladled with the oil until it is crisp and deeply, glossily red on the outside but still tender within. This same term can also refer to pouring sizzling-hot oil over spices as one stage of cooking.

### 19. qiang (炝)

Stir-frying vegetables in oil flavored with dried chiles and Sichuan pepper.

*Examples*: stir-fried water spinach with chiles and Sichuan pepper (p. 271), stir-fried lotus root with chiles and Sichuan pepper (p. 276).

### 20. hong (烘)

Frying gently in a little oil, first over medium heat and then low heat, until the food, usually an omelet or eggy pancake, is crisp and fragrant on the outside but fluffy within (as for stuffed eggy pancakes, p. 397). Informally, Sichuanese people also use this term to describe a method where they sizzle chile bean paste and other aromatics in oil, add the main ingredient and a little liquid, then cover the wok and cook everything gently for a while.

### 21. cuan (汆)

Boiling slices or strips of food, or meatballs and fishballs, in water until they are cooked, either as a soup or as part of a more complex cooking process.

*Example*: chicken balls in clear soup (p. 318).

### 22. tang (烫)

Scalding small pieces of food briefly in boiling water until just done, sometimes as a stage in a longer cooking process.

*Example*: hotpot (p. 407).

### 23. chong (冲)

Cooking runny paste-like foods in oil or water, until they are cooked and can hold their shape.

*Example*: chicken "tofu" (p. 203).

### 24. dun (simmering 炖)

Simmering large pieces of food or whole fowl in water, usually with a little ginger and scallion, over low heat and for some time, until they are extremely tender. Brings out the original, essential flavor (*yuanwei*) of the main ingredient.

*Example*: clear-simmered oxtail soup (p. 313).

25. zhu (boiling 煮)
Boiling ingredients in plenty of water until they are done, either as a preliminary stage of cooking or to make simple vegetable soups.
*Example*: boiled pumpkin “soup” (p. 315).

26. shao (braising 烧)
One of the most universal Chinese cooking methods, which involves bringing food to a boil in a seasoned liquid and then simmering it over medium or gentle heat until the food is tender and the sauce reduced and glossy. The sauce may be thickened with starch just before serving. The main ingredients are usually pre-cooked by any one of a number of methods.

27. hongshao (“red-braising” 红烧)
A type of braising found across China where soy sauce—or sometimes caramel coloring—gives the dish a deep “red” hue. In Sichuan, red-braised dishes are also made with Sichuan chile bean paste, which gives them a much more pronounced reddish color.
*Examples*: red-braised pork (p. 143), red-braised beef with daikon (p. 168).

28. baishao (“white-braising” 白烧)
A type of braising without strongly colored seasonings, so the pale natural color of the main ingredient, often fish, chicken or vegetables, is emphasized in the finished dish.
*Example*: chicken with ginkgo nuts (p. 326).

29. congshao (“scallion braising” 葱烧)
A braising method that begins with the frying of scallions in oil before stock and other ingredients are added. The final dish has a strong scalliony flavor.

30. jiangshao (“braising with fermented sauce” 酱烧)
Begins with the frying of a little sweet fermented paste before the addition of stock and seasonings; the main ingredients are often deep-fried before they are added to the pot.
*Example*: tofu with ground meat in fermented sauce (p. 252).

31. jiachang shao (“home-style braising” 家常烧)
This method starts by stir-frying chile bean paste until the cooking oil is red and fragrant, then adding stock and other ingredients; everything is simmered gently over low heat until the food has absorbed the rich flavors of the sauce.
*Examples*: fish braised in chile bean sauce (p. 218), duck braised with konnyaku “tofu” (p. 208).

32. shengshao (“raw braising” 生烧)
Braising tougher ingredients, which are simmered slowly with seasonings until soft, at which point the heat is increased to reduce the liquid.

33. shushao (“cooked braising” 熟烧)
A faster type of braising used to cook small pieces of food.

34. ganshao (“dry-braising” 干烧)
In this method, the main ingredient and flavorings are simmered over medium heat until the liquid has almost completely reduced. Starch is never added as a thickener.
*Examples*: dry-braised beef tendons (p. 173), dry-braised fish with pork in spicy sauce (p. 226).

35. du (㸅,𤆵)
A Sichuanese folk method of cooking, really a type of braising, but named after the noise made by the sauce bubbling in the wok.
*Example*: mapo tofu (p. 245).

36. ruandu (“soft du” 软 㸅)
Also known as “soft-braising” (*ruanshao*). Like *du*, except that the food is not pre-fried but is either directly added to simmering sauce or briefly dunked in warm, not hot, oil. Often used for fish cooking: for example, if the fish for fish braised in chile bean sauce (p. 218) is not fried beforehand.

37. hui (烩)
Similar to white-braising, but with a shorter cooking time and more liquid. Used to cook two or more ingredients, often cut into slivers, together in a pale, gentle sauce.
*Example*: stir-fried mixed mushrooms (p. 297).

**38. men ("smothering" 焖)**
Stewing pre-fried ingredients in a closed pot, over low or medium heat. The liquid—not as much as for other stewing methods—is added at the start of the cooking and not reduced. It can be thickened with starch before serving.

**39. wei (煨)**
Stewing chunks of food with stock, flavorings and caramel color or dark soy sauce over extremely low heat, until they are cooked and beautifully brown, and the liquid much reduced.

**40. kao (㸆)**
Another kind of stewing, in which large chunks of rather tough food (including classic banquet delicacies such as bear's paw or shark's fin) are simmered very gently with stock and flavorings.

**41. zheng (steaming 蒸)**
*Example*: leaf-wrapped glutinous rice dumplings (p. 387).

**42. qingzheng ("clear steaming" 清蒸)**
Pale foods steamed with pale-colored flavorings: ginger, scallions, salt, wine and fine stock.
*Example*: steamed egg custard with ground pork topping (p. 211).

**43. hanzheng ("dry-steaming" 旱蒸)**
Steaming food, often wrapped in paper or in a covered dish, with seasonings but no liquid.
*Example*: "sweet cooked white" rice pudding with pork fat (p. 438).

**44. fenzheng ("ricemeal steaming" 粉蒸)**
In which meat or poultry is mixed with marinade ingredients and ricemeal, and then steamed.
*Example*: spicy steamed beef with ricemeal (p. 165).

**45. kao (烤)**
Roasting meat, poultry or fish over a radiating heat source. The main ingredient is usually whole, and sometimes stuffed or wrapped in leaves or clay. This is the method used for the traditional fork-roasting of a large tranche of pork belly.

**46. gualu kao ("hanging-oven roasting" 卦炉烤)**
Roasting fowl by hanging them in a closed oven. This is the method used for both Peking duck and the similar Sichuanese roast duck.

**47. minglu kao (明炉烤)**
Barbecuing meat, poultry or fish over an open-topped heat source such as a grill full of embers.

**48. kaoxiang kao ("oven-roasting" 烤箱烤)**
Roasting in a closed oven.

**49. tangzhan ("sugar crusting" 糖粘)**
Encrusting food in a seasoned sugary paste or syrup.
*Example*: "strange flavor" peanuts (p. 123).

**50. zhashou ("deep-fry and receive" 炸收)**
Simmering deep-fried foods in seasoned broth until they absorb or "receive" the flavors of the liquid.
*Examples*: numbing-and-hot dried beef (p. 120), "rabbit eaten cold" (p. 116).

**51. lu (卤)**
Stewing foods in a spiced broth.
*Examples*: "man-and-wife" offal slices (p. 97), spiced chicken hearts (p. 100).

**52. ban (拌)**
Tossing raw or cooked foods in a dressing, like a salad. *Example*: smacked cucumber in garlicky sauce (p. 106). A variant of this is "dry-tossing" (*ganban*), where dry spices are used, rather than a sauce.
*Example*: Dry-tossed beef (p. 101).

**53. pao (pickling in brine 泡)**
*Example*: Sichuanese pickled vegetables (p. 420).

**54. zi ("steeping" 渍)**
Steeping in a flavored liquid.
*Example*: coral-like snow lotus (p. 81).

**55. zaozui (糟醉)**
Steeping in a mildly alcoholic brine (*zao* means wine-pickled, *zui* means drunken).

**56. dong (jellying or freezing 冻).**

# Bibliography

## Chinese-language sources

The vast majority of works consulted during the research for both editions of this book are only available in Chinese, and are therefore useful for just a small minority of readers. For this reason, my publishers and I decided not to devote valuable space in the book to a full bibliography.

If any Chinese-proficient researchers wish to see a full bibliography, they are invited to contact me via my website.

I am much indebted to Gwenaële Chesnais's *Les Maisons de Thé de Chengdu* (unpublished manuscript, Institut National des Langues et Civilisations Orientales, Paris), and also to Dr. Francesca Tarocco, for sharing with me her research on Buddhist vegetarian food.

## English-language sources

Administration of Quality and Technology Supervision of Sichuan Province, *Culinary Standard of Sichuan Cuisine,* 2011

Chang, K. C. (ed.), *Food in Chinese Culture,* Yale University Press, New Haven, 1977

Cost, Bruce, *Foods from the Far East,* Century, London, 1990

Davidson, Alan, *The Oxford Companion to Food,* Oxford University Press, Oxford, 1999

Delfs, Robert A., *The Good Food of Szechwan: Down-to-Earth Chinese Cooking,* Kodansha International Ltd., New York, 1974

McGee, Harold, *On Food and Cooking: An Encyclopaedia of Kitchen Science, History and Culture,* Hodder & Stoughton, London, 2004

Phipps, Catherine, *The Pressure Cooker Cookbook,* Ebury, London, 2012

Schrecker, Ellen, *Mrs. Chiang's Szechwan Cookbook,* Harper & Row, New York, 1976

So, Yan-kit, *Classic Chinese Cookbook,* Dorling Kindersley, London, 1984

So, Yan-Kit, *Classic Food of China,* Macmillan, London, 1992

Zong Shi (ed.) *Selected Poems from the Tang Dynasty,* Beijing: Chinese Literature Press, 1999

# Acknowledgments

My acknowledgments for this book now extend, incredibly, over a quarter of a century, and revisiting them has brought back many happy memories. Once again with this new edition, the most important ingredient has been the generosity of my friends and teachers in China and in England. Without them, the book, and indeed my entire Chinese food-writing career, would never have existed. I cannot begin to express how much I owe to Wang Xudong, retired editor of Sichuan Pengren magazine, who has helped and encouraged me in my work for nearly 20 years. His kindness, good humor and resourcefulness have been limitless, and his influence shines through on every page of this new edition.

Chef Yu Bo and his brilliant wife Dai Shuang have been an inspiration for many years, opening my eyes to the glories of Sichuanese haute cuisine, as well as its gorgeous folk cooking. They have fed me with a thousand delicacies and answered countless questions. I'm also grateful for the friendship and support of their team, including Huang Wenyan, Guan Liao and He Rong. Chef Lan Guijun of Yuzhilan has been unbelievably generous and patient with his time and expertise. I am constantly amazed by the depth of his knowledge and his passionate and philosophical approach to cooking. I've been touched by his kindness in helping me to resolve numerous recipe issues. I'm thankful also to his wife and sous-chef, Lü Zhongyu.

My knowledge of the history of chiles and Sichuan pepper in Sichuanese cuisine derives almost entirely from the exhaustive research of Professor Jiang Yuxiang of Sichuan University, who is a human treasurehouse of knowledge about local customs and culture, as well as brilliant and entertaining company. Growing up with my old Sichuan University classmates Liu Yaochun and Xu Jun, both now professors at the university, has been an enriching experience; Liu Yaochun and his students have also helped me source research materials on many occasions. The writer and photographer Lai Wu has been a fantastic friend and colleague, and has taught me so much about Chengdu life and culture. Professor Du Li of the Sichuan Institute of Higher Cuisine has been a longstanding friend and colleague. Deng Hong and Sichuan pepper expert Cai Mingxiong have both helped me on my way. Li Shurong has been an adopted Sichuanese aunt, feeding me delicious food, nurturing me and putting me up during my stays in Chengdu. The designer Yuan Longjun, a fervent advocate of Sichuanese cuisine, has been generous in his support in recent years. It was the music of the *erhu* player Zhou Yu of the Sichuan Conservatory of Music that lured me to Chengdu in the first place, and he and his wife Tao Ping were my earliest friends in Chengdu.

I have been immensely privileged to have enjoyed the support of a great network of chefs, food experts and food-lovers across Sichuan. In Chengdu, particular thanks to Liu Deyao, Li Renguang, Li Qi, Zhang Guobin, Cao Jing and Wen Xing. In Chongqing, the city of fire and spice, thanks to Wang Bin, Yi Faming and Li Qinshui (Tony) for being the best possible companions, and particularly to Wang Bin for his generous hospitality. In Pixian, Chen Shucheng and Chen Wei of the Shaofenghe factory helped me understand the intricacies of their famous family invention, chile bean paste. In Luzhou, Luo Jun, Xiao Luo, veteran chef Li Liangshu and his son Li Jin all introduced me to local delicacies and food culture. In Leshan, Yang Xia and Yang Ge fed me tofu and street snacks, while in Jiajiang, Ru Ju, Yu Zhu and Wu Shasha entertained me and helped me understand fermented tofu. In Shuangliu, Liu Shaokun amazed me with his pickles and country cooking. Wang Qiang and the staff at the Shining Autumn restaurant, and Ren Qiang at the Lingering Fragrance in Li Zhuang, taught me several local recipes. Chef Li Zhuang was a wonderful astronomic guide to Yibin and the Bamboo Sea, and I particularly appreciated his advice on *yacai*. In Zigong, Chen Maojun, Chen Weihua and Wang Xiaojing helped me understand "salt-gang" cooking, particularly "rabbit eaten cold," and the famous local salt. In Langzhong, the home of Baoning vinegar, Meng Wan, Wang Congdu and Yang Yan kindly showed me around.

The godfather of the first edition of this book was Professor Feng Quanxin, who shepherded my friend Volker and me through our first classes at the Sichuan Institute of Higher Cuisine. He and his wife Qiu Rongzhen have been my Chengdu family and have been tireless in their support of my work. The late Professor Xiong Sizhi, renowned authority on Sichuanese food culture, was generous with his time and his library. Fan Shixian, head chef of the Dragon Wonton restaurant in Chengdu, was an unforgettable teacher. Special-grade chef Zhang Shechang was endlessly patient in answering my questions. Yu Weiqin, Zhou Xiaowei, Kou Caijun, Peng Rui, Liu Chun and Zeng Bo all contributed recipes, ideas and contacts. Shang Meng kindly helped with some of my translations.

I would also like to extend heartfelt thanks to my other teachers at the Sichuan Institute of Higher Cuisine—Gan Guojian, Lü Maoguo, Long Qingrong and Li Daiquan—for their inspiring lessons and their kindness to the only foreigner among their students. Huang Weibing, Lu Yi and Li Yunyun have also been most supportive. At the Sichuan Minorities Institute, I'm indebted to Qin Heping. The veteran journalist Che Fu and food critic Zhang Changyu both helped me on my way. I was privileged to enjoying a cooking class in the legendary Shufeng Garden restaurant, thanks to manager Li Lin and his staff. I'm also grateful to manager Yu De and the staff of the Chengdu Restaurant, Feng Rui and his family at the wonderful Bamboo Bar, Xiao Jianming and Xiao Ming of Piaoxiang, everyone at the Dragon Wonton (especially waiter Xu Gang) and everyone at the Mousehole. In Chongqing, I was helped by Mao Xinning, the manager of Old Sichuan, and the head chef at Xiao Dongtian. It would be impossible to name individually all the other chefs, tofu-makers, market vendors, snack-sellers and restaurateurs who have contributed to this book.

I would like to thank heartily all the other laowai in China and at home in England who have spurred me on, especially Francesca Tarocco, Nunzia Carbone, Gwenaële Chesnais, Volker Dencks, Jari Grosse-Ruyken, Davide Quadrio, Seema Merchant, Mara Baughman, Lipika Pelham, Penny Bell and Simon Linder, Rebecca Kesby, Louise Beynon, Ian Cumming, Jo Forkin, Rachel Harris, Susan Jung, Nigel Kat, Jakob Klein, Angie Knox, Rose Leng, Marianne Bek Phiri, Pietro Piccoli, Maria af Sandeberg, Monica de Togni, Clemens Treter, Elena Valussi and Alessandro Zelger. In London, I'm thankful for the support and encouragement of the late, great food writer Yan-kit So, and I will be eternally grateful to her son Hugo Martin for the extraordinary gift of Yan-kit's library and kitchenware, which I treasure and use on a near-daily basis.

Thank you also to Norman Fu, the late Alan Davidson, Helen Saberi, Anissa Helou, Huw Prendergast at Kew Gardens, Lindsey Jordan, Sara Marafini, Tom Weldon and the rest of the team at Michael Joseph, Tara Fisher, Qu Lei Lei and Dodie Miller. Nick Wilson ensured that the first edition of this book made it to publication. Jeremy Carpenter, Martin Toseland, Sue Bale, Ann Barr and Angela Atkins all provided me with valuable advice in the early stages. At the BBC, I am much indebted to Alan Le Breton, Larry Jagan, Lillian Landor, Nikki Johnson, Lucy Walker, Jo Floto and Lucy Perez. Wu Xiaoming and Kai Wang helped with some knotty translation issues. Adam Lieber, Sam Chatterton Dixon, Cathy Roberts, Simon Robey, Jimmy Livingstone and Sophie Munro performed the arduous task of tasting many of the recipes!

The staff of the Barshu restaurant group in London have been stalwart friends during a decade of collaboration, and always ready to help with culinary queries: my heartfelt thanks to Shao Wei,

the fabulous Juanzi, Sherry Looi, Anne Yim, Ting,
Li Xue, Zhou Bo, Zheng Qingguo, Li Liang, Zhang
Chao, Zhang Huabin and the rest of the team,
past and present. Chef Zhang Xiaozhong, formerly
of Barshu and now owner of Tian Fu restaurant,
helped me work out several key recipes. Chef Fu
Bing of Baiwei has been generous with his expertise.

It has been a delight to work on this new edition
with the wonderful team at Bloomsbury, including
Natalie Bellos, Richard Atkinson, Kitty Stogdon
and Alison Cowan. Happily, for the photo shoots,
we were able to reassemble our crack team of
photographer Yuki Sugiura and props stylist Cynthia
Inions, assisted by photographer Clare Lewington,
who were an absolute joy to work with. In cooking
for the photography, I was exceptionally lucky to be
assisted by chef Guirong Wei, chef-patron of Xi'an
Impression in north London and one of very few
female Chinese chefs in London; I'm so grateful
for her support, friendship and calm presence in
the kitchen. Thanks also to Charlotte Heal Design
for the stunning designs. I'm extremely grateful to
Maria Guarnaschelli at W. W. Norton for publishing
all my US editions and for championing my work
for so many years, and also to her colleagues
Erin Sinesky Lovett and my new editor Melanie
Tortoroli. A huge thanks also to my agent, friend
and confidante Zoe Waldie, and to her assistant
Miriam Tobin.

Finally, I would like to thank my parents, Bede and
Carolyn Dunlop, for bringing me up in a house full
of extraordinary food and for giving me the run of
the kitchen from a very early age.

# Glossary of Chinese Characters

*baba rou* 粑粑肉 – meatloaf

*babaxi* 坝坝席 – rural feast, served on the flat ground
outside a Sichuanese farmhouse

*baiguo shu* 白果树 – ginkgo tree (*Ginkgo biloba*)

*baijiu* 白酒 – strong vodka-like grain liquor

*bailu* 白卤 – "white" or uncolored spiced broth

*baimu'er, bai'erzi* 白木耳，白耳子 – alternative names
for silver ear fungus

*bairong* 白茸 – "white paste" of ground chicken,
used to clarify stock

*baiwei* 白味 – "white-flavored" (dishes without
dark colorings such as soy sauce)

*bai youcaitai* 白油菜薹 – "white" (actually green)
rape shoots

*banyou* 板油 – leaf fat used for making lard

*baorong* 包容 – open, adaptable and inclusive

*bashu* 巴蜀 – the ancient Ba and Shu kingdoms of Sichuan,
and a poetic name for Sichuan

*benwei* 本味 – essential or "root" taste of ingredients

*benwei pian* 本味篇 – "The Root of Tastes" section of the
*Lü Annals* or *Spring and Autumn Annals* (*lüsi chunqiu* 吕氏
春秋 c. 239 BC), compiled by Lü Buwei

*bosi* 波斯 – Persia

*candou* 蚕豆 – fava bean (literally "silkworm bean")

*cangying guanzi* 苍蝇馆子 – "fly" restaurants

*caoyu* 草鱼 – grass carp (*Ctenopharyngodon idella*)

*changjiang* 长江 – Yangtze River, literally "long river"

*changjiang xun* 长江鲟 – Yangtze sturgeon
(*Acipenser dabryanus*)

*changjiu* 长久 – long-lasting

*chaotianjiao* 朝天椒 – "facing-heaven chile" (a variety of chile)

*chase* 茶色 – "tea color"

*chashugu* 茶树菇 – tea-tree mushrooms, brown mushrooms
with small caps and long stems

*chen mapo* 陈麻婆 – pock-marked Mother Chen,
inventor of mapo tofu

*chicu* 吃醋 – to be cuckolded (literally "to eat vinegar")

*chifan* 吃饭 – to eat a meal (literally "to eat cooked rice")

*chiku* 吃苦 – to "eat bitterness" (to suffer)

*chongcai* 冲菜 – mustardy greens (young mustard shoots)

*chongcao* 虫草 – caterpillar fungus (*Cordyceps sinensis*)

*chongcao yazi* 虫草鸭子 – duck stewed with caterpillar fungus

*chuanyi* 穿衣 – "putting on some clothes," coating pieces
of food in batter

*chuan'er* 串儿 – skewer on which food is impaled
before cooking

*chui* 捶 – to pound with the back of a cleaver blade

*chunpan* 春盘 – "spring platters," the ancestors of spring rolls

*chunsun* 春笋 – spring bamboo shoot

*chunya* 椿芽 – the tender shoots of the Chinese toon tree
(*Toona sinensis*)

*chushi de tang, changxi de qiang* 厨师的汤，唱戏的腔 –
"the chef's stock, the voice of the opera singer"
(phrase expressing the importance of stock in a chef's art)

*ciba haijiao* 糍粑海椒 – *ciba* chiles, dried chiles that
have been soaked and then pounded with other seasonings

*conghua* – scallion "flowers" (thin slices)

*cuanhe* 攒盒 – decorative hors d'oeuvre box

*cui* 脆 – a type of crispness

*cuo haijiao* 搓海椒 – "rubbed" chiles, dried chiles that
have been roasted and then rubbed into flakes

*dabaicai* 大白菜 – "big cabbage," Chinese cabbage

*dahe bang* 大河帮 – "Great River clique" (style of cooking)

*danba* 胆巴 – bittern, mineral salts used for setting tofu
(also known as *yanlu*, Japanese nigari)

*dang* 檔 or *shi zhuyu* 食茱萸 – an old variety of Sichuan
pepper (*Zanthoxylum ailanthoides*)

*daokou haijiao* 刀口海椒 – "knife-mouth chiles,"
chiles that are fried and then finely chopped

*datoucai* 大头菜 – preserved turnip-like vegetable
(*Brassica juncea* var. *napitormis*)

*denglongjiao* 灯笼椒 – "lantern peppers," a variety of
chile (also used for sweet capsicum peppers)

*dengzhanwo xing* 灯盏窝形 – "lamp-dish slices" (of pork)

*ding baozhen* 丁宝桢 – nineteenth-century governor
of Sichuan, after whom Gong Bao chicken is named

*ding pei ding, si pei si* 丁配丁，丝配丝 –
"cubes with cubes, slivers with slivers"

*dingxiang* 丁香 – cloves

*dongcai* 冬菜 – "winter vegetable" (preserved mustard greens,
a specialty of Nanchong)

*donggao* 冻糕 – steamed rice cakes

*donggu* 冬菇 – alternative name for dried shiitake mushrooms

*donghancai* 冬寒菜 – cluster mallows (*Malva verticillata*),
an ancient Sichuanese vegetable also known as *kuicai* 葵菜

*dongsun* 冬笋 – winter bamboo shoot

*doufucai* 豆腐菜 – "tofu vegetable," Malabar spinach
(*Basella alba*), also known as *mu'ercai* 木耳菜
("wood ear vegetable")

*doufugan* 豆腐干 – "dry" (firm, pressed) tofu

*doufu lianzi* 豆腐帘子 – tofu "curtains," molded rolls of tofu

*doufunao* 豆腐脑 – "tofu brain" (standard Chinese name
for "flower" tofu)

*doufupi* 豆腐皮 – tofu skin

*douhua* 豆花 – "flower" tofu (silken tofu)

*douhua bu yong dou, chi ji bu jian ji* 豆花不用豆，吃鸡不见鸡
– "flower tofu without the beans,
chicken without the appearance of chicken"

*doumiao* 豆苗 – pea shoots (also known as
"dragon's whiskers")

*dounai* 豆奶 – soy milk

*douzha* 豆渣 – soy-bean residue (known in Japanese as okara)

*douzha yazi* 豆渣鸭子 – duck with soy-bean residue, a Sichuanese dish

*duansheng* 断生 – to "break the rawness" of food

*dunjitang* 炖鸡汤 – chicken broth

*duo chi shucai, shao chi rou* 多吃蔬菜，少吃肉 – "eat more vegetables, eat less meat"

*dusuan* 独蒜 – Sichuanese single-cloved garlic

*ercai* 儿菜 – "sons vegetable," a type of Brassica consisting of tiny round mustard heads clustered around a "mother" stem (a bit like Brussels sprouts)

*erdao rou* 二刀肉 – "second-cut pork," a particular cut of pork rump

*erjie tuding* 二姐兔丁 – "second-sister rabbit cubes" (a cold dish)

*erjingtiao* 二荆条 – a local variety of chile (also given as *erjintiao* 二金条, "two golden strips")

*erpingzhuang* 二平桩 – the variety of mustard green used to make Yibin *yacai* preserved vegetable

*fanghun cai* 仿荤菜 – Buddhist dishes of imitation meat and fish

*fanjiao* 番椒 – "barbarian peppers" (Ming-dynasty name for chiles)

*fan, shai, lu* 翻，晒，露 – "turn, sun-dry, bask in dew," traditional process for making Pixian chile bean paste

*fan zaiyang* 饭灾殃 – "Rice Apocalypse" (restaurant, Chengdu)

*feichang fen* 肥肠粉 – sweet potato noodles with stewed pork intestines

*fei er bu ni* 肥而不腻 – "richly fat without being greasy"

*feisi* 飞丝 – "flying silks," hair-like strands of sugar syrup

*fengwei tiao* 凤尾条 – "phoenix tail" strips

*fuhewei* 复合味 – compound flavors

*furong jipian* 芙蓉鸡片 – "hibiscus-blossom chicken slices," a Sichuanese delicacy

*gaiwancha* 盖碗茶 – lid-bowl tea (Sichuanese style of tea-drinking)

*ganban mian* 干拌面 – "dry-tossed noodles," noodles without broth

*gan hong* 干红 – dry red wine

*ganlan shu* 橄榄树 – Chinese olive tree (*Canarium album*)

*gaoliangjiang* 高良姜 – galangal

*geng* 羹 – a kind of thick soup

*gepeng* 割烹 – "to cut and to cook"

*gongfu cha* 功夫茶 – southeastern Chinese tea-drinking ritual

*gongjiao* 贡椒 – "tribute pepper," Sichuan pepper sent to court

*gua* 刮 – to scrape

*guguting* 姑姑筵 – "Auntie's Feast," legendary old Chengdu restaurant

*guiyu* 鳜鱼 or 鲑鱼 – Chinese perch (*Siniperca chuatsi*)

*guokui* 锅魁 in Sichuan or 锅盔 elsewhere in China – general term for a variety of flatbreads and pastries

*gupai pian* 骨牌片 – "domino slices"

*haijiao* 海椒 – "sea peppers" (Sichuanese dialect for chiles)

*hao xinxiang* 好辛香 – to like hot and fragrant tastes

*haozidong zhang yazi* 耗子洞张鸭子 – "Mr. Zhang's Mousehole Duck" (restaurant, Chengdu)

*hei douhua* 黑豆花 – black silken tofu

*hewei* 和味 – to "harmonize" or round out flavors

*hongbai cha* 红白茶 "red-and-white tea," also known as "eagle tea"

*hongbao jiding* 烘爆鸡丁 – fast-fried chicken cubes

*hongrong* 红茸 – "red paste" made from ground pork, used to clarify stock

*hongtang* 红糖 – brown sugar, literally "red sugar"

*hongtanglu* 红汤卤 spicy "red" hotpot broth

*hongyou caitai* 红油菜薹 – "red" (actually purple) rape shoots

*hongyou douban* 红油豆瓣 – "red-oil" bean sauce, a popular type of chile bean paste

*huacha* 花茶 – "flower tea" (jasmine blossom tea)

*huagu* 花菇 – dried shiitake mushrooms with fissured caps

*huajiao tuding* 花椒兔丁 – rabbit cubes with Sichuan pepper

*huanghou* 黄喉 – pig's or cow's aorta

*huanghua* 黄花 – day-lily flowers

*huangshan* 黄鳝 – yellow eel (see also *shanyu*)

*hudou* 胡豆 – Sichuanese dialect for fava bean (literally "barbarian bean")

*huguang tian sichuan* 湖广填四川 – literally "filling Sichuan from Hu and Guang," term used for the great migration of people from more than a dozen provinces to Sichuan in the early Qing dynasty

*huihuicai* 灰灰菜 – wild green, known in English as fat hen or lamb's quarters (*Chenopodium album*)

*hula jiding* 煳辣鸡丁 – chicken cubes with seared chiles

*hunheyou* 混合油 – blended oil, typically a mixture of lard and vegetable oil

*huobianzi niurou* 火边子牛肉 – "fireside beef," a specialty of Zigong

*huoge* 火哥 – "Brother Fire," Sichuanese internet chef

*huoguo diliao* 火锅底料 – hotpot soup base

*huohou* 火候 – literally "fire and waiting," the control of heat in cooking

*huolu* 火炉 – furnace

*huorou* 活肉 – "live" meat, meaning taut, muscular meat

*huoxiang* 藿香 – Korean mint (*Agastache rugosa*)

*jiangan qingcai* 箭杆青菜 – type of mustard green used to make *dongcai*

*jiang* 酱 – general term for thick fermented sauces

*jianghu cai* 江湖菜 – "river-and-lake" dishes, Chongqing-style folk cooking

*jiangtuan* 江团 – long-snout catfish (*Leiocassis longirostris*)

*jiaofang* 椒房 – "pepper houses"

*jijing* 鸡精 – "chicken essence," a yellow flavoring powder

*jimeng kuicai* 鸡蒙葵菜 – mallow tips coated in chicken paste and served in clear broth, a Sichuanese delicacy

*jinjiang* 锦江 – Brocade River

*jinsimian* 金丝面 – "golden-thread" noodles, very fine noodles made with an egg-yolk dough

*jiucaiye miantiao* 韭菜叶面条 – chive-leaf noodles

*jiu dawan* 九大碗 – "nine big bowls," colloquial name for a rural feast *jiugongge* 九宫格 – "nine-chambered [metal] frame" used for dividing space in a Chongqing hotpot

*jiuhuang* 韭黄 – yellow Chinese chives (*Allium tuberosum*)

*jiumi* 酒米 – "wine rice," southern Sichuanese name for glutinous rice

*jiuniang* 酒酿 – alternative name for *laozao*

*jiuqu* 酒曲 – yeast starter used for making Chinese wines

*jiuyeqing* 九叶青 – "nine-leaf green," a variety of green Sichuan pepper

*jiyu* 鲫鱼 – crucian carp (*Carassius carassius*)

*juecai* 蕨菜 – fiddlehead ferns

*kaihua* 开花 – to split or, literally, "burst into flower"

*kaishui baicai* 开水白菜 – "white cabbage in boiling water"

*kaiwei* 开胃 – to "open the stomach" (whet the appetite)

*kan* 砍 – to chop

*kandao* 砍刀 – heavy chopping cleaver

*konghua tang* 空花糖 – "hollow-flower toffee," a kind of honeycomb toffee made from malt sugar

*kongque kai ping* 孔雀开屏 – "peacock spreading its tail"

*kougan* 口感 – mouthfeel

*koukoucui* 口口脆 – "crisp in the mouth," Sichuanese term for rabbit stomachs

*ku* 苦 – bitter

*kuaizi tiao* 筷子条 – "chopstick" strips

*kujiao* 苦藠 – "bitter shallot," a variety of *Allium Chinense*

*kusun* 苦笋 – bitter bamboo shoot

*la meizi* 辣妹子 – "spice girls"

*lao* 老 – overcooked, tough (literally "old")

*laochou* 老抽 – dark soy sauce

*laomuji* 老母鸡 – "old mother chicken," mature hen used to make stock

*laoying cha* 老鹰茶 – alternative name for *hongbaicha*

*layue* 腊月 – the last lunar month, the month of winter sacrifices

*la zhong you xianwei* 辣中有鲜味 – "savory, umami flavors in the midst of spiciness"

*lengdanbei* 冷淡杯 – "a few cold dishes and a glass of beer" (Sichuanese tapas)

*liandaopian* 连刀片 – linked or "sandwich" slices

*liang* 两 – tael, a traditional Chinese measurement (about 2 oz/50g)

*liangtouwang* 两头望 – "frantic glances in both directions," old nickname for the dish of "man-and-wife" offal slices

*lianzi* 莲子 – lotus seeds

*liji* 礼记 – *The Book of Rites*

*linghuo* 灵活 – spirited, flexible

*liyu* 鲤鱼 – carp (*Cyprinus carpio carpio*)

*long chaoshou* 龙抄手 – "Dragon Wonton" (restaurant, Chengdu)

*lucai* 卤菜 – dishes cooked in a spiced, aromatic broth (*lushui*)

*lushui* 卤水 – aromatic broth

*luzhou laojiao* 泸州老窖 – Luzhou "Old Cellar" sorghum liquor

*mahua* 麻花 – deep-fried dough twists

*malatang* 麻辣烫 – "numbing-hot-and-scalding," a spicy broth in which skewers of food are cooked

*mantou* 馒头 – steamed bun

*mantou* 蛮头 – "barbarian head"

*maobi su* 毛笔酥 – crisp "calligraphy brushes"

*maodu huoguo* 毛肚火锅 – beef-tripe hotpot (the original Chongqing hotpot)

*maofeng cha* 毛峰茶 – Mao Feng tea

*maozhu* 毛竹 – a type of bamboo with edible shoots

*meimao* 眉毛 – "eyebrows"

*meizi* 梅子 – Chinese plum

*mengding ganlu* 蒙顶甘露 – Meng Ding sweet dew tea

*miansao* 面臊 – noodle topping

*miantang* 面汤 – "noodle broth," the silky liquid in which noodles have been boiled

*miliangfen* 米凉粉 – rice jelly, a Sichuanese snack

*mujiangcai* 木姜菜 – a variety of mint (*Elsholtzia souliei*) used as a herb in southern Sichuan

*nanzhu* 楠竹 – a type of bamboo with edible shoots

*neibu faxing* 内部发行 – "for internal circulation only"

*nen* 嫩 – tenderness, delicacy (of meat, fish, etc)

*niannian you yu* 年年有余 – "having a surplus every year" (sounds the same as 年年有鱼, which means "having fish every year")

*nianyu* 鲇鱼 – Amur catfish (*Silurus asotus*)

*niqiu* 泥鳅 – loach or weatherfish (*Misgurnus anguillicaudatus*)

*niuganjun* 牛肝菌 – ox-liver mushroom (*Boletus* genus)

*niupicai* 牛皮菜 – "ox-leather" greens, chards

*niushe pian* 牛舌片 – "ox-tongue" slices

*niushipo* 牛市坡 – "Ox Market Slopes," an area in Hanyuan County where the finest Sichuan pepper is said to be grown

*nong* 浓 – strong, dense, concentrated (in flavor)

*nongjiale* 农家乐 – "the happiness of rural homes," meaning a farmhouse restaurant

*nuo* 糯 – soft, huggy and glutinous in texture

*pa* 粑 – Sichuanese dialect term for the texture of food that has been cooked until it is very soft

*pa'erduo* 粑耳朵 – "soft ears," colloquial Sichuanese term for hen-pecked husbands

*pa la* 怕辣 – "fear of chile-hotness"

*paocai tanzi* 泡菜坛子 – Sichuanese pickle jar

*paoge rou* 袍哥肉 – "Secret Society Meat" (a nickname for twice-cooked pork)

*paojiao sancui* 泡椒三脆 – "three crisp ingredients (goose intestines, duck gizzards and wood ear mushrooms) with pickled chiles"

*pa wandou* 粑豌豆 – "soft peas," a mash of cooked dried yellow peas used in soups and sauces

*pingdi yi sheng lei* 平地一声雷 – "a sudden clap of thunder," nickname for pork in "lychee" sauce with crispy rice

*qiaojiao niurou* 跷脚牛肉 – "crossed-legs" beef hotpot of Leshan

*qingcai* 青菜 – green vegetables

*qingcaitou* 青菜头 – crisp, fleshy mustard stalks or "heads"

*qingcheng xueya* 青城雪芽 – Qingcheng Mountain snow-shoot tea

*qingdun niubian tang* 清炖牛鞭汤 – clear-simmered ox penis soup

*qingshiqiao* 青石桥 – Green Stone Bridge (wholesale market, Chengdu)

*qingsun* 青笋 – another name for *wosun* (celtuce)

*qingtang* 清汤 – clear stock

*qixingjiao* 七星椒 – "seven-star chile" (a variety of chile)

*qujiu* 曲酒 – generic term for strong vodka-like wines

*rongleyuan* 荣乐园 – legendary old Chengdu restaurant

*roudoukou* 肉豆蔻 – nutmeg

*ruwei* 入味 – "send the flavors in"

*san nen* 三嫩 – "three tender bites"

*sanzheng jiukou* 三蒸九扣 – "three steamed dishes and nine steamed bowls" (folk name for a rural banquet)

*sanzi* 馓子 – deep-fried noodles (used as a crunchy topping)

*saowei* 臊味 – "foul" odor or taste

*sewei* 涩味 – astringent taste

*se xiang wei xing* 色香味形 – "color, fragrance, flavor and form"

*shancheng xiao tangyuan* 山城小汤圆 – "mountain city little glutinous rice balls"

*shanghuo* 上火 – "rising fire," excess of internal heat, seen as a cause of disease in Traditional Chinese Medicine

*shangtang* 上汤 – superior stock

*shang ziwei* 尚滋味 – "to appreciate flavors"

*shanwei* 膻味 – "muttony" odor or taste

*shanyu* 鳝鱼 – yellow or paddy eel (*Monopterus albus*)

*shanzhen haiwei* 山珍海味 – "treasures of the mountains and flavors of the seas"

*shaocai* 烧菜 – braised dishes

*shaocai* 苕菜 – a wild green, winter vetch (*Vicia hirsuta*)

*shaoxing jiu* 绍兴酒 – Shaoxing wine

*shengchou* 生抽 – light soy sauce

*shipayu* 石爬鱼 – a type of catfish (*Euchiloglanis kishinouyei*)

*shi zai zhongguo, wei zai sichuan* 食在中国，味在四川 – "China is the place for food, but Sichuan is the place for flavor"

*shi zhurou* 食猪肉 – "Eating Pork" (a poem by Su Dongpo)

*shu* 蜀 – the name of the ancient kingdom centered on today's Chengdu (and a poetic name for the Chengdu area)

*shunan zhuhai* 蜀南竹海 – Bamboo Sea, a nature reserve in southern Sichuan

*shu quan fei ri* 蜀犬吠日 – "Sichuanese dogs bark at the sun"

*sifang cai* 私房菜 – "private kitchen"

*sirou* 死肉 – literally "dead meat," meat that has not been active muscle, such as chicken breast

*su* 酥 – a type of crispness

*suanhao* 蒜毫 – alternative name for *suantai* (garlic stems)

*suanni* 蒜泥 – crushed garlic in water

*suantai* 蒜薹 – garlic stems

*sucai hunzuo* 素菜荤做 – "vegetable ingredients cooked meatily"

*suji* 素鸡 – sausage-shaped roll of tofu (literally "vegetarian chicken")

*surou* 酥肉 – "crisp pork," slices of fatty pork clothed in egg batter and deep-fried

*tan douhua* 谭豆花 – "Mr. Tan's Flower Tofu" (restaurant, Chengdu)

*tanzi rou* 坛子肉 – clay-jar pork, a kind of confit pork preserved in lard

*tangmian* 汤面 – noodles served in broth

*tangmian* 烫面 – "scalded dough," a type of dumpling dough made with boiling water

*tedian* 特点 – distinguishing characteristics

*tengjiao* 藤椒 – green Sichuan pepper

*tianfu zhi guo* 天府之国 – "land of plenty"

*tianji* 田鸡 – "field chicken," meaning frog

*tianjiu* 甜酒 – alternative name for *laozao*

*tiantang* 天堂 – "paradise," a nickname for pigs" upper palates

*tianxi* 田席 – rural banquet (literally "field feast")

*tongcai* 通菜 – Mandarin Chinese for water spinach

*tongxue* 同学 – "same-school," classmate

*tu* 土 – rustic, earthy, free-range (literally "earth")

*tuanyuan* 团圆 – reunion

*tuji* 土鸡 – farmhouse or free-range chicken

*tu naoke* 兔脑壳 – Sichuanese dialect term for rabbit heads

*wan* 剜 – to gouge

*weijing* 味精 – monosodium glutamate, MSG (literally "the essence of flavor")

*weiqi* 围棋 – the game Go

*wosun* 莴笋 – celtuce, a type of lettuce with a thick stem (*Lactuca sativa* var. *angustata*)

*wowotou* 窝窝头 – a type of steamed bun, usually made from cornmeal

*wuguji* 乌骨鸡 – "black-boned chicken," silkie chicken

*wu han bu cheng cai* 无咸不成菜 – "you can't make a dish without saltiness"

*wuhua rou* 五花肉 – pork belly meat (literally "five-flower meat")

*wuhun* 五荤 – the so-called "five pungent" ingredients avoided by strict Buddhists, including garlic, scallions and other alliums

*wuliangye* 五粮液 – Sichuanese five-grain wine

*wu tan guoshi* 勿谈国事 – "do not discuss national affairs"

*wuxiang fen* 五香粉 – five-spice powder

*xiafan cai* 下饭菜 – "send the rice down" dishes

*xiancai* 咸菜 – general term for salt-preserved vegetables

*xiang chuzi* 乡厨子 – village chef

*xiangliao* 香料 – "fragrant things" (collective name for spices)

*xiangya tiao* 象牙条 – "elephant tusk" strips

*xiaochi* 小吃 – "small eats" (snacks)

*xiaohe bang* 小河帮 – "Small River clique" (style of cooking)

*xiaomila* 小米辣 – "little rice chile" (a type of chile)

*xingwei* 腥味 – "fishy" odor or taste

*xionghuangjiu* 雄黄酒 – realgar wine (liquor with traces of an arsenic compound), traditionally drunk at the Dragon Boat Festival

xiongmao zhan zhu 熊猫战竹 – "panda fighting bamboo"

xuehua jinao 雪花鸡淖 – "snowflake chicken custard,"
a Sichuanese delicacy

yanbang cai 盐帮菜 – "salt gang" cooking, Zigong cuisine

yandu 盐都 – "salt capital" (Zigong city)

yangrou 羊肉 – sheep or goat meat

yangyu chao tudou 洋芋炒土豆 – "spud-fried potatoes"

yanli 岩鲤 – rock carp (*Procypris rabaudi*)

yanlu 盐卤 – bittern, mineral salts used for setting tofu
(also known as *danba*, Japanese nigari)

yansui 芫荽 – Mandarin Chinese name for cilantro

yayu 雅鱼 – a type of carp (*Schizothorax prenanti*)

yeshanjiao 野山椒 – "wild mountain chile," small, pale
green pickled chiles

yicai yige, baicai baiwei 一菜一格，百菜百味 –
"each dish has its own style,
a hundred dishes have a hundred different flavors"

yifeng shu 一封书 – "a book," description used for
slices of food arranged in shallow steps on a board

yinmi 阴米 – "shady rice"

yinxing 银杏 – "silver apricots," ginkgo nuts
(also known as *baiguo*)

yinzhen si 银针丝 – "silver needle" sliver

yiwei 异味 – peculiar smell, off-taste

youlazi 油辣子 – "oily chiles," chile sediment in
chile oil

youmaicai 油麦菜 – Indian lettuce (*Lactuca indica*)

yulajiao 鱼辣椒 – "fishy chiles," red chiles pickled
in brine with a few crucian carp

yulan pian 玉兰片 – "jade magnolia slices,"
slices of dried bamboo shoot

yuxiang 鱼香 – "fish-fragrant"

yuxiang 鱼香 – spearmint, also known as *liulanxiang*
留兰香

yuyan cong 鱼眼葱 – "fish-eye" scallion slices

zaojiao shu 皂角树 – Chinese honey locust tree
(*Gleditsia sinensis*)

zaojun 灶君 – the Kitchen God

zaozui 糟醉 – "drunken," used of dishes flavored
with glutinous rice wine

zengzi 甑子 – wooden rice steamer

zhan 斩 – to chop

zhandao 斩刀 – heavy chopping cleaver

zhang 樟 – camphor

zhang mu 章穆 – Zhang Mu, author of *tiaoji yinshi bian*,
调疾饮食辨 (1823)

zhangzhou 漳州 – city in Fujian Province

zharou 鲊肉 – alternative name for pork steamed in
ricemeal

zhashou 炸收 – to "deep-fry and receive," cooking method

zhe'er gen 折耳根 – *Houttuynia cordata* (a salad vegetable),
also known as *ze'er gen* 则耳根

zhengroufen 蒸肉粉 – "steam-meat powder," spiced ricemeal
for steaming meat

zhengxingyuan 正兴园 – famous old Chengdu restaurant run
by a Manchu chef

zhengzheng gao 蒸蒸糕 – literally "steamed steamed cakes,"
a favorite street snack made of ground rice

zhenzhuba 珍珠粑 – "pearly cake," festive rice cake made
in western Sichuan

zhijia pian 指甲片 – "thumbnail" slices

zhu'er ba 猪儿粑 – "piglet" dumplings

zhuhua 竹花 – bamboo flower lichen

zhusun 竹荪 – bamboo pith fungus (*Phallus indusiatus*)

zhusun 竹笋 – bamboo shoot

zhusundan 竹荪蛋 – volvae or "eggs" of the bamboo pith fungus

zhutongfan 竹筒单 – rice cooked inside sections of bamboo

zhu yanwo 竹燕窝 – "bamboo bird's nest," a kind of fungus

zhuye qing 竹叶青 – green bamboo-leaf tea

zidantou 子弹头 – "bullets" (a variety of chile)

zinei bang 自内帮 – "Zigong-Neijiang clique"
(style of cooking)

zongzi 粽子 – leaf-wrapped parcels of glutinous rice,
eaten around the time of the Dragon Boat Festival,
on the fifth day of the fifth lunar month

# Index

# For my mother, Carolyn

Text copyright © 2019 by Fuchsia Dunlop
Photographs on pages 2, 6, 18–19, 22, 28–29, 60, 128, 130–131, 180–181, 242–243, 264–265, 306–307, 332–333, 343, 344–345, 402, 413, 414, 418–419, 436–437 and 466–467 © Ian Cumming, 2019; photograph on page 15 © Ming-hsiung Tsai, 2019; all other photographs © Yuki Sugiura, 2019

Acknowledgments on pages 480–82 constitute an extension of this copyright page.

First published in the UK in 2001 by Michael Joseph as *Sichuan Cookery* and in the US in 2003 by W. W. Norton & Company as *Land of Plenty*.
This revised and updated edition first published in 2019 by Bloomsbury Publishing.
First American Edition 2019

For information about permission to reproduce selections from this book, write to Permissions, W. W. Norton & Company, Inc., 500 Fifth Avenue, New York, NY 10110

For information about special discounts for bulk purchases, please contact W. W. Norton Special Sales at specialsales@wwnorton.com or 800-233-4830

Project editor: Alison Cowan
Design: Charlotte Heal Design, charlotteheal.com
Photography: Yuki Sugiura, yukisugiura.com
Additional location photography: Ian Cumming
Props stylist: Cynthia Inions
Indexer: Vanessa Bird

Printed in China by RR Donnelley Asia

ISBN: 978-1-324-00483-7

W. W. Norton & Company, Inc., 500 Fifth Avenue, New York, N.Y. 10110
www.wwnorton.com

W. W. Norton & Company Ltd., 15 Carlisle Street, London W1D 3BS

1 2 3 4 5 6 7 8 9 0